Federal Resume Guidebook

FOURTH EDITION

*Strategies for Writing a Winning Federal
Electronic Resume, KSAs, and Essays*

Kathryn Kraemer Troutman

jist
Works
America's Career Publisher

Federal Resume Guidebook, Fourth Edition

© 2007 by Kathryn Kraemer Troutman

Published by JIST Works, an imprint of JIST Publishing
7321 Shadeland Station, Suite 200
Indianapolis, IN 46256-3923
Phone: 800-648-JIST   Fax: 877-454-7839   E-mail: info@jist.com

Visit our Web site at www.jist.com for information on JIST, free job search tips, book chapters, and ordering instructions for our many products!

See the back of this book for information on ordering this book's resume samples on CD. Quantity discounts are available for JIST books. Have future editions of JIST books automatically delivered to you on publication through our convenient standing order program. Please call our Sales Department at 800-648-5478 for a free catalog and more information.

Trade Product Manager: Lori Cates Hand
Cover Designer: Nick Anderson
Cover Photo: Hisham F. Ibrahim/Photographers Choice/Getty Images
Interior Designers: Aleata Howard, Marie Kristine Parial-Leonardo
Proofreaders: Linda Seifert, Jeanne Clark
Indexer: Kelly D. Henthorne

Printed in the United States of America
13 12 11 10 09 08   9 8 7 6 5 4 3

    Library of Congress Cataloging-in-Publication Data
Troutman, Kathryn K.
    Federal resume guidebook : strategies for writing a winning federal electronic resume, KSAs, and essays / by Kathryn Kraemer Troutman. -- 4th ed.
      p. cm.
    Includes index.
    ISBN 978-1-59357-426-0 (alk. paper)
    1. Civil service positions--United States. 2. Résumés (Employment)--United States. I. Title.
    JK716.T73 2007
    650.14'2--dc22
                            2007005242

We have been careful to provide accurate information in this book, but it is possible that errors and omissions have been introduced. Please consider this in making any career plans or other important decisions. Trust your own judgment above all else and in all things.

Trademarks: All brand names and product names used in this book are trade names, service marks, trademarks, or registered trademarks of their respective owners.

ISBN 978-1-59357-426-0

Contents

Index of Sample Resumes

Chapter	Resume Format	Name	Career Transition	Current Job Title	Grade/ Salary
1	USAJOBS	Sara Jacobs	Fed. to fed.	Management Assistant	GS-07
1	Paper	Mark Eriksson	Fed. to fed., prior military	Transportation Security Officer (Screener)	SV-D
8	Electronic	Mary Simons	Fed. to fed.	Administrative Specialist	GS-09
13	CV/paper federal	David Raikow	Fed. to fed.	Research Aquatic Biologist	GS-11
14	Paper	Matthew Chan	Private industry to fed.	Lead Computer Technician	$27,500
14	Electronic	Janet Johnson	Fed. to fed.	Senior IT Specialist	GS-13
15	Electronic	George Daimlar	Private industry to fed.	Subcontract Administrator	$60,000
16	Paper	Mary Stone	State to fed.	Inspection Aide	$29,200
16	Paper	Barbara Taylor	Private industry to fed.	Business Process Analyst	$47,000
16	Paper	Carol Deeter	Fed. to fed.	Secretary	GS-07
16	Electronic	Debra Jones	Private industry to fed	Customer Service Representative	$40,000
17	Electronic	Christine Dietrich	Fed. to fed.	Management Analyst	GS-11
18	Electronic	Becky Wallace	Private industry to fed.	Human Resources Benefits Administrator	$29,000
20	Paper	Jane Myers	Military to fed.	Surveillance Case Officer	$30,000
20	Electronic	Bob Becker	Military to fed.	Lt. Colonel	$100,500
21	Electronic	Wayne Hart, Jr.	Fed. to fed.	Air Conditioning/ RefrigerationMechanic	WG-10
22	Paper	Michael Smith	Fed. to fed.	Natural Resource Specialist	GS-09
Appendix	USAJOBS	Caroline Martin	Fed. to fed.	DFAS, Accounting Technician	GS-05
Appendix	Paper, USAJOBS	Mark Etheridge	Fed. to fed.	TSA Screener	SV-1802-D/D
Appendix	Paper	Stephanie Haines Glasgow	Private to fed.	General Attorney, Education Spec.	$65,000
Appendix	USAJOBS	Jeanna Simpson	Private to fed.	RPCV, Industry, Business Development	$49,500

Years of Experience	Target Job Title	Target Series	Target Grade	Target Agency
1 yr., GS-07	Management Analyst	343	GS-09/11/12	Immigration and Customs Enforcement
1 yr. SV-D, 24 yrs. military	Transportation Security Manager, Bomb Appraisal Officer	1802	H-H	Transportation Security Agency
4 yrs., GS-09	Human Resources Specialist	0201	GS-09	Department of Energy
1.5 yrs.	Aquatic Ecologist	0401	GS-12	National Oceanic and Atmospheric Administration
2.5 yrs.	Information Technology Specialist	2210	GS-07	Agricultural Research Service
3 yrs.	Senior IT Specialist (OS)	2210	GS-14	Department of Education
3 yrs., GS-13	Contract Specialist	1102	GS-13	General Services Administration
12 yrs.	Secretary, Office Assistant	0318	GS-06	Department of Justice
4.5 yrs.	Management Assistant	0344	GS-07	Department of Housing and Urban Development
9 yrs., GS-07	Secretary	0318	GS-08	Farm Service Agency
11 yrs.	Procurement Support Assistant	0303	GS-04	Department of Energy
4.5 yrs., GS-11	Management and Program Analyst	0343	GS-12	U.S. Navy
5.5 yrs.	Human Resources Assistant	0203	GS-07	Federal Trade Commission
9.5 yrs.	Intelligence Operations Specialist	132	GS-07/09	Transportation Security Agency
23 yrs., military	Supervisory Logistics Management Specialist	346	GS-14/15	U.S. Army
8 yrs., GS-9/11	Vocational Instructor (HVAC)	1712	GS-09/11	U.S. Navy
11 yrs., GS-11	Biologist or Natural Resources Manager	401	GS-11	Bureau of Land Management
5 yrs.	Accounting Technician	0525	GS-07	Defense Finance and Accounting Service
1 yr.	TSA Lead Screener or FAM	1802	SV-1802-F/F	Transportation Security Agency
3 yrs.	General Attorney	0905	GS-11/12	Department of Education
3 yrs.	Economist	0110	GS-02	Any

Foreword

Ten years ago one of my brighter cousins asked if I could help her get a government job. She figured that with 20 years of covering the federal establishment I would have special insights. That I would know who to see, where to go, and what to do when she got there.

I told her to get a copy of the *Federal Resume Guidebook.*

Two weeks ago the very bright son of an old friend asked if I could help him get a government job. They, the father and son, figured that with 30 years of covering the federal establishment I would have special insights. That I would know who to see, where to go, and what to do when he got there.

I told him to get a copy of the *Federal Resume Guidebook.*

There was a time, eons ago, when you went to a federal agency, filled out a form, took a test, and maybe, maybe, maybe, heard back and got a job. But that was then and this is now.

This is not your father's government anymore.

Computers have made things easier and tougher at the same time. The government is no longer an army of clerks in green eyeshades (if it ever was). Now there are more scientists than secretaries. People who can speak exotic languages are in demand. Individuals who know how to launder money (and thus catch tax cheats and terrorists) are needed.

In many ways the federal establishment is the most sophisticated, well-educated, cutting-edge, often exciting operation in the nation.

Government workers do everything, including taking the temperature of polar bears (a hazardous job at best) as part of a program for long-range space trips. Government workers are alongside troops around the world. The first person on the moon was a GS, NASA civilian.

So if you want to be one, to be a fed, and you want my expert advice, it is this:

Get yourself a copy of the *Federal Resume Guidebook.*

—Mike Causey, Federal NewsRadio

About This Book

The fourth edition of the *Federal Resume Guidebook* has two objectives: first, to teach you how to target your resume content, and second, to help you format your content for online applications. With so many federal agencies requiring that the federal resume, KSAs, Essays and Questions be submitted online, the format of your job application is almost as important as the content.

Part 1 is dedicated to the USAJOBS resume builder, which is the leading method to apply for federal jobs. This section teaches you how to write an electronic federal resume for online builders. All sample USAJOBS screenshots, preview samples, and content will apply to all of the agency federal builders, such as CPOL, Navy CHART, AF, DFAS, DLA, and other electronic resume application systems and online builders. This section is critical for your success in applying correctly, being ranked "Best Qualified," and getting referred to the supervisor. By seeing the builder sections, preview excerpts, insights, and samples, you can create competitive content and learn how to use resume builders to your advantage.

Part 2 helps you take your federal resume to the next step and make your application stand out above the competition. Your writing style and value-added core competencies will allow your resume to rise to the top of electronic keyword hiring systems.

In part 3 and all new to this edition, essays and KSAs are the narratives that demonstrate your performance level. The KSAs are still rated and ranked, but the Essays will support your "self-assessment" questions. Learn how to get ready to answer questions: multiple choice, check all that apply, and true or false. The government application process is complex, but you can master it if you are ready to write examples of your experiences. These two chapters will help you understand the resume and questions/essay application process.

Analyzing the vacancy announcement for critical information can be confusing. In part 4, discover the critical sections of a federal announcement and how you can use language from the announcement in your federal resume. The all new resume builder chapter gives you easy-to-understand Work Experience character counts and headings for the resume builders—invaluable for your copy-and-paste resume building!

In part 5, we further analyze certain occupational series for core competencies, specialized experience, skills, and formats. These specialized chapters provide insight to break into a series, get promoted, and write federal resumes especially for these positions. Sample resumes demonstrate the writing style, skills, and accomplishments or projects that demonstrate specialized knowledge.

Part 6 has strategies for transitioning job seekers: wage-grade, military-to-federal, and SES. Part 7 presents insights for managing your federal career and job search.

In summary, the *Federal Resume Guidebook* is a comprehensive federal career resource with instruction, insight, and samples, written to help you write a competitive federal resume in today's online federal application process. I hope this book helps you apply successfully and efficiently for many positions. Write to me with your success stories when you get hired as a result of the insights in this book.

—Kathryn K. Troutman, author, kathryn@resume-place.com

Acknowledgments

I want to thank The Resume Place, Inc., clients for trusting our Certified Federal Resume Writers with their future federal careers and sharing their experiences and feedback with us. Since 1974, the Resume Place, Inc., has supported hundreds of thousands of federal job seekers. Our customers' first-hand experiences helped us learn important lessons about how to write the best federal resumes, get referrals, nail interviews, and correctly apply online. The *Federal Resume Guidebook* would not exist without *your* feedback and support.

My continued thanks to Ligaya Fernandez, Senior Policy Analyst at the Merit Systems Protection Board, for her expertise and tips for the most complex federal human resources questions.

Thanks also go to the numerous representatives of federal agencies and military bases who have coordinated and introduced my programs at their facilities:

To Lori Smith, who coordinated the Resumix Resume Writing courses for hundreds of Accounting Technicians from the Vendor Pay Division at the Defense Finance and Accounting Service.

To SueEllen Bunting, Gilda Grant, Renee Harrington, and Gaby Reiling of the EEO Staff at Defense Logistics Agency (for many years) where I learned about the behavior-based interview and now teach an effective course on this topic.

To Faith Skordinski from HHS and CMS, who coordinated more than 50 Federal Resume & KSA Writing workshops.

To Ed Roscoe, Christine DeGraw, and Dave DuBois of the Commander, Fleet and Family Support Center, Millington, Tennessee, for believing in the new Outline Electronic Resume format and *Ten Steps to a Federal Job* curriculum for U.S. Navy, Fleet and Family Support Centers worldwide.

To Gretchen Shannon and Kathy Knight of AF Ramstein, who implemented the Certified Federal Job Search Trainer™ program for the AF MAJCOM Europe, taught by Emily Troutman in Alconbury, England.

To training coordinators at the National Science Foundation, Bureau of Land Management, National Institutes of Health, Environmental Protection Agency, Department of Energy, National Credit Union Administration, Department of Agriculture, National Resources Conservation Service, Animal and Plant Health Inspection Service, Department of Homeland Security, Pension Benefit Guarantee Corporation, Immigration and Customs Enforcement, Federal Emergency Management Agency, Centers for Medicare and Medicaid Services, Social Security Administration, Department of Interior, U.S. Marine Corps HQ/Albany, Kanaohe, Naval Air Station Pensacola, and many more agencies for inviting me to teach federal resume, Resumix, QuickHire, USAJOBs, and KSA writing to thousands of federal employees.

I also want to thank the 250 Certified Federal Job Search Trainers (CFJST) who have brought *Ten Steps to a Federal Job* to more than 150 military bases, universities, and federal agencies worldwide.

Thanks to the producers of Monster.com, where I manage the Public Service/Government Board and answer hundreds of federal job search questions.

To the RP Certified Federal Resume Writing Team for helping produce this book. Especially to Sarah Blazucki for the development of our samples; Craig Taylor for production coordination of the CD-ROM; and Mark Hoyer for the screenshot production in chapters 1, 2, 3, 4, 5, and 11 and CD-ROM production.

I especially want to thank my family for coping with me through the writing and production of another federal resume book!

About the Contributors

Author **Kathryn Troutman** is a federal resume expert and career consultant and government human resources career trainer with more than 30 years of experience in the specialized federal job market. She is Founder and President of The Resume Place, a leading resume writing service in Baltimore that originated in 1971. A sought-after trainer of federal job seekers and HR professionals, Troutman has written ten career books and produces www.resume-place.com.

Jacqueline Allen, CFRWC, is a Senior Executive Service consultant and writer. Jacqueline authored the Program and Management Analyst chapters for the third and fourth editions of the *Federal Resume Guidebook,* as well as the Management Analyst series samples for the *Military to Federal Career Guide.* Jacqueline is an expert in the Analyst/Specialist series, as well as SES applications. She spent 20+ years in marketing management positions in the private sector, directing major federal proposal efforts for multimillion-dollar contracts. She taught career communications at the college level and developed and presented numerous business writing courses to corporate executives and midlevel managers.

Patricia Alvarez, CFRWC, is a retired federal human resources specialist. Patricia has more than 20 years of federal human resources experience. Her federal career included a broad array of human resources responsibilities, with a specialization in federal recruiting and many years of providing career coaching to federal applicants. During her career, Pat received numerous awards, including the Distinguished Career Service Award from both the Bonneville Power Administration and the U.S. Department of Energy. Pat contributed samples to the fourth edition of the *Federal Resume Guidebook, Military to Federal Career Guide,* and *Jobseeker Guide.*

Sarah Blazucki, CFRWC, CPRW, is an expert federal resume and KSA writer and project analyst. She has more than nine years of writing experience and is an expert in federal resumes (paper and electronic), KSAs, ECQs, cover letters, and private-industry resumes. Sarah served as an editor and proofreader for *The Student's Federal Career Guide; Federal Resume Guidebook,* Fourth Edition; and *Ten Steps to a Federal Job.* She also served as resume sample developer and editor for *The Military to Federal Career Guide* and *Resumes for Dummies,* Fifth Edition, by Joyce Lain Kennedy.

Diane Burns, CCMC, CPRW, IJCTC, CEIP, CCM, is a nationally recognized author and has been quoted on CareerBuilder and other national periodicals. Diane is a member of the Professional Association of Resume Writers (PARW) International Resume Certification committee and is the facilitator for the Certified Professional Career Coach program. As an award-winning resume writer, her achievements include Best Executive Resume Award by PARW. Her resumes are published in more than 30 books and periodicals, including the chapter on military to civilian in the *Military to Federal Career Guide* and the *Federal Resume Guidebook,* Third and Fourth Editions.

Rita Chambers, PMP, MS, Computer Science, CFRWC, is a Senior Executive Service consultant and writer. Rita has more than 15 years of technical writing expertise in the IT field. She is currently an active IT project manager in government and has extensive knowledge of project management and defense contracting. Before moving into the technical career field, Rita taught public school adult education classes and courses at the college level. She authored the IT and KSA chapters of the third and fourth editions of the *Federal Resume Guidebook, Ten Steps to a Federal Job, Student's Federal Career Guide, Military to Federal Career Guide,* and *Jobseeker Guide.*

Jessica Coffey, CFJST, CPRW, is the *Federal Career Corner* newsletter editor and an interview training consultant. For more than 10 years, Jessica has provided career-management strategies to all levels of government and private-sector employees. She graduated from Virginia Tech with a B.S. in Business Management and an M.Ed. in College Student Personnel Administration. Jessica wrote the interview chapter for the *Federal Resume Guidebook,* Fourth Edition; *Ten Steps to a Federal Job;* and *Student's Federal Career Guide.*

Susan Custard, CFRWC, is a Senior Executive Service consultant and writer, and federal human resources manager. With more than 27 years of federal human resources experience, working for several executive agencies (Navy, Interior, Energy), Susan has developed an outstanding reputation for her knowledge and expertise in executive-level staffing and selection. As both an employment manager and human resources director for several large organizations, Susan uses her knowledge and insight of the requirements of the SES process to design successful and focused job search strategies and competitive application materials for each client. Susan has contributed to the SES chapter of the third and fourth editions of *Federal Resume Guidebook,* as well as to *The Student's Federal Career Guide* and *Military to Federal Career Guide.*

Christopher Juge, JD, is an award-winning author, lecturer, and trial attorney. Christopher has nearly 20 years of professional writing experience in the corporate, legal, and government spheres. Currently Christopher is a federal administrative judge and federal employment expert. He authored the "Plain-Language Resumes" chapter in *Federal Resume Guidebook.* This chapter was cutting edge in the 2001 publication of the *Electronic Federal Resume Guidebook* and plain-language lessons have been used in Resumix courses worldwide since then.

Elizabeth Juge, CFJST, CFRW, is an experienced federal resume writer trained in federal human resources recruitment and selection. Elizabeth is an expert in federal resume project assessments and client communication concerning qualifications and experience. Elizabeth's communication and writing credentials are extensive. Applying her degree in mass communication from Tulane University, Elizabeth honed her skills in persuasive and influential writing as a marketing and public relations director for an international luxury hotel chain. Her writings there included business plans, marketing plans, and budget justifications, adding to her skill set in writing for private-industry job seekers as well as all types of federal management positions. Elizabeth contributed to the plain language and career survival chapters of the fourth edition of *Federal Resume Guidebook* and samples for the *Military to Federal Career Guide.*

David Raikow received his Ph.D. in zoology and ecology, evolutionary biology, and behavior from Michigan State University. A research aquatic biologist by trade, David currently works for the National Oceanic and Atmospheric Administration. His scientific work has appeared in *Limnology & Oceanography* and other journals. As a Certified Federal Job Search Trainer, he has written federal resumes, other federal application materials, articles for the Web, and books.

Emily Troutman, MPP, CFRWC, CFJST, is Co-Leader, Certified Federal Job Search Trainer Program; and Vice President, Federal Career Training Institute. Emily graduated from the College of the Atlantic in Bar Harbor, Maine, with a B.A. in human ecology and specializes in writing, publishing, public policy, and international affairs in the Middle East. Emily completed her Master of Public Policy from the Hubert Humphrey Institute, University of Minnesota. Writing ECQs for senior executives has become one of her specializations, along with book editing and training curriculum design for the family business. Emily co-authored *The Student's Federal Career Guide* with Kathryn, as well as the *Military to Federal Career Guide* and the second edition of the *Jobseeker Guide,* the publication used at more than 150 military bases worldwide. She was also the curriculum designer for *Ten Steps to a Federal Job,* Second Edition.

Carla Waskiewicz, CPRW and CFRW, has more than 20 years of professional writing experience. She provides full-service resume writing and career consultation to The Resume Place clients, including private-industry and federal resumes, KSAs, and Resumix writing and editing services. She holds a B.A. in Communications from Penn State University. Carla authored the Administrative chapter for the third and fourth editions of the *Federal Resume Guidebook,* multiple samples for the *Military to Federal Career Guide, The Student's Federal Career Guide, Creating Your High School Resume,* and *Ten Steps to a Federal Job.*

Part 1

Writing a USAJOBS Resume and Other Electronic Federal Resumes

CHAPTER 1

What Is a Federal Resume?

This chapter introduces you to the unique resume format for applying for federal jobs, known as the federal resume, which I developed 10 years ago and published in the first edition of *Federal Resume Guidebook* in 1996, and which remains the standard despite various changes in the application process.

Most federal agencies now require applicants to submit their resumes through "resume builders" on the Internet. This chapter introduces you to the concept of resume builders and briefly describes the most popular ones, especially the USAJOBS Resume builder.

Because USAJOBS and federal agencies are providing "resume builders" for your federal resume and require an electronic submission, you will learn how to write and build (or format) your electronic federal resume at the same time. Our goal is that you will be ready to "copy and paste" your well-written, focused content, which will be correctly formatted and at the right length, into USAJOBS and other agency builders.

No matter how confusing and complex the announcement "how to apply" instructions are, if you have a good electronic federal resume that is focused toward your job (occupational series) and salary (grade), you will be ready to apply (copy and paste) for the positions. And then, of course you will follow the directions for the additional application elements.

Some agencies still accept a paper resume that is mailed, e-mailed, or faxed. This format is the traditional paper format, which is easy to read and looks great.

> **Note:** The next four chapters give instructions for certain sections of the USAJOBS builder. Because more than half of the federal agencies are using the USAJOBS builder, we give you an orientation on this builder throughout the "how to write an outstanding federal resume" content.

What Is a Federal Resume?

A "federal" resume is a resume written to apply for a job with the federal government. The federal resume is usually three to five pages in length, which is longer than a typical business resume. The reason for the additional length is that federal human resources specialists require that you prove in writing the skills that you have. Each generalized and specialized skill that you have developed in your career has to be written into the document. We cover content development for your federal resume further in the rest of part 1.

The History of the Federal Resume

In 1995, then Vice President Al Gore initiated Reinvention Government, which called for the simplification of forms and language in government procedures. One of the best recommendations from this initiative was to eliminate the SF-171, which had gotten out of control. Federal employees were writing 171s that were up to 30 to 50 pages long and were placed into three-ring binders with indexes and tabs, and mailed in large jiffy bags with return receipts. The human resources offices were stacked with up to eight feet of large envelopes all the way down the hallways. The Reduction in Paperwork Act was here; but yet the federal job application was still gargantuan. The electronic revolution was coming, and at that time it would be impossible to e-mail or browse and upload a 30- to 50-page employment form.

Mr. Gore stated that the federal government should recruit and hire people like the rest of the world. Private-industry job seekers typically write a one- to two-page resume, which is a summary of their career focused toward a particular job. Applicants for federal jobs should be able to write a resume to apply for a federal job, Gore reasoned.

The question initially was what would the federal resume look like? Initially the Office of Personnel Management created the OF-510 brochure, which stated "What to Include in Your Resume." This three-panel brochure still did not give a sample or say how this resume should be organized.

I met with a senior manager at the Office of Personnel Management and we discussed a book that would give guidance to federal employees and external applicants about the new resume that would replace the SF-171. I wanted to write a book about it and create samples of the best possible federal resume. My friend and colleague Dick Whitford said, "Kathryn, write your book." So I wrote the first edition of the *Federal Resume Guidebook* and put the cover of the OF-510 on the cover of the book. Now I've written the fourth edition, which focuses on OPM's USAJOBS Resume Builder.

The Original Instructions for Writing a Federal Resume Still Stand

In 1994, the Office of Personnel Management published a brochure called "OF-510: Applying for a Federal Job," which provided guidance to the general public on how to apply for federal jobs and how to construct a federal resume (what necessary work, education, and other information applicants should include in their resumes or other applications). The same instructions contained in the OF-510 have now been incorporated into the USAJOBS resume builder, other agency builders, vacancy announcements, and agency career Web sites. See the OF-510 Federal Resume Chart later in this chapter.

Your Federal Resume Is Your Federal Application and Examination (and Sometimes the Interview, Too)

The federal resume is your application for a federal job. The federal resume is also an examination of sorts. Your federal resume will be assessed for your qualifications and skills; and possibly will be graded by the human resources specialist to determine the level of your qualifications. The federal resume could even be your job interview. On some occasions, supervisors make hiring decisions based on the resume.

A Federal Resume Is Not an OF-612 or SF-171

The federal resume is a resume, not a form. If you read instructions on vacancy announcements stating that you can submit an OF-612 form or a resume, it would be best to use a resume to apply for this position. The agencies that will accept only an OF-612 obviously are not accepting resumes online because the OF-612 is not a form that you can copy and paste or browse and pick up online.

Are You Qualified or Best Qualified?

Prove it in your federal resume. Your resume will be reviewed by the human resources specialist to see whether you have the qualifications for the position and a certain grade level. See "What's Important in your Federal Resume" for a list of what the HR specialist will be looking at when determining which candidates are Best Qualified. The time, research, writing, and editing you put into your federal resume should demonstrate your qualifications in a way that makes the human resources specialist rate your resume Qualified or Best Qualified.

From a Vacancy Announcement: How You Will Be Evaluated

"Resumes will be evaluated for basic qualifications requirements and for the skills needed to perform the duties of the position, as described in this vacancy announcement and identified by the Selecting Official for the position."

The Office of Personnel Management has published a Qualifications Standard (search for this at www.opm.gov), which states the years of experience, specialized experience, generalized experience, education, and certification that are required for certain jobs at certain salaries. The human resources specialist will review your resume to see whether you are Minimally Qualified with the basics, and then Best Qualified with excellent experience that is proven with examples and specifics. You can refer to the Qualifications Standard to make sure you cover all of the job elements in your federal resume.

Federal Human Resources List of What's Important in Your Federal Resume

The human resources staffing specialist will determine your qualifications for the position by looking at the following items in your federal resume. Qualification determinations are based on the following areas of your resume and experience:

Education

- Major field of study
- Number of years completed or number of semester hours completed
- Grade-point average (GPA)

Training

- Related to job only
- Number of days or hours

> **Experience**
> - Quality of experience
> - Directly related to the job or general nature of work
> - Complexity of assignments (what, for whom, why)
> - Decision-making authority or span of control
> - Knowledge, skills, and abilities used
> - Length of experience
> - Full-time or part-time
> - Number of hours per week

The Difference Between Federal Resumes and Private-Industry Resumes

One of the biggest differences between a private-industry resume and a federal resume is the length. The federal resume includes longer and more detailed descriptions of your work experience so that the human resources specialist can ensure that you have performed work at the specific level of the job you are seeking.

Table 1.1: Federal Resume to Private-Industry Resume Comparison

Private Industry	Federal Resume
One to two pages	Three to four pages
No specific description	Include specific qualifications for certain jobs and salary levels
Concise	Detailed and descriptive
Industry language	Federal keywords and skills
Few acronyms	Many acronyms for everything
Targeted toward corporate mission	Targeted toward agency mission
Profit focused	Budget focused
Striving to increase sales	Service within a budget
Corporate mission driven	Legislative, congressional, regulation, compliance driven
Compliant with federal regulations	Federal regulations are interpreted, ensured, complied with, and enforced
Performance analysis	Qualitative and quantitative analysis

(continued)

(continued)

Private Industry	Federal Resume
Business analysis	Program and management analysis
Presentations	Briefings
Writing	Same
Technical details	Same
Customer focused	Same
Project based	Same
Recommendations and solutions	Same
IT database, systems management	Same
Communications skills	Same
Teamwork, team leader	Same

The three biggest differences between federal and private-industry resumes are the following:

★ **Length:** The biggest difference is the length of the resume. The federal resume is usually two times longer than the average private-industry resume. The reason for this difference is that the federal human resources specialists must see your skills, abilities, and experience written on paper.

★ **Writing style:** The second biggest difference is the way you write a federal resume. The federal resume includes more details about your experience. See the difference between the following two private-industry and federal resume sentences:

> ## IT SPECIALIST, GS-12

Private-industry sentence:

> Supervise staff managing information management systems through phases of System Development Life Cycle.

The federal resume sentence includes more details and descriptions:

> Develop and implement plans, and manage, direct, and supervise staff involved in working on information management systems through phases of System Development Life Cycle, including inception, elaboration, construction, transition, and maintenance.

★ **Keywords:** The third biggest difference is the federal language and detailed descriptions of a skill or duty. You can read more about how to find and analyze keywords in chapter 6. The private-industry or short version of a sentence on a Postal Service Worker's resume would be the following:

> CUSTOMER SERVICE: Provide customer service to Defense agency offices and postal lobby customers. Provide quality services, investigate complaints, and advise on cost-effective and efficient ways to mail and ship items.

The federal resume sentence should include specific keywords for this postal service position:

> CUSTOMER SERVICE: Provide **customer service** to a large number of Department of Navy and other Department of Defense agencies as well general customers through **postal lobby services**. **Investigate complaints**, trace lost or damaged mail, and **recommend resolution**. **Provide advice** to customers concerning the most **cost-effective** and **efficient ways** to mail and ship items.

OF-510 Federal Resume Chart: What to Include in Your Federal Resume

Job Information

Announcement number, and title and grade(s) of the job you are applying for

Personal Information

Full name, mailing address (with ZIP code), and day and evening phone numbers (with area codes)

Social Security number

Country of citizenship (most federal jobs require United States citizenship)

Veterans' preference

Reinstatement eligibility (if requested, attach SF-50 proof of your career or career-conditional status)

Highest federal civilian grade held (also give job series and dates held)

Education

Colleges or universities

- Name, city, and state (ZIP code if known)
- Majors
- Type and year of any degrees received (if no degree, show total credits earned and indicate whether semester or quarter hours)
- Send a copy of your college transcript only if the job vacancy announcement requests it.

(continued)

(continued)

Work Experience

Give the following information for your paid and nonpaid work experience related to the job you are applying for (do not send job descriptions):

- Job title (include series and grade if it was a federal job)
- Duties and accomplishments
- Employer's name and address
- Supervisor's name and phone number
- Starting and ending dates (month and year)
- Hours per week
- Salary
- Indicate whether we may contact your current supervisor

Other Qualifications

Job-related training courses (title and year)

Job-related skills, for example, other languages, computer software/hardware, tools, machinery, and typing speed

Job-related certificates and licenses (current only)

Job-related honors, awards, and special accomplishments; for example, publications, memberships in professional or honor societies, leadership activities, public speaking, and performance awards (give dates but do not send documents unless requested)

Federal Resume Formats

There are two federal resume formats: electronic and paper (see the sample formats at the end of this chapter). The USAJOBS resume gets separate billing (even though it is also an electronic format) because the USAJOBS Web site is the official Office of Personnel Management job recruiting Web site and resume builder. To submit a resume to the USAJOBS builder, you simply copy and paste your electronic federal resume version into the OPM's builder (see figure 1.1).

You can submit five resumes to your My USAJOBS account. You can name the resumes with a different occupational series and submit different resumes to different announcements.

The USAJOBS resume has a distinctive look, which is pretty good and is becoming popular among job seekers and agency human resources recruiters. Eventually, most or all agencies will use the USAJOBS resume builder for resume collection. Now, however, only approximately 50 percent of all agencies are using it.

You will learn how to write a template electronic resume that you can copy and paste into all the agency resume builders. The builders may have different character and page length requirements, but you can adjust your content to fit their directions. This chapter introduces you to the various resume builders and their official names, so that you can begin to recognize different formats and systems. Some of the names you will see are USAJOBS, QuickHire, Resumix, and Avue Central. These licensed names are owned by companies that work with federal agencies to help manage recruitment. These systems post vacancy announcements, collect resumes, and help manage the assessment process for the best-qualified candidates. No matter how many names the agencies use for their resume builders and job sites, you can still copy and paste your electronic federal resume into their system as your application.

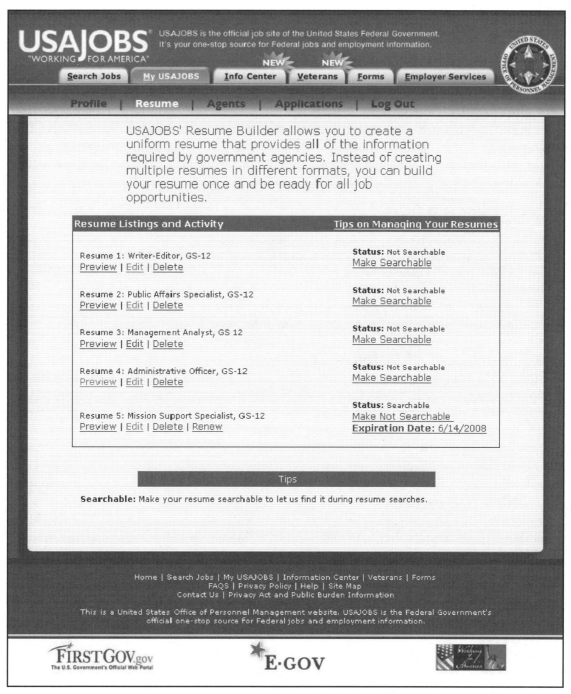

Figure 1.1: The USAJOBS resume builder.

The USAJOBS Resume

The chapters and samples in this book will teach you how to write a successful, focused USAJOBS resume. You will submit your USAJOBS resume to the USAJOBS Web site, which is the federal government's official one-stop source for federal jobs and employment information. The USAJOBS resume is the No. 1 resume builder. USAJOBS is operated by OPM and provides job vacancy information, employment fact sheets, job applications/forms, and online resume development. Job seekers can create a "My USAJOBS" account, where they can create up to five resumes. These resumes are stored in one location, where they can be updated, saved, or sent at any time. The five resumes can be focused toward different federal job titles. This is an excellent feature of the USAJOBS resume builder.

Each resume can be five pages and each job block in your work experience section can be 3,000 characters long.

The Electronic Federal Resume

One focused electronic federal resume basically works for all the resume builders on the agency Web sites. You can count the agency resume builder character count instructions and copy and paste the resume into all of the resume builders. This electronic resume can be versatile for many resume builders. You can see a sample of a focused electronic federal resume on pages 12–14.

The "Paper" Federal Resume

Some agencies still request a paper resume, which can be submitted by mail, by e-mail as an attached file, by fax, or in person. This is the formatted "paper" resume that is impressive for human resources managers and supervisors. The paper resume is usually in Microsoft Word format, and sometimes it can be uploaded into a resume system. When applying for jobs, you might see instructions to "browse" and upload your Word formatted resume. This is unusual for federal applications at this point in the progression of automated resume collectors; however, it occasionally still happens.

The Department of Defense Resumix

The Resumix is a "keyword" resume format written for Department of Defense agencies, including U.S. Navy, Army, Air Force, Marine Corps, and other DOD agencies. (See chapter 6 for more about keywords.) The Resumix is challenging for many job seekers who have not spent time searching for the most prominent skills for their target position. The Resumix is a keyword resume where the human resources specialist searches for the Best Qualified people with keywords. You will learn more about Resumix in chapter 11, "Vacancy Announcement Analysis Techniques."

The QuickHire Resume

Many agencies are using the QuickHire automated resume system, with questions. The QuickHire resume is a 16,000-character, five-page resume that is flexible and very easy to copy and paste into the QuickHire builders. You can see samples of the QuickHire resumes throughout this book.

> ⭐ **Note:** QuickHire and Avue Central are both commercial automated human resources recruiting software systems and databases. Certain agencies choose to use certain companies to recruit candidates and manage resumes. I have introduced them both in this book so that you will know that they are not the same, and it is important to submit your resume to all of the resume builders if you are interested in jobs in many different agencies.

The Avue Central Resume

The Avue Central federal jobs and automated staffing Web site (www.avuecentral.com) is a copy-and-paste resume builder format. This system also enables you to upload a Word-format resume or a paper-format resume. The average length is three to four pages.

> ⭐ Tip: The good news about your electronic federal resume is this: You really need one good three- to four-page electronic federal resume to apply to most federal jobs. Most resume builders will accept this length and content.

Federal Resume Case Studies

Following are samples of federal resumes along with background information about the candidates.

1. USAJOBS Format: Management Assistant Seeking Management Analyst Promotion

Sarah Jacobs is currently a GS-7 with the FBI's Weapons of Mass Destruction Office. She managed to get into the government with an outstanding resume summarizing her administrative experience as the office manager of an embroidery shop. Her prior experience demonstrated analytical, document, database, and customer service experience. Now she is ready for a career-ladder position and has identified a Management Analyst position, GS-9/12. Her skills are excellent for this target position. You will notice that her Summary is written to closely match this list of desired qualifications. Specialized skills and keywords for her target position include the following:

> **Providing assistance to higher-graded analysts by developing** background information for studies; researching **official documents;** compiling and charting **statistical data;** interviewing employees **and supervisors; gathering, summarizing, and** analyzing information **for incorporation into final reports; carrying out specified portions or segments of** specific projects; **and** identifying **and** recommending solutions **to problems.**

Target Job: Management Analyst, Immigration and Customs Enforcement, GS-0343-09.
Career Ladder Position, GS-09/11/12 from current position of Management Assistant GS-07.
Resume format: USAJOBS resume, federal-to-federal career promotion.

Sara Jacobs
4567 Dandelion Way
Apt. 2B
Washington, DC 20009
Mobile: 202-222-2323
Email: smjacobs@verizon.net

Country of citizenship: United States of America
Veterans' Preference: No
Highest Grade: GS-0344-07, 08/2005-present
Contact Current Employer: Yes

AVAILABILITY

Job Type: Permanent
Work Schedule: Full Time
US

DESIRED LOCATIONS

WORK EXPERIENCE

Federal Bureau of Investigation, Weapons of Mass Destruction Directorate
Washington, DC US

8/2005 - Present

Grade Level: GS-07

Salary: 52,794 USD Per Year

Hours per week: 40

Management and Program Assistant, 0344

TECHNICAL MANAGEMENT AND PROGRAM SUPPORT to an analytical workforce. As the sole Management Assistant to 10 Analysts, I support higher-level analysts in research and analysis of weapons of mass destruction. Conduct special research projects as assigned or as a team member. Support analysts with administrative tasks and assist in conducting studies concerning research on weapons of mass destruction.

DATA COLLECTION: Gather, evaluate, and compile variety of data and information to report progress. The analysts depend on me to compile and write drafts of final reports to include editing for obvious omissions or errors, as well as compliance with established format. Produce charts and graphics with content provided by analysts and original research.

REPORT PRODUCTION AND DATABASE ADMINISTRATION: I am the quality-control check and proofread reports and other documents for correct information. Coordinate administrative requirements with other Dept. of Homeland Security offices. I maintain the WMD databases, identify trends/patterns, compile reports, and apply data-gathering methods to collect information.

CUSTOMER SERVICES AND OFFICE ADMINISTRATION: I am the primary point of contact for the Directorate Analysts. I also hold primary responsibility for administrative programs and ensure compliance with all procedural requirements.

ACCOMPLISHMENTS:
+ Updated the WMD database with more than 2 months of data collected by the analysts. Created a spreadsheet with the updated information to summarize data collected, as well as news summaries from major news outlets. Received recognition from my supervisor for attention to detail.
+ Developed a spreadsheet to maintain project status of the Analysts' research, which was posted for easy access and 24x7 viewing. This resulted in less repetition in research and immediate information on available date. (Contact Supervisor: Yes, Supervisor's Name: Joette Zimmerman, Supervisor's Phone: 202-222-2222)

Premier Sportswear, Inc.　　　　　2/2003 - 8/2005

Fredericksburg, VA US　　　　　Salary: 900 USD Per Week

　　　　　　　　　　　　　　　　Hours per week: 40

Office Manager

Managed busy satellite office of screen-printing and embroidery company.

OFFICE ADMINISTRATION AND EFFICIENCY EXPERT: Managed all administrative and operational aspects of office. As Office Manager, I prioritized and balanced workload to complete all tasks for an administrative staff of 6. Answered phones, managed incoming and outgoing correspondence, collected payments, handled basic bookkeeping, and took inventory and ordered supplies. Prepared letters, e-mails, memos, invoices, proposals, contracts, and other internal and external communications using MS Word, Excel, and Works. Established flow and control system for correspondence and files; created and maintained files and records. Tracked performance data in spreadsheets; analyzed data and prepared monthly summary and narrative interpretations for main office.

CUSTOMER SERVICE: I served as the primary contact and account manager for customers, responding to inquiries with attention to detail and efficiency. Scheduled, coordinated, and conducted on- and off-site client meetings and consultations. Assessed needs, advised clients on product selection, and secured orders. Collected design information and forwarded to graphic artists and main office (regularly used scanner, copier, and fax machine). Tracked orders to ensure timely delivery, resolved problems, and followed up with customers to ensure satisfaction. (Contact Supervisor: Yes, Supervisor's Name: Jun Takio, Supervisor's Phone: 540-222-1313)

College Funding Solutions, Inc.　　　9/2001 - 2/2003

Spotsylvania, VA US　　　　　Salary: 26,200 USD Per Year

　　　　　　　　　　　　　　　　Hours per week: 40

Student Loan Consultant

Served as federal and private loan expert, providing information and services to students.

ACCOUNT MANAGEMENT: As a student account representative, I serviced accounts through entire life-cycle; assessed needs, sent student consolidation loan applications to customer, and followed up to make sure literature was understood. Answered all customer inquiries and repeated and interpreted legal and regulatory policies related to joint consolidation loans, grace periods, deferment, forbearance, and promissory notes for private loans.

CUSTOMER SERVICE: Seeking financial help, I provided expertise and counseling to students via phone, explaining their federal rights and privileges, as well as legal, regulatory, and technical aspects of loan consolidation. After gaining explicit consent and necessary personal information, accessed Department of Education's National Student Loan Data System.

ADMINISTRATION: Maintained confidential electronic and paper records, cataloging, routing, and controlling sensitive data. Prepared internal and external correspondence as well as spreadsheets to track activities. Used variety of office software, including Word, Excel, and Outlook.

KEY ACCOMPLISHMENT:
+ Received award for Outstanding Customer Service and Focus. (Contact Supervisor: Yes, Supervisor's Name: Matthew Levy, Supervisor's Phone: 540-333-9595)

(continued)

(continued)

First Credit, Inc.	**1/1999 - 3/2001**
Fredericksburg, VA US	**Salary: 45,000 USD Per Year**
	Hours per week: 40

Direct Banking Associate / Product Specialist

Provided customer care and account management for global Fortune 500 financial services provider. Originally hired as Direct Banking Associate; promoted to Product Specialist.

ACCOUNT MANAGEMENT: Established, maintained, and managed investment accounts and home equity lines of credit, as well as personal, small business, and secured credit card accounts. Disclosed all legal and regulatory policies related to Certificates of Deposit and Money Market Accounts, as well as privacy and income disclosures. Applied knowledge of Truth in Lending Act, Regulation Z (designed to help customers comparison shop), and Regulation X (which regulates certain credit card practices).

CUSTOMER SERVICE: Prescreened applicants via phone with basic questionnaire, provided disclosures and obtained customer's consent, and pulled credit reports. Created, updated, and maintained detailed, sensitive records and files. Ensured confidentiality and proper handling of records. Prepared correspondence, letters, memos, spreadsheets, and other documents. Utilized MS Office (Excel, PowerPoint) and Outlook Express; Lotus WordPerfect and Organizer.

KEY ACCOMPLISHMENTS:
+ One of 10 associates selected for Internet chat test from Marketing & Analysis Department for delivering proactive sales techniques and gaining expertise on Capital One policies and procedures. (Contact Supervisor: Yes, Supervisor's Name: Rafael Henna, Supervisor's Phone: 540-777-4545)

EDUCATION

Strayer University

Fredericksburg, VA US

Some College Coursework Completed - 5/2003

18 Semester Hours

Major: Business Administration

GPA: 3.8 out of 4.0

Germanna Community College

Fredericksburg, VA US

Some College Coursework Completed - 5/1999

21 Semester Hours

Major: General Studies

GPA: 3.3 out of 4.0

James Monroe High School

Fredericksburg, VA US

High School or equivalent - 6/1997

Honors: cum laude

ADDITIONAL INFORMATION

PROFILE: Administrative professional with over 6 years of developing background information for analytical studies, researching official documents, and updating databases and creating spreadsheets to manage information. Possess skill and experience in summarizing and analyzing information for incorporation into final reports and supporting analysts with research, data compilation, project coordination, and tracking. I am an experienced professional administrator with outstanding skills in identifying and resolving problems. Strong analytical and communications skills; expertise in multitasking, working under pressure, and teamwork.

Figure 1.2: A sample resume in the USAJOBS format.

2. Paper Federal Resume Format: Transportation Security Administration Screener Seeks Promotion as Transportation Security Manager—Bomb Appraisal Officer

Mark Eriksson is ready to move up already within TSA. He came from real estate and prior to that was a Master Sgt. in the USMC as an Instructor, Armorer, Special Operations. Mark would like to use his TSA and military training, supervision, and teamwork experience and move up to the H/H level. This Bomb Appraisal Officer is a new position and he would like to leverage his prior military experience, as well as his knowledge of TSA. He offers knowledge of the technical subject, as well as serving as a consultant and an instructor on these devices.

Target skill examples in the Lead position are: Bomb Appraisal Officer (BAO): **Manages** local BAO **Program** and serves as **technical consultant** for the assigned FSD and subordinate managers on all issues involving explosives; **problem-solving; analytical skills; communications** and **teamwork**; improvised explosive devises (IEDs); and Chemical, Biological, Radiological, and Nuclear (CBRN) threats.

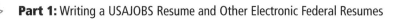

Target Job: Transportation Security Manager—Bomb Appraisal Officer, SV-1801-H/H, from current position as Lead Transportation Security Officer, SV-1802-D/D.
Mark is going to qualify for the H/H Pay Grade based on his military experience as an Instructor/Armorer at Aberdeen Proving Ground.
Resume format: Federal Paper Resume.
Federal-to-federal career promotion.

Mark G. Eriksson

564 Fairmount Ave. • Boston, MA 02045
Residence: 777-222-2323 • Cell: 333-555-1212
E-mail: markge@msn.com

SSN: 000-00-0000	Federal Status: SV-1802-D, 01/2006 to present
Citizenship: U.S.	Veterans' Preference: 5 points

OBJECTIVE: Transportation Security Manager, Bomb Appraisal Officer
Announcement Number: TSA-HQ-2006-0195

PROFILE: More than 20 years of experience in administration, military instruction, special operations, customer service, and knowledge of Transportation Security Administration airport missions. Demonstrated experience in task operations, testing, training, assessments of situations, security precautions, and coordination with law enforcement agencies. At TSA, I am experienced in incident analysis and able to ensure minimal disruption to passengers, checkpoints, and terminals.

Military experience at Aberdeen Proving Ground in Instructor, Armorer, Special Warfare Division. Proven skills in solving problems, leading teams, and managing staff. Strong administrative skills, able to manage office workload, prepare correspondence, maintain records, and coordinate events. Excellent interpersonal and verbal communication skills, able to lead change and build trust. Active Secret Clearance 1991 to 2001.

PROFESSIONAL EXPERIENCE

Transportation Security Officer (Screener), SV-1802-D   01/2006 to present
Transportation Security Administration, Boston, MA   40 hours/week
Supervisor: Jasmine Franks, 777-666-4545. May be contacted.

- Lead Screener: Volunteer to serve as Lead for Screener Checkpoint on daily or as-needed basis, including equipment and personnel. Calibrate equipment and perform shift maintenance. Identify, distribute, and balance workload among 5 employees, making adjustments for workflow and skill level. Schedule employee breaks, ensuring adequate coverage to efficiently and effectively screen travelers. Rotate employees to ensure attentiveness and equal workload, accomplishing goals and meeting established priorities. Monitor flow of passengers through screening checkpoint to facilitate orderly and efficient processing. (Acting Lead 10 hours per week on average.)

- Screener: Screen passengers and carry-on baggage. Technically proficient operating Walk Through Metal Detector, X-ray Machine, Explosive Threat Detection, Explosive Detection System, hand-held metal detector, and other screening equipment. Ensure safe air transport of passengers and baggage. Discover, prevent, and deal with threats to aviation security through complete screening of passengers and baggage, supporting TSA mission of protecting the traveling public. Implement security-screening procedures central to TSA objectives, identifying any deadly or dangerous objects and preventing them from being transported onto an aircraft.

- Communications / Customer Service: Build customer rapport and trust through professional and courteous communications. Answer questions and resolve simple, informal complaints of employees and traveling public; refer others to supervisor or appropriate official. Participate in information briefings on security-sensitive or classified information, and relay information to co-workers as needed. Assist management with inquiries for information or investigations. Maintain

- 1 -

communication with supervisors regarding issues that might reveal weaknesses or vulnerability of security screening discovered during screening duties.

Key Accomplishments / Special Projects:
- Selected to conduct off-site screening of Maryland and Duke women's basketball teams for the Final Four Championship in April. Set up portable screening station at teams' hotel and screened players, coaches, and other staff before they were escorted by state troopers to a chartered plane. Ensured all communications were professional and exceeded customer service expectations.
- Rotate assignment to collect, sort, mark, and store prohibited and lost-and-found items for entire airport. Complete records, both paper and electronic, for tracking purposes, and prepare prohibited items for disposal.

MILITARY EXPERIENCE

Master Sergeant, E-8　　　　　　　　　　　　　　　　　　08/1995 to 10/2001
U.S. Marine Corps　　　　　　　　　　　　　　　　　　　　　40 hours/week
Supervisor: Stanley Swenson, 910-333-5656.

Senior Instructor / Operations Chief, Aberdeen Proving Ground, MD, 07/1998 to 10/2001

- <u>Administration:</u> Coordinated, directed, and completed full range of clerical and administrative duties in support of training and instruction programs. As key member of management staff, served as point of contact for executive officers and subordinate staff. Responded to inquiries and provided staff guidance on policies and procedures.
- <u>Senior Marine Instructor:</u> Served as lead strategist for training support for 2 military occupational specialty schools, managing staff of 21 instructors with 87 students. Ensured department adhered to Marine Corps and Army regulations and standards.

Operations Manager, Quantico, VA, 08/1995 to 07/1998

- <u>Instructor / Armorer:</u> Piloted logistics, operations, administration, and security for 13 individual armories with million-dollar inventories. Reviewed operations and implemented new policies and procedures to ensure tracking of weapons. Ensured new policies were understood and followed, including procedures for physical security, personnel access, and possession monitoring. Troubleshot problems and applied innovative solutions. Provided training and operations support to FBI and DEA. Led public relations and community outreach programs.

Key Accomplishments:
- Brought on as Senior Military Instructor / Operations Chief at Aberdeen Proving Ground, after department failed Inspector General inspection due to poor recordkeeping, resulting in termination of predecessor. Revamped training program, armory recordkeeping policies and procedures, and drug-testing program data collection. Passed subsequent inspections.
- Revised Electro-Optical course, assessing presentation, materials, tests, course objectives, and student learning. Condensed class, eliminating extraneous information and streamlining teaching agenda and presentation. Received Meritorious Service Award, 07/2001.
- Provided support to Coalition and Special Warfare Division in pre-deployment of Riverine Training Team (RTT)/Operation Rompadour to Republic of Colombia, in fighting the war on drugs. Instrumental in efficient and smooth transfer of weapons. Received Letter of Appreciation, 05/1996.

- 2 -

(continued)

(continued)

Mark G. Eriksson | Cell: 333-555-1212
Announcement Number: TSA-HQ-2006-0195 | SSN: 000-00-0000

Staff Sergeant/Various Ranks, E-1 through E-6   08/1977 to 06/1995

State Department Instructor / Trainer, Saudi Arabia, 04/1994 to 06/1995
Selected to lead Small Arms Repair Course and train the trainer for this esteemed assignment. Revised, planned, coordinated, and supervised course instruction. Coordinated resources to build Saudi Royal Marines readiness, providing guidance to develop and implement training course. Formulated innovative periods of instruction and resolved numerous maintenance issues to maximize training opportunities and ensure mission success. Introduced new, cutting-edge equipment. Held additional duty of maintaining armory. Promoted strengthened relationships with allies.

Instructor / Inspector, Dallas, TX, 05/1991 to 04/1994
Held operations and security authority for 23 locations, personnel, inventories, and budgets. Grew reserve armory section into effective, cohesive, and independent group. Team leader and liaison in multiple community programs, including Drug Free campaign and Toys for Tots.

Ground Ordnance Chief, El Toro, CA, 05/1989 to 05/1991
Led resource allocation and operations management for 19 armory locations, inventories, and budgets in support of Desert Storm. Developed and implemented Wing Armed Awareness Safety Program (which became Third Marine Air Wing policy) and Standard Operating Procedures. Fully accountable for personnel and ordnance materials valued at over $9 million. Streamlined arrival/departure processes of 200 aircraft and interactions among several units.

Key Accomplishments:
- Overcame language and culture barriers to train 6 Saudi nationals as small arms repair and weapons maintenance personnel. Awarded Navy and Marine Corps Achievement Medal, 04/1996.
- Successfully spearheaded design of new armory, including supervision of construction. Researched and designed weapons issue ports, resulting in improved efficiency and armory flow. Received Navy Achievement Award, 05/1994.
- Volunteered for additional assignment during Desert Storm, staying on as 3rd MAW Embarkation Chief. Coordinated and assisted loading of 200+ aircraft; led team of 15 embarkation specialists and provided critical logistical coordination between 3rd MAW units, the arrival/departure control group, and Logistics Movement Control Center. Awarded Navy Commendation Medal, 06/1991.

BUSINESS EXPERIENCE

Real Estate Agent | 11/2001 to 12/2005
First Coast Realty, Jacksonville, FL | 40 hours/week
Salary: $50,000/year
Supervisor: Madeline Connor, 904-555-4545. May be contacted.

- Customer Service: Maintained full knowledge of real estate process from buying and selling perspectives. Interviewed clients to determine needs, objectives, and financial resources; researched property listings and recommended appropriate options.

- Communications: Served as instructor for North East Florida Association of Realtors. Taught Ethics, Fair Housing, Antitrust, and Personal Security seminars for 60 to 90 people. Developed curriculum and prepared materials including tests and handouts.

- 3 -

- Contract Review / Recordkeeping: Prepared and reviewed complex legal documents for clients, including representation contracts, purchase agreements, closing statements, deeds, and leases. Ensured data accuracy and completeness.

EDUCATION

Undergraduate Coursework, Computer Science, Park College, Parkville, MO, 1997, 51 credits
Diploma, Westbury Senior High, Houston, TX, 1977

TRAINING

TSA Screener, 40 hours of classroom training plus 60 hours of on-the-job training, 01/2006
Substance Abuse Counseling 09/1999 to 10/2001
Small Arms Weapons Instructor Class, 01/1993 to 10/2001
Advanced Course, 5 weeks, 09/1996
Communications Material Security School, 6 weeks, 09/1993
Senior Military Customs Inspections Course, 4 weeks, 03/1991
Small Arms Repairs, 4 weeks, 03/1983
Engineer Equipment Operator, 9 weeks, 02/1978

Advanced training in Leadership, Communications, Public Speaking, Administration, Operations, Technical Issues, Applied Management, Physical Education, and Military Science.

AWARDS

Meritorious Service Medal, 07/2001
Navy Commendation Medal, 06/1991
Navy and Marine Corps Achievement Medal with one star, 04/1996 and 05/1994
National Defense Service Medal, 02/1991
Marine Corps Good Conduct Medal with five stars, 1977 to 2001
Kuwait Liberation Medal, 02/1992
Armed Forces Expeditionary Medal, 12/1995
Navy and Marine Corps Overseas Service Ribbon with two stars, 07/1995
Joint Meritorious Unit Award, 06/1994
Southwest Asia Service Medal with three stars, 10/1991 to 09/1992

COMPUTER PROFICIENCIES

MS Office: Word, Excel, Outlook, PowerPoint, Access

- 4 -

Figure 1.3: A sample Bomb Appraisal Officer resume.

Summary

One complete, compliant, focused electronic federal resume will get you started with your federal job search campaign. It is best if you edit the resume slightly for each announcement so that you can pick up the keywords from the announcement (see chapter 5 for more on focusing your resume). The next resume writing chapters give you more strategies on how to write an outstanding federal resume in the USAJOBS resume builder that will result in you being Best Qualified and landing an interview and ultimately a job offer and a career opportunity with the U.S. government. You should follow the USAJOBS builder lessons for other builders as well. You will read about all of the builders in chapter 12, "Applying for Jobs with USAJOBS and Other Federal Resume Builders."

CHAPTER 2

Work Experience: The Most Important Section of Your Resume

The Work Experience section is the most important section of your federal resume. Writing the descriptions of work experience is also the most challenging part of writing a federal resume. People ask questions such as these: How much should I write? How much detail? How do I write about my experiences so that the federal HR specialist will understand my job and see that I have the experience for the announced position?

This chapter introduces several ways *not* to write your federal resume, with solutions for a new style. The before-and-after formats are typical problems that I see in my federal resume consulting practice. These presentations enable you to visualize a better way to write your federal resume very quickly.

Federal Job Seekers Write About Their Work Experiences in Many Formats

Is your current federal resume in the "big block" style? Or is it a laundry list of bullets? Is your resume a skeleton? Is it too short? Or is it so generic that the supervisor won't be able to understand what you do all day? Is your resume filled with acronyms, causing a supervisor in another agency to not understand your job duties?

It's time to learn how to write a great federal resume—especially now, with the extensive use of the electronic resume. The electronic resume is fairly new. Many agencies are now collecting resumes online instead of accepting paper submissions. Despite what you might think, an electronic resume *can* look good, read well, be focused, and include highlights. The electronic resume formats in this chapter are successful in all of the resume builders.

For first-time federal job seekers, this chapter will be an eye-opening experience. You will learn how to expand your private-industry resume into the longer, more descriptive text that the HR specialists require to determine whether you are Best Qualified for the position.

What Do You Really Do?

A Defense Finance & Accounting Supervisor told me this: "When I read resumes I sometimes can't tell what they really do." This chapter is dedicated to helping the supervisor understand what you do in your job. In fact, the supervisor will be impressed with your top-level skills and accomplishments, and the excellent match of your past experience to the new position's duties.

The before-and-after samples in the following section will show you how to rewrite your resume so that it is on target with the job, filled with the right keywords, descriptive in the area of critical skills and duties, and includes accomplishments.

The USAJOBS Builder

The USAJOBS Builder provides space for 3,000 characters for your work experience description (see figure 2.1). This is about one full page. The instructions above the block say "Duties, Accomplishments and Related Skills." This chapter focuses on how to write about these components of your experience.

Work Experience ⑦

Note: If your resume is **confidential**, the name of your current employer (indicated by an end date of "present") will not be visible to recruiters performing resume searches. Learn more.

* **Employer Name**	
* **Employer City/ Town**	
* **Employer State/ Province**	
* **Employer Country**	US
* **Formal Title**	
* **Start Date**	December 2006
* **End Date**	Present
Salary	$00,000 USD Per Year
* **Average Hours per week**	
May we contact your supervisor?	○ Yes ⦿ No
Supervisor's name:	
Supervisor's phone number (including area code):	
Is this a Federal Position?	○ Yes ⦿ No
Series:	
Pay Plan and Grade:	

* **Duties, Accomplishments and Related Skills**

(You have 3000 characters remaining for your description...)

✦ ADD WORK EXPERIENCE

— OR

☐ **I have no relevant work experience.**

Figure 2.1: The USAJOBS Resume Builder Work Experience section—Duties, Accomplishments and Related Skills.

Do you want to make the job of the HR specialist and supervisor easier? Yes you do, because it will give you a better chance of being hired. The "after" resumes in the next section represent an excellent perfect mix for the federal human resources specialist who is the first reviewer of your resume.

This detailed, on-target writing style is also excellent for the supervisor who might have 20 to 50 resumes to read and determine the best candidates to interview, or who might on occasion hire based on the resume qualifications.

Resume Success

Your federal resume can be successful in three ways:
- By getting you referred to the supervisor
- By getting you selected by the supervisor for an interview
- By getting you a job offer

OPM's Qualification Standards: Understanding the Importance of Generalized, Specialized Experience and Level of Experience

The HR specialist reviews the description of your work to determine the years of experience, the complexity of your experience, the generalized experience, and the specialized experience. They refer to the Qualification Standards written by the Office of Personnel Management to ensure that the level of your experience is equal to the target job duties and grade level of the position. You can refer to the Qualification Standards yourself when writing your federal resume. Just search for the Standards at www.opm.gov.

The easiest way for you to make sure your resume "hits" the critical skills, specialized experience, and matching duties is to carefully analyze the target vacancy announcement. In chapter 11, we analyze vacancy announcements for the top critical skills the HR specialist will be looking for in your resume.

The following chart comes from the Qualification Standards from OPM. You can read how an HR specialist must decipher your work experience/duties section to determine the Minimally Qualified or the Best Qualified candidates. You can read about General and Specialized Experience and how they look at the Level of Experience in your resume. Hint: If your work is complex, say so.

Qualification Standards for General Schedule Positions

General Policies and Instructions

3. Experience Requirements

Experience is typically described in a qualification standard as either general or specialized experience.

(a) General experience is usually required at grade levels where the knowledge and skills needed to perform the duties of a specific position are not a prerequisite, but where applicants must have demonstrated the ability to acquire the particular knowledge and skills.

(b) Specialized experience is typically required for positions above the entry level where applicants must have demonstrated that they possess the ability to perform successfully the duties of a position after a normal orientation period. Specialized experience is typically in or related to the work of the position to be filled.

(continued)

(continued)

(c) Describing experience in vacancy announcements—The following factors should be considered in describing experience in vacancy announcements:

- Since a published OPM qualification standard may cover hundreds of positions in dozens of organizations, it must be broad enough to cover the range of work classified to the occupational series. Therefore, agencies and examining offices should clearly describe the specific experience or education required to qualify for the positions covered by an examination or vacancy announcement. This will better attract applicants with appropriate qualifications to agencies, thereby greatly improving the effectiveness of the examination process.

- The description of qualifying general experience will vary in its degree of specificity from one series to another. For some occupational series, any progressively responsible work experience may be qualifying. Others may require experience that provided a familiarity with the subject matter or processes of the broad subject area of the occupational series. For example, an entry-level medical technician position may require general experience that provided a basic knowledge of the procedures and equipment in a chemical or clinical laboratory.

- A position description or a position classification standard can usually provide information related to the duties and responsibilities typical of work in an occupational series or position. This information is useful in the staffing process in identifying specialized experience requirements and also in determining the level of experience possessed by applicants.

  1. Determining level of experience—Most qualification standards require that a certain amount of the qualifying experience be at a level of difficulty and responsibility equivalent to the next lower or second lower grade. The grade-level criteria in the position classification standard or guide help in making this determination, particularly for applicants with experience outside the federal government.

  2. Identifying specialized experience—As indicated in (b) above, many qualification standards describe specialized experience as experience "related to the work of the position." This is to allow agencies to pinpoint the specific requirements in the vacancy announcements for their positions. For example, to meet the specialized experience requirements for a medical technician position, the applicant would likely be required to have a specific level of experience performing duties such as preparing culture media and stains and performing certain laboratory tests. The description of duties and responsibilities contained in the position classification standard, along with the position description, help in identifying the kinds of work experience that would meet this requirement. In addition, the knowledge, skills, and abilities required to perform the work may also be described.

Five Ways Not to Write Your Work Experience Section—and Solutions

We will look at a few of the most popular ways not to write your federal resume. The "before" resumes obviously do not clearly describe the candidates' specialized experience and might not describe the level of their experience. We'll study the correction strategies to turn around your federal job search success and improve your ratio of being referred to the supervisor, selected by the supervisor for an interview, and getting hired.

Resume Writing Problem	Federal Resume Writing Solutions
The big block	Outline with headlines and keywords
Laundry list	Outline with accomplishments
Generic with semicolons	Special projects featured
Too short	Specialized experience featured
Filled with acronyms	Plain language

1. The Big Block

The big block format is a popular, hard-to-read format written for the Department of Defense's Resumix system. This resume makes it difficult for the supervisor to decipher the specialized experience, critical skills, and accomplishments, and this is generally not impressive. The keywords for this resume may be integrated into the text (see chapter 6 for more on keywords). This resume could be referred to the supervisor, but because it is difficult to read, this candidate might not be selected for an interview.

WORK EXPERIENCE   **Commander Navy Installations Command**   **1/2005 - Present**
Millington, Tennessee US

Hours per week: 40

Management Analyst, GS-0341-11
Management Analyst for the Family Readiness Programs that include Navy Family Ombudsman Program and Deployment Readiness Program. Responsible for program development and strategic initiatives that have led to improvements and delivery of all Family Readiness Programs at 62 delivery sites worldwide. Conducted and researched issues that required modifications to regulations and policy development. Assisted in the development, implementation, maintenance, and evaluation of the Navy Family Ombudsman Program and Deployment Readiness Program. Analyzed issues; identified best course of action; determined potential impact on retention, readiness, and subordinate organizations; and provided recommendations for corrective actions. FAMILY READINESS: Developed numerous program initiatives that directly impacted retention, readiness, and career progression. Served as Subject Matter Expert for the revision of the Ombudsman Program Manual and Instructor's Guide. SURVEYS: Created three surveys to be completed by Ombudsmen, Fleet and Family Support Center Ombudsmen Coordinators, and Command Leadership. Collected and reviewed data, analyzed data, and exported it into Excel spreadsheets and PowerPoint for use at the annual Ombudsman Quality Management Board meeting for discussion on how to improve the Navy Family Ombudsman Program. DATABASE MANAGEMENT: Administrator of Ombudsman Registry (CNO initiative). Oversee database implementation, evaluation, and quality control. Conduct formal and informal surveys of field sites. Consolidate and analyze statistical data and trends utilizing data to develop reports for Navy Leadership, DoD, and Congress regarding the status of the Ombudsman Program. Additional responsibilities include developing contract mod, approving and administrating user access levels, and ensuring command data is accurate. ACCOMPLISHMENTS: During supervisor's two-month absence, functioned as Program Manager. Responsible for reviewing and making recommendations/corrections to revised OPNAVINST, Ombudsman Program Manual, Ombudsman Instructor's Guide, and Ombudsman video. (Contact Supervisor: Yes, Supervisor's Name: John Smith, Supervisor's Phone: (804) 333-3333)

Figure 2.2: Before.

After: Outline Format with Keywords and Headlines

This is the new electronic resume format, which is organized into critical skill sets to emphasize the candidate's top specialized experience. This format targets the future position, includes headlines with keywords, and is easy to read—even in an electronic resume builder system. The ALL CAPS words are keywords found in the vacancy announcement and the Qualifications Standards. This resume is also interesting to read!

WORK EXPERIENCE	Commander Navy Installations Command Millington, Tennessee US	1/2005 - Present Grade Level: GS-11 Salary: 49,559.00 USD Per Year Hours per week: 40

Management Analyst, GS 0341-11 , 0341
During the Program Manager of Commander Navy Installations Command's 2-month absence, I served as Acting Program Manager, continuing to implement significant change, efficiency, and service initiatives for a growing customer base (military families in transition), with a dramatically decreased budget for the Family Employment Readiness Managers located at 62 military bases worldwide.

PROGRAM MANAGEMENT: Management Analyst for the Navy Headquarters Family Readiness Programs, including Navy Family Ombudsman Program and Deployment Readiness Program.

PLAN AND DEVELOP STRATEGIC INITIATIVES that have led to improvements and delivery of Family Readiness Programs at 62 delivery sites worldwide. I continued the management of improved programs and initiatives for Family Employment Readiness Program Managers and military families worldwide. Evaluate effectiveness of programs and efficiency of management. Plan and conduct in-depth studies, analyze data, and develop policy recommendations.

CUSTOMER COMMUNICATIONS: Extensive communications, problem-solving, and program implementation with program personnel located at U.S. Navy Fleet and Family Support Centers worldwide. Prepare and present briefings and presentations on analytical findings and recommendations; represent agency at meetings and conferences.

FAMILY READINESS STAFF TRAINING: Developed, oversaw, coordinated, and presented numerous program initiatives that directly impacted retention, readiness, and career progression. Maintain contact within DoD and professional community to utilize latest ideas, methodologies, and issues.

DATA MANAGEMENT AND ANALYSIS: Administrator of Ombudsman Registry. Serve as advisor on development of the database. Oversee database implementation, evaluation, and quality control. Conduct formal and informal surveys of field sites. Consolidate and analyze statistical data and trends, utilizing data to develop reports for Navy Leadership, DoD, and Congress regarding the status of Ombudsman Program. Additional responsibilities include developing contract mod, approving and administering user access levels and ensuring command data is accurate.

ACCOMPLISHMENTS AND SPECIAL PROJECTS:

+ POLICY IMPROVEMENTS AND MODIFICATIONS: Navy Family Ombudsman Program and Deployment Readiness Program. Researched issues that required modifications to regulations and policy development. Analyzed issues; identified best course of action; determined potential impact on retention, readiness, and subordinate organizations; and provided recommendations for corrective actions.

+ OMBUDSMAN PROGRAM MANUAL. Served as Subject Matter Expert for the revision of the Ombudsman Program Manual and Instructor's Guide. Reviewed and provided recommendations and corrections to revised OPNAVINST, Ombudsman Program Manual, Ombudsman Instructor's Guide and Ombudsman video, 2nd Edition.

+ SURVEY DESIGN AND DEVELOPMENT: Created three surveys. (Contact Supervisor: Yes, Supervisor's Name: John Smith, Supervisor's Phone: (703) 000-0000)

Figure 2.3: After.

2. The Laundry List

The work experience section of your Federal resume should not be a list of bulleted short sentences that do not complete the skill set and will not impress the human resources specialist or supervisor. This resume needs to be described in more detail to cover the critical job elements.

WORK EXPERIENCE	NIH Office of Extramural Activities Support Bethesda, Maryland US	8/2005 - Present Grade Level: GS-8 Hours per week: 40

LEAD EXTRAMURAL SUPPORT ASSISTANT (TASK LEADER) , 0303
• Supervise a seven-member administrative support team providing meeting and special events planning, purchasing, and travel.
• Coordinate staff assignments and ensure deadlines are met.
• Team with Program Officers, Administrative Technicians, and the Director's Executive Secretary to identify and resolve administrative issues.
• Process and review travel and training using NBS Travel Manager and NIHITS.
• Evaluate staff performance and recommend training to increase individual and organizational performance.
• Serve on a staff training committee tasked with creating a curriculum catalogue for DEAS staff training and establishing an intranet service.
• Volunteered to serve as co-interviewer for selecting potential Grants Clerk candidates in 2006.
• Recognition and Appreciation Special Achievement Award, NINDS, NIH, 8/2003.
• Windows operating system; MS Office suite; WordPerfect Office suite; Adobe Acrobat; HPScanJet; Adobe Photoshop; CorelDRAW; Microsoft Access; Corel Paint Shop Pro 8; Roxio Easy CD Burning software. Federal Database Systems: NBS Travel Manager, NIHITS, AMBIS, IMPAC II, QVR, and ECARES. Hardware and Software installations. Keyboard Rate: 60 wpm. (Contact Supervisor: Yes, Supervisor's Name: Ron White, Supervisor's Phone: (301) 888-8888)

Figure 2.4: Before.

After: Outline Format with Top Skills and Accomplishments

This Outline Electronic Resume format is far more impressive, with small skill paragraphs that also match the top skills in the target vacancy announcement. The sentences are complete and cover the specialized qualifications of the new position. The ALL CAPS words are top critical skills and keywords for the position.

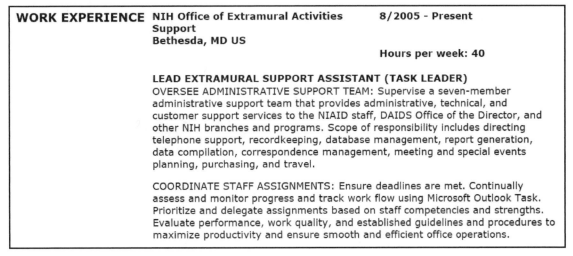

WORK EXPERIENCE	NIH Office of Extramural Activities Support Bethesda, MD US	8/2005 - Present Hours per week: 40

LEAD EXTRAMURAL SUPPORT ASSISTANT (TASK LEADER)
OVERSEE ADMINISTRATIVE SUPPORT TEAM: Supervise a seven-member administrative support team that provides administrative, technical, and customer support services to the NIAID staff, DAIDS Office of the Director, and other NIH branches and programs. Scope of responsibility includes directing telephone support, recordkeeping, database management, report generation, data compilation, correspondence management, meeting and special events planning, purchasing, and travel.

COORDINATE STAFF ASSIGNMENTS: Ensure deadlines are met. Continually assess and monitor progress and track work flow using Microsoft Outlook Task. Prioritize and delegate assignments based on staff competencies and strengths. Evaluate performance, work quality, and established guidelines and procedures to maximize productivity and ensure smooth and efficient office operations.

(continued)

(continued)

ADMINISTRATIVE LIAISON: Team with Program Officers, Administrative Technicians, and the Director's Executive Secretary to identify and resolve administrative issues and develop strategies, processes, and procedures to improve administrative operations.

OVERSEE TRAVEL: Process and review travel and training using NBS Travel Manager and NIHITS. Ensure all documentation is accurate and complete for forwarding to the Administrative Technicians. Review 15-20 travel authorizations and 10 vouchers per week. Access AMBIS for conference registrations and office supplies.

MENTOR & MOTIVATE STAFF, FACILITATE TRAINING: Evaluate staff performance and recommend training to increase individual and organizational performance. Review and recommend training to improve staff competencies. Coach and mentor staff to resolve workplace issues. Facilitate problem solving and collaboration. Recommend staff for awards and ensure accomplishments are recognized. Provide monthly status report of team activities and success in achieving the program plan. Coordinate and chair monthly DEAS meetings for up to 20 attendees. Set up room, write agendas, and take minutes.

ACCOMPLISHMENTS:
++ Selected by supervisor to serve on a staff training committee tasked with creating a curriculum catalogue for DEAS staff training and establishing an intranet service.
++ Commended by the former director for "Demonstrating a clear grasp on level of attention to detail...the foundation of good customer relations."
++ Nominated by a supervisor in 2005 for a monetary Special Achievement Award for outstanding contribution as DAIT's Acting Task Leader.
++ Volunteered to serve as co-interviewer for selecting potential Grants Clerk candidates in 2006.

Figure 2.5: After.

3. Generic with Semicolons

This resume format is not organized into skill sets. Nothing stands out and the words become blurred. It's simply a list of phrases and semicolons without direction.

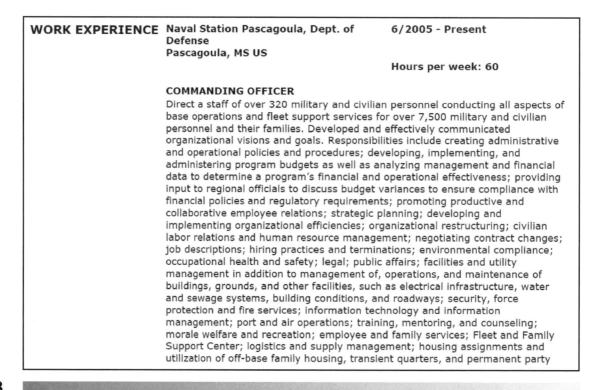

WORK EXPERIENCE	Naval Station Pascagoula, Dept. of Defense	6/2005 - Present
	Pascagoula, MS US	
		Hours per week: 60

COMMANDING OFFICER
Direct a staff of over 320 military and civilian personnel conducting all aspects of base operations and fleet support services for over 7,500 military and civilian personnel and their families. Developed and effectively communicated organizational visions and goals. Responsibilities include creating administrative and operational policies and procedures; developing, implementing, and administering program budgets as well as analyzing management and financial data to determine a program's financial and operational effectiveness; providing input to regional officials to discuss budget variances to ensure compliance with financial policies and regulatory requirements; promoting productive and collaborative employee relations; strategic planning; developing and implementing organizational efficiencies; organizational restructuring; civilian labor relations and human resource management; negotiating contract changes; job descriptions; hiring practices and terminations; environmental compliance; occupational health and safety; legal; public affairs; facilities and utility management in addition to management of, operations, and maintenance of buildings, grounds, and other facilities, such as electrical infrastructure, water and sewage systems, building conditions, and roadways; security, force protection and fire services; information technology and information management; port and air operations; training, mentoring, and counseling; morale welfare and recreation; employee and family services; Fleet and Family Support Center; logistics and supply management; housing assignments and utilization of off-base family housing, transient quarters, and permanent party

> quarters. Lead, monitor, and direct administration and operation of all departments as well as developing and exercising financial and management control; providing technical advice, guidance, and assistance; analyzing, developing, evaluating, and promoting improvements in the policies, plans, methods, and procedures of all programs. Developing and implementing courses of action to be taken to resolve deficiencies. Supporting tenant functions: medical and dental clinic operations; ship-repair services; Navy exchange operations; U. S. Coast Guard support, which includes ship and shore station support; Commander Destroyer Squadron Six and U.S. Navy ships.

Figure 2.6: Before.

After: Federal Resume with Projects Featured

This resume is impressive, presents the top skills that will be of the most interest for future positions, and includes the most challenging accomplishments during this time period. Again, this uses an Outline format with critical skills of the job featured. The critical skills are found in the Duties and Specialized Experience section of the job announcement.

WORK EXPERIENCE	Naval Station Pascagoula, Dept. of Defense Pascagoula, MS US	6/2005 - Present Hours per week: 60

COMMANDING OFFICER

MANPOWER/MANNING MANAGER. Fully implemented the Navy's Human Capital Strategy by constantly assessing the required core competencies of a staff of over 320 military and civilian personnel conducting base operations and fleet support services for over 7,500 military and civilian personnel.

EMPLOYEE DEVELOPMENT. Provided continuous personnel development based on job requirements and individual competencies to meet the demands of a dynamic work environment to enhance the necessary knowledge and skills required in the workplace.

PERSONNEL PROGRAM MANAGER. Supervised programs for the recruitment, hiring, orientation, and payroll of AFP and NAF employees. Ensured that all Equal Employment Opportunity programs were satisfied.

ACCOMPLISHMENTS:

HURRICANE KATRINA RECOVERY (2005). Hurricane Katrina is considered one of the costliest and deadliest natural disasters to hit the United States. I led Naval Station Pascagoula in recovery efforts to stabilize and bring all resources back online by rapidly modifying personnel and financial strategies. Developed logistics chains that delivered over 1,400 tons of food and other supplies to support base and community recovery efforts. Reorganized base and tenant functions to address immediate personnel needs; established a support structure that aided over 9,200 military and civilian personnel and their families.

The major challenge in the recovery efforts was clearing the waterways so that base operations could return to operational capability while balancing the needs of personnel for home and financial recovery in their personal lives. The support structure process and design was adopted by the Chief of Naval Installations Command as a best practice. I was awarded the DEFENSE MERITORIOUS SERVICE MEDAL and the Humanitarian Service Medal for resourcefulness, creativity, and leadership during the crisis.

BASE REALIGNMENT AND CLOSURE (BRAC) (2005). BRAC is the congressionally authorized process DoD has previously used to reorganize its base structure to more efficiently and effectively support our forces, increase operational readiness, and facilitate new ways of doing business. Due to the level of destruction of Naval Station Pascagoula from Hurricane Katrina, I realized that the cost of reconstruction far outweighed the current and/or future capability of Naval Station Pascagoula. Conducted a detailed and comprehensive manpower

(continued)

(continued)

assessment to meet the requirements of the congressionally mandated base closure. Ultimately winning approval for the comprehensive closure and redevelopment plan that will save over $120 million.

ACTIVITY BASED COSTING (ABC) MANAGEMENT. ABC is a more accurate cost-management system than traditional cost accounting used to identify, describe, assign costs to, and report on agency operations. ABC identifies opportunities to improve business process effectiveness and efficiency by determining the "true" cost of a product or service.

Figure 2.7: After.

4. Too Short

This work experience description did not cover all the elements of the position. Multiple areas of responsibility were not even mentioned.

WORK EXPERIENCE	Dept. of Homeland Security, Citizenship and Immigration Newark Asylum Office, 120 Wall Street West, Lyndhurst, NJ US	11/2006 - Present
		Hours per week: 40

IT SPECIALIST (CUSTOMER SUPPORT)
Systems analyst for the Local Area Network. Reconfigured system and updated user authorities. Redesigned directory structure on the primary server, increasing throughput significantly. Removed excess systems, software, and documentation. Upgraded system support library. Configured users and machines into a Microsoft domain server to ensure compatibility with exchange server to enhance the migration from cc:Mail to Outlook. I am the ISSO, PICS, TECS, and LEA for the office. T1 DHS/USCIS Security Clearance.

Figure 2.8: Before.

After: Expanded—Specialized Experience Featured

This IT Specialist/Systems Analyst held multiple responsibilities for networking, systems analysis, customer service, and special projects. This description now covers all of the elements in the 2210 job series.

WORK EXPERIENCE	Dept. of Homeland Security, Citizenship and Immigration Newark Asylum Office, 120 Wall Street West, Lyndhurst, NJ US	11/2006 - Present
		Hours per week: 40

IT SPECIALIST (CUSTOMER SUPPORT)
SYSTEMS ANALYST FOR THE LOCAL AREA NETWORK. Serve as the Local Area Network (LAN) manager for the organization. Identify and control all LAN hardware and software configuration requirements. Develop technical standards and procedures for LAN development, implementation, and management. Establish performance management metrics. Evaluate overall LAN performance against relevant standards. Provide technical advice and consultation to users. Manage the design, security assessment, configuration, installation, setup, and certification of intranet/Internet servers and software. Manage the utilization of 3270 emulation programs, A2B, Access 95, and other web-based programs.

MANAGE THE INSTALLATION, TESTING, OPERATIONS, troubleshooting, and maintenance of computer systems and associated hardware and software; evaluate problem areas and offer technical guidance for hardware and software, including analyzing and diagnosing systems problems.

MANAGE HELP DESK SUPPORT. Provide synchronization of operations between Tier 1 Help Desk support using Remedy. Act as Tier 2 and 3 support provider for all program, security, and systems issues. Manage the configuring, maintenance, and administration of a networked MS Windows system. Provide guidance for e-mail, office software applications, databases, and word-processing applications. Assess the total need for additional computers and analyze a variety of problems and questions to make recommendations for an optimum communication plan to satisfy functional needs.

TECHNICAL SUPPORT FOR 100 USERS. Assigned as the ISSO, PICS, TECS, and LEA for the office. Provide technical support to 100 users (with two servers, 40 printers, and two locations) who need advice, assistance, and training in applying hardware and software systems. Manage difficult and complex problems in customer support. Provide professional and courteous customer service to users in person and/or via the telephone.

TECHNICAL SUPPORT FOR USERS. Provide complex technical support and assistance to the office staff / users with installing and troubleshooting, new software, versions and updates, and acceptance of communication/network facilities; and configure and test software, hardware, and other user systems for effective integration of software systems.

EVALUATE NEW TOOLS. Evaluate and report on new tools and trends in the customer support field and recommend purchase of new tools to enhance the delivery of customer support services as required.

MANAGEMENT ADVISOR. Consult on major aspects of ADP system design, including what system interrelationships must be considered, or what operating mode, system software, and/or equipment configuration is most appropriate for a given project.

SPECIFIC ACHIEVEMENTS...

CONTINUED IN ADDITIONAL INFORMATION ...

Figure 2.9: After.

5. Acronyms in a Big Block

This DFAS Resumix is a giant description of a complex position. The real job is described in the "after" resume. One of the biggest problems with this version is that the reader does not know the "who" in this accounting description. Who are the customers? What are the biggest challenges? How complex is this work? The Accounting Technician series is very competitive, and the most successful applicants get promoted and hired with resumes that feature skills in technical skills and customer service/solutions.

WORK EXPERIENCE	Defense Finance & Accounting Service	1/2005 - Present
	St. Louis, MO US	Grade Level: GS-07
		Hours per week: 40

ACCOUNTING TECHNICIAN , 0525
In Reports and Analysis, I work all appropriations for four commands, including Defense Working Capital Fund. I retrieve errors from the Electra Subsystem Program (Electronic Error Correction and Transactions Analysis) monthly. I research and correct edit errors using Defense Finance and Accounting Service (DFAS), Indianapolis Manual 37-100, Army regulations, to accurately identify the correct data to upload in the Electra Subsystem Program the same day. I research and interpret the Army Regulations 37-1 to identify obligations exceeding funds for different appropriations. I contact the customer to facilitate correction. I retrieve the Funding Authorization Documents (FADS) from the Program and Budget Accounting System (PBAS) daily. I research SOMARDS (Standard Operations and Maintenance Army Research and Development System) daily to reconcile the funding with Funding Authorization Documents. I contact the customer in a written memo identifying any funding discrepancies

(continued)

(continued)

within the reporting cycle. I attach my queries to show which Army Management Structure Codes (AMSCO) are out of balance to assist them in correcting the database. I access the BEIS (Business Enterprise Information Services) system daily to retrieve suspended transactions for all appropriations. I analyze and research suspended data using the Army's regulations to clear suspended transactions in the BEIS system. I communicate with the customer in writing, providing them with the invalid transactions for them to correct in the database. I follow up with a telephone call. I submit footnote requests from Headquarters Indianapolis for abnormal balances to appropriate office in transmittal format with attached spreadsheets identifying lines requiring footnotes monthly. Use Microsoft Word to format the footnotes into the appropriate document. I submit completed footnotes to Headquarters Indianapolis Department of the Army reporting level within the established time frame. I use the File Transfer Protocol Server (FTP), a subsystem, to retrieve Command Expenditure Reports (CER). I use Excel to prepare spreadsheets showing disbursements discrepancies between the database and Data Element Management Accounting Report (DELMAR – treasury). I am responsible for researching disbursement discrepancies differences and providing all information necessary to perform correction to the proper area. I assist accountants in analyzing, researching, and resolving abnormal balance conditions to facilitate resolution by command or functional area prior to month end. I accurately prepare various mathematical spreadsheets using formulas to calculate required data to submit to customers and accountants. I retrieve access reports weekly for the accountants and supervisor. I answer inquiries in person, telephonically, or through written correspondence in a courteous and timely manner. (Contact Supervisor: Yes, Supervisor's Name: John Smith, Supervisor's Phone: (301) 000-0000)

Figure 2.10: Before.

After: Plain Language and Structured

This new Outline format is easier to read and understand. It clearly presents the customer commands in the first paragraph. Then the major duties are separated into paragraphs. The complexity of the work is clear and specialized experience is easier to find. The accomplishments demonstrate outstanding service; the human resources specialist will be impressed with the "above and beyond" work performance.

WORK EXPERIENCE	Defense Finance & Accounting Service	1/2005 - Present
	St. Louis, MO US	
		Hours per week: 40

ACCOUNTING TECHNICIAN
REPORTS AND ANALYSIS OF APPROPRIATIONS FOR FOUR DEPARTMENT OF DEFENSE ARMY COMMANDS: Communications Electronics Command, Ft. Monmouth, NJ; Tank Automotive and Armament Command, Warren, MI; Tank Automotive and Armament Command, Rock Island, IL; Research, Development Command, Picatinny Arsenal, Dover, NJ; and Defense Working Capital Fund.

RESEARCH, RETRIEVE, VALIDATE, AND RECONCILE ERRORS from Electronic Error Correction and Transactions Analysis (Electra Subsystem Program) monthly, using Army regulations to identify correct data to upload in Electra program. Research Military Interdepartmental Purchase Requisitions (MIPR). Submit footnote requests monthly from Headquarters Indianapolis for abnormal balances to appropriate office in transmittal format with attached spreadsheets identifying lines requiring footnotes. Research automated and manual files. Resolve discrepancies and complete reconciliation of invoices on contracts. Coordinate work of the Contracting Officer Representative (COR). Reconcile invoices on contracts. Create, format, edit, and modify footnotes into appropriate documents. Submit completed footnotes to Headquarters Indianapolis.

ANALYZE AND RESEARCH SUSPENDED DATA daily to clear suspended transactions in Business Enterprise Information Services (BEIS) system for all appropriations. Retrieve Funding Authorization Documents (FADS) from the Program and Budget Accounting System (PBAS) daily. Research Standard Operations and Maintenance Army Research and Development System (SOMARDS) weekly to reconcile funding with Funding Authorization Documents submitted according to Army Management Structure Codes. Assist accountants in analyzing, researching, and reconciling abnormal balances.

IDENTIFY FUNDING DISCREPANCIES within the reporting cycle by contacting customers. Use File Transfer Protocol Server (FTP) to retrieve Command Expenditure Reports (CER). Prepare spreadsheets showing disbursement discrepancies between SOMARDS and Data Element Management Accounting Report (DELMAR). Research CER differences and provide information to perform corrections. Assist DFAS by researching and reconciling disputed vendor bills. Research SOMARDS for over-obligated funds and contact the appropriate office to facilitate correction. Accurately prepare variety of mathematical spreadsheets using formulas to calculate required data to submit to customers and accountants. Answer inquiries in person, via phone, or through written correspondence.

ACCOMPLISHMENTS
SPECIAL ACT AWARD for outstanding contributions to DFAS and exceptional support to the mission of the General Funds Reports Branch during the fiscal-year-end processing. Assisted accountants in completing the AMCOM-Missile year-end TABS and Edits--

OTHER ACCOMPLISHMENTS CONTINUED IN ADDITIONAL INFORMATION...

Figure 2.11: After.

Federal Resume Writing Lessons

Federal HR specialists like the Outline format a lot! The all-new, popular Outline approach is based on the concept of "how many hats do you wear at work"? The electronic resume Outline format presented in training classes by the author more than 1,000 times in 100 federal agencies where the Resumix and electronic resume format are required. Federal HR specialists attend these classes frequently and say this about the new format: "I love the cause-and-effect style of writing." "This is great, easy to read." "I love it!" "This is so much easier to read." "I can see what people actually do." "This will work for us."

The New Concept: How Many Hats Do You Wear at Work?

The Outline format was created at a meeting I had with a management consultant in 1999. In order to advise me in my business management, he asked me what I did at work. At first I was overwhelmed with the question (and realized why writing a resume was overwhelming) and didn't know where to start with the answer. Then I thought of a quick way to answer the question just by giving him the "hats I wear at work." I answered him simply with this list. I am a

★ Webmaster

★ Author/publisher

★ Small-business owner

★ Career counselor

★ Trainer

This list would ultimately become the description of my current work experience if I wrote a resume. This is a perfect outline for my job and is very true. I would then fill in the outline with my duties and responsibilities.

Nouns and Headlines for Interest, Critical Skill, Keyword, and Duty Descriptions

In 2005, I traveled to more than 20 Defense Finance and Accounting Service agencies U.S.-wide to teach DFAS employees how to write a Resumix. Their agencies were restructuring in the BRAC from 29 agencies to about 4 in the U.S. During this time of extensive travel, I was checking yahoo.com news to stay in touch with the world. I read the five-word headlines with great interest; and one day it dawned on me that the five-word headlines would be great in the popular Outline Electronic resume format, instead of using a simple noun.

Write Your Outline Format Work Experience Description

Here are three easy steps for writing your Outline-format work experience description.

1. CREATE AN OUTLINE OF YOUR CURRENT JOB

In the case of the USAJOBS sample for Sara Jacobs in figure 1.2 in chapter 1, the candidate's current work experience outline would be the following:

★ Reports Analyst for Commands

★ Researcher—Research Errors

★ Suspense Analyst

★ Problem-solver–Identify funding discrepancies

The following Outline resume format was expanded from a noun to a headline for the Accounting Technician's resume. We converted the nouns into headlines with a few more words to describe the content of the work.

Mar 01 – Present; ACCOUNTING TECHNICIAN, GS-0525-07 (GS-6 promotion 03/2001; GS-7 03/2002), Defense Finance and Accounting Service, St Louis, MO 63120, Supervisor: Learlene Riley, (314) 260-3059; may contact, Annual Salary: $00,0000; Weekly hours worked: 40 hrs

REPORTS AND ANALYSIS OF APPROPRIATIONS FOR FOUR DEPARTMENT OF DEFENSE ARMY COMMANDS:

RESEARCH, RETRIEVE, VALIDATE, AND RECONCILE ERRORS

ANALYZE AND RESEARCH SUSPENDED DATA

IDENTIFY FUNDING DISCREPANCIES

---

2. FILL IN THE OUTLINE WITH A DESCRIPTION OF EACH CRITICAL SKILL

Write two to five sentences about each major skill area to describe your duties. You can use content from your current resume or language from vacancy announcements to help you describe your duties.

Mar 01 – Present; ACCOUNTING TECHNICIAN, GS-0525-07 (GS-6 promotion 03/2001; GS-7 03/2002), Defense Finance and Accounting Service, St Louis, MO 63120, Supervisor: Learlene Riley, (314) 260-3059; may contact, Annual Salary: $00,0000; Weekly hours worked: 40 hrs

---

REPORTS AND ANALYSIS OF APPROPRIATIONS FOR FOUR DEPARTMENT OF DEFENSE ARMY COMMANDS: Communications Electronics Command, Ft. Monmouth, NJ; Tank Automotive and Armament Command, Warren, MI; Tank Automotive and Armament Command, Rock Island, IL; Research, Development Command, Picatinny Arsenal, Dover, NJ; and Defense Working Capital Fund.

RESEARCH, RETRIEVE, VALIDATE, AND RECONCILE ERRORS from Electronic Error Correction and Transactions Analysis (Electra Subsystem Program) monthly, using Army regulations to identify correct data to upload in the Electra program. Research Military Interdepartmental Purchase Requisitions (MIPR). Submit footnote requests monthly from Headquarters Indianapolis for abnormal balances to appropriate office in transmittal format with attached spreadsheets identifying lines requiring footnotes. Research automated and manual files. Resolve discrepancies and complete reconciliation of invoices on contracts. Coordinate work the Contracting Officer Representative (COR). Reconcile invoices on contracts. Create, format, edit, and modify footnotes into appropriate documents. Submit completed footnotes to Headquarters Indianapolis.

ANALYZE AND RESEARCH SUSPENDED DATA daily to clear suspended transactions in the Business Enterprise Information Services (BEIS) system for all appropriations. Retrieve Funding Authorization Documents (FADS) from the Program and Budget Accounting System (PBAS) daily. Research Standard Operations and Maintenance Army Research and Development System (SOMARDS) weekly to reconcile funding with Funding Authorization Documents submitted according to Army Management Structure Codes. Assist accountants in analyzing, researching, and reconciling abnormal balances.

IDENTIFY FUNDING DISCREPANCIES within the reporting cycle by contacting customers. Use File Transfer Protocol Server (FTP) to retrieve Command Expenditure Reports (CER). Prepare spreadsheets showing disbursement discrepancies between SOMARDS and Data Element Management Accounting Report (DELMAR). Research CER differences and provide information to perform corrections. Assist DFAS by researching and reconciling disputed vendor bills. Research SOMARDS for over-obligated funds and contact the appropriate office to facilitate correction. Accurately prepare a variety of mathematical spreadsheets using formulas to calculate required data to submit to customers and accountants. Answer inquiries in person, via phone, or through written correspondence.

3. ADD ACCOMPLISHMENTS AT THE END OF EACH OF YOUR MOST RECENT TWO OR THREE POSITIONS

ACCOMPLISHMENTS

SPECIAL ACT AWARD for outstanding contributions to DFAS and exceptional support to the mission of the General Funds Reports Branch during the fiscal year-end processing. Assisted accountants in completing the AMCOM-Missile year-end TABS and Edits; helped key the pen-and-ink changes sent in by the commands; and keyed and monitored General Ledger changes. Member of Missile team. Met customer's year-end demands and all year-end processes one week ahead of schedule. Dedication allowed the General Funds Reports Branch to meet the FY-05 year-end deadlines with quality and accurate reports. 2005

More on the All-Important Accomplishments: What Have You Accomplished?

When the supervisor has 30 to 50 resumes on his desk, he will need to choose the to three or five Best Qualified. What is the one question a prospective employer is most interested in when interviewing you for a job—the question that comes up in every job interview you will ever have? You guessed it; it's the "What have you accomplished recently," or "What have you done in the past year or so" inquiry that every employer wants to know about—and for a good reason.

From an employer's point of view, accomplishments, unlike the duties and responsibilities outlined in every job description and resume ever submitted (which an applicant might or might not have done well), show what you have actually done. And it is only by your actions and your accomplishments that an employer can make an educated guess as to whether you can actually do the job for which you are applying.

This cannot be overstated. Your accomplishments and the way you present them are the keys to securing employment and then to advancing your career.

What Are Accomplishments?

Your accomplishments

- ★ Are what set you apart from all other candidates.

- ★ Show the hiring authorities that you are the most qualified applicant for the job.

- ★ Form the foundation of your "skill sets" and your "Knowledge, Skills, and Abilities" responses (see chapter 9).

Accomplishments are the "headlines" of your career experience and the measure of how well your current skills and abilities will fit the requirements of the job you are applying for. They are anything you have done or are doing: work, projects you have completed, classes you have finished, or volunteer programs you are involved with. In short, accomplishments are descriptions of anything you have done and the results of those actions.

How to Write About Your Accomplishments

As you can see from the preceding samples, the best accomplishments are *specific* descriptions. In every case, they describe a specific action or steps you have taken to resolve a problem or to do your job. You will also note that the applicants used numbers, dollars, and percentages to describe what they had accomplished. This is important because by describing your accomplishments and projects in *measurable and quantifiable terms,* you give prospective employers the tools they need to figure out the scale and scope of your accomplishments and see how your accomplishments relate to the job they want to fill. For example, in the preceding Accounting Technician example, how much of a difference would it make in your mind if this job seeker just met the customer's year-end demands versus meeting the demands and working one week ahead of schedule? Would you be more or less impressed with the applicant's ability to meet and exceed deadlines and expert knowledge? Would you imagine there was a challenge in completing the year end one week prior to deadline? If you were looking for someone who could work under deadlines, would this impress you enough to make you want to meet this person and possibly have them on your accounting team?

The easiest way to write about your accomplishments is to make a list of projects and tasks that you have worked on and completed over the past few years. Begin with an outline like this:

1. Project or task—what problem did the project or task solve?

2. What you did (the steps you took to solve the problem).

3. The results (what happened as a result of the steps you took).

Make a list of five to ten projects or tasks you have worked on over the past few years. Then write and apply three-to-four-line accomplishment statements to your resume and KSAs (see chapter 9).

Guidelines for Writing Job-Winning Accomplishments

There are three major things to keep in mind when you are writing about your accomplishments:

1. Be specific. For example:

> Selected to conduct off-site screening of Maryland and Duke Women's basketball teams for the Final Four Championship in April. Set up portable screening station at teams' hotel and screened players, coaches, and other staff before they were escorted by state troopers to a chartered plane. Ensured all communications were professional and exceeded customer service expectations.

2. Describe your accomplishments in measurable and quantifiable terms whenever possible. For example:

> SMS UPGRADE: Led the project team tasked to upgrade from SMS 2.0 to SMS 2003 with minimal interruption to the production environment. Developed and executed a detailed project plan and led a 15-person technical team through the configuration, integration, pilot, and rapid deployment stages to upgrade 80 SMS servers providing enterprise management for over 250 servers and 5,000 client workstations (2005).

3. Target the vacancy you are applying for.

In chapters 8 and 11, you learn how to analyze vacancy announcements and how to research your core competencies and keywords. That work is the "blueprint" for writing about your accomplishments (and later, your electronic resume or KSA responses).

Keep the keyword list you developed in your vacancy analysis close to your computer. As you turn your project and task outline into narrative statements, make sure you include some of that language in your accomplishments. This strategy will pay big dividends when your application package is being read and scored later in the application process.

Project Lists

In some professions, such as engineering, architecture, and computers, applicants have long used "project lists" as part of their application packages. Project lists are just collected accomplishments, but they can be very effective if used judiciously as an addendum to your resume and as the basis for KSA responses.

The form the lists take can vary considerably because they are targeted to specific audiences. What makes sense for a senior IT person might not make sense for an auditor, architect, or social services executive.

As with your accomplishments, make sure your project statements relate directly to the vacancy you are applying for and that you use words you identified in the vacancy analysis.

Know Your Audience: Who's Going to Read Your Resume?

In the private sector, the audience of a resume is the hiring official. Personnel staff might do some preliminary screening, but that's all. The hiring official hires whomever she or he wants, and the personnel staff simply processes the paperwork. In the federal government, the personnel function is much more important.

The HR specialist will review your resume for qualifications for the job. He or she will look at the months and years of specialized experience and required education to determine whether you are Best Qualified. And if you are Best Qualified, you will then possibly be forwarded (referred) to the supervisor. There are two important readers of your resume in a government application: the HR specialist and the supervisor.

Do Your Research

Before you can start writing, it is vital that you do your research, both on your own work experience and on the agency that you are targeting.

Go to your computer, your files, your bookcases, and your briefcase and gather your latest resume, KSAs, SF-171, OF-612, and any other agency employment form. This will be helpful information for the chronology, overview, and compliance details. Also look for the following information:

- ★ **Position descriptions (PD) for your last two positions.** Beware of depending on the PD for the duties and responsibilities of your job. Is the PD up-to-date? Does it really say what you do? You should not write directly from the PD—this could result in a 171 life-history document. Use the PDs to ensure you include the most important aspects of your jobs.

- ★ **Supervisory evaluations.** Look for the text and keywords used in the evaluations. Read the evaluations to find out where your strengths are. If your evaluations are "pass/fail," look at the key elements of the evaluation—these probably reflect your major duties.

- ★ **Independent Development Plans.** Many critical skills, keywords, and accomplishments included in IDPs can be used in your resume.

- ★ **Annual Achievements List or Yearly Annual Reports** (if you write one). This is great information for the accomplishments portion of your job description and also for KSA statements.

- ★ **Agency brochures and mission statements** (from the Web site or your office). This description can give you insight into customers, services, programs, and future plans that you can use in your work experience write-up.

- ★ **Letters of commendation and appreciation awards.** Hopefully you saved these letters and awards to remind yourself of your value as an employee. The awards and letters are written by others about you and your accomplishments. These descriptions can be great resume and KSA material. Remember that you are trying to "sell" yourself. If you have received recognition for outstanding service, this is a demonstration of your work excellence!

- ★ **Vacancy announcements.** The announcements include keywords, skills, and information that you can use to build your federal resume and KSAs.

- ★ **Transcripts of college courses and college course catalog descriptions.** If you are a recent college graduate or a returned college graduate, you might need to describe your courses. You can find wonderful keywords and language in the course descriptions that might help you write your critical skills.

Popular Questions and Answers About the Federal Resume Work Experience Section

★ **How far back should I go?** Focus on the last 10 years. You will need to cover 10 years of work experience and include all compliance details. The most important positions will be within the last five years. Positions 10 years and prior can be included, but with shorter descriptions.

★ **Should each description be the same length?** The present or most recent position should be the longest—if this job is relevant to your new job objective. The second position should be somewhat shorter. The third position should be shorter yet, and so on. You can summarize positions 15 years ago and beyond.

★ **What about gaps in dates?** The OF-510 brochure states that you should include Recent and Relevant jobs. If you have a gap in dates, just leave out the time period. Then list your positions before and after this period of time. If you wish to state something about this time period, it is a personal preference. Many people take breaks from their career for care giving, travel, or education. You can simply skip this time period. The HR specialist will be reading your jobs and education to determine your qualifications for their position.

★ **What if the most important job I held in relation to my current objective was five years ago?** If you are returning to a job/career you held five years ago, list this position first if you can. The HR specialist and supervisor will want to read this position, which is relevant. You can probably also submit the work experience out of reverse chronology into the resume builders. For instance:

> 9/2001 to 9/2003
>
> 9/2003 to present
>
> 1/1995 to 9/2001

This way, the HR specialist will see the relevant position first and understand why you are applying for this position.

★ **How long should my current job description be?** Most of your time and energy will be spent writing this description (if it is your highest level and is most closely related to your objective). The "after" samples in this chapter are typical length.

The resume builders vary in character length:

USAJOBS (www.usajobs.gov): 3,000 characters.

Navy (https://www.donhr.navy.mil): 6,500 characters.

Army (www.cpol.army.mil): 12,000 characters for all the work experience descriptions. If you have been in your current position for five years, most of the difficult, important writing will be over when you finish this description.

★ **Is the Work Experience section the most important section?** Yes, this is the section that will get you rated as Qualified or Best Qualified for the job (in addition to your KSAs). You generally can use the following list, but you won't necessarily use all the headings. You can adapt this list for writing about your major and most recent positions.

  ☆ Job Information and Compliance Details (title of job, agency, office, address, supervisor, supervisor's phone, salary, hours per week)

  ☆ Introduction (overview of the office's mission and service)

☆ Outline of your top-level skills: "hats you wear at work"

☆ Accomplishments/projects

☆ Teams/collateral duties

★ **How long should my second job description be?** This description will be approximately half as long as the first position, unless it is your most job-related position.

★ **Can I include community service and volunteer positions or unpaid experience?** Remember to include both paid and unpaid work experience related to the job for which you are applying, for positions within the last 10 years. You can include the following: community and civic leadership positions, association or nonprofit leadership positions, teaching, consulting, and small-business experiences. Don't follow the format of the preceding list for these positions—just give compliance details and a few descriptive lines. In chapter 4, "Additional Information," you will see examples of other information that you can add to your resume in the USAJOBS Resume Builder.

★ **What about jobs I held prior to the last 10 years?** It's your choice whether to show a short chronology of your early career. If this experience is job related, you need to describe the positions in detail so that you will qualify for the position.

Summary

Writing your work experience in the new Outline format will help you cover the critical skills of the target job, use the keywords for the new position, demonstrate specialized experience, and feature your accomplishments. This all-new resume format is also a great format for resume builders. The next chapter steers you toward organizing your education, training, and certifications to meet and exceed the requirements of the position.

CHAPTER 3

Education and Job Related Training

Your educational background is an important part of your federal resume. The amount of information you provide, the way you present the information, and the organization of this section can impress HR professionals and hiring managers. HR professionals are looking for specific degrees, majors, courses, and specialized training to determine whether you are qualified for the position.

Some federal jobs require degrees; other federal positions will accept specialized or generalized experience in place of college degrees. The federal job announcement is clear about the qualifications for the position. Read the "Specialized or Generalized Qualifications" section of the vacancy announcement to see whether you have the necessary educational qualifications for the position. If the qualifications require that you have 25 credits in accounting for a Staff Accountant position, you *must* have these credits. List them in your resume and add up the credits.

Here is the education information that *must* be on your federal resume, according to OPM brochure OF-510:

> College or universities (name and address, majors, type and year of degree; if no degree, show total credits earned and whether semester or quarter hours)

Considerations for Organizing Your Educational Background

The resume builders are usually rigid about the amount of information you can supply concerning your education. The Education section gives you space for college degrees, majors, universities, and dates.

In order to add your relevant course list, course descriptions, significant papers, team projects, and activities, you might have to write this information in the Additional Information section toward the end of the builder.

The vacancy announcement might mandate the inclusion of classroom hours. Read the announcement to determine the information required, or include the hours just in case. Some announcements require you to fax your transcripts; others don't. You can attach a course list if you feel that your courses are significant in showing your qualifications and performance for a particular federal job.

Education Section Samples

Each of the samples shown here is from the USAJOBS resume builder. We have included a screenshot of the builder, followed by a screenshot of the "preview" of your resume that will appear in the resume builder. These are three examples of how you will submit your content into the Education field and then preview your Education section.

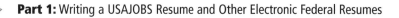

Target Job: GS-12 Biologist position, Environmental Protection Agency.
Resume Format: USAJOBS.
Federal to federal career promotion.
This candidate landed the job promotion. See chapter 13 for the complete resume.

Education ❓

* **School or Program Name** — `MICHIGAN STATE UNI`
* **City/Town** — `East Lansing`
* **State** — `MI`
* **Country** — `US`

Degree/Level Clarifications

* **Degree/Level Attained** — `Doctorate`

Completion Date — `June` `2002`

Major — `Ecology, Evolutionary E`

Minor — [ ]

GPA — [ ] of [ ] **GPA Max.**

Total Credits Earned — [ ]

System for Awarded Credits
- ○ Semester Hours
- ○ Quarter Hours
- ○ Other [ ]

Honors — `Select`

Relevant Coursework, Licensures and Certifications

Advisor:
Stephen K. Hamilton, Dissertation: "How the feeding ecology of native
and exotic mussels affects freshwater ecosystems."

(You have 1871 characters remaining for your description...)

✔ UPDATE

School	City, State	Country	Degree Level	Completion Date	
MICHIGAN STATE UNIVERSITY, Dept. of Zoology and W.K. Kellogg Biological Station	East Lansing, MI	US	Doctorate	6/2002	✖
University of Pittsburgh, Department of Biological Sciences	Pittsburgh, PA	US	Master's Degree	6/1996	✖
University of Pittsburgh	Pittsburgh, PA	US	Bachelor's Degree	6/1993	✖
University of Pittsburgh, Department of Biological Sciences	Pittsburgh, PA	US	Bachelor's Degree	6/1993	✖

Figure 3.1: Sample Education form for a Biologist position.

EDUCATION	MICHIGAN STATE UNIVERSITY, Dept. of Zoology and W.K. Kellogg Biological Station East Lansing, MI US Doctorate - 6/2002 Major: Ecology, Evolutionary Biology and Behavior (EEBB) and Zoology (dual degree) Relevant Coursework, Licensures and Certifications: Advisor: Stephen K. Hamilton, Dissertation: "How the feeding ecology of native and exotic mussels affects freshwater ecosystems." University of Pittsburgh, Department of Biological Sciences Pittsburgh, PA US Master's Degree - 6/1996 Major: Biological Sciences, Ecology and Evolution Program Relevant Coursework, Licensures and Certifications: Advisor: William Coffman, Thesis: "macroinvertebrate diversity and substrate heterogeneity in Linesville Creek" University of Pittsburgh, Department of Biological Sciences Pittsburgh, PA US Bachelor's Degree - 6/1993 Major: Biological Sciences Relevant Coursework, Licensures and Certifications: Senior Thesis: "Factors that affect coarse particulate organic matter retention in an Appalachian mountain stream." University of Pittsburgh Pittsburgh, PA US Bachelor's Degree - 6/1993 Major: History and Philosophy of Science

Figure 3.2: Sample preview of Education section for a Biologist position.

Target Job: Program Analyst or International Relations Specialist position with USAID or State Department.
Resume Format: USAJOBS.
Peace Corps to federal career transition.

This returning Peace Corps Volunteer has an MBA in International Management and is seeking a position with USAID or the State Department.

Education ⓘ

✳ **School or Program Name**	Monterey Institute of Int
✳ **City/Town**	Monterey
✳ **State**	California
✳ **Country**	US
	Degree/Level Clarifications
✳ **Degree/Level Attained**	Master's Degree
Completion Date	December 2005
Major	MBA, International Man
Minor	
GPA	☐ of ☐ GPA Max.
Total Credits Earned	
System for Awarded Credits	○ Semester Hours ○ Quarter Hours ○ Other ☐
Honors	Select

Relevant Coursework, Licensures and Certifications

Peace
Corps Masters International Program (PCMI): Completed joint program
with the US Peace Corps emphasizing small enterprise
development

(You have 1322 characters remaining for your description...)

✅ **UPDATE**

School	City, State	Country	Degree Level	Completion Date	
Monterey Institute of International Studies (MIIS)	Monterey, California	US	Master's Degree	12/2005	✄
Arizona State University	Tempe, AZ	US	Bachelor's Degree	5/2005	✄

Figure 3.3: Sample Education form for a Program Analyst or International Relations Specialist.

EDUCATION	Monterey Institute of International Studies (MIIS) Monterey, California US Master's Degree - 12/2005 Major: MBA, International Management Relevant Coursework, Licensures and Certifications: Peace Corps Masters International Program (PCMI): Completed joint program with the US Peace Corps emphasizing small enterprise development, language proficiency, and cultural adaptability. To fulfill program requirements, served two years in Africa with the Peace Corps before completing final semester at MIIS under a half-tuition scholarship. International Curriculum: Graduate coursework focused on international business management. Worked with an intercultural team on a Business Plan capstone project for a domestic company wishing to extend its services abroad; worked intimately with colleagues from other cultures and gained exposure to global market challenges. Arizona State University Tempe, AZ US Bachelor's Degree - 5/2005 Major: Economics GPA: 3.7 out of 4.0 Relevant Coursework, Licensures and Certifications: Barrett Honors College Graduate: Magna Cum Laude: 3.7 GPA. Completed (1) 15 hours of lower division honors credit, (2) 15 hours of upper division honors credit, and (3) an HONORS THESIS that discussed the costs and benefits of using low labor standards to achieve ECONOMIC DEVELOPMENT goals. International Business Certificate: Completed thirty-hour international business certificate (beyond baccalaureate) focusing on three areas of competency: (1) international business, (2) cultural sophistication, and (3) language proficiency. Possess understanding of input/output accounts and the Gross Domestic Product.

Figure 3.4: Sample preview of Education section for a Program Analyst or International Relations Specialist.

Target Job: Librarian at National Institutes of Naval Medicine Library.
Resume Format: USAJOBS.
Military to federal transition.
This retired Navy musician with a new master's in Library Science and internships in library science got the interview!

Education ⓘ

✱ **School or Program Name**	Catholic University of A
✱ **City/Town**	Washington
✱ **State**	District of Columbia
✱ **Country**	US
	Degree/Level Clarifications
✱ **Degree/Level Attained**	Master's Degree
Completion Date	October 2006
Major	Library and Information
Minor	
GPA	3.60 of 4.00 **GPA Max.**
Total Credits Earned	33.00
System for Awarded Credits	⦿ Semester Hours
	○ Quarter Hours
	○ Other
Honors	Select

Relevant Coursework, Licensures and Certifications

Coursework
in organization of information, cataloging, information literacy, reference service provision, science and technology, collection development, information systems and library technology assessment, and

(You have 1766 characters remaining for your description...)

✓ **UPDATE**

School	City, State	Country	Degree Level	Completion Date	
Catholic University of America, School of Library and Information Science	Washington, District of Columbia	US	Master's Degree	10/2006	✖
University of Maryland University College	Adelphi, Maryland	US	Certification	12/2003	✖
Arizona State University	Tempe, AZ	US	Master's Degree	5/1993	✖
Eastman School of Music	Rochester, NY, New York	US	Bachelor's Degree	5/1989	✖

Figure 3.5: Sample Education form for a Librarian position.

EDUCATION	Catholic University of America, School of Library and Information Science Washington, District of Columbia US Master's Degree - 10/2006 33.00 Semester Hours Major: Library and Information Science GPA: 3.60 out of 4.00 Relevant Coursework, Licensures and Certifications: Coursework in organization of information, cataloging, information literacy, reference service provision, science and technology, collection development, information systems and library technology assessment, and government documents. Arizona State University Tempe, AZ US Master's Degree - 5/1993 40.00 Semester Hours Major: Music GPA: 3.61 out of 4.0 Relevant Coursework, Licensures and Certifications: Graduate Teaching Assistantship. Coursework in advanced topics in the field of music. Eastman School of Music Rochester, NY, New York US Bachelor's Degree - 5/1989 131 Semester Hours Major: Music GPA: 3.14 out of 4.00 Relevant Coursework, Licensures and Certifications: Coursework in English, German, psychology, music instruction, and performance. University of Maryland University College Adelphi, Maryland US Certification - 12/2003 15 Semester Hours Major: Technology in Distance Education and Instruction in Distance Education GPA: 3.60 out of 4.00 Relevant Coursework, Licensures and Certifications: Coursework in the foundations of distance education including both traditional and emerging theories and practices in instruction. Coursework in instructional design and multimedia production.

Figure 3.6: Sample preview of Education section for a Librarian position.

Job Related Training Section Samples

Each of the Job Related Training sections samples shown are from the USAJOBS builder. You can see that you can add training courses organized by type of training, classroom hours, and impressive training information. The training can result in the human resources specialist adding points to your application score. Each example includes the resume builder screen shot and the preview screen shot, so that you can see how your training list will look in the builder as well as in the actual resume.

Target Job: Contract Specialist.
Resume Format: USAJOBS.
Military to federal transition.
This Attorney and Contract Specialist lists military honors and awards and bar memberships.

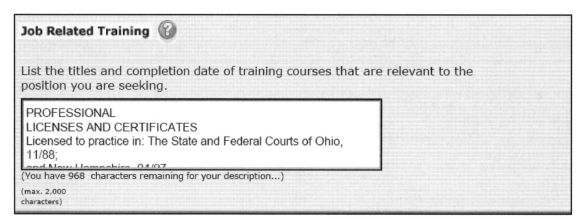

Figure 3.7: Sample Job Related Training form for an Attorney/Contract Specialist.

JOB RELATED TRAINING	PROFESSIONAL LICENSES AND CERTIFICATES
	Licensed to practice in: The State and Federal Courts of Ohio, 11/88; and New Hampshire, 04/97 The State Courts of Massachusetts, 02/97; and Colorado, 05/04 The District of Columbia, 05/05
	MILITARY SERVICE
	U.S. Air Force, 10/92 to 01/96, Honorable Discharge Highest Military Grade Held: Captain
	AWARDS AND HONORS
	Military Honors and Awards: Air Force Commendation Medal, 1995 Air Force Achievement Medal, 1992 Top Gun Award for litigation and advocacy skills, 1992
	Professional Honors and Awards: Lawline Honor Roll, 1999 (donating time and legal services to the needy and indigent) Speaker, Continuing Legal Education presentation in 1997; selected by New Hampshire Bar Association to teach Continuing Legal Education (CLE) courses in Administrative Law and Procedures Appointed Legal Customer Service Representative for LEXIS/NEXIS, Mead Data Central, 1988 to 1989 Certificate of Appreciation, University of New Hampshire, for Presentation on Trial Advocacy and Constitutional Rights

Figure 3.8: Sample Job Related Training preview for an Attorney/Contract Specialist.

Target Job: Program Analyst, SV-343-H, with Transportation Security Agency.
Resume Format: USAJOBS.
Federal to federal career transition.
This Acting Human Resources Manager had extensive training. She got the interview!

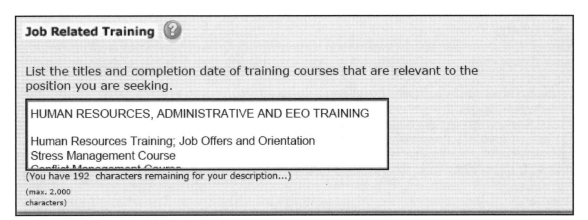

Job Related Training ❓

List the titles and completion date of training courses that are relevant to the position you are seeking.

HUMAN RESOURCES, ADMINISTRATIVE AND EEO TRAINING

Human Resources Training; Job Offers and Orientation
Stress Management Course
Conflict Management Course

(You have 192 characters remaining for your description...)

(max. 2,000 characters)

Figure 3.9: Sample Job Related Training form for a Program Analyst.

JOB RELATED TRAINING	HUMAN RESOURCES, ADMINISTRATIVE AND EEO TRAINING
	Human Resources Training; Job Offers and Orientation
	Stress Management Course
	Conflict Management Course
	Sensitive Security Information (SSI) Awareness
	Model Workplace Training, 2005
	Interim Policy on Employee Responsibilities and Conduct
	Introduction to Civil Rights
	Records Management
	SCREENER TRAINING
	Guidance Regarding the Use of Race for Law Enforcement Officers
	Respecting Privacy, Preserving Freedom
	Bloodborne Pathogens Awareness
	Identification and Reporting of Security Violations, Threat Information, and Criminal Activity
	Computer Access Agreement
	IT Security Awareness Training
	Excellence in Screener Performance Series: ETD & Physical Bag Search-Checked Bag Screener Specific
	Excellence in Screener Performance Series: Basic Supervisor Technical Training
	Excellence in Screener Performance Series: ETD & Physical Bag Search Checkpoint Screener Specific
	Hazardous Material Awareness and Hazard Communication Training
	Excellence in Screener Performance Series: ETD & Physical Bag Search – Common Component
	Safety Awareness: Checked Baggage Safety
	Safety Awareness: Checkpoint Safety
	TIP Job Aids for Screeners
	Excellence in Screener Performance Series: Customer-Focused Security
	Excellence in Screener Performance Series: X-Ray Operator
	Safety Awareness: Lifting Techniques
	Suspected Improvised Explosive Device Component Discovery
	Selected Searches of Individuals
	Threat Area Search Procedures
	Ergonomic Solutions: Baggage Handling
	Excellence in Screener Performance Series: Checkpoint and Checked Baggage Operational Differences
	Excellence in Screener Performance Series: Customer-Focused Security
	OPSEC Awareness for TSOs
	TSA Screener Improvised Explosive Device (IED)
	Basic Checked Baggage Screening Procedures Practical Skills – Classroom

Figure 3.10: Sample Job Related Training preview for a Program Analyst.

Target Job: IT Specialist (GS-2210-12): Network Manager, Systems Administrator, or Database Management positions.
Resume Format: USAJOBS.
Private industry to federal career transition.

Job Related Training ❓

List the titles and completion date of training courses that are relevant to the position you are seeking.

> ScriptLogic Desktop Authority, 2006
> SQL Server 2000 Database Design and Implementation, 2005
> Microsoft Word 2002 (Intermediate and Advanced), 2004
> Microsoft Excel 2002 (Intermediate), 2004
> Microsoft PowerPoint 2002 (Intermediate), 2004

(You have 1151 characters remaining for your description...)

(max. 2,000 characters)

Figure 3.11: Sample Job Related Training form for an IT Specialist.

JOB RELATED TRAINING	ScriptLogic Desktop Authority, 2006
	SQL Server 2000 Database Design and Implementation, 2005
	Microsoft Word 2002 (Intermediate and Advanced), 2004
	Microsoft Excel 2002 (Intermediate), 2004
	Microsoft PowerPoint 2002 (Intermediate), 2004
	Microsoft Access 2002 (Intermediate), 2004
	Microsoft Outlook 2002 (Intermediate), 2004
	Windows Server 2003 MCSE/MCSA Boot Camp, 2003
	Cisco Router 1 and 2, Cisco Networking Academy - CCNA Track, 2003
	Exchange 2000 Administration, 2002
	Transact SQL for SQL 2000, 2002
	Network and Operating Essentials, 2001
	Windows 2000 Active Directory Services
	Windows 2000 Networking Infrastructure, 2001
	Windows 2000 Security, 2001
	Windows 2000 Server and Windows 2000 Professional, 2001
	Microsoft Word, Excel, PowerPoint, Acces, Outlook 2000 (Beginner, Intermediate, Advanced), 2001
	A+, 2001
	SQL Server 7.0 Administration, 2000

Figure 3.12: Sample Job Related Training preview for an IT Specialist.

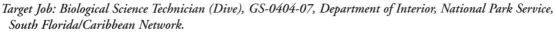

Target Job: Biological Science Technician (Dive), GS-0404-07, Department of Interior, National Park Service, South Florida/Caribbean Network.
Resume Format: USAJOBS.
Private industry/government partnership to federal career transition.
This Biologist/Research Assistant with the National Coral Reef Institute was seeking a new position with the National Park Service.

Job Related Training (?)

List the titles and completion date of training courses that are relevant to the position you are seeking.

CERTIFICATIONS:
-- American Academy of Underwater Sciences, Scientific Diver, June
2003-present. -- Enriched Air Diver, Professional Association of
Diving

(You have 373 characters remaining for your description...)

(max. 2,000
characters)

Figure 3.13: Sample Job Related Training form for a Biological Science Technician.

JOB RELATED TRAINING

CERTIFICATIONS:
-- American Academy of Underwater Sciences, Scientific Diver, June 2003-present.
-- Enriched Air Diver, Professional Association of Diving Instructors, November 2003.
-- Rescue Diver, PADI, May 2002.
-- Advanced Scuba Diver, National Association of Underwater Instructors, May 1999.
-- Oxygen First Aid for Scuba Diving Injuries, Divers Alert Network, August 2005.
-- Cardiopulmonary Resuscitation/First Aid, Emergency First Response, May 2005.
-- United States Power Squadron, America's Boating Course, April 2006.
-- State of Florida Certificate of Boating Education, July 2004.
-- Basic Sailing, American Red Cross, March 2004.

MEETINGS AND WORKSHOPS:
-- Florida Reef Resilience Program-Coral Bleaching Training Session, Dania Beach, FL, July 2006.
-- Society for Sedimentary Geology-Quaternary Reefs and Platforms, Houston, TX, April 13-14, 2006.
-- Florida Reef Resilience Program Community Workshop, Homestead, FL, March 9, 2006.
-- Ocean Sciences Meeting, Honolulu, HI, February 20-24, 2006.
-- Rosentiel School of Marine and Atmospheric Science/Atlantic and Gulf Rapid Reef Assessment Coral Disease Symposium, Miami, FL, January 24, 2006.
-- Coral Reef Restoration, Scientific Frameworks for Rehabilitation, Miami, FL, October 18-19, 2005.
-- U.S. Coral Reef Task Force Meeting, Miami, FL, December 1-4, 2004.
-- Diseases of Corals and Other Reef Organisms, Summerland Key, FL, July 10-18, 2004.
-- Florida Fish and Wildlife Conservation Commission 6th Annual Sea Turtle Permit Holder Meeting, Orlando, FL, February 21-23, 2003.
-- Marine Ornamentals '99, Kona, HI, November 16-19, 1999.

Figure 3.14: Sample Job Related Training preview for a Biological Science Technician.

Summary

Your Education and Job Related Training sections will support your qualifications for the federal jobs you are applying for. Try to remember and include your conferences, courses, and self-development courses for continual learning. The next chapter shows you how to maximize your Additional Information toward a winning total federal resume presentation.

CHAPTER 4

Additional Information

Outside your 9-to-5 position, you might have another life. That's what "Related Information" is about: the experience and qualifications you've gathered outside of work experience, formal education, and training. Among the many possibilities to include here are specialized skills, other languages, honors and awards, accomplishments, publications, professional memberships, community involvement or leadership, and public speaking. HR professionals might be impressed or interested in what you do above your job description. There's no guarantee that this information will qualify you for a position; however, many outside activities demonstrate leadership, communications skills, planning, and the ability to manage time and resources. It is important to present the whole picture.

Be sure to notice, however, the number of times the phrase "job-related" is repeated in government requirements. Your federal resume should emphasize recent and job-related information. Federal HR professionals are looking for skills, accomplishments, and professional involvement that qualify you for a specific federal position.

A federal vacancy announcement will ask for "Related Information" in the following sections of the USAJOBS Resume Builder:

★ Additional Language Skills

★ Affiliations

★ Professional Publications

★ Additional Information, which can include job-related honors, awards, leadership activities, skills (such as computer software proficiency or typing speed), or any other information requested by a specific job announcement

Resume Sections for Additional Information

The following section of this chapter contains discussions of various resume sections for your honors, awards, memberships, public speaking, and publications.

Job-Related Honors, Awards, or Special Accomplishments

Your honors, awards, and special accomplishments might be important in qualifying you for certain positions. This section on your resume can include such items as publications, memberships in professional or honor societies, leadership activities, public speaking, and performance awards, as well as the dates you received them. Here is an overview of the items you might list and describe in this section on your federal resume:

★ **Honors and awards** demonstrate career or educational excellence and recognition.

★ **Affiliations** demonstrate involvement, motivation to learn about specific industries, and knowledge of state-of-the-art industry information through reading newsletters and attending conferences and meetings.

★ **Public speaking and presentations** show communications skills before groups and the ability to write and present information orally.

★ **Publication lists or written works** illustrate your ability to research, write, edit, use computers, and study a specific topic area.

★ **Collateral duties and details** in your federal job can be listed in this section. These additional responsibilities might lead to new careers and positions. The responsibilities you carry out 5 to 20 hours per week can provide the skills you need to make a career change.

★ **Community or civic activities** demonstrate personal interest, dedication, and time committed to helping others. Involvement in community activities might give you valuable responsibilities such as leading groups, planning, promoting and coordinating events, managing budgets, negotiating contracts, directing volunteers, and achieving organizational goals.

Sports, Activities, and Special Interests

You might wonder why this information should go on your federal resume. This information will not help you qualify for the position. However, if the hiring manager is an avid golfer, sailor, or Orioles fan, you'll give him or her a short vacation from the serious side of candidate reviews. These outside activities usually show leadership, communications ability, organizational skills, creativity, entrepreneurial spirit, planning, management, budgeting, mentoring, counseling, teamwork, and interpersonal-relations skills. Outside activities also show energy, interest, enthusiasm, community spirit, involvement, caring, giving of time, the ability to manage multiple functions, and commitment and service to others. That's a lot. If this information makes your resume stand out, you should include it, just in case.

Public Speaking

If you've been quoted in a newspaper, spoken before a class or association on your area of expertise, been interviewed on the radio, or presented an impressive briefing, write it in your resume and include it again in your KSA statement. The popular KSA statement, "Ability to communicate orally and in writing" can be answered with detailed statements regarding your public speaking and articles.

Other Work Experience

It's best if you keep your Work Experience to five or six job listings. Summarize relevant positions in the Additional Information field. Keep the lists short. But the experience could be of interest to a supervisor.

Examples of Additional Information Sections

The following examples show the kinds of additional information you can provide in your federal resume.

Administrative Officer with Civic and Community Activities

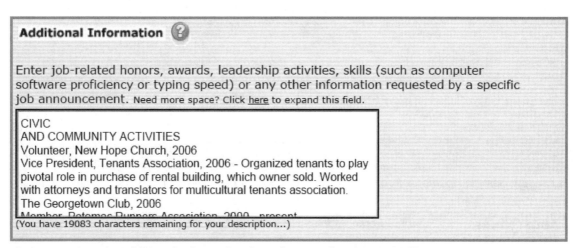

Additional Information

Enter job-related honors, awards, leadership activities, skills (such as computer software proficiency or typing speed) or any other information requested by a specific job announcement. Need more space? Click here to expand this field.

CIVIC
AND COMMUNITY ACTIVITIES
Volunteer, New Hope Church, 2006
Vice President, Tenants Association, 2006 - Organized tenants to play pivotal role in purchase of rental building, which owner sold. Worked with attorneys and translators for multicultural tenants association.
The Georgetown Club, 2006
Member, Potomac Runners Association, 2000 - present
(You have 19083 characters remaining for your description...)

Figure 4.1: Sample Additional Information form for an Administrative Officer.

ADDITIONAL INFORMATION

CIVIC AND COMMUNITY ACTIVITIES

Volunteer, New Hope Church, 2006

Vice President, Tenants Association, 2006 - Organized tenants to play pivotal role in purchase of rental building, which owner sold. Worked with attorneys and translators for multicultural tenants association.

The Georgetown Club, 2006

Member, Potomac Runners Association, 2000 - present

Volunteer Coach, "Run Into Spring" Program, Spring 2004. Part of coaching team that organized and coached runners, from beginner to experienced for a successful training program for ten-mile race. Educated runners on speed work, nutrition, endurance running, injury prevention, sports psychology, cross and weight training. Successfully completed six-month marathon training program to become qualified coach.

Volunteer, Washington Animal Rescue League, 2001 - 2002

Member, Board of Directors, American Scandinavian Association, 2001 - 2002

Figure 4.2: Sample preview of Additional Information section for an Administrative Officer.

Attorney with Licenses, Certifications, Military Service, and Awards and Honors

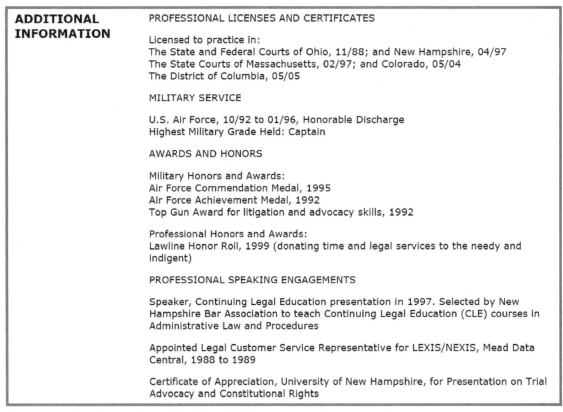

Figure 4.3: Sample Additional Information form for an Attorney.

ADDITIONAL INFORMATION	PROFESSIONAL LICENSES AND CERTIFICATES
	Licensed to practice in: The State and Federal Courts of Ohio, 11/88; and New Hampshire, 04/97 The State Courts of Massachusetts, 02/97; and Colorado, 05/04 The District of Columbia, 05/05
	MILITARY SERVICE
	U.S. Air Force, 10/92 to 01/96, Honorable Discharge Highest Military Grade Held: Captain
	AWARDS AND HONORS
	Military Honors and Awards: Air Force Commendation Medal, 1995 Air Force Achievement Medal, 1992 Top Gun Award for litigation and advocacy skills, 1992
	Professional Honors and Awards: Lawline Honor Roll, 1999 (donating time and legal services to the needy and indigent)
	PROFESSIONAL SPEAKING ENGAGEMENTS
	Speaker, Continuing Legal Education presentation in 1997. Selected by New Hampshire Bar Association to teach Continuing Legal Education (CLE) courses in Administrative Law and Procedures
	Appointed Legal Customer Service Representative for LEXIS/NEXIS, Mead Data Central, 1988 to 1989
	Certificate of Appreciation, University of New Hampshire, for Presentation on Trial Advocacy and Constitutional Rights

Figure 4.4: Sample preview of Additional Information section for an Attorney.

Biologist's Publication List

Professional Publications

Enter any professional publications in the space provided

ABSTRACTS
& REPORTS:
HODEL, EC and Vargas-Ángel, B. 2006. Histopathological
assessment and

(You have 619 characters remaining for your description...)

(max. 2,000 characters)

Figure 4.5: Sample Professional Publications form for a Biologist.

PROFESSIONAL PUBLICATIONS

ABSTRACTS & REPORTS:

HODEL, EC and Vargas-Ángel, B. 2006. Histopathological assessment and comparison of sediment and phosphate stress in the Caribbean Staghorn Coral, Acropora cervicornis. Eos Trans. AGU 87(36), Ocean Sciences Meeting Supplement, Abstract OS26G-09.

Vargas-Ángel, B, Halter, HA, HODEL, EC. A histopathological index as an indicator for sedimentation stress on scleractinian corals. 10th International Coral Reef Symposium Abstracts, Okinawa, Japan, June 28-July 2, 2004, pp. 13.

Vargas-Ángel, B., Riegl, B.M., Dodge, R.E., Blackwelder, P., Snell, T., Gilliam, D. S., Fisher, L., HODEL, E.C., Renegar, D.A. 2005. A higher resolution, multi-layered approach to assessing sedimentation stress in reef corals. American Society of Limnology and Oceanography Summer Meeting Abstracts, Santiago de Compostela, Spain, pp 159.

HODEL, EC and Menezes, S. Tidal effects on phytoplankton in the Pettaquamscutt River Estuary. Papers from the Summer Undergraduate Research Fellowship Program in Oceanography, 2001. Graduate School of Oceanography, University of Rhode Island, Narragansett, RI. GSO Technical Report 2001-02

HODEL, EC, Longmore, W, Sonnenschein, L. Effects of organic and inorganic compound levels in miniature coral reef systems. Marine Ornamentals '99: Collection, Culture, Conservation Abstracts, Kona, Hawaii, November 16-19, 1999, pp 45.

Figure 4.6: Sample preview of Professional Publications section for a Biologist.

Biologist's Affiliations List

Affiliations ?

* **Organization Name**	The International Society for Reef Studies
* **Affiliation/Role**	Member

✓ **UPDATE**

Organization Name	Affiliation/Role	
The International Society for Reef Studies	Member	✖
American Society of Limnology and Oceanography	Member	✖
American Academy of Underwater Sciences	Member	✖
Divers Alert Network, joined May 2001	Member	✖

Figure 4.7: Sample Affiliations form for a Biologist.

AFFILIATIONS	The International Society for Reef Studies	Member
	American Society of Limnology and Oceanography	Member
	American Academy of Underwater Sciences	Member
	Divers Alert Network, joined May 2001	Member

Figure 4.8: Sample preview of Affiliations section for a Biologist.

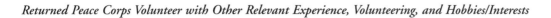

Returned Peace Corps Volunteer with Other Relevant Experience, Volunteering, and Hobbies/Interests

ADDITIONAL INFORMATION	OTHER RELEVANT POSITIONS - ADVOCATE, INSTRUCTOR, CURRICULUM DEVELOPMENT: SHELTER ADVOCATE, Support Committee for Battered Women, Waltham, MA, US, 1/1998 - 9/1998; Salary: 18,000 USD Per Year; Hours per week: 40 Staffed 24-hour crisis hotline and performed intake procedures for potential guests. Provided shelter orientation, advocacy, and crisis intervention for guests. WILDERNESS INSTRUCTOR, Hurricane Island Outward Bound School, Hurricane Island, FL, US, 1/2001 - 10/2002; Salary: 22,000 USD Per Year; Hours per week: 40 + Managed 9 wilderness courses and provided at-risk youth and juvenile offenders between the ages of 13-18 with the necessary training, guidance, and support to fulfill the educational objectives of Outward Bound. Promoted from intern to assistant instructor to lead instructor within 6 months of hire. Received a Course Director recommendation on final course. Facilitated 10-day instructor training on facilitation skills, group dynamics, and effective communication skills for 7 newly selected interns. Supervised the development of assistant instructors and interns over 9 30-day courses. LEARNING LAB INSTRUCTOR, Brown Middle School, Atlanta Outward Bound Center, Atlanta, GA, 12/2002 - 5/2003 Salary: 15.00 USD Per Hour; Hours per week: 10 Designed and instructed 13-week after-school program for 20 Brown Middle School students aged 10-14 developing their communication, team building, and decision making skills through group facilitation and experiential education techniques. PUBLICATIONS/PRESENTATIONS Selected as an oral presenter for the 132nd American Public Health Association's Annual Meeting: Traditional birth attendants: A look at the transition to skilled attendants in Safe Motherhood in Cambodia. Washington, DC, November 10, 2004. CARE Presentation: An Evaluation of CARE Cambodia's Training Tools and Referral Procedures for Traditional Birth Attendants, CARE Atlanta, November 2003. VOLUNTEER Big Brothers Big Sisters Program, 10/02-11/04 HOBBIES/INTERESTS Hiking, Running, Soccer, Reading, Rock Climbing, Canoeing

Figure 4.9: Sample preview of Additional Information section for a returned Peace Corps Volunteer.

Returned Peace Corps Volunteer with Distinctions, Other Positions, and Interests

ADDITIONAL INFORMATION	DISTINCTIONS
	Monterey Institute of International Studies: 3.8 GPA; Half tuition academic scholarship 2002-2003; Masters International Scholarship 2005; Net Impact 2005, affiliate.
	Arizona State University: 3.7 GPA, Magna Cum Laude, ASU President's Scholar 1996-1999; ASU Dean's List, every semester; National Dean's List, 1998-2000; Student Economics Association, President Fall 2000, Vice President 1999-2000; Beta Gamma Sigma National Honor Society, inducted 1998.
	Peace Corps: Small Enterprise Development (SED) Steering Committee, selected member 2004; Peace Corps Trainer 2004, 2005.
	PROFICIENCIES
	Languages: English (native), French (written, proficient; spoken, fluent).
	Computer: Extensive use of MS Word, Excel, Outlook, Publisher, and PowerPoint; past extensive use of scheduling and billing systems; high proficiency in Internet research; general knowledge of statistical analysis software.
	FREELANCE EDITORIAL WORK:
	Editorial/Research Assistant
	06/01–08/01; 08/05–present
	Counseling & Consultation/Testing Support Services Arizona State University, Tempe, AZ
	Provide editorial and research support to authors writing career testing and career development curricula.
	EARLY WORK EXPERIENCE:
	GRADUATE ASSISTANT
	09/02–05/03
	International Commercial Diplomacy Project, Monterey Institute of International Studies, Monterey, CA
	Compiled, researched, and summarized international economics, trade, and commercial diplomacy Internet links now used as a resource for trade officials, negotiators, and students in the field; designed trade negotiation simulations that allow students and practitioners to participate in mock trade negotiation and dispute resolution exercises.
	ADMINISTRATIVE ASSISTANT
	08/97–07/98; 06/99–05/00; 06/01–08/02
	Counseling & Consultation/Testing Support Services, Arizona State University, Tempe, AZ
	Provided front office and customer service support for the counseling and testing center; performed data management using both Access and Excel; organized a data collection project and created outcome report for the Director; created marketing materials on MS Publisher; managed intern application process under the general direction of the Training Director; and assisted on special projects.
	BUSINESS INTERN
	01/01–05/01
	L'ESSEC, Paris, France
	Assisted in the preparation of corporate training programs in France's leading business school; served as an expert on English grammar, business jargon, and American culture.

Figure 4.10: Sample preview of Additional Information section for a returned Peace Corps Volunteer.

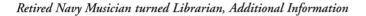

Retired Navy Musician turned Librarian, Additional Information

Additional Information ⑦

Enter job-related honors, awards, leadership activities, skills (such as computer software proficiency or typing speed) or any other information requested by a specific job announcement. Need more space? Click here to expand this field.

> AWARDS
> AND HONORS
> • Navy Achievement Medal and Letter of Commendation. U.S. Navy Band.
> Awarded for performance in the positions of Library Assistant, Application Developer, Command Assessment Team, Public Affairs Office

(You have 17935 characters remaining for your description...)

Figure 4.11: Sample Additional Information form for a retired Navy Musician turned Librarian.

ADDITIONAL INFORMATION

AWARDS AND HONORS

• Navy Achievement Medal and Letter of Commendation. U.S. Navy Band. Awarded for performance in the positions of Library Assistant, Application Developer, Command Assessment Team, Public Affairs Office Assistant, and Musician First Class. 2005.

• Ruth Fine Memorial Scholarship. The District of Columbia Library Association. 2005.

• Global War on Terrorism Service Medal. U.S. Navy. 2004.

• National Defense Service Medal. U.S. Navy. 1996.

• Navy Good Conduct Medals. U.S. Navy. 1997, 2000, 2003.

OTHER QUALIFICATIONS

• Qualified typist/word processor with a typing speed of 48 words per minute with three or fewer errors in a five-minute period.
• Experienced information professional with proven strong work ethics and documented professional decorum.
• Able to multi-task. Simultaneously worked two part-time library positions while performing complex tasks in an internship at the National Library of Medicine and completing a Master of Library and Information Science degree over the past year and a half.
• Nine months of experience creating, maintaining, and editing MARC-21 bibliographic records using Endeavor's Voyager Cataloging Module in an internship for the National Library of Medicine, History of Medicine Division.
• 10 years of progressive professional and academic experience using library and office related technologies.
• 10 years of active-duty military service in the U.S. Navy.

TECHNICAL SKILLS

• Word processing: Microsoft Word, Corel WordPerfect.
• Project development and data entry: Microsoft Excel, Access, PowerPoint; Adobe Acrobat, Photoshop; Macromedia Dreamweaver, Fireworks.
• Integrated library systems: Endeavor's Voyager, InMagic.
• Bibliographic searching utilities: LexisNexis, EBSCOhost, Proquest, OCLC First Search, and Dialog.
• Web development: HTML, Macromedia Dreamweaver.
• Operating Systems: Microsoft Windows, 96, 98, Me, 2000, and XP.
• Scanning equipment and software: HP scanning equipment and software; Adobe Acrobat, Photoshop.

Figure 4.12: Sample preview of Additional Information section for a retired Navy Musician turned Librarian.

Summary

The Additional Information you add to your resume will complete the picture of your qualifications, experience, and background. This information can tell the human resources specialist and supervisor more about you than the job duties. The next chapter tells you how to focus your resume toward a particular job while emphasizing the critical skills, qualifications, and accomplishments that will help you stand out.

CHAPTER 5

Focusing Strategies: Profile Statements, Top Skills, and Specialized Qualifications

Focusing your resume is important whether you are changing your career, seeking a promotion, or hoping to move to a lateral position. There are four ways to focus your resume toward your next position:

★ **Write a profile statement.** Summarize your career into a Profile narrative that will serve as your "elevator speech" and present a total picture of your relevant career.

★ **Feature top critical skills.** You may have eight top skills, but only five of them are relevant for your target position. You need to feature the five that are relevant.

★ **Highlight specialized experience.** The announcement might ask for specialized experience and examples that demonstrate this specialized experience. You can add these very clear examples in your focusing section. In the USAJOBS resume builder, the Focusing section is called "Additional Information."

★ **Emphasize important accomplishments.** You may have two or three outstanding accomplishments that you want to make sure the HR specialist and the supervisor read. These accomplishments could result in an interview.

Overview of the Four Types of Focusing Sections

Here is a brief description of each of the four focusing sections that I recommend for your resume. You can choose to use one or all these focusing techniques.

Profile Statement

The Profile statement is an abstract of your career. It addresses the interviewer's inevitable statement, "Tell me about yourself." The federal resume format allows you to strengthen your application by summarizing your qualifications in an opening Profile statement, an option that the OF-612 did not give you. You can use this profile of your career to feature your experience and skills, as well as keywords taken directly from the vacancy announcement. Private-industry resumes almost always include a Profile statement to introduce the reader to the applicant's qualifications and background. This section can save the human resources professional's time. Do you want the reader to be interested in you and keep reading your resume? Then you need a Profile statement on your resume. You can write your Profile statement in your Additional Information field in the USAJOBS Resume Builder.

Critical Skills List

The Critical Skills list is easier to write than the Profile statement. This is a list of skills that you have that are also in the vacancy announcement. This simple list of skills should be easy to read. The Critical Skills section is especially useful for technical positions where certain skills are mandatory. Do you have specific expertise that is required for your desired position? Make a list and copy and paste this into the Additional Information field in the USAJOBS resume builder.

Specialized Experience List

If the vacancy announcement asks for specialized experience in a certain area of work, be sure to list it clearly for the human resources specialist. This could help you support a Best Qualified consideration and your resume could be forwarded to the supervisor. Make this information easy to find and read. This specialized experience should be written in your Work Experience section; or if you run out of character space, you can add it to Additional Information.

Accomplishments List

Accomplishments can be included in two places in your federal resume. You can include them in your Work Experience section, as discussed in chapter 2, or you can list them in Additional Information.

Do you have an accomplishment that demonstrates you are an excellent and valuable employee to your office? Was this project challenging, interesting, and successful? Did it result in new methods or processes in your agency? Would you like this accomplishment to stand out? Do you want to impress someone with your abilities and experience in a particular area? You can write a three-to-five-line statement focusing on the results of your accomplishment. You can include between three and five statements before the list becomes too long.

Your resume accomplishments can be the same as your KSA accomplishments, except that your accomplishments will be longer and more detailed in your KSAs. (See chapter 9 for more on writing KSAs.)

Targeting Your Resume to Each Announcement

You should target your resume to each announcement you apply to by changing your Profile statement. It takes only about an hour or so to customize your federal resume for each vacancy announcement.

Reading, understanding, and valuing the information in the announcement are important when you are focusing your resume. Read and analyze the Duties and Responsibilities section of the announcement. Read between the lines, too! If you don't understand the position description, go to the agency's Web site and find out the agency's functions and programs. Think about the agency's and the hiring manager's needs. You will be the person who will perform this job. Whatever problems or special situations exist in this office, you will be person who will solve them. Chapter 11 reviews how to analyze the announcement in more detail.

Federal Resume Case Studies with Additional Information Focusing Sections

The applicants in the resume case studies that follow focused their resumes toward a specific position by using the Profile statement, Critical Skills list, Specialized Experience list, or Accomplishments list.

Case Study 1: Profile with Certifications, Core Competencies, and Technical Skills

IT Specialist in private industry targeting an IT Specialist government position, GS-2210-12.

Additional Information ⑦

Enter job-related honors, awards, leadership activities, skills (such as computer software proficiency or typing speed) or any other information requested by a specific job announcement. Need more space? Click here to expand this field.

PROFILE
Results-oriented information technology professional with a proven track record in providing effective customer service, desktop management, network administration, and systems analysis demonstrated
through more than five years in help desk support and systems administration. Qualifications include the following:
– Highly skilled in providing excellent customer service to all levels

(You have 18114 characters remaining for your description...)

Figure 5.1: Sample Additional Information form for an IT Specialist.

ADDITIONAL INFORMATION

PROFILE

Results-oriented information technology professional with a proven track record in providing effective customer service, desktop management, network administration, and systems analysis demonstrated through more than five years in help desk support and systems administration. Qualifications include the following:

= Highly skilled in providing excellent customer service to all levels of users.
= Proficient in mastering sophisticated software and tools while regularly identifying and implementing the latest industry innovations.
= Success at reviewing, analyzing, testing, and maintaining computer and network systems.
= Demonstrated experience preserving system integrity utilizing a variety of proactive backup and recovery strategies.
= Proven abilities in administering security to protect data and access to company network.

CERTIFICATIONS

Microsoft Certified Systems Engineer (MCSE), Windows Server 2000/2003, Received 2003
Microsoft Certified Systems Administrator (MCSA), Windows Server 2003, Received 2003

CORE COMPETENCIES
Network Administration
User Support and Training
Managing Security to Network
Business Systems Administration
Proactive Data Recovery and Management
Software Configuration, Installation, and Upgrade

TECHNICAL SKILLS

Maufacturers: 3COM; Cisco; Compaq; Dell; Gateway; Hewlett-Packard; Intel

Environments: CITRIX Mainframe XP; Windows 9x/NT/2000/XP

Software: Active Directory; Adobe Acrobat; Filemaker Pro; McAfee (Netshield, VirusScan ASAP); Microsoft Office Suite 9x/XP/2003; Norton (Antivirus & Ghost 5x/7x); Veritas Backup Exec

Databases: SQL Server 7.0/2000/2005

Mail Programs: Exchange 5.5/2000/2003

Networking DHCP; DNS; firewalls; hubs; routers; switches; TCP/IP; WINS

Applications: ADP, Business Objects; GIFTS; Great Plains; HRIS; ULTIMUS

Peripherals: Blackberry; Palm; Treo

Figure 5.2: Sample Additional Information section preview for an IT Specialist.

Case Study 2: Profile with Certifications, Expertise, and Significant Accomplishments

IT Specialist, Team Coordinator, GS-2210-14, seeking new IT Systems Specialist position, GS-2210-14.

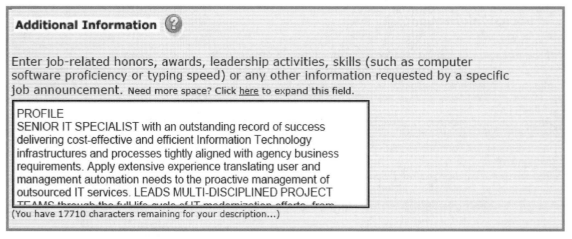

Figure 5.3: Sample Additional Information form for an IT Specialist.

ADDITIONAL INFORMATION	PROFILE
	SENIOR IT SPECIALIST with an outstanding record of success delivering cost-effective and efficient Information Technology infrastructures and processes tightly aligned with agency business requirements. Apply extensive experience translating user and management automation needs to the proactive management of outsourced IT services.
	LEADS MULTI-DISCIPLINED PROJECT TEAMS through the full life cycle of IT modernization efforts, from requirements capture, through design, implementation, and ongoing administration. Apply innovation and persistence to consistently deliver project objectives on time and within budget. Self-motivated and goal-oriented, with a demonstrated ability to handle complex responsibilities in a demanding work environment.
	CERTIFICATIONS
	Information Security Officer (ISO) Certification, National Defense University, 2005 Chief Information Officer (CIO) Certification, National Defense University, 2004
	EXPERTISE
	IT Operations: Direct enterprise data, computing, and networking operations to support critical business functions.
	Technical and Project Management: Provide technical direction and oversight to IT Operations and modernization projects.
	User Support: Provide customer service, technical assistance, and training on all aspects of software applications, systems, and network infrastructure.
	IT Consultation: Recommend industry best practices in the implementation of new technologies.
	SIGNIFICANT ACCOMPLISHMENTS
	EPA SERVER OPERATIONS MOVE: Project Manager to relocate EPA Server Operations following facility damage in the aftermath of Hurricane Katrina. Targeted for completion in Month, 200x, this move has required detailed planning for a fully renovated network, server, and office infrastructure.
	EPA ENTERPRISE IT OPERATIONS: Manage all IT services for multiple EPA buildings and facilities in the Washington, D.C., area, including the Ronald Reagan Building. Coordinate network, telecommunications, systems, and user services for over 2,000 users in a high-paced and demanding work environment.
	EMERGENCY OPERATIONS CENTER (EOC): Led the design, implementation, management, and oversight of the computing infrastructure for a state-of-the-art Emergency Operations Center for the EPA (2005).

Figure 5.4: Sample Additional Information section preview for an IT Specialist.

Case Study 3: Profile with Specialized Functional Skills Targeted Toward New Position

Contractor Operations Specialist seeking Logistics Management, Systems Analyst positions, GS-11/12-level.

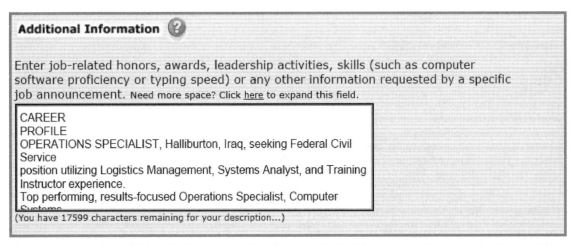

Figure 5.5: Sample Additional Information form for a Logistics Management/Systems Analyst position.

ADDITIONAL INFORMATION

CAREER PROFILE

OPERATIONS SPECIALIST, Halliburton, Iraq, seeking Federal Civil Service position utilizing Logistics Management, Systems Analyst, and Training Instructor experience.

Top performing, results-focused Operations Specialist, Computer Systems Analyst, and Training Instructor with over 20 years of multidimensional private-sector and U.S. military experience.

Highly successful supervisor with cross-functional expertise in Operations Analysis, Project Management, Information Technology, Education/Training, Personnel Administration, and Organizational Development. Experience managing, mentoring, evaluating, and coordinating the work of up to 90 employees.

Successful working with and across multiple functions, countries, and cultures to achieve goals. Flexible in dynamic, challenging, and multicultural business environments. M.S., Education. Education/Instructional Design Doctoral candidate.

INFORMATION TECHNOLOGY: Over three years of experience as a Computer Analyst supervising help desk operations and providing customer service support for computer operations. Record of success designing computer information systems to improve production and work flow. Skilled in network troubleshooting and support. Expertise planning, developing, implementing, and maintaining programs, polices, and procedures to protect the integrity and confidentiality of systems, networks, and data. A+ Network Certification.

TRAINING & INSTRUCTIONAL TECHNOLOGY & DESIGN: Experience developing and implementing college-level training and instructional programs. Excel in curriculum design, program evaluation, and instructor coordination. Comprehensive knowledge of technology-based e-learning, adult learning techniques, needs assessments, learning technologies, and performance improvement systems.

OPERATIONS MANAGEMENT/PROJECT MANAGEMENT: Proven ability to plan, manage, and coordinate resources and large-scale infrastructure, services, facilities maintenance, and operational support projects. Expertise in quality assurance, best practices, project lifecycle monitoring, and facilities process development.

COMPUTER/TECHNICAL EXPERTISE: A+ Certified. Proficient in MS Office, HTML, JAVA, ActionX.

SECURITY CLEARANCE: Top Secret (SCI) (Expired)

PERSONAL INTERESTS: Physical fitness training

TRAVEL / RELOCATE: Willing to travel and relocate. Flexible.

Figure 5.6: Sample Additional Information section preview for a Logistics Management/Systems Analyst position.

Case Study 4: Qualifications Summary Featuring Specialized Experience in Contracting

Contract Attorney focusing on contracting and procurement experience seeking Contractor Specialist positions, GS-12/13.

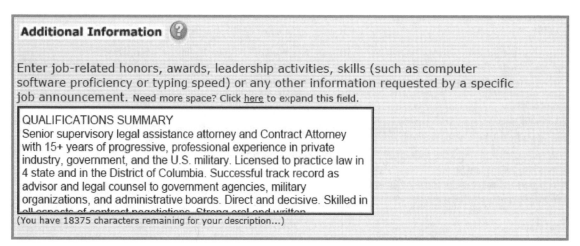

Additional Information ?

Enter job-related honors, awards, leadership activities, skills (such as computer software proficiency or typing speed) or any other information requested by a specific job announcement. Need more space? Click here to expand this field.

> QUALIFICATIONS SUMMARY
> Senior supervisory legal assistance attorney and Contract Attorney with 15+ years of progressive, professional experience in private industry, government, and the U.S. military. Licensed to practice law in 4 state and in the District of Columbia. Successful track record as advisor and legal counsel to government agencies, military organizations, and administrative boards. Direct and decisive. Skilled in all aspects of contract negotiations. Strong oral and written

(You have 18375 characters remaining for your description...)

Figure 5.7: Sample Additional Information form for a Contractor Specialist.

ADDITIONAL INFORMATION	QUALIFICATIONS SUMMARY Senior supervisory legal assistance attorney and Contract Attorney with 15+ years of progressive, professional experience in private industry, government, and the U.S. military. Licensed to practice law in 4 state and in the District of Columbia. Successful track record as advisor and legal counsel to government agencies, military organizations, and administrative boards. Direct and decisive. Skilled in all aspects of contract negotiations. Strong oral and written communications skills. Excellent organizational, analytical, and research capabilities. PC proficient. CONTRACT PROCUREMENT: Currently administering over $1 million in contracts for five U.S. military installations. Juris Doctorate and Master of Law degrees. Outstanding record of performance in contract administration and procurements. Including four years of experience as Judge Advocate General for the U.S. Air Force, Strategic Air Command (SAC). Expert knowledge of federal contracting laws, regulations, policies, and procedures, including Government Procurement Procedures and Federal Acquisition Regulations (FARs). Demonstrated ability to manage and administer all facets of the contract process from pre-award to post-award including acquistion strategy, acquistion planning, procurement package input and validation, solicitation, negotiation, contract award, administration, and closeout/termination. Experienced in all contracting/procurement methods and types. Strong skills in working with logistics managers, product quality managers, engineers, and other subject-matter experts and stakeholders.

Figure 5.8: Sample Additional Information section preview for a Contractor Specialist.

Case Study 5: Profile for an Administrative Professional

Administrative Assistant summarizing top-level administrative skills and competencies, seeking GS-9 positions.

Additional Information ⓘ

Enter job-related honors, awards, leadership activities, skills (such as computer software proficiency or typing speed) or any other information requested by a specific job announcement. Need more space? Click <u>here</u> to expand this field.

> PROFILE:
> Administrative professional with over 6 years of developing background information for analytical studies, researching official documents, and updating databases and creating spreadsheets to manage information. Possess skill and experience in summarizing and analyzing information for incorporation into final reports and supporting analysts with research, data compilation, project coordination, and tracking. I am an experienced professional administrator with outstanding skills in

(You have 19361 characters remaining for your description...)

Figure 5.9: Sample Additional Information form for an Administrative Assistant.

ADDITIONAL INFORMATION	PROFILE: Administrative professional with over 6 years of developing background information for analytical studies, researching official documents, and updating databases and creating spreadsheets to manage information. Possess skill and experience in summarizing and analyzing information for incorporation into final reports and supporting analysts with research, data compilation, project coordination, and tracking. I am an experienced professional administrator with outstanding skills in identifying and resolving problems. Strong analytical and communications skills; expertise in multitasking, working under pressure, and teamwork.

Figure 5.10: Sample Additional Information section preview for an Administrative Assistant.

Case Study 6: Relevant Skills for a Biologist

Biologist summarizing top-level field, clinical, and research skills, seeking GS-7/8 positions.

Additional Information ⓘ

Enter job-related honors, awards, leadership activities, skills (such as computer software proficiency or typing speed) or any other information requested by a specific job announcement. Need more space? Click <u>here</u> to expand this field.

> RELEVANT SKILLS:
> 1. FIELD SAMPLING AND INVESTIGATION: Underwater scientific data collection Survey, taxonomic identification and sampling of Atlantic/Caribbean corals, reef fish, invertebrates, and macroalgae; coral reef monitoring and restoration; water quality testing using field/laboratory equipment (Hobos, pH meter, dissolved oxygen meter, etc.); Use of radio telemetry to monitor terrestrial wildlife.
> 2. DOCUMENTATION AND DATA MANAGEMENT: Perform

(You have 17409 characters remaining for your description...)

Figure 5.11: Sample Additional Information form for a Biologist.

<table>
<tr><td valign="top">

ADDITIONAL INFORMATION

</td><td valign="top">

RELEVANT SKILLS:

1. FIELD SAMPLING AND INVESTIGATION: Underwater scientific data collection Survey, taxonomic identification and sampling of Atlantic/Caribbean corals, reef fish, invertebrates, and macroalgae; coral reef monitoring and restoration; water quality testing using field/laboratory equipment (Hobos, pH meter, dissolved oxygen meter, etc.); Use of radio telemetry to monitor terrestrial wildlife.

2. DOCUMENTATION AND DATA MANAGEMENT: Perform underwater photography and videography, using transect and quadrat methods. Skilled in using image processing and enhancement software (Adobe Photoshop, Jasc Paint Shop Pro). Use MS Excel and Statistica to manage and maintain data. Make field notes, record observations, and take size measurements. Prepare and classify collected samples.

3. STATISTICAL ANALYSIS AND REPORTING: Substantial experience analyzing tissues for signs of disease, stress, reproduction, and other factors; draw conclusions of environmental impact. Perform field analysis to determine next steps. Utilize computer programs such as MS Word to draft project reports and perform data manipulations. Statistical programs (Statistica, MS Excel, SAS). Statistical data analysis (e.g. ANOVA, Regression, t-test, non-parametric statistics, etc.). Coral reef assessment (Coral Point Count with Excel extensions 3.4) and mapping software (ArcGIS, ENVI).

4. WRITING AND PUBLIC SPEAKING: Design and present informative audiovisual presentations at scientific meetings using MS PowerPoint; lecture to undergraduate students and lead discussions regarding animal and plant biology/ecology/taxonomy; lead educational outreach tours and field trips regarding resource management issues. Write and edit project reports. Good experience with abstracts.

HONORS:
-- Fellowship, Summer Undergraduate Research Fellowship in Oceanography, Graduate School of Oceanography, University of Rhode Island, 2001.
-- Golden Key National Honor Society, University of Missouri, 2000-2001.
-- Allen Greenberg Biology Scholarship, University of Missouri, 1999, 2000.
-- University Scholar Scholarship, University of Missouri, 1998, 1999, 2000.
-- Dean's List, all semesters, University of Missouri, 1998-2001.

VOLUNTEER COMMUNITY SERVICE:
-- Florida Keys National Marine Sanctuary, Reef Medics Program, volunteer since July 2005. Perform bleaching, disease, and small-scale damage assessments within the sanctuary.
-- Reef Environmental Education Foundation, member since January 2005. Perform reef fish surveys via SCUBA in South Florida/Florida Keys.

</td></tr>
</table>

Figure 5.12: Sample Additional Information section preview for a Biologist.

Summary

Congratulations! You have just finished focusing your resume toward the position you are seeking next. You can refocus your resume for each announcement that you find by selecting and using some of the skills, competencies, and keywords you find in the announcements. The next chapter focuses on selecting the appropriate keywords. Continue to review your Profile, Skills, and Qualifications and see whether you can add a few more keywords into these paragraphs.

CHAPTER 6

Keywords for 12 Occupational Series: What Are Your Keywords?

Federal resume writers, Resumix resume writers, and private-industry writers all know that the keywords and skills included for a certain job are critical for the success of the resume. They are especially critical for the Department of Defense Resumix automated system.

The Department of Defense automated resume system is called Resumix, and it is known as a "keyword system." The supervisor and HR specialist decide on five to eight keywords/skills that are most important for the position. They search the database of all of the candidates for resumes that contain all of the keywords. If the resume does not contain the keywords for the position, the resume might not be selected in the system. Therefore, the applicant will not be referred to a supervisor for consideration for an interview.

Resumix is very much like CareerBuilder.com or Monster.com, where the HR recruiter searches for candidates based on job title, skills, and specific experience.

Keywords are critical for all resumes—electronic or paper. The HR specialist reviews paper resumes for top critical skills (and the right keywords) for the best candidates. The words in the announcement should be in your resume. Chapter 11 shows you how to analyze an announcement for keywords.

How These Keyword Lists Were Selected

My process for building the keyword lists was the following: I decided on a job series. Then I went to USAJOBS and did a search on that job title for all locations and all agencies. Then I selected three vacancy announcements to analyze. I copied and pasted the following sections from the announcement to analyze for keywords: Duties, Specialized Qualifications, KSAs, and Questions. I set up an account at the www.dla.mil ASP Resume Builder (which may or may not continue this keyword feature). I copied and pasted the language into the Duties section of the builder and submitted the resume to the DLA builder. I didn't actually apply for a job; I just submitted the resume. After about three minutes, I received an e-mail with the list of keywords that were abstracted from my "duties" sections. We then took the keyword list and eliminated some of the nonsense. We alphabetized the list and the final list is printed right here in this chapter.

The keyword analysis for the Logistics Management Specialist was done by a professional indexer, Pilar Wyman of www.wymanindexing.com, who said the following about the keyword analysis and selection process for the Logistics Management Specialist List:

> I put the keywords into a table, pulled out the junk, and then sorted them alphabetically in the attachment. I also eliminated place names (which could be innumerable) and Defense Department agencies, and some that were just gobbledygook, incomplete terms. You'll see that some don't necessarily occur in the job announcement, but are clearly related. "Teaching" for example, isn't in the job announcements (I think), although training is, and both are covered,

if only conceptually. What's left is indeed relevant to logistics management and to these announcements. More than 25 percent, I believe. You can see a variety of forms for some concepts, and many terms are very specific: WPM, communication, military experience, library experience, logistics, equipment management, creative writing, MIS, crime prevention, conflict resolution, teamwork, customer support, damage analysis, textiles, and so on.

⭐ **Note:** Many job seekers don't spend the time to research and analyze keywords and series language that should be included in the resume. They write their resumes from their memory of their job. And they don't actually do an analysis of the top skills from their current job to their target job. The matching of transferable skills can be done with a set of keywords.

---

12 Occupational Series Analyzed for Keywords/Skills

When you are writing your federal resume, you will learn how to analyze a vacancy announcement to use the terminology from the announcement in your resume. These lists demonstrate that the keywords for certain jobs or occupational series can be developed from vacancy announcements, the agency mission statement, and the OPM's Qualification Standards. If you are applying for an Accounting Technician, GS-7, it would be great to develop a list of keywords from several vacancy announcements before you start writing. The abbreviations that you will see in the lists came from the Resumix Knowledge Base.

The abbreviations shown in the keyword lists came out of the Resumix Knowledge Base. They are searchable abbreviations. But it is always better to spell out abbreviations in your resume.

In this section you'll find keyword lists for the following positions/series:

★ Accounting, GS-510

★ Administrative Series, GS-303

★ Administrative Officer, GS-341

★ Budget Analyst, GS-560

★ Continuity Exercise/Operation Specialist, FEMA GS-301

★ Contract Specialist, GS-1102

★ Criminal Investigator, GS-1811

★ Education Specialist, GS-1701

★ Health Administration Series, GS-0670

★ Human Resources Assistant, GS-203

★ Logistics Management Specialist, GS-346

★ Public Affairs Specialist, GS-1035

Accounting, GS-510

Accounting Systems
Accounts Payable
Accounts Receivable
Accruals
Acctg/Finance Ops
Acct'ing Principles
Amer w/ Disabil Act
Analytical Ability
Appraise
Assets
Audit
Budget Terms
Budget Transaction
Bus Strategy Trms
Business Acumen
Business Terms
Cntrct Modif Analys
Coach MentorMotiv
Commercial Law
Communications
Communicat'n Skills
Comptrollership
Concept Development
Continuous Imprvmt
Contract Assessmn
Contract Fin
Contrct Modif
Contrct Monitoring
Contrct Oversight
Cost Accounting
Cost Allocation
Cost Control
Cost Terms
Course of Study
CPA
Degree Requirements
Design & Dev
Disbursement
Effectiveness Eval
Electricity
Emerg Computr Tec
Emerging Technology
Engineering Exp
Entrprs Rsrc Pln SW
Ethical Standards
Evaluation Method
Evaluation Plan
External Audit
Facilities Maint
Fed Energy Reg Comm

Fed Mgr Fin Int Act
Federal Agencies
Federal Regs
Finance
Financial Accountg
Financial Auditing
Financial Exp
Financial Mgmt
Fin'l Laws/Regs
Fin'l Principl/Proc
Fixed Assets
Follow Policy/Proc
Force Management
Fund Management
Funding Documents
Funds Allocation
Funds Appropriation
Funds Distrib/Disbr
Funds Mgmt/Control
Funds Utilization
Gas Pipeline
Gen Accounting Off
General Ledger
Government Exp
Group Instruction
Group Leadership
Information Tech/IS
Innovtn&Initiatve
Insp General
Inspection
Internal Audit
Internal Controls
Language Arts
Law/Regs Interp
Laws
Leadership
Lease
Legal Documents
Legislative
Liaison
Maintenance System
Management Systems
Microsoft Cert Prof
MIS
Negotiating Skills
Network Development
Obligate Funds
Oil Pipelines
Oper Terms
Oral Written Comm
Organiz Development
Organizat'nl Skills
Payroll

PeopleSoft
Performance Awards
Performance Imprvmt
Pol&Proc Dev&Rev
Policies & Proced
Policy Admin
Policy Analysis
Policy Development
Policy Planning
Policy/Proc Review
Printing Exp
Procedure Develop
Procurement
Professional Dev
Prog Effectiveness
Prog Proj Plan
Program Advising
Program Coord
Program Implementn
Program Management
Program Planning
ProgrmDev Imp Obj
Proofreading
Public Accounting
Public Administratn
Purchase Order
Purchasing Docs
Purchasing Exp
Quality Analysis
Quality Issue Sys
Reconcile
Records Management
Regulat Affairs
Regulations
Spec Dev Rev
State & Fed Regs
Strategic Focus
Strategic Planning
Subsystem Design
Supervision
System Control
System Implmntn
Systems Accounting
Team Management
Treasury

Administrative Series, GS-303

Ability to Plan
Accounting Exp
Accounting Systems
Admin Assistance
Admin Functions

All Bachelors
Analytical Ability
Answer Phones
Appointments
Automation SW
Billeting
CAR
Career Counseling
Civ Per Mgmt
Civilian Pay
Clerical Skills
Coach MentorMotiv
Collect Stats
Communctns,Military
Communications
Communicat'n Skills
Computer Literate
Conduct Studies
Conf Scheduling
Conference Organiz
Conference Support
Confidential
Corrective Action
Correspondence
Creative Writing
Data Collect Tool
Data Collection
Data Retrieval
Data Storage
Data Utilization
Database
Database Mgmt
DBMS
Discrepancy Repor
Disposition
Distribution Oper
Document Distrib
Document Prep
Document Production
Document Retrieval
Document Review
DoD Policy
Edit Writing
Efficient
Employee Records
Employee/Labor Rel
English
Equipment Operation
Facilities Maint
Facility Util
FF&V
File Maintenance
Follow Policy/Proc

Follow Rules/Regs
Formatting
General Supply
Graphics
Greet Visitors
Grievance
HR Communications
HR Leadership
Info Reporting
Informatn Retrieval
Inspection Report
Investigate
Labor Relations
Labor/Mgmt Relatns
Language Arts
Law Enforcement
Leadership
Logistics Mgmt Exp
Logstcs Emrg Tech
Mail Sorting
Materials Rev
Mgmt Analysis
Mgmt Assistance
Military Experience
Military Police
Network
Office Administratn
Office Automation
Op Efficiency
Oper Terms
Oral Written Comm
PC Applications
PCS
Performance Goal
Performance Terms
Personal Computer
Personnel Actions
Personnel Mgmt
Planning
Pol&Proc Dev&Rev
Police
Policy Development
Policy/Proc Review
Position Analysis
Procedure Develop
Process Impr
Produce Spec
Professional
Prog Proj Plan
Program Data
Program Evaluation
Program Objective
Program Policy

Program Support
Programming
ProgrmDev Imp Obj
Proofreading
Publication
Quantitative Meth
Query System
Receiving
Records Management
Regulations
Regulatory Dev
Report Compilation
Reporting Procedure
Reporting System
Rept Discrep
Resource Stewardshp
Respnsbl&Acctblty
Schedule Calendar
Screen Calls
Secretarial
Self-Managing
Shadowing
Software Support
Software Use
Spreadsheet
Staffing
Staffng/Recruitng
Stat Analysis Sys
Statistic Terms
Statistical Data
Statistical Typing
Statistics
Storage & Retrieval
Supervision
Traffic Mgt
Train Authoriz Form
Training Experience
US Air Force
Wage & Salary Grade

Administrative Officer, GS-341

Ability to Plan
Achieves Goals
Admin Operation
Administratv Supply
Advise and Guidan
Analytical Ability
Benefit Terms
Budget Admin
Budget Estimate
Budget Execution
Budget Execputn

Budget Formulatio
Budget Justfcations
Budget Plan/Forecst
Budget Requests
Budget Systems
Budgeting Process
Civ Per Mgmt
Civilian Personnel
Coach MentorMotiv
Communicat'n Skills
Conduct Studies
Conflict Resolutn
Contract Methods
Contract Negotiatn
Correspondence
Credit Card
Credit Record
Decision Making
Design & Dev
Distribution Oper
Document Control
Efficiency Imprvmt
Efficiency Review
Emerg Computr Tec
Employee Benefits
Employee Counseling
Employee Promotion
Employee/Labor Rel
English
Estimating
Facilities Mngmnt
Fact Finding
Fast-Paced Environ
Finance
Financial Mgmt
Financial Reporting
Fin'l Principl/Proc
Follow Policy/Proc
Follow Rules/Regs
Fund Development
HR Administration
HR Bus Strategy
HR Communications
HR Leadership
HR Systems
Identifies Problems
Information Mgmt
Information Tech/IS
Innovtn&Initiatve
Installation Mgmt
Interpersonal Skill
Investigate
Labor Relations

Liaison
Loan/Credit Review
Logistics Mgmt Exp
Long Range Plan
Management Systems
Methods Analysis
Office Administratn
Op Effectiveness
Op Efficiency
Oral Written Comm
Organiz Assessment
Organiz Change
Organiz Design
Organiz Development
Performance Eval
Performce Monitor'g
Pers Security
Personnel Actions
Personnel Mgmt
Presents Findings
Problem Solving
Procedural Analysis
Procedure Develop
Process Design
Process Improvement
Procurement
Procurement Regs
Productivity
Prog Proj Plan
Program Needs
Program Objective
Program Planning
Program Reviews
Programming
Property Disposal
Property Management
Purchase Agree
Purchase Equipment
Purchasing Docs
Purchasing Proced
Reconcile
Records Management
Regulations
Regulatn Maintenanc
Relationship Buildr
Requirements Analy
Requirements Verif
Requisition Proc
Research
Resource Stewardshp
Resource Allocation
Resource Coord
Resource Management

Resource Mgmt Sys
Resource Mgt Plng
Resource Steward
Respnsbl&Acctblty
Results Oriented
Safety Management
Secure Facility
Space Utilization
Staffing Efficiency
Staffing Needs
Staffing Planning
Staffng/Recruitng
Strategic Focus
Supply Mgmt Exp
Supply Policy
Support Services
System Planning
Teaching
Team Leader
Teamwork
Technical Ops
Workers Comp
Written Comm
WrkrCompConfResol

Budget Analyst, GS-560

Ability to Plan
Accounting Exp
Accounting Systems
Accounts
Acct Reconciliation
Achieves Goals
Advise and Guidan
All Bachelors
Alternative Budget
Analytical Abilit
Analytical Ability
Analyze Expenditure
Assets
Budget
Budget Adjustment
Budget Analysis
Budget Docs
Budget Estimate
Budget Execution
Budget Executn
Budget Formulatio
Budget Formulatn
Budget Info/Data
Budget Justfcations
Budget Mgmt
Budget Plan/Forecst

Budget Policy
Budget Prep
Budget Presentatn
Budget Reporting
Budget Requests
Budget Restrictions
Budget Review
Budget Systems
Budget Terms
Budgetary Goals
Budgetary Issues
Budgetary Laws/Regs
Budgeting Process
Business Policies
Business Terms
Capital Assets
Coach MentorMotiv
Comm Skill
Comparative Cost
Computer Lit
Conflict Resolutn
Cost Analysis
Cost Control
Cost Terms
Cost-Benefit Analys
Creative Writing
Credits/Debits
Crime
Cust Acct Mgr
Data Collect Tool
Economic Analysis
Emp Dev
Estimating
Federal Budget
Federal Prison
Finance
Financial Analysis
Financial Exp
Financial Mgmt
Financial Policy
Financial Reporting
Fin'l Principl/Proc
Fiscal Law
Forecasting
Formulation Develop
Fund Development
Funding Documents
Funding Needs
Funding Review
Funds Allocation
Funds Analysis
Funds Appropriation
Innovtn&Initiatve

Language Arts
Logistics Mgmt Exp
Logstcs Emrg Tech
Mfg Terms
Mgmt Assistance
Mgmt Consulting
Military Experience
Network
Oral Written Comm
Performance Analys
Performance Goal
Performance Terms
Planning
Pol&Proc Dev&Rev
Policies & Proced
Policy Development
Policy Interpretatn
Policy/Proc Implemt
Position Analysis
PPBS
Presentation Skills
Prg Budget Acct Sys
Prison
Problem Analysis
Problem Solving
Procedural Analysis
Process Impr
Procurement
Professional
Prog Proj Plan
Program Advising
Program Development
Program Direction
Program Evaluation
Programming
ProgrmDev Imp Obj
Quantitative Meth
Regulations
Reimbur Budget
Reimburse Analysis
Requirements Analy
Requirements Verif
Resource Stewardshp
Resource Management
Resource Mgt Plng
Resource Steward
Respnsbl&Acctblty
RFID AIT Requrmnt
Rsource Mgm
Satellite
Security Procedure
Social Services
Staff Education

Statistic Terms
Statistics
Status of Funds
System Control
System Planning
Teamwork
Tech Skills
Technical Mgmt
Technical Support
Trend Analysis
US Air Force
US Dept Commerce
US Dept Defense
US Dept Justice
US Executive Branch

Continuity Exercise/ Operation Specialist, FEMA GS-301

Ability to Plan
Achieves Goals
Advise and Guidan
All Bachelors
Analytical Abilit
Assets
Budget
Budget Execution
Bus Strategy Trms
Business Terms
Civ Per Mgmt
Cntrct Office Rep
Coach MentorMotiv
Comm Skill
Communicat'n Skills
Con Oper Plan
Concept Development
Conduct Studies
Conflict Resolutn
Contingency Oper
Continuity Gvmt
Continuity Operat
Contract Assessmn
Contract Developmt
Contract General
Contract Negot
Contract Surv
Contrct Monitoring
Contrct Offcr
Contrct Oversight
Co-Op Program

Coord Facilities
Creative Writing
Daily Operations
Decision Making
Distribution Oper
Emergency Response
Emp Dev
Evaluation Method
Exercise Program
Facility Util
Fed Emgncy Mgmt
Federal Agencies
Federal Government
Goal Setting
Government Exp
Group Instruction
Group Leadership
HR Bus Strategy
HR Communications
HR Leadership
HR Program Implemnt
Innovtn&Initiatve
Investigate
Job Description
Language Arts
Leadership
Logistics
Logistics Mgmt Exp
Military Experience
Mission Analysis
National Security
Natural Disaster
Negotiating Skills
Network
Oper Terms
Operational Policy
Oral Comm
Oral Written Comm
Performance Plan
Pers Security
Plan of Action
Planning
Pol&Proc Dev&Rev
Policies & Proced
Policy Analysis
Policy Development
Policy Planning
Policy/Proc Implemt
Population
Problem Solving
Procedural Analysis
Process Impr
Professional

Prog Proj Plan
Program Coord
Program Development
Program Evaluation
Program Implementn
Program Management
Program Mgmt
Program Operations
Program Planning
Program Policy
Program Support
Programming
ProgrmDev Imp Obj
Project Planning
Regulations
Resource Stewardshp
Resource Allocation
Resource Management
Resource Mgt Plng
Respnsbl&Acctblty
Rsource Mgmt Term
Secure Facility
Security Policies
Security Procedure
Security Reqmt
Setting Priorities
Shipping
Staff Mgmt
Strategic Focus
Strategic Planning
Supervision
System Planning
Team Leader
Team Management
Teamwork
Tech Skills
Technical Support
Terrorism
Test & Eval
Tools
Traffic Mgt
Train Prg Plan/Pres
Training
Training Coordinatn
Training Design
Training Evaluation
Training Experience
Training Schedule
US Air Force
Writing Skills

Contract Specialist, GS-1102

Ability to Plan
Accounting Exp
Acquis Plan
Acquisitions
Acquisitn Logist
Acquistn Strategy
Advise and Guidan
All Bachelors
Analytical Ability
Bidding
Budget
Bus Strategy Trms
Business Terms
C&E
Coaching/Mentoring
Comm Skiils
Construction Work
Constructn Contract
Contract Administr
Contract Assessmn
Contract Award
Contract Complexity
Contract Developmt
Contract General
Contract Law
Contract Negot
Contract Negotiatn
Contract Plan
Contract Problems
Contract Surv
Contract: $100K+
Contract: $1M+
Contract: $500K+
Contrct Close-Out
Contrct Monitoring
Contrct Offcr
Contrct Oversight
Contrct Terminatn
Co-Op Agreement
Cost Accounting
Cost Analysis
Cost Survey
Cost Terms
Cost/Price Analysis
Creative Writing
Cust Svc
Customer Service
Damage Analysis
Distance Learning

Distribution Oper
Document Prep
E Learning
Emerg Computr Tec
Emergency Logis
Employee/Labor Rel
Equipment Acquis
Excel
Fact Finding
Federal Procurement
Federal Regs
Finance
Financial Analysis
Financial Exp
General Supply
Interagency Agrmnts
Investigate
Labor Relations
Land Survey
Large Purchases
Leadrship
Legal Experience
Logistics Mgmt Exp
Long-Term Contract
Meet Timeline
Microsoft Outlook
Microsoft Word
Milestone Sched
Military Experience
Monitor Schedule
MS PowerPoint
Multitasking
Negot Positn Determ
Negotiating Skills
Network
Operating Systems
Oral Written Comm
Outplacement
Performce Monitor'g
Performing Acty
Planning
Pol&Proc Dev&Rev
Position Analysis
Post Award
Pre-Award Admin
Price Analysis
Price Negotiation
Price Terms
Pricing
Problem Solving
Procedural Analysis
Process Impr
Procurement

Procurement Negot
Procuremnt Contract
Prog Proj Plan
Programming
Progress Pymt
Progress Report
ProgrmDev Imp Obj
Purchase Agree
Purchase Equipment
Purchasing Exp
Purchasing Negot
R&D
Regulations
Regulatory Analysis
Research
Resource Stewardshp
Respnsbl&Acctblty
Service Contract
Service Plan
Settlement
Shipping
Small Purchase
SOW
Space Flight
Specialized Cntrct
Spreadsheet
SSEB
State & Fed Regs
Strat Acq Plan
Strategic Focus
Strategic Planning
Strategic Sourcing
Supervision
Supply Operation
Supply Plan
Survey Analysis
Team Leader
Teamwork
Tech Skills
Technical Contract
Technical Data
Term for Conv
Traffic Mgt
US Air Force
Vendor Selection
Voucher
Windows
Writing Skills

Criminal Investigator, GS-1811

Ability to Plan
Accident Invest
Agency Intl Develop
All Bachelors
Analytical Abilit
Analytical Ability
Analytical Method
Antitrust
Applications Mgmt
Apprehend Detain
Arrest Procedures
Arrest Warrant
Assembly Exp
Budget
Budget Analysis
Budget Execution
Budget Formulatio
Budget Terms
Career Planning
Civil Law
Communications
Communicat'n Skills
Compensation
Conflict Interest
Containment
Contract Surv
Corp Communication
Cost Analysis
Cost Control
Cost Terms
Creative Writing
Crime Prevention
Criminl Investigatn
Data Collect Tool
Data Collection
Develop Briefing
Discrepancy Repor
Distribution Oper
Document Prep
E-Banking
Elec Funds Transfer
Evidence Collection
Exec Communications
Fact Finding
Fed Law Enf Agys
Finance
Financial Analysis
Financial Exp
Financial Mgt

FMS Con & Log Mgt
Fraud
Funds Transfer
Gaming Exp
General Supply
Government Exp
Govt-Owned Property
Information Mgmt
Informat'l Material
Innovtn&Initiatve
Insp General
Inspection
International Law
Interview Skills
Intl Govt
Investigative
IRM
Kitting
Language Arts
Law Enforcement
Leadrship
Legal Documents
Liaison
Logical
Logistics
Logistics Mgmt Exp
Logstcs Emrg Tech
Military Experience
Negotiating
Negotiating Skills
Office Auto
OOU
Op Efficiency
Oper Terms
Oral Written Comm
Overseas Service
Performing Acty
Planning
Police
Presentation Skills
Presents Findings
Presidential
Proactive
Problem Solving
Procurement
Professional
Prog Proj Plan
Program Implementn
Programming
ProgrmDev Imp Obj
Promotions
Property Terms
Regional Pay

Regulations
Report Writing
Research
Resource Stewardshp
Resource Management
Resource Mgt Plng
Resource Steward
Resourceful
Respnsbl&Acctblty
Rsource Mgmt Term
Schedule Work
Search & Seizure
Search Warrant
Secretarial
Securities
Self-Accountable
Subpoena
Supervision
Suspect Interrogtn
Tactful
Takes Initiative
Team Leader
Teamwork
Tech Skills
Technical Documents
Technical Equipment
Telecomm Exp
Telecommunication
Telemarketing
Tools
Traffic Mgt
Training Experience
Typing
Undercover Ops
United States
US Air Force
US Citizen
US Dept State
US Dept Treasury
US Postal Service
Vacancy Announcemnt
Warrant
Witness Interview

Education Specialist, GS-1701

Acquisitions
Annual Report
Any Community Exp
Audio Video Exp
Audio Visuals

AV Production
Baseline
Biology Exp
Bioresearch
Budget
Budget Execution
Budget Formulatio
Budget Prep
Budget Terms
Bus Strategy Trms
Business Terms
Caribbean
Civ Per Mgmt
Civil Service
Coach MentorMotiv
Comm Skill
Communicat'n Skills
Community Program
Contract General
Correspondence
Course Development
Course of Study
Creative Writing
Data Analysis
Data Collect Tool
Data Collection
DEU
Develop Briefing
Distance Learning
Distribution
Diversity
Document Prep
Documentation
E Learning
Edu. Program Devel
Educ Deg/Major/Cert
Educ Principles
Education Dept
Educational Progs
Educational Psych
Educationl Research
EEO
Emp Dev
English As 2nd Lang
Equip Maint/Monitor
Equipment Eval
ESL/EFL/ESOL
Executive Orders
Fnl Overhead Rate
Gateway
GED
General Supply
Goal Setting

Group Instruction
Hardware Install
Instructional Dvlp
Instructional Tech
Internet
Inventory Stock
Investigate
Jamaica
Layout Design
Leadrship
Learning Theory
Lesson Plan
Liaison
Logistics
Logistics Mgmt Exp
Logstcs Emrg Tech
Resource Stewardshp
Maint Agreement
Media Preparation
Mfg Terms
Military Experience
Multimedia
National/State Park
Network
Network Mgt
North America
Office Auto
Offsites
Oper Terms
Operational Methods
Oral Written Comm
Organizat'nl Skills
Outreach Recruiting
Performance Analys
Performance Eval
Performance Terms
Performce Monitor'g
Peripheral
PLAN
Planning
Presentation Skills
Prev Maint
Problem Solving
Process Impr
Prod Methods
Product Terms
Prog Integrator
Prog Proj Plan
Program Coord
Program Development
Program Implementn
Program Reviews
Programming

ProgrmDev Imp Obj
Project Analysis
Project Execution
Quantitative Meth
Questionnaire
Referral Coord
Regulations
Research
Research Experience
Research Project
Resource Management
Resource Mgt Plng
Resource Steward
Respnsbl&Acctblty
Results Oriented
RFID AIT Requrmnt
Rsource Mgmt Term
Service Contract
Shipping
Short Range Plan
Software
Software Install
Staff Education
Staffng/Recruitng
Statistic Terms
Strategic Focus
Strategic Planning
Student Development
Supervision
Supply Maintenance
Supply Program
System Design
System Installation
Teaching
Team Leader
Training Assistance
Training Experience
Troubleshoot Hrdwre
Troubleshoot Sftwre

Health Administration Series, GS-0670

Accreditation
All Bachelors
Allied Health
Ambulatory Care
Analytical Ability
Analytical Method
Assist Physician
Awareness
Budget

Budget Admin
Budget Formulatio
Budget Mgmt
Budget Prep
Budget Proposal
Budget Terms
Career Counseling
Career Planning
Civ Per Mgmt
Clinic Management
Comm Corps Pers Mnl
Comm Skiils
Complaint Inv
Conflict Resolution
Contin Med Educatn
Contract Assessmn
Contract Fin
Contract Negotiatn
Contrct Oversight
Cost Center
Cost Control
Cost Terms
Creative Writing
Credentialing
Decision Making
Delegate Mgmt
Dental Health
Dental X-Rays
Dietary
Disciplinary Action
Distribution
Edu. Program Devel
EEO
Emp Dev
Employee Counseling
Employee Promotion
Employee/Labor Rel
EMS
EMT
Equal Opportunity
Estimating
Fac Organization
Facilities Mngmnt
Facilities Reqs
Facility Util
Finance
First Aid
First-Line Suprvsn
Fiscal Mgmt
Follow Policy/Proc
Funds Allocation
Health Clinic Exp
Health Requirement

Health Services
Healthcare
Hospital
HR Administration
HR Leadership
HR Policy
HSA
Innovtn&Initiatve
In-Patient
Interpersonal Skill
Investigate
JCAHO
Labor Relations
Language Arts
Leadership
Logistics
Logistics Mgmt Exp
Management Systems
Medical Equipment
Medical Management
Medical Records
Medical Supplies
Medical Unit
Meet Timeline
Mgmt Practices
Military Experience
Motivates Others
Multi-Discip Team
Negotiating
Network
North America
Off Personnel Mgmt
Office Administratn
Organiz Assessment
Organiz Development
Organiz Planning
Out-Patient
Patient Care
Patient Relations
Performance Eval
Performance Stndrds
Performance Terms
Personnel Practices
Personnel Regs
Pharmaceutical
Pharmaceutical Mkt
Pharmacy Exp
Planning
Pol&Proc Dev&Rev
Policy Admin
Policy Development
Policy Interpretatn
Policy/Proc Implemt

Prev Maint
Procurement
Prod & Svcs Quality
Prod Ctrl Svc Eva
Prod Methods
Prod Qlty Def Rep
Product Terms
Professional
Professional Dev
Prog Proj Plan
Program Coord
Program Direction
Program Evaluation
Program Implementn
Program Management
Program Objective
Program Policy
Program Reviews
Programming
ProgrmDev Imp Obj
Promotions
Public Health Svc
Public Relations
Purchasing Mgmt
Quality Improvement
Quality Issue Sys
Quality of Care
Radiological Med
Respnsbl&Acctblty
US Dept Health
Wellness
Work Direction
X-Ray

Human Resources Assistant, GS-203

Ability to Delegate
Ability to Plan
Acctg Discrepancy
Admin Assistance
Admin Operation
Advise and Guidan
AIS
All Bachelors
Automatic Tools
Automation Suppor
Automation Support
Automation SW
Benefit Determine
Benefit Evaluation
Benefit Terms
Budget
Civ Per Mgmt

Civilian Issues
Civilian Personnel
Clerical Skills
Coach MentorMotiv
Coding Data
Compensation
Compensation Analys
Conduct Studies
Conflict Resolution
Conflict Resolutn
Containment
Creative Writing
Customer Service
Data Analysis
Data Utilization
Death Benefit
DEU
Disability Benefits
Disciplinary Action
Distribution Oper
Document Location
Document Prep
Documentation
Drug Screening
Edit Writing
Emerg Computr Tec
Employee Assistance
Employee Benefits
Employee Merit
Employee Promotion
Employee Records
Employee Relations
Employee Relocation
Employee Services
Employee Terminatn
Employee/Labor Rel
Error Correction
Evaluation Method
Facility Util
FedBen Admin Insu
FedBenAdmn Sep/Rtm
FEGLI
File Maintenance
Filing
Focal Review
Government Exp
Health Insur Prog
HR Communications
HR Leadership
HR Policy
Human Resources Exp
Identifies Problems
Inc Awd Liaison

Information Tech/IS
Innovtn&Initiatve
Inspection
Insurance Benefits
Labor Relations
Language Arts
Law/Regs Interp
Leadrship
Life Insurance
Logistics
Logistics Mgmt Exp
Merit Promotion
Mfg Terms
Microcomputers
Military Experience
Military HRM
New Hire Orientat'n
Office Automation
Payroll Systems
Paysetting
PCS
Performance Analys
Performance Eval
Performance Mgmt
Performance Terms
Personal Computer
Personnel Actions
Personnel Practices
Personnel Regs
Personnel Systems
Planning
Privacy Act
Problem Solving
Process Impr
Prog Proj Plan
Program Support
Programming
ProgrmDev Imp Obj
Proofreading
Qual Analysis
Quantitative Meth
Query System
Receiving
Records Management
Recruiting
Regulations
Regulatory Reqmt
Relationship Buildr
Reprographics
Resource Stewardshp
Resource Mgt Plng
Resource Utilizatn
Respnsbl&Acctblty

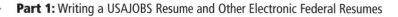

RFID AIT Requrmnt
Rsource Mgmt Term
Secur. Withholding
Social Security
Software Support
Software Use
Special Pay
Staffing Planning
Staffng/Recruitng
Stat Analysis Sys
Statistic Terms
Statistical Data
Statistics
System Administratn
Systems Training
Technical Support
Thrift Plan
Thrift Sav Prog
Tools
Training
Training Experience
Wage & Salary Grade
Withholding
Workers Compenstn
WrkrCompConfResol
WrkrCompLaws

Logistics Management Specialist, GS-346

Ability to Plan
Acctg Discrepancy
Accurate
Achieves Goals
Admin Functions
Aircraft
AIS
Am Soc Train & Dev
Analytical
Apparel
Armament
Arms Monitoring
Asn Supv & Curr Dev
Authorization Doc
Auto Data Process'g
Automotive Exp
Awards
Bachelors
Battle
Billeting
Budget
Budget Estimate

Budget Plan/Forecst
Budget Terms
C&E
Call Detail Record
Civ Per Mgmt
Clothing & Textil
Coach MentorMotiv
Comm
Comm Skill
Command
Communicat'n Skills
Community Center
Community Exp
Computr Tec
Conflict
Conflict Resolutn
Construction Work
Contact Person
COSIS
Course Development
Creative Writing
Crime
Crime Prevention
Cust Rel Mgmt
Customer Service
Customer Support
Damage Analysis
Data Analysis
Data Collection
Data Processing
Depreciation
Dept Housing
Design
Develop Briefing
Development
Dir Engineer
Distribution
Document Prep
Documentation
Documents
DoD Policy
Economics
Effectiveness
Effectiveness Eval
Elementary Sch Exp
Email
Emerg
Emp Dev
Emp Sfty and Welf
Employee
Employee Activities
Eng
Engineering Exp

Equip Maint/Monitor
Equipment Mgmt
Estimating
Evaluation
Evaluation Method
Experience
Facilities
Family Housing
Finance
Financial
Financial Status
Fiscal Mgmt
Follow Policy/Proc
Follow Rules/Regs
Forces
FORSCOM
Funding
Funds Allocation
Funds Analysis
Funds Mgmt/Control
General Supply
Goal Setting
Government Exp
Govt-Owned Property
Group Leadership
Health & Safety
HR
HR Communications
Identifies Problems
Identify
Information Tech/IS
Innovtn&Initiatve
Inspection
Interpersonal Skill
Intgratd Log
Inv Dist Mgmt
Item Mgmt
Job Description
Key Control
Language Arts
Law/Regs Interp
Leadership
Legal Documents
Liability
Liaising
Liaison
Library Exp
Logistics
Logistics Analysis
Logistics Data
Logistics Integratn
Logistics Issues
Logistics Mgmt Exp

Logistics Mgmt Sys
Logistics Operation
Logistics Plan
Logistics Principls
Logistics Support
Logistics System
Logstcs Emrg Tech
Maint/Repair Reqmt
Maintenance
Maintenance Support
Management
Management Systems
Management Training
Material Production
Material Storage
Materials
Meet Timeline
Member
Middle School Exp
Military Cmd
Military Experience
MIS
Mission Analysis
Monitor
Multi-Family
Obligate Funds
Occupational Health
Offcr
Operational
Oral
Organiz Change
Organiz Design
Performance
Performance Eval
Performing Acty

Public Affairs Specialist, GS-1035

Ability to Plan
Acquisitions
Advise and Guidan
Analytical Abilit
Analytical Method
Awareness
Broadcast Media
Broadcasting Exp
Brochure Prep
Brochures
Budget Execution
Bus Strategy Trms
Business Terms

Coach MentorMotiv
Comm Skill
Communications Plan
Community Affairs
Community Leader
Community Org
Community Outreach
Community Program
Conf Scheduling
Conference Organiz
Cong Relations
Content Developmnt
Correspondence
Creative Writing
Develop Briefing
Distribution Oper
Document Prep
Effectiveness Eval
Emerg Computr Tec
Event Planning
Fact Finding
Fed Law Enf Agys
Follow Policy/Proc
Identifies Problems
Information Tech/IS
Innovtn&Initiatve
Interchange
Internatl Logis

Interpersonal Skill
Interview
Investigate
Investigative
Leadership
Leadrship
Letter Composition
Liaison
Logistics
Logistics Mgmt Exp
Material Command
Material Selection
Mgmt Assistance
Mgmt Consulting
Multimedia
Network
News Release
Op Readiness
Operational Plans
Operational Plns
Oral Written Comm
Performing Acty
Photography
Planning
Pol&Proc Dev&Rev
Policy Development
Policy Interpretatn
PowerPoint

Presentation Skills
Presents Findings
Proactive
Problem Solving
Procedure Develop
Professional
Prog Effectiveness
Prog Proj Plan
Program Advising
Program Coord
Program Data
Program Development
Program Direction
Program Evaluation
Program Implementn
Program Leadership
Program Management
Program Mgmt
Program Operations
Programming
ProgrmDev Imp Obj
Project Mgmt
Public Affairs
Public Speaking
Publication
Quantitative Meth
Regulations
Relationship Buildr

Release of Info
Reprographics
Request for Info
Research
Resource Stewardshp
Resource Mgt Plng
Resource Reqmt
Respnsbl&Acctblty
Rsource Mgmt Term
Speech Writing
Staff Education
Staff Liaising
Statistic Terms
Statistics
Strategic Focus
Strategic Planning
Subj Matter Expert
Supervision
Target Identificatn
Target Recognition
Team Leader
Teamwork
Tech Skills
Technical Support
Training
Training Experience
Video
Writing Skills

Summary

You will add your keywords to your resume when you are creating your outline, writing your accomplishments, and using language from the job announcement to improve the description of your duties. Using keywords shows that you are qualified for the job and that you took the time to analyze the target announcement. Two more strategies will help you improve your resume content: writing with plain language (see chapter 7) and adding your core competencies (see chapter 8).

Part 2

Plain Language and Value-Added Lessons

Plain-Language Writing Lessons

How do you look on paper? How impressive is your resume? It's high time for civilians and current federal employees to learn to write about their career accomplishments in a concise, clear, and nonbureaucratic style. You must communicate your skills and accomplishments, and even brag a little. However, a three- to five-page resume does not afford space for every detail of your work. You must select the key experiences and write the resume in a new style, which I call *plain language*.

This chapter might be one of the most important in this book. By following the 10 resume-writing principles spelled out in this chapter, you will produce a well-written, easy-to-read, likable, impressive, factual, concise, and marketable resume. And a well-written resume will help you be selected for a promotion, increase your salary, and add to your retirement fund. All of your writing and editing effort will pay off!

Although this chapter is primarily about writing resumes, the tips apply equally well to other types of writing. These tips are useful for writing KSAs, a memorandum in justification of your promotion, your annual performance review statement of accomplishments, or even an SES package.

Most people don't give themselves enough credit in their resumes. Sometimes this is due to misplaced modesty. Sometimes it's because of the "I can't take full credit for that because we work as a team" attitude. More often, though, it's either a failure to recognize the significance of your performance or an inability to articulate your performance in a way that sounds meaningful.

Fortunately, writing a good resume can be manageable, simple, and even easy, if you follow a few guidelines. Although there's no substitute for experience, even a first-time resume writer can produce a perfectly fine resume. And the more you practice, the better you will become.

To write a good resume, you have to be able to do three things:

★ Write well. Face it: you can't make a good resume out of poor sentences. You will learn how to write well by following the principles in this chapter. If you work at it, you can do it.

★ Perceive your abilities and accomplishments clearly and objectively, neither diminished through false modesty nor exaggerated through undue pride.

★ Assemble the well-written and accurate description of your qualifications into a compact, focused package.

Many people feel that their writing is not good. Even professional writers struggle with this feeling. And many people who need to put together a resume don't do much writing and have had little practice. At the same time, however, most people are good at telling a story to a friend—perhaps a funny thing that happened at the market, or an interesting program they saw on television. This ability is all you need to write a good resume. Your resume is really just a story about you.

You start with good content. If you are a poor worker and have accomplished little, your resume will not be impressive. But the fact that you are reading this book means that you are dedicated to improving your situation, and that's a sign of a good worker. If you have been reading and working with the chapters in part 1 of this book, you have some good content by now. Now let's make it work for you.

I have identified 10 principles of good writing. They are neither hard nor complicated to learn and follow, and they work. Apply them yourself and see!

First Principle: Use Plain Words and Write About What You Really Do at Work

The purpose of a resume is to impress the reviewer with your qualifications for the job. But before you can impress them, they have to understand what you are writing. Overly embellished writing can be a turn-off or make you seem pompous. If used incorrectly, you fail to seem impressive; you might even appear obtuse. Unspecific writing will not reach the essence of your duties, fails to explain the correlation between actions and results, and prevents the reader from understanding your job.

Here's an example of some generic writing that does not explain the "real job":

Halliburton (KBR) Operations (IRAQ)

Operations Specialist (01/06-present)

Ensure reports are completed in accordance with deadlines and undertake report editing where necessary. Ensure all security incidents are appropriately recorded and reported to project managers and relevant parties. Receive, analyze, disseminate, and submit to higher headquarters significant activity reports.

The real story is here:

Halliburton (KBR) Operations (IRAQ)

Operations Specialist (01/06-present)

FACILITY SUPPORT CUSTOMER SERVICES REPRESENTATIVE:

As one of 20 Operations Services Staff, I ensure a high quality of life and living services for contractors and federal civilians supporting the fighters in Iraq, Afghanistan, Kosovo, and other international sites. Receive requests for new services and solve problems for facilities maintenance requests. Provide accommodations for incoming staff. Oversee support for morale and health activities. I manage the status of more than 50 incoming project requests on a daily basis.

Tip: Here's a simple way to test whether your resume contains any overblown or nonspecific writing. Read it aloud to a friend. Can you keep a straight face? Or are you embarrassed? If you read it out loud to someone else, do they understand your job?

Plain language is the single most important key to good resume writing. But if your resume does not pass the "straight face" test, how do you go about making it simple? You must look critically at *every single word* in your resume. Every word must pull its weight. You must mercilessly chop out every word that does not pack a punch. Use the fewest words possible to say the most.

Second Principle: Use Short Sentences

Long sentences are confusing and boring. They do not belong in your resume. Short sentences crackle with excitement! Abraham Lincoln once made the statement, "If you need me to give a long speech, I am ready now. If you want me to give a short speech, it will take me some time to prepare." No wonder the Gettysburg Address consists of just 10 short sentences. What is true of speeches is even more true of resumes. The last thing you need in your resume is a string of long sentences that take the reviewer a lot of time and effort to figure out.

Ideally, a sentence conveys only one clear thought. It flows logically from the preceding sentence and leads into the next sentence. There is no magically prescribed length for a good sentence. Good writing generally alternates between sentences of medium length and sentences that are much shorter. This creates variety and can set up a rhythm that keeps the reader's attention. See?

If your sentences have grown too long, you can break them into smaller sentences. Each small sentence can convey one piece of the full thought. Don't put a "laundry list" of ideas into one sentence. Here's an example:

Before:

> Provide logistics and information management support for designated programs/projects managed by the Advanced Undersea Systems Program Branch in order to identify specific requirements for money, manpower, material, facilities, and services for logistics and information management through one or more of the following phases of the program/project life cycle: concept formulation, demonstration and validation, full-scale development, and production development.

After:

> As the Logistics Management Specialist in the Advanced Undersea Systems Program Logistics Branch, I directed logistics and information management support. Administered funding for manpower, materiel, facilities, and services. Managed full lifecycle projects from concept formulation, demonstration and validation, full-scale development, and production development.

Third Principle: Use "I" Intelligently

In the old days, there was no *I* in *resume*. The personal pronoun "I" was taboo. This was probably because it is easy to fall into the trap of starting every sentence with "I," which quickly becomes tedious and egocentric-sounding. The downside to avoiding "I" is that the sentences can end up as verbal contortionism. Today, the resume writer must strike a balance between these extremes.

This week, we received a copy of an e-mail from a USMC civilian employee regarding the use of "I" in resumes for the U.S. Department of the Navy online application system (DONHR) system:

> Human resources has passed the word that all resumes submitted through Resumix should be in first person (worded as if you are speaking). The person does affect the pulling of the resumes.

Many reviewers still cringe at an "I" in a resume, but there is a growing trend toward including it. This is part of an overall shift away from a stilted resume, and toward a resume that flows more naturally. The modern rule of thumb is to use "I" to personalize your resume, but not so often as to become obnoxious.

Electronic federal resumes have become bureaucratic, filled with acronyms and position description-like language, and mostly devoid of accomplishments. Federal HR specialists are trying to encourage writing that reflects what an employee really did in his or her job. What were the challenges? Who were the customers? What extra value did you bring to the job? This more personal style of writing can result in telling the "real story" about their job.

New Resume Use of "I Rules™"

- **Don't** use "I" to start every sentence.
- **Don't** use "I" twice in the same sentence, or in two sentences in a row.
- **Do** use "I" when it makes your sentence flow smoothly.
- **Do** use "I" three to five times per page.
- **Do** use "I" with descriptions of accomplishments or "KSAs in the resume."
- **Do** use "I" in a compelling sentence emphasizing complexity, uniqueness, challenge, or outstanding service.
- **Do** use "I" in a summary of skills or competencies.
- **Do** use "I" in project descriptions where you are performing a particular role.
- **Do** use "I" in your Other Qualifications or Summary of Skills section. You can use "I" more frequently in a summary of your personal values, core competencies, and skills.

Here's an example in which it makes good sense to use "I" in a specific project description:

> My Division Director ordered an audit to be conducted within two business days. The task appeared nearly impossible. After getting input from other team members, I proposed a division of labor that made the challenge more manageable. We completed the audit a half-day ahead of schedule, and the Director awarded me a Certificate of Recognition for my contribution.

Notice that in this example, the last sentence does not say "I received a Certificate…." By saying "the Director awarded me," I avoided "I" and also made the sentence active rather than passive (see the Tenth Principle). This example also showcases a more personalized writing style.

Following are some other examples of the use of "I," which personalizes the example of success.

Project Example:

> After extensive research I was able to convey to all personnel covering 7 different agencies the proper use/dispatch of government vehicles within Europe. Status of Forces Agreement (SOFA) stipulates if a European Country is not part of this agreement, government vehicles cannot be driven there without proper authorization.

Compelling Example:

> As a Natural Resource Specialist, I complete difficult and innovative assignments, including unparalleled watershed analysis partnerships and a unique outreach partnership with Nestucca High School. Provide effective liaison to the public in wildlife and forest conservation issues. Fulfill a variety of roles centered on team leadership, fostering partnerships, providing expertise and advice on animal populations, performing wildlife surveys, and supervising summer crews for timber sale layout.

In the Summary or Profile or Other Qualifications sections:

> ### PROFILE
> Natural Resource Specialist with 24 years of extensive Bureau of Land Management ecosystem-based management experience. I am valued by managers for my expertise in completing innovative and challenging special projects. Possess strong skills in coordinating interagency partnerships and interdisciplinary team efforts. Specialize in public speaking, timber project layout leadership, wildlife surveys, habitat restoration, cooperative agreements, public outreach to school groups, and representing BLM goals to outside interest groups. My experience includes successful resolution of multiple-use conflicts involving wildlife, forest, and botanical resources. I have excellent communication, supervision, and negotiation skills.

First sentence in Work Experience after title:

> As a Wildlife Biologist, I practiced ecosystem-based management in a self-directed work team atmosphere. Wildlife Biologist on the Lower Deschutes eco-team assigned to evaluate and improve wildlife and fish habitat. The last four months of this employment period were spent detailed to the wildlife staff of the Lakeview District BLM, Klamath Falls Resource Area.

Fourth Principle: Use Powerful Words

If you use plain language in short sentences, how is your resume going to impress anyone? Through the use of powerful words! Powerful words convey strong and unambiguous meaning. You should use a thesaurus to find stronger substitutes for weak words in your resume. This is even more important in the age of the resume builder, where the character count may be strictly limited. But this won't take you all the way. To clear away the debris of weak words, you need to think about writing in a new way. For example, consider the following statement:

> Serve as point of contact for all matters pertaining to personnel.

Serve as is not impressive. It does not tell the reader anything. Chop it. *Point of contact* is good, but *chief liaison* is better. *Sole liaison* is better still (if true). *Pertaining to* adds nothing, so eliminate it. Just say *all personnel matters*. Thus, the following statement is a good phrase:

Sole liaison on all personnel matters.

Every single word in it contributes significantly to the idea. See how if you remove any word, the sentence becomes weaker? That's how you know your sentence is truly strong.

Here are a few examples of powerful words that you might see frequently in federal vacancy announcements:

★ Complex or highly complex

★ Unique

★ Energetic

★ Creative

The following list is a compilation of more than 100 powerful words for resume writing based on more than 15 years of professional resume writing experience. There are undoubtedly many more. Keep this list near your computer or wherever you work on your resume as a handy reference. It will be a great tool when you are stuck for a word. The list is arranged into categories. Just by picking words for the various categories and modifying them as needed, you will be already halfway to a quality resume.

These words are nouns and verbs, quantifiers, interpersonal traits, abilities, core competencies, and industry jargon. These exceptional words will demonstrate your level of independence and impress the reader.

Creation

These verbs demonstrate initiative, resourcefulness, organizational skills, and creativity.

assemble	conceive	convene	create	design
forge	form	formulate	invent	implement
initiate	realize	spearhead	plan	

First or Only

The Navy Job Kit gives these instructions: "Use modifiers to define the frequency at which you perform tasks, i.e., occasionally, regularly, once or twice per year, monthly, weekly, daily. Use words that define the level and scope of your experience and skills." These quantifiers are important. If you do not tell readers you were the sole support for 15 professionals, how will they know it?

chief	first	foremost	greatest	most
leading	number one	singular	one	only
prime	single	sole	unparalleled	top
unique	unrivaled			

Outcomes

To demonstrate that you can "get things done," use these words to demonstrate action and results.

communication	cooperation	cost-effective	efficiency	morale
outcomes	output	productivity		

Employment

These words demonstrate movement, action, and decision-making abilities.

deploy	employ	exercise	use	utilize

Leadership

Leaders are in demand—whether you are a manager, administrative staffer, or tradesperson. If you are a team leader, foreman, supervisor, or lead, define your leadership responsibilities.

(be) chief (of)

(be) in charge of

(be) responsible for

administer	control	direct	govern	head up
lead	manage	oversee	run	supervise

Primacy

How important are you to the project? Are you a subject-matter expert? If you are, say so.

advisor	co-worker	key	major	expert
primary	principal	subject matter	source person	lead
sole source				

Persuasion

The ability to persuade is a significant trait for success. Persuasive skills and language can be used in describing teamwork.

coach	galvanize	inspire	lobby	rally
persuade	(re)invigorate	(re)vitalize	unify	unite

Success

The word "success" suggests results and positive thinking. The reader believes you are successful because you have written it in your resume.

accomplish	achieve	attain	master
score (a victory)	succeed	sustain	

Authorship

Writing is one of the principal skills needed in a civilian job. If you write and edit documents, include these skills.

author	create	draft	edit
generate	publish	write	

Newness

Are you part of a project that is being done for the first time? Tell readers or they won't know this is an innovative, state-of-the-art program designed to improve services and enhance the program.

creative	first-ever	first-of-its-kind	innovative	novel	state-of-the-art

Degree

Quantify your successes and results—with a percentage, if possible. Your resume will be more interesting, complete, and exciting.

100% (or other percentage that is impressive)

completely	considerably	effectively	fully
especially	extremely	outstanding	greatly
particularly	powerful	seasoned	highly
significantly	strongly	thoroughly	solidly

Quality

Qualify your work efforts. Was it excellent, outstanding, or high quality? Positive thinking and writing about outstanding achievements will sell the selecting official on your capabilities.

excellent	great	good	high quality
outstanding quality	special	superb	

Competencies

Writing about your knowledge, skills, and abilities in your resume requires that you state you are adept in concise, focused writing; expert in certain laws and regulations; capable in facilitating meetings; and skilled in network administration.

able	adept at	capable	competent	demonstrated
effective	expert	knowledgeable	proven	
skilled	tested	trained	versed in	

Words to Edit Out of Your Resume

Just as there are powerful words that serve you well in a resume, there are simple words and phrases to avoid. Here are a few "before" and "after" examples of the old writing style and the new, more succinct writing style.

Currently I am working as the Manager of Operations.
Manage operations.

I also have experience with planning meetings.
Plan and coordinate meetings.

I have worked for the Office of Training Programs.
Cooperate with Office of Training Programs.

I have helped set up office systems.
Organized new office systems.

Major duties include working with other staff.
Cooperated with staff.

I used a variety of equipment.
Equipment skills include….

Major duties were to write and edit.
Write and edit….

I provide….
Select a verb that will be more descriptive than "provide," such as design, research, coordinate, or facilitate.

Worked in the capacity of management analyst.
Management Analyst.

I was responsible for managing the daily operations.
Managed daily operations.

I also have experience in designing audit reports.
Design audit reports.

When needed, supervise team members.
Supervise team members on occasion.

As the department's user support….
User support for the department.

Worked with team members.
Member of a team.

Being the timekeeper for the office.
Timekeeper for the office.

Assume duties of the education specialist.
Education specialist planning programs and curriculum.

Also responsible for preparing payroll information.
Prepare payroll for 250 employees.

Helped with writing, editing.
Wrote, edited, planned, coordinated… any verb that describes the activity.

Tasks included compiling, organizing, and researching information.
Compile, organize, and research information.

Assisted with planning, researching, and designing.
Co-planned, researched, and designed….

As a member of a team, planned, researched, and designed.
Planned, researched, and designed as a member of the interagency team.

Responsible for all aspects of the critical reviews and narrative reports.
Wrote critical reviews and narrative reports.

(continued)

(continued)

> *I provide the leadership to maintain benchmarks to meet project deadlines.*
> Plan and lead team to maintain benchmarks to meet project deadlines.
>
> *Concurrently monitored project….*
> Managed details for the _____ project.
>
> *My other duties consist of customer services, research, and problem-solving.*
> Research and resolve problems for customers.
>
> *The information is gathered from….*
> Complied, organized, and managed information gathered from….
>
> *I have to do systems analysis and planning.*
> Manage systems analysis and planning for projects.
>
> *Assisted in all aspects of….*
> Involved in all aspects of….

Those are just some of the phrases to avoid; there are stronger ways to express yourself. The key is to review every single word and phrase in your resume. Then ask yourself two questions:

★ If I cut it out, would the sentence be less meaningful?

★ Is there any shorter or clearer way to say it?

If you can honestly answer no to both questions, leave it in. I look at it this way: You have to work hard; so should each word in your resume!

Fifth Principle: Beware of Acronyms

We know that Federal employees depend on acronyms to communicate. And this is okay at work among your co-workers. But in a resume where you may be applying to another agency, your resume could be Greek to the new HR specialist. And, the electronic Resumix system at DOD might not recognize your acronyms as keywords. The Resumix keyword system does not include any of the unusual acronyms.

Solution: Describe your experience with both acronyms and descriptions to be safe. The Defense Finance & Accounting Service human resources specialist gives this advice to employees to maximize success with the Resumix resume system:

> Please write a generic description of your proprietary systems, so that the automated system can search for your software and skill knowledge.

Here's an example. WAWF (Wide Area Work Flow) should be described this way in your resume:

> Train and provide technical assistance to customers in the use of Wide Area Work Flow (WAWF), Department of Defense Receipts & Acceptance system.

Sixth Principle: No Bureaucratese or Position Description (PD)–Style Writing

If you are writing a federal electronic resume based on your position description, beware of the temptation to write your resume the same way the HR specialist wrote the position description. You can write in a more clear and meaningful style without the bureaucratese or position description–style writing.

No Bureaucratese or PD-Style Writing

Bureaucratese is a style of language characterized by jargon and euphemisms that is used especially by bureaucrats. It is often confusing, cold, intimidating, and cloudy. All of us, but particularly those of us who work for the public, have a responsibility to handle language with care. We need to be accessible and clear. We need to avoid jargon and bureaucratese. Examples of jargon include the following:

★ Overuse of the passive voice (see the Ninth Principle for more on this)

★ Using federal and state program names without explaining what the programs are

★ Using and misusing words such as *impact, interface, prioritize, modality,* and *ascertain*

★ Using phony words and phrases such as *analyzation, conduit, augment,* and *determine the nature of*

Before: Bureaucratic Writing Style

Administrative Support Specialist: Serves as deputy to the supervisor of the Administrative Personnel Processing Office (APPO), with responsibility for overseeing and assuring the quality and accuracy of a variety of support functions associated with the APPO of the Transatlantic Program Center (TAC). Manages assigned activities through a continuous review of operations support program accomplishments, against established objectives and goals. This process encompasses every aspect of personnel deployment to include temporary change of station (TCS) and temporary duty (TDY) requirements; pre-deployment package actions; travel itineraries; timekeeping; and final return to home station actions. Provides technical advice on operations support functions and quality assurance oversight to the supervisor. Plans, organizes, coordinates, and assists in the implementation of the mission Requirements of the APPO. Manages, coordinates, and oversees the quality and accuracy for day-to-day support operations.

After: Active Writing Style That Is More Friendly and Direct

As the deputy to the supervisor of the Administrative Personnel Processing Office (APPO), I oversee efficient administrative and support operations for the Transatlantic Program Center (TAC). Coordinate deployment services for an average of 1,500 U.S. Army Corps of Engineers civilians deployed to Iraq and other reconstruction areas per year. As the lead of the Support Team, we ensure continuous review and update for the following deployment services: temporary change of station and temporary duty requirements. The team also manages customer services for predeployment package actions, travel itineraries, and final return to home station actions. I am the technical advisor to the supervisor on all mission requirements of the APPO.

Seventh Principle: Tell a Story or Describe a Project

The best resumes flow with well-written, interesting prose—almost like a story. Many federal employees are involved in major projects in their work. Their entire resumes can be composed of descriptions of projects.

What Is Your Top Ten List of Accomplishments?

The human resources specialists and supervisors enjoy a good story that demonstrates your accomplishment, outstanding service to the office or customer, and added value to the office. If you write 10 accomplishments and combine them into your resume, you will achieve a genuine personal statement of success, demonstrate your skill level, and keep the HR specialist spellbound.

Here's an impressive story:

Project: National Emergency Response Team (NERT):

Currently assigned to the NERT activated by the Director, FEMA; respond to incidents of national significance. I am a key participant in the design and implementation of IT and telecom solutions to meet the needs of emergency-management teams in response to critical events, including Hurricane Katrina. Prepared an Interagency Operations Plan that coordinated the joint operations of multiple federal and civil organizations including FEMA, the FBI, the U.S. Secret Service, the Port Authority NY/NJ, and the New York City Police.

Story: Irate Passenger at BWI

As a Lead Security Screener, I negotiated a solution with an unruly passenger recently at BWI airport. The passenger was highly irate because he could not take a special garden cutting tool to his mother for Mother's Day. When the screener originally presented the passenger with his options, he quickly escalated to the point where he was intimidating the female officer. I was presently on another lane and quickly went over to the location, where I immediately assumed control of the situation. Again in a calm, firm, clear, and precise manner, I explained all of the passenger's options. After the passenger took the information in, he yielded, decided to relinquish the item, and then apologized to the female TSO and to me for his actions.

Project: TSA Customer Service Survey

As the Lead Screener, I have created a TSA New Customer Service Survey and have trained more than 27 screeners in the survey administration. The survey information is managed in Excel and tracks problem data and monitors trends. **RESULTS:** These surveys have proven to be a valuable two-way tool to both gather data on the screening process and give the screening officers who have administered the survey valuable insight into passenger behavior.

Technology Out of This World

A potential customer approached me to design a new type of aerial imaging equipment. I explained that I was well qualified for this job, as I had designed a similar instrument, which was already in use. The customer asked to see the instrument. I explained, "I'd love to show it to you, but it's aboard MIR, the Russian Space Station." I got the account.

These stories show that you can work under pressure, can lead teams, can handle and negotiate problems, are resourceful, and can multitask very well. They also show you are a decision-maker and proven leader. Examples like these demonstrate that you can negotiate working partnerships with a plan of action. They also show you are highly technically skilled.

Eighth Principle: Be Consistent with Verb Tenses

The rule about tense in resumes is to use the present tense for all present responsibilities and skills and the past tense for all past responsibilities. Here are a few samples:

SENIOR COMPUTER TECHNICIAN (September xxxx to present)

- Senior Computer Technician serving a fast-paced metropolitan retail outlet for CompUSA, one of the nation's leading retailers and resellers of technology products and services. Lead for the Technical Service Group, a 7-person team providing warranty repair services for the broad range of computer and personal electronics products sold by the company. Repair desktop and laptop computer systems, including digital camera equipment, cellular phones, Personal Digital Assistants (PDAs), printers, and other computer peripherals.

SENIOR COMPUTER TECHNICIAN (September xxxx to June xxxx)

- Systems administrator for a scientific workgroup computing environment. Planned and delivered customer support services to the organization. Installed, upgraded, delivered, and provided troubleshooting for hardware and software components. Performed file backups and restores, system and peripherals troubleshooting, and component repair.

- Provided a high level of customer service for a wide variety of computer and network problems. Monitored, analyzed, and resolved end-user issues and provided informal training and assistance.

  Researched and reported on new technologies, equipment, and software with application to the Naval Surface Warfare Center.

Ninth Principle: Avoid the Passive Voice and Words to NOT Use in Your Resume

Human resources professionals write vacancy announcements in the passive voice. Many civilians became accustomed to writing their resumes in the passive voice. Now, however, you should avoid doing so. Use the active voice whenever possible. It's best if you can start your sentences with a verb or noun.

Terms to Eliminate from Your Resume

- Responsible for *or* Responsibilities include
- Duties include
- Additional duties include
- Tasks include
- Helped with, worked with, assisted with

Here is a typical example of passive voice followed by the more impressive version rewritten in active voice. The passive-voice example does not reflect that the employee really did anything. Someone else did the work, or the statement is simply a statement without action.

Before:

Lead Security Screener, TSA

Responsible for oversight of Security Screener operations to ensure performance of security screeners; provide security and protection of air travelers, airports, and aircraft. Tasked with oversight of passenger screening and baggage screening. Serve as primary interface between senior management and workforce and communicate operational and administrative information up and down chain of command. Other duties include obtaining and collating passenger flight data. Assisted with correcting the improper use or application of equipment, provided guidance to subordinates, and answered routine and non-routine questions. Additional duties include collecting performance metrics to process improvement areas.

After:

Lead Security Screener

Provided direct leadership to approximately 60 screeners per shift.

Operations Management: Optimized situational awareness, serving as primary interface between senior management and workforce; communicated operational and administrative information up and down chain of command. Obtained and collated passenger flight data and flight departure information, and interacted with checkpoint supervisors to ensure operational readiness. Recognized and recommended correction of improper use or application of equipment, provided guidance to subordinates, and answered routine and non-routine questions. Managed and supported collection of performance metrics to process improvement areas and systemic or individual weaknesses, vulnerabilities, or inefficiencies in screening processes. Recognized customer service needs of traveling public and balanced them with safety and security. Moved screener forces to accommodate and balance wait times. Ensured accountability at all levels. Monitored individual performance and provided frequent communication to promote screener development.

Tenth Principle: Tell the Truth and Brag a Little

People are taught by their mothers and grandmothers to not brag about themselves. But in a federal job search, you have to be confident, proud, and able to talk about your best accomplishments.

In the same category, avoid superlatives as a general rule. Phrases such as *all, very, every, the greatest, the only,* and so forth raise a red flag. Use superlatives only for objectively quantifiable accomplishments or when reciting the opinion of a knowledgeable person. Example: "My supervisor has praised me as being the most efficient office manager he has ever known." Though subjective, the opinion of a supervisor is meaningful.

Summary

Because your resume reflects who you are, you should feel comfortable with it. Can you speak it out loud without embarrassment? If not, you could end up being embarrassed if the interviewer asks you about your accomplishments as recorded on the resume.

Resumes should be written in a way that allows you to read them aloud in a natural and comfortable fashion. What works for one person might not work for another. How would you speak about your experience to a friend? Look at the passive-voice examples in the Ninth Principle section. Do you see the difference in readability between the passive voice and the active voice?

The new writing style is more personal without being too casual, the flow of the prose tells a story, and the sentences are complete and written in active voice. These paragraphs are written as you would speak them.

CHAPTER 8

Researching the Agency's Core Competencies

Many federal agencies have developed a list of the top core competencies desired in employees. The agencies might integrate the competencies with their applications. The core competencies are used for recruiting the best candidates, for promoting employees to the next level, and as "behavior-based" interview questions (read more in chapter 23). This chapter shows you how important core competencies are to your application for a federal job, in terms of your resume and the essays or examples that you will be asked to write to demonstrate your performance.

If you read the vacancy announcement, it gives you the technical "duties" of the job. It then lists the "specialized qualifications" desired for the job. Some vacancy announcements mention core competencies, and others do not. This chapter includes the core competencies for five federal agencies, including the Transportation Security Agency, which focuses a lot of emphasis on the core competencies and KSAs published in the announcements. In the case of the TSA, the core competency examples are not "value-added"; they are required as part of the application.

In some agencies, the competencies seem like "value-added" skills to a technical set of skills. To stand out, it's great to include top competencies in your resume within various sections, such as Work experience, Other Qualifications, or Summary.

What Are Your Core Competencies and How Can You Include Them in Your Resume?

As you read this chapter, underline the competencies that you consider to be yours as well. Because federal agencies are using the new behavior-based interview style, you should be prepared to write your best examples and practice speaking them for the interview.

> ⭐ **Note:** Dr. Daniel Goleman wrote a great book that focuses on work-based competencies: *Working with Emotional Intelligence* (Bantam). He makes it clear that your core competencies are critical to the success of your job performance.

When including your core competencies in the text of your resume, you should blend them with language from your current and past position descriptions, the vacancy announcement's "duties" section, and your own statements of responsibility. Resume sections that can include core competencies are Work Experience descriptions, your Profile or Summary of Skills section, or a section near the end of the resume called Other Qualifications.

Using Core Competencies as Transferable Skills When Changing Careers

If you are changing careers, you will want to use this chapter to find your "transferable skills," which can take you from one job series to another. Most jobs require skills in customer service, project management, teamwork, working under deadlines, and attention to detail. You can integrate these competencies to match your current skills to the skills that the new job requires.

Every agency has its own list of required competencies and its own interests. If you study the various core competency lists and agency descriptions, you will see that they require diverse values, soft skills, knowledge, and specialized skills for particular occupations. Some of the competencies are similar between agencies, such as customer service, flexibility, decision-making, problem-solving, teamwork, and resourcefulness.

> **Note:** The OPM's definition of core competencies is the following: "Observable, measurable pattern of skills, knowledge, abilities, behaviors, and other characteristics that an individual needs to perform work roles or occupational functions successfully." (U.S. Office of Personnel Management, Op. Cir., Glossary.)

Agency and Company Core Competencies

More and more agencies are developing their own sets of competencies. You can find a few of these lists by going to www.opm.gov and searching for "core competencies." You can also go to the sites for specific agencies and use their search engines to find "core competencies." Some agencies list them on their sites; others do not.

> **Note:** Chapter 19, "Senior Executive Service, Executive Core Qualifications," includes samples and descriptions of OPM's Executive Core Qualifications. These are the core competencies for executives in government.

In this section we provide example sets of core competencies for five federal agencies:

- ★ **Transportation Security Administration:** Focuses extensively on the core competencies at each "pay band" level and position.
- ★ **Veteran's Administration:** Developed one of the first sets of core competencies and still looks for these competencies in applications.
- ★ **Department of the Interior, U.S. Forest Service:** Its core competencies have been widely used as KSAs and interview questions for years.
- ★ **Central Intelligence Agency—Clandestine Agent:** These core competencies were found in a job announcement.
- ★ **Defense Logistics Agency:** Uses these core competencies for management promotions, evaluations, and interviews.

Core Competency Set 1: Core Competencies for Transportation Security Administration

This section is a case study of core competencies for Transportation Security Administration promotions. Many job seekers are mystified by the Core Competencies and KSA narratives that are required for promotion and getting hired for the first time. It's very helpful to analyze the significant core competencies that the HR specialist and supervisors will recognize as important for the performance of that position.

TSA Competencies Get More Complex for Each Higher-Level Pay Band

The TSA competencies for each of the grade and experience levels is interesting to consider when you are trying to get promoted to the next grade level. Think about the next highest level of competencies needed in any position and think about examples that will demonstrate your skill at the next highest level. Most agencies have not defined their competencies as clearly as the TSA has. This set of competencies shows you that each level has higher-level competencies and examples. Use this as an example for the competencies and top-level skills that your target agency desires.

The Most Critical Skills Needed at TSA

The HR specialist and supervisor would like to read examples of experience in each of these critical areas:

★ Accountability

★ Oral Communication

★ Written Communication

★ Administration and Management

★ Decisiveness

★ Operations Management

★ Problem Solving

★ Security Directives and Regulations

How to Write the Best Answers

Read chapter 9, "New Essay Writing: The KSA Way," to learn how to write examples that demonstrate your experience in each competency. You will read about three styles for writing the examples: Narrative, Outline, and List. Choose one of those styles and give your best, most complex, and most impressive example that demonstrates your skill in each core competency area.

Transportation Security Agency Announcement Excerpt

HOW YOU WILL BE EVALUATED:

Applicants will be evaluated on their total background including experience, education, awards, training, and self-development as it relates to the position. Responses to the evaluation criteria may be ranked according to relative merit for this position and identified as being "qualified" or "best qualified." Selection for this position will be made only from among candidates possessing the best qualifications.

EVALUATION CRITERIA:

In order to receive further consideration applicants MUST address, in a concise narrative statement on a separate sheet of paper, each of the knowledge, skills and abilities (KSAs and competencies) listed below. Failure to address any KSA described below will disqualify applicants from receiving further consideration.

Your description should explain the nature of experience, accomplishments, education, and training opportunities that best illustrate how, to what degree, and with what impact you have applied/used each of the knowledge, skills, abilities, and competencies needed for successful performance in this position. Your description may include one or more examples of accomplishments, problems resolved, risks/threats averted, or processes improved as a result of your efforts.

There are four sets of competencies at various levels of performance, which are analyzed in this chapter:

★ Federal Security Director—SV-0340-K

★ Assistant Federal Security Director—SV-0340-J

★ Screening Manager—SV-1801-H

★ Supervisory Transportation Security Officer (Screener)—SV-1802-G/G

FEDERAL SECURITY DIRECTOR—SV-0340-K

Examples for this level of position should demonstrate this experience: "day-to-day direction for federal airport security staff and operations at a large airport with few checkpoints."

1. Accountability—Ensures that effective controls are developed and maintained to ensure the integrity of the organization. Holds self and others accountable for rules and responsibilities. Can be relied upon to ensure that projects within areas of specific responsibility are completed in a timely manner and within budget. Monitors and evaluates plans; focuses on results and measuring attainment of outcomes.

2. Oral Communication—Makes clear and convincing oral presentations to individuals or groups; listens effectively and clarifies information as needed; facilitates an open exchange of ideas and fosters atmosphere of open communication.

3. Written Communication—Expresses facts and ideas in writing in a succinct and organized manner.

4. Administration and Management—Knowledge of planning, coordination, and execution of business functions, resource allocation, and production.

(continued)

(continued)

5. Decisiveness—Exercises good judgment by making sound and well-informed decisions; perceives the impact and implications of decisions; makes effective and timely decisions, even when data are limited or solutions produce unpleasant consequences; is proactive and achievement oriented.

6. Operations Management—Application of specialized knowledge of laws, procedures, practices, relevant to managing and executing programs in an operational environment.

7. Problem Solving—Identifies and analyzes problems; distinguishes between relevant and irrelevant information to make logical decisions; provides solutions to individual and organizational problems.

8. Security Directives and Regulations—Knowledge of TSA's air transportation security policies, directives, and regulations, including ongoing regulations and new or emerging directives, as well as understanding of how to implement the policies, directives and regulations in local TSA airport operations.

Duties:

The Federal Security Director (FSD) is responsible for providing day-to-day direction for federal airport security staff and operations at a large airport with few checkpoints. The FSD is the ranking TSA authority responsible for the leadership and coordination of TSA security activities. These responsibilities and accompanying authority include tactical planning, execution, and operating management for coordinated security services and other duties as prescribed by the Under Secretary of Border and of Transportation Security. The FSD is responsible for activities such as organizing and implementing the Federal Security Crisis Management Response Plan; implementation, performance, and enhancement of security and screening standards for airport employees and passengers; oversight of passenger, baggage, and air cargo security screening; airport security risk assessments; security technology implementation and maintenance within established guidelines; crisis management; data and communications network protection and recovery as it impacts on federal security responsibilities; employee security awareness training; supervision of federal law enforcement activities within the purview of the FSD and TSA; and coordination of applicable federal, state, and local emergency services and law enforcement.

ASSISTANT FEDERAL SECURITY DIRECTOR—SV-0340-J

Examples at this level should demonstrate that you can "support the FSD" in operations: "The Assistant Federal Security Director (AFSD) is responsible for supporting the Federal Security Director (FSD) by providing day-to-day direction for airport security and operations at airports with multiple checkpoints and a workforce ranging from 126 to 250 employees."

1. Accountability—Ensures that effective controls are developed and maintained to ensure the integrity of the organization. Holds self and others accountable for rules and responsibilities. Can be relied upon to ensure that projects within areas of specific responsibility are completed
in a timely manner and within budget. Monitors and evaluates plans; focuses on results and measuring attainment of outcomes.

2. Administration and Management—Knowledge of planning, coordination, and execution of business functions, resource allocation, and production.

3. Security Directives and Regulations—Knowledge of TSA's air transportation security policies, directives, and regulations, including ongoing regulations and new or emerging directives, as well as understanding of how to implement the policies, directives, and regulations in local TSA airport operations.

4. Written Communication—Expresses facts and ideas in writing in a succinct and organized manner.

5. Oral Communication—Makes clear and convincing oral presentations to individuals or groups; listens effectively and clarifies information as needed; facilitates an open exchange of ideas and fosters atmosphere of open communication.

6. Problem Solving—Identifies and analyzes problems; distinguishes between relevant and irrelevant information to make logical decisions; provides solutions to individual and organizational problems.

7. Operations Management—Application of specialized knowledge of laws, procedures, practices, relevant to managing and executing programs in an operational environment.

8. Knowledge of Human Resources Programs and Functions—Knowledge of employment staffing, benefits, workers compensation, and methods used to evaluate their effectiveness.

Duties:

For the J Band: The Assistant Federal Security Director (AFSD) is responsible for supporting the Federal Security Director (FSD) by providing day-to-day direction for airport security and operations at airports with multiple checkpoints and a workforce ranging from 126 to 250 employees. Provides support in the following areas: tactical planning, execution, and operating management for coordinated security services. Participates in briefings concerning sensitive security information. Serves as a Principal Advisor to the FSD on all matters concerning operational support. Develops plans, coordinates, and manages support operations that include customer service/stakeholder programs, training, and engineering services. He/she confers with the FSD and/or appropriate staff personnel to outline work plans, provide technical advice to resolve problems, review status reports, and modify schedules in order to meet workload fluctuations. Provides analysis of airport human resources (HR) programs and recommends and implements strategies to enhance program effectiveness. Evaluates new policies, procedures, and requirements to determine impact and ensure appropriate and timely implementation. Uses program knowledge to provide guidance and advice regarding day-to-day HR operations. Monitors program results and provides advice to FSD.

SCREENING MANAGER—SV-1801-H

Examples at this level should demonstrate your ability to manage operations at multiple screening sites: "Screening Manager responsible for screening procedures, processes (passenger, baggage, cargo, et al), and performance. Uses good judgment while making decisions in the field. Manages multiple locations simultaneously, including off-site locations."

1. Accountability—Ensures that effective controls are developed and maintained to ensure the integrity of the organization. Holds self and others accountable for rules and responsibilities. Can be relied upon to ensure that projects within areas of specific responsibility are completed in a timely manner and within budget. Monitors and evaluates plans, focuses on results, and measures attainment of outcomes.

2. Administration and Management—Knowledge of planning, coordination, and execution of business functions, resource allocation, and production.

3. Security Directives and Regulations—Knowledge of TSA's air transportation security policies, directives, and regulations, including ongoing regulations and new or emerging directives, as well as understanding of how to implement the policies, directives and regulations in local TSA airport operations.

4. Written Communication—Expresses facts and ideas in writing in a succinct and organized manner.

(continued)

(continued)

5. Oral Communication—Makes clear and convincing oral presentations to individuals or groups, listens effectively, and clarifies information as needed; facilitates an open exchange of ideas and fosters atmosphere of open communication.

6. Problem Solving—Identifies and analyzes problems; distinguishes between relevant and irrelevant information to make logical decisions; provides solutions to individual and organizational problems.

7. Operations Management—Application of specialized knowledge of laws, procedures, practices, relevant to managing and executing programs in an operational environment.

Duties:

The incumbent functions as a Screening Manager responsible for screening procedures, processes (passenger, baggage, cargo, et al), and performance. Uses good judgment while making decisions in the field. Manages multiple locations simultaneously, including off-site locations (i.e., spoke airports), in addition to the following duties: Manages screening checkpoints that are central to Transportation Security Administration (TSA) objectives that serve to protect the traveling public by preventing any deadly or dangerous objects from being transported onto an aircraft. Recognizes and recommends correction of improper use or application of the equipment, provides guidance to subordinates, and answers routine questions presented by subordinates. Manages and supports the collection of various performance metrics in an effort to identify areas in need of process improvement and systemic or individual weaknesses, vulnerabilities, or inefficiencies in the screening process. Coordinates national and local crisis management and incident response protocols. Recognizes and understands the customer service needs of the traveling public and balances these needs with safety and security in mind. Works cooperatively with airport stakeholders in furtherance of the TSA mission. Monitors individual performance and provides frequent communication in order to promote screener development.

SUPERVISORY TRANSPORTATION SECURITY OFFICER (SCREENER)— SV-1802-G/G

These core competencies are assessed in a questionnaire format. You will learn more about questionnaires and self-assessment methods in chapter 10, "Questions and Self-Assessment Essays." A total of 33 questions and 10 essays are required with this application. The essays are examples that demonstrate experience. The HR specialist will be looking for experience that demonstrates a specific skill level.

These core competencies for the G/G level are slightly different (a longer list): Conflict Management, Conscientiousness, Customer Service, Flexibility, Interpersonal Skills, Listening, Manages and Organizes Information, Oral Communication, Organizational Awareness, Problem Solving, Resilience, Teambuilding, Written Communication, Maintaining Command Posture (Screening-Specific), Operations Management, Safety Policies and Procedures.

You will see that many of the questions give you the opportunity to select your skill level, or to "self-assess" your skill level. On occasion, to save space, I have written "Self-Assessment List" under the question to indicate that a self-assessment list follows in the original core competencies list.

Examples at this level should demonstrate "Level 1 Supervisory Transportation Security Officer (Screener) responsible for supervising personnel performing pre-board security screening of persons and their carry-on and checked baggage. Oversees the screening checkpoint on a day-to-day basis to include equipment and personnel. Schedules an adequate number of screener personnel to provide for efficient and effective screening of all persons, their baggage, and cargo."

1. Do you have at least six months of full-time equivalent work experience as a Lead Transportation Security Officer (Screener), SV-1802-F (formerly SV-0019-F, GS-9 level) OR six months of full-time equivalent or higher security experience in the federal government or private sector? Full-time experience is based on a 40-hour work week. Part-time experience is credited proportionately.

   Yes   *No*

2. I am a TSA employee working at Norfolk International Airport (ORF) or Newport News/Williamsburg International Airport (PHF).

   True   *False*

Conflict Management

1. From the following activities that involve conflict management, please identify those you have performed.

   Check all that apply

   1. I have applied TSA guidance to resolve complaints of Screeners.

   2. I have referred formal grievances to the appropriate officials.

   3. I have resolved conflicts arising among Screeners.

   4. I have resolved conflicts over the enforcement of security rules with the traveling public.

   5. I have resolved conflicts with other employees or team members that required cooperation, coordination of activities, and reaching consensus.

2. In the space provided, please describe briefly an example of your conflict-management skills.

   (Essay Question)

Conscientiousness

3. Which of the following best reflects how you routinely use equipment, supplies, and resources in your work?

   1. I use equipment, supplies, and resources according to standard operating procedures.

   2. I oversee the day-to-day use of equipment, supplies, and resources.

   3. I coordinate and schedule the use of equipment, supplies, and resources with others.

   4. I plan, monitor, and make necessary adjustments for the efficient use of equipment, supplies, and resources.

   5. None of the above.

Customer Service

4. Which best describes your skills in providing customer service to the traveling public?

   1. I answer customer inquiries in a timely and courteous fashion and when I do not know the answer, I seek the assistance of a supervisor.

   2. I respond to customer inquiries completely, timely, and courteously without need of a supervisor.

   3. I help customers understand the security-screening policies and procedures.

   4. I interact with passengers with disabilities, wheelchairs, baby strollers, child passengers, or others in need of special assistance.

   5. I resolve difficult passenger situations, such as an irate passenger.

   6. None of the above.

(continued)

(continued)

5. In the space provided, please support your choice by briefly describing an example of your customer service skills.

(Essay Question)

Flexibility

6. From the following list please identify those situations where you have adapted your behavior or work methods to adjust to other people or to changing situations or work schedules.

Check all that apply

1. To facilitate the amicable resolution of competing or conflicting interests among parties whose cooperation is needed to meet an objective.

2. To interact effectively in situations where frequent changes, delays, or unexpected events arise that cause major shifts in priorities, timetables, or work assignments.

3. To provide direction, guidance, or instruction to staff.

4. To persuade and/or inspire others to adopt new methods, procedures, or techniques to improve operations.

5. To diffuse confrontational situations with people who are difficult, hostile, or distressed.

6. To develop trusting, productive working relationships with subordinates, colleagues, and supervisors to achieve goals and objectives.

7. To work cooperatively with others as a team to achieve a project or program goal.

8. None of the above.

Interpersonal Skills

7. Select one description that best represents your highest level of experience in interacting with various groups and individuals.

1. Experience that involves working with management officials to resolve unique or complex issues, such as sharing options and initiating ongoing contacts with managers to foster strong working relationships, or developing new policies and procedures.

2. Experience that involves assisting management officials with inquiries for information or communicating potential security issues to management.

3. Experience that involves routinely working with managers to resolve issues and problems that arise on a daily basis.

4. Experience that involves routinely educating, advising, or participating in meetings with groups or individuals when contacted to address issues or problems.

5. Experience that involves explaining agency policy and regulations and providing background of the rationale for such policies, and using negotiating techniques to ensure full compliance.

6. None of the above.

Listening

8. Please select the response that best describes your experience or training interpreting verbal communications and directions.

(Self-Assessment List)

Manages and Organizes Information

9. From the list below, please identify the ways you have obtained facts, information, or data relevant to a particular problem, question, or issue.

   Check all that apply

   1. Observation of events or situations.

   2. Discussion with others.

   3. Research or retrieval from written electronic sources.

   4. I do not have experience with this task.

10. Please provide a specific example of how you obtained facts, information, or data relevant to a particular problem, question, or issue.

   (Essay Question)

11. In which of the following events have you communicated orally or made oral presentations?

   Check all that apply

   1. Speeches

   2. Conferences

   3. Meetings

   4. One-on-one discussions

   5. Telephone inquiries

   6. Training

   7. Technical assistance

   8. Interviews

   9. Briefings

   10. None of the above

12. From the list below, identify all of the types of audiences with which you have experience communicating orally or making oral presentations.

   Check all that apply

   1. Senior agency officials

   2. Managers

   3. Colleagues

   4. Subordinates

   5. Government organizations

   6. Private industry

   7. General public

   8. Technical experts

   9. Professional organizations

   10. None of the above

(continued)

(continued)

Organizational Awareness

13. Please select the response that best describes your experience applying TSA policies and procedures and applicable federal laws while conducting the screening process.

    1. I have completed training on applying TSA policies and procedures and applicable federal laws related to the screening process, but have not yet applied it on the job.

    2. I have applied TSA policies and procedures and applicable federal laws related to the screening process while under close supervision by a supervisor, manager, or senior employee.

    3. I have applied TSA policies and procedures and applicable federal laws related to the screening process while working independently and usually without review by a supervisor, manager, or senior employee.

    4. Applying TSA policies and procedures and applicable federal laws related to the screening process has been a central or major part of my work. I have performed it myself routinely.

    5. I have trained others in applying TSA policies and procedures or applicable federal laws related to the screening process and (or) others have consulted me as an expert for assistance in performing this area.

    6. None of the above.

Problem Solving

14. From the following list of problem-solving activities, please identify those you have recently performed.

    Check all that apply

    1. Identified a security issue and its cause.

    2. Anticipated a security problem and implemented a procedure to avoid the problem.

    3. Recommended an improvement in security-screening procedures with options for implementation.

    4. Worked closely with individuals and groups to resolve problems, analyze alternatives, negotiate differences, and make improvements.

    5. None of the above.

15. In the space provided, please support your answer by providing a brief example of your experience in problem-solving.

(Essay Question)

Resilience

16. From the list below, please identify those situations you have encountered on the job.

    Check all that apply

    1. Pressure

    2. Stress

    3. Emergencies

    4. Hostile individuals

    5. Setbacks

    6. Personal problems

7. Work-related problems

8. None of the above

17. Please provide two detailed examples of how you handled unexpected or stressful situations in the workplace.

(Essay Question)

Team Building

18. Which of the following best describes your work experience in a team environment?

1. I have no experience working in teams.

2. I have worked effectively as part of a team in meeting common team goals.

3. I have frequently worked in team environments and have led teams in non-work-related activities.

4. I occasionally work in team environments and have led teams in work-related projects.

5. I regularly work in team settings and frequently lead teams in work-related projects

19. Briefly describe a team that you worked on, including the nature and purpose of the team and your responsibilities for the team.

(Essay Question)

Written Communication

20. Which of the following types of documents have you written?

Check all that apply

1. Correspondence

2. Technical reports

3. Regulatory/statutory material

4. Policy or procedures

5. Analyses of proposed policy, legislative, or management initiatives

6. Memos

7. Newsletter

8. Training materials

9. None of the above

21. In the space provided, please describe two specific examples of documents you have written.

(Essay Question)

Maintaining Command Posture (Screening-Specific)

22. Please select the response that best describes your experience issuing instructions and making requests to individuals.

(Self-Assessment List)

23. Please provide a specific example of a situation where you have issued instructions and made requests to individuals.

(Essay Question)

(continued)

(continued)

Operations Management

24. Which of the following have you done as a routine part of your professional work experience?

    Check all that apply

    1. Identify needed tasks to be performed.

    2. Assign tasks and monitor performance.

    3. Schedule adequate personnel.

    4. Monitor flow and make necessary adjustments.

    5. Distribute tasks among employees according to skill level.

    6. Make resource decisions for periods of high demand.

    7. Anticipate and resolve problems.

    8. None of the above.

25. In the space provided, please describe an example of a time when you had to balance workloads and tasks among yourself and others.

    (Essay Question)

Safety Policies and Procedures

26. Please select the response that best describes your experience completing safety logs, incident reports, and other records.

    1. I have not had experience or training on completing safety logs, incident reports, and other records.

    2. I have completed training related to completing safety logs, incident reports, and other records, but have not yet applied it on the job.

    3. I have completed safety logs, incident reports, and other records while under close supervision by a supervisor, manager, or senior employee.

    4. I have completed safety logs, incident reports, and other records while working independently and usually without review by a supervisor, manager, or senior employee.

    5. Completing safety logs, incident reports, and other records has been a central or major part of my work. I have performed it myself routinely.

    6. I have trained others in completing safety logs, incident reports, and other records and (or) others have consulted me as an expert for assistance in performing this area.

27. Please provide a specific example of a situation where you had to complete safety logs, incident reports, and other records as part of your job.

    (Essay Question)

Security Equipment Knowledge

28. Please select the response that best describes your experience or training with security screening equipment.

    (Self-Assessment List)

Security Screening Policies and Procedures

29. Please select the response that best describes your experience overseeing screening operations and ensuring the correct application of screening procedures.

30. Please select the response that best describes your experience providing on-the-job correction and instruction on screening procedures.

    (Self-Assessment List)

Visual Observation—Screening-Specific

31. Please select the response that best describes your experience or training distinguishing between relevant visual cues or information and irrelevant or distracting information.

    (Self-Assessment List)

32. Please select the response that best describes your experience or training visually inspecting persons, property, or equipment.

    (Self-Assessment List)

33. Please select the response that best describes your experience or training recognizing differences, similarities, or patterns in circumstances or events.

    (Self-Assessment List)

Duties:

Functions as Level 1 Supervisory Transportation Security Officer (Screener) responsible for supervising personnel performing pre-board security screening of persons and their carry-on and checked baggage. Oversees the screening checkpoint on a day-to-day basis to include equipment and personnel. Schedules an adequate number of screener personnel to provide for efficient and effective screening of all persons, their baggage, and cargo. Conducts screening of passengers and/or baggage, and/or cargo. Works with a full team of Transportation Security Officers (Screeners), supervisors, law enforcement personnel at checkpoints, airport security staff, and management.

Implements security-screening procedures that are central to Transportation Security Administration (TSA) objectives that will serve to protect the traveling public by preventing any deadly or dangerous objects from being transported onto an aircraft. Participates in information briefings concerning security-sensitive or classified information. Assists management with inquiries for information or investigations that may be initiated against a regulated party. Maintains communication with management regarding issues that might reveal a weakness or vulnerable area of security screening that is discovered in the course of screening duties.

Directs the work of subordinate employees. Sets priorities; assigns tasks, monitors and evaluates performance, coaches and develops employee capabilities; approves leave; and takes or recommends corrective/disciplinary action, as appropriate. Provides guidance to staff on resolving difficult technical issues. Coaches staff in customer service, technical approaches, and other duties related to passenger screening. Resolves all but unique technical problems without the intervention of management or a more experienced technical specialist, but consults with higher-level management when existing guidelines are not available or applicable for complex problems. May be called upon to assist in the development of new policies and procedures.

Summary of TSA KSA/Core Competencies

The total application for TSA positions is a federal resume and the examples to support the KSA core competencies. Your answers and examples will make the difference between being referred for consideration and not being referred. Think carefully about examples that demonstrate your accountability, flexibility, or customer services skills.

Core Competency Set 2: Veterans Administration

Read the entire descriptions of these core competencies at the Department of Veterans Affairs Web site at www1.va.gov/visns/visn02/education/hpdm/index.html. If you are applying for jobs at the Veterans

Administration or other federal agencies, you can include some of this language in your federal resume and KSAs. Definitions are described here: www1.va.gov/visns/visn02/education/hpdm/CoreCompetencyDescriptions.doc.

★ Interpersonal Effectiveness

★ Customer Service

★ Systems Thinking

★ Flexibility/Adaptability

★ Creative Thinking

★ Organizational Stewardship

★ Personal Mastery

★ Technical Competency

Core Competency Set 3: Department of the Interior, National Park Service, Universal Competencies

These competencies are a combination of employee competencies/values and specific knowledge of the agency policies, legislation, and programs. You can read more about this agency at the National Park Service Web site: www.nps.gov/training/uc/home.htm.

Mission Comprehension—This competency requires a thorough background and understanding of the 1916 NPS Organic Act and its many ramifications and the additional responsibilities that have been added to the NPS throughout its history; and a perspective of how the National Park System began as a part of the Conservation Movement that continues today.

Agency Orientation—This competency requires a basic comprehension of the structure and organization of the NPS at the park, cluster, field area, and Washington Office levels; an understanding of the structure and organization of the Department of the Interior and its place in the federal government; and the development of an insight into an individual employee's role in the NPS in particular, and in the federal government in general.

Resource Stewardship—This competency requires an overall understanding of the spectrum of resources protected by the NPS; the range of NPS responsibilities in managing these resources; the individual's role in resource stewardship; the planning process and its purpose in the NPS; and working with partners outside the agency to promote resource stewardship.

NPS Operations—This competency encompasses a general comprehension of the basic operations of the NPS, especially at the park level; how these operations interact to fulfill the mission of the NPS; and why visitors come to parks and how the NPS "manages" them.

Fundamental Values—This competency focuses on an employee's ability to exhibit certain attitudes and behaviors to accomplish an assigned job and to contribute to the overall health of the organization. These include leadership and teamwork behaviors; ethical behavior toward people and the organization; support of cultural diversity and fairness issues in the workplace; support of accessible parks and workplaces; an attitude towards safe behavior for one's self and for others; and mental and physical fitness.

Communications Skills—This competency encompasses the ability to communicate effectively with the public and employees in writing and speech; to use interpersonal skills to be an effective employee; and to exhibit basic computer abilities.

Problem-Solving Skills—This competency deals with the ability to analyze a problem, build consensus, make decisions, and practice innovation in various aspects of one's job.

Individual Development and Planning—This competency considers an individual's being able to work with one's supervisor and agency to plan a course of action for one's performance, career, and ultimately, retirement.

Core Competency Set 4: Central Intelligence Agency

The CIA's top competencies are a combination of specialized, technical skills and soft skills, including spirit, self-starter, and courage. This is a great list of competencies.

Qualifications: Central Intelligence Agency's Clandestine Service Trainee Program is the gateway to a unique overseas experience. To qualify you must have first-rate qualifications: a bachelor's degree with an excellent academic record, strong interpersonal skills, the ability to write clearly and accurately, and a burning interest in international affairs. A graduate degree, foreign travel, foreign language proficiency, previous residency abroad, and military experience are pluses. We are particularly interested in candidates with backgrounds in Central Eurasian, East Asian, and Middle Eastern languages, and those with degrees and experience in international economics and international business as well as in the physical sciences. Entrance salaries range from $43,500 to $60,400, depending on credentials.

They also require the following core competencies:

For the extraordinary individual who wants more than just a job, we offer a unique career—a way of life that will challenge the deepest resources of your intelligence, self-reliance, and responsibility. It demands an adventurous spirit, a forceful personality, superior intellectual ability, toughness of mind, and a high degree of personal integrity, courage, and love of country. You will need to deal with fast-moving, ambiguous, and unstructured situations that will test your resourcefulness to the utmost. It takes special skills and professional discipline to produce results.

Core Competency Set 5: Defense Logistics Agency

These competencies are a combination of employee competencies/values and specific knowledge of the agency policies, legislation, and programs.

★ Mission Comprehension

★ Customer Services

★ Professionalism

★ Resource Stewardship

★ Innovation and Initiative

★ Leadership

★ Teamwork

★ Oral and Written Communications

★ Strategic Focus

★ Responsibility/Accountability

Other Agency Core Competencies

The Office of Personnel Management Web site (www.opm.gov/hrd/lead/trnginfo/trnginfo.htm#core) offers core competency resources for a few other federal agencies.

Sample Resume with Core Competencies

This sample federal resume is for an administrative person who is seeking to emphasize her human resources skills. The resume also mentions continuous improvements, developing new policies and procedures, efficiency, and productivity. She has great technical and soft skills.

Target Job: Human Resources Specialist, GS-0201-09, from current position as Administrative Specialist, GS-0301-09.
Resume Format: Electronic Federal Resume.
Federal administrative career seeking career change. Core competencies are marked in bold.

Mary P. Simons

SKILLS SUMMARY

Administrative Specialist and Executive Secretary with 11 years of federal government experience, including 4 years of human resources services to employees and managers. Exceptional communications, **customer service,** organizational, and administrative skills. Independently demonstrate excellent **interpersonal skills, meet deadlines,** manage office workflow, and **implement new** administrative procedures. **Advisor** to employees concerning retirement and personnel matters. **Adaptable and flexible** in **meeting changing deadlines** and priorities.

PROFESSIONAL HISTORY

12/2002 to Present: **ADMINISTRATIVE SPECIALIST,** GS-301-09/6
Department of Energy, Office of the Secretary, Homeland Security Staff
EPA Region 3 Regional Office, 1650 Arch Street, Philadelphia, PA 19103-2029
Salary: $47,711, 40 hours/week, Supervisor: Jim Smith. Please do not contact.

EXECUTIVE SECRETARY for Director and Deputy Director of Department of Agriculture, Homeland Security Staff, who report directly to the Secretary of Agriculture. **Support continuous improvements** in staff's management of homeland security operations. Collaborate with management to **develop new or modified administrative policies,** goals, and objectives. Serve as staff representative with organizations within and outside the agency.

HUMAN RESOURCES MANAGEMENT: Complete general human resources tasks for the office of 350 employees and 55 managers. Identify resources and advise on available resources required to provide administrative support to meet office operations. Serve as **team member** in planning and conducting studies and analyses of employee/organizational **efficiency** and **productivity** and **recommending changes or improvements** in organization, staffing, work methods, and procedures.

Keep time and attendance records. Prepare SF-50s. Write award letters and standards for performance appraisals. Prepare paperwork and determine cash bonuses and compensation. **Troubleshoot** human resource problems, including **resolving** health and retirement benefits and pay and leave **discrepancies.**

Recognize staffing issues and advise management on possible solutions. Conduct job analysis and create position descriptions and vacancy announcements as needed. **Resolve problems** for special employee needs regarding pay and benefit issues.

OFFICE ADMINISTRATION: Fully support staff of seven in day-to-day operations. Implement technology to **improve efficiency** of administrative support and/or program operations. Under senior staff direction, review actions to determine compliance with agency regulations, procedures, and sound administrative practices.

KEY ACCOMPLISHMENTS:
+ During Hurricane Isabel, took **initiative** and projected impact of storm on area crops and farms; created PowerPoint summary for emergency staff meetings.

Figure 8.1: A resume for a Human Resources Specialist featuring core competencies.

Summary

To stand out with your federal resume, including relevant core competencies that you have developed (and that the agency is seeking) will help you get referred and selected for an interview. If you can add some of the critical competencies for an agency into your resume, KSA, or essays, you will be closer to being referred and selected for an interview. If you can write examples for the top competencies, you will be prepared for job interviews. Many agencies use their core competencies as a basis for interview questions. You will clearly be including specialized experience; to stand out, however, a few significant core competencies will help you to be more competitive.

Part 3

Questions, KSAs, and Essays in the Resume

CHAPTER 9

New Essay Writing: The KSA Way

Do you have a fear of writing KSAs and Essays? There are new, easier options for writing KSA and Essay narratives. KSA writing has been a detriment for some federal job seekers. A job seeker might not apply for a job that requires KSAs as part of the application process because of the fear of writing full-page narratives about experiences that support the KSAs. With the new Essay requirements, your fear of writing might have just gotten better and worse. The situation is better because the Essays are shorter—sometimes only 500 words, one example, or 1,500 characters. But the situation can also be thought of as worse: Some of the announcements ask for 10 or more Essays.

KSAs and Essays are important parts of your total application. Most federal applications are composed of two or three parts. First is the federal resume (usually in electronic format). Then there is often a requirement for Knowledge, Skills, and Abilities (KSA) narratives. More recently, agencies have been adding Questionnaires with Self-Assessment Questions and Essay Answers as a part of the application process. The third part is faxes of additional information.

What's New in This Chapter?

New Questionnaires and Essays: Application Questionnaires, Essays, and Short and Long Answers are relatively new since the publication date of the preceding edition of this book. Increasingly these questionnaires include "self-assessment" questions followed by a request for an essay or short answer to validate the performance level you entered on your self-assessment.

Your Skills Assessment and Examination: The KSAs, Questionnaire, and Essays are an "assessment" or "examination" of your specialized qualifications and skills for the targeted position. The examples you provide will help the human resources specialist determine whether you are Best Qualified or just Minimally Qualified.

Your Pre-Interview: It is possible to get hired from your resume and assessment questionnaire answers. In some cases the federal supervisor may even hire a person without an interview. So think of the KSAs and Essays as being your first interview; only in this case, you aren't put on the spot and required to answer the questions without preparation. You actually get to think them through thoroughly and in advance. For this "interview," you can entirely avoid the regret of "I wish I had thought about telling them about that!"

What Is a KSA?

KSA stands for *knowledge, skills,* and *abilities.* KSA statements form the second part of some applications for a federal job or promotion. In the resume, you tell about your specific job history and skills and how they relate to the targeted position. In the KSAs, you give examples that demonstrate your performance. The KSA narratives exemplify the critical job elements that require specialized experience. Supervisors are looking for examples that demonstrate your highest level of experience.

KSAs are "rated and ranked" with a scoring system based on the complexity of your experience. The highest scoring applicants are placed on the "List of Certified Eligibles," and the resumes are forwarded to the hiring manager.

What Is an Essay?

An Essay is an answer to a Question on the new Questionnaire Assessment component of the federal application. Essays ask you to assess your skills to a certain level. If you rate yourself as being expert or almost expert, you may be asked to provide an example or essay. As of the publication of this book, most of the essays are not "rated and ranked." They are requested so that the human resources specialist can determine whether you really are an expert in this area. You are proving your assessment rating with your example. If you say that you are an expert in a certain task, the example you provide should demonstrate this level of competence.

> **Note:** Read more about the Questionnaires and Self-Assessment Questions in chapter 10, "Questions and Self-Assessment Answers."

Introducing Three KSA/Essay Writing Styles

Some agencies are asking for up to 12 (or more) essays in the Questionnaire. So, as a result of the number of essays required, the length of the essays can now be shorter than the previous paper KSAs required in vacancy announcements. When there were only three or four KSAs, the narratives would typically be one page or one-and-a-half pages. Now with 6, 8, or 12 essays, you should consider the length of time it will take the human resources specialist to read them.

Now there are shorter, easier ways to write KSAs and Essays. The Questionnaire instructions could direct you to write 500 words, half a page, a short answer, one example, or 1,500 characters (each agency is different). Now you can write one good example, two good examples, a short list of several examples that demonstrate your performance, or you can write a full-page narrative that includes an introduction, CCAR examples, and a closing statement.

There are three different KSA/Essay styles:

* **Narrative CCAR KSA (long—one page):** The narrative writing style is a traditional writing style that has been used for KSA writing since the first edition of this book in 1996. This style includes full sentences, descriptions, details, and long and short sentences. It could include the full Context, Challenge, Action, and Results (CCAR) formula that tells a complete story, or an example that demonstrates your competency in this area. The narrative is slightly longer because of the transition sentences, introduction, and fully explained examples. The narrative may include full project details either in the CCAR or partial CCAR formula. Read "Driving Your KSAs and Essays with the CCAR Format" later in this chapter for more details about how to write KSAs in the CCAR "storytelling" style.

* **Example KSA—shorter style (medium—half page):** Project details are similar to the narrative style, but presented in a shorter format. The example may not include a CCAR story, just an example demonstrating performance.

★ **List KSA (shortest—half page):** This response provides a list of relevant examples that will prove your skill level for the Question or KSA request. The list should include the name of the project or item, plus a description. Each list entry should include a short description.

Following are examples of KSA and Essay narratives using three different styles: Narrative KSA/Essay with CCAR, Example Essay, and List Essay.

Writing Style 1: Narrative KSA/Essay with CCAR
Narrative CCAR KSA for Program Analyst, GS-301-9, seeking Grant Management Specialist, GS-11.

> ESSAY QUESTION: Briefly describe your experience(s) as a team member within an organization. Include information about the purpose of the team and your efforts to work effectively with others to accomplish the team's objectives.

4136 characters with spaces:

As the Task Leader for the Division of Extramural Activities Support (DEAS) at the Division of AIDS (DAIDS), 2005-present, I oversee a team of seven administrative support personnel providing administrative, technical, and customer support services to the NIAID staff, DAIDS Office of the Director, and other NIH branches and programs. As team lead, I work in cooperation with the Administrative staff, Program Officers, Administrative Technicians, and the private secretary for the Director of the DAIDS to identify and resolve administrative issues.

I believe that a team is more than a group of people who work together at the same time. As a team leader, I try to show each team member how important his or her skills are, and how important their contribution is to achieving the established goals. I believe in leading by example and by fostering open communication among all team members.

As the Task Leader for the Division of Extramural Activities Support (DEAS) at the Division of AIDS (DAIDS), 2005-present, I work in cooperation with the Administrative staff, Program Officers, Administrative Technicians, and the private secretary for the Director of the DAIDS to identify and resolve administrative issues.

Context: For example, I recently led a team of 7-10 staff members for the planning and execution of a major conference. I was the Task Leader and my team included Program Officers, the Program Manager, and DEAS staff assigned to process the data in the NBS Travel system.

Challenge: I was challenged to communicate each person's role for the conference and all procedures to the DEAS staff and Program Officers. This included a timeline with deadlines and a plan of action. We had 90 days to plan the conference to be attended by 60 international scientific experts from the U.S. and Europe.

Actions: The tasks assigned included securing location logistics, establishing dates and times of the events, negotiating hotel accommodations, and scheduling travel for speakers and participants. We also produced conference materials, and secured audiovisual equipment. The team managed on-site registration, logistics, and catering.

We divided key tasks and set timelines to ensure all goals and deadlines were met. The DEAS staff completed their part of the project, and I used my computer graphics background to create nameplates, labels, charts, and mail-merge data to create quality, detailed communications for conference attendees.

RESULTS: The conference was a complete success. Our entire team was recognized for their dependability and professionalism. The DEAS Director wrote "This conference was the most detailed, time-efficient, and complication-free conference we have held. Thank you for your dedication and perseverance." Henry Summit, M.D., Ph.D., Director, DEAS.

This conference is representative of my team leadership philosophy. My goal is to create an environment of shared values that allows each DEAS employee to effectively develop the optimal performance skills and abilities needed to get the job done, and to feel a sense of accomplishment.

I have been recognized throughout my career for my effectiveness as a team leader and team player. Following are several additional examples:

OTHER RECOGNITIONS:

In 2003-2004, I was nominated by my peers to serve as President of the 37-member NINDS Administrative Support Staff Group. I worked to promote employment interests for program and grants technical assistants.

In 2003, as a Program Support Assistant for the NIH, NINDS, Division of Extramural Research, I was awarded a "Special Achievement Award" for outstanding volunteer contribution to the NINDS program support staff response to the A-76 questionnaire survey. I was part of a team that volunteered to work throughout the weekend to achieve our goal of completing the project ahead of schedule.

This year, I was honored to be selected by my supervisor to serve on a staff committee that will work together as a team to drive improvements in staff training. We will be working together to create a curriculum catalogue for DEAS staff training and to establish an Intranet service.

Writing Style 2: Example KSA/Essay—Shorter Style (Medium—Half Page)

Example KSA for Lead Extramural Support Assistant (Task Leader) Seeking Program Analyst Position.

ESSAY QUESTION: Please describe examples of work performed in software applications and databases.

AMBIS SYSTEM POWERPOINT TRAINING CURRICULUM: As a Lead Extramural Support Assistant (Task Leader) for the NIH, I am skilled in manipulating data to develop a variety of formats and specialized communications to support training, conferences, meetings, or special projects. I designed a PowerPoint presentation to teach the DEAS staff. The PowerPoint included curriculum lessons for proper protocol for e-mail and voice-mail etiquette. I created the electronic version, which included text and animated graphics. I incorporated different fonts, letter sizes, and margins to create visual interest and enhance key points. I also created a PowerPoint presentation to train staff in use of the AMBIS system.

DESIGNED EXCEL TABLES FOR TRAVEL REVIEWS REQUIRING DATA MANAGEMENT: I also developed Excel tables for logging my travel reviews. I created a matrix to track the program or branch to which the DEAS support staff was assigned. On numerous occasions, I have created and merged letters, mailing labels, tent cards, and name badges using the Microsoft Excel database in a text-file format for meetings and conferences. For

(continued)

(continued)

example, for a recent meeting held by one of our IC customers, I merged data directly from our Excel database into letter format in MS Word. I used the same database to create mailing labels in a script font. My extensive technical knowledge of the database and ability to integrate the data with other programs such as Word and PowerPoint significantly reduced the amount of time needed to prepare the letters, forms, and envelopes.

Writing Style 3: List KSA/Essay

List KSA for Grants Management Specialist (GS-7) seeking career change to Human Resources Specialist (GS-7).

ESSAY QUESTION: Describe the training and/or education you have completed, including the dates if applicable. Indicate where this is reflected on your resume (i.e., identify the specific experience), but do not paste your resume here.

Over the past four years, I have completed nine federal professional development courses. This training complements my more than 15 years of professional experience as an executive-level Administrative Assistant. I have completed certification training toward a new career in human resources.

College Coursework:

42 credit hours at Strayer University (1992-1994) toward a B.S. in Business Administration with a minor in Accounting. My coursework included Accounting, English, and Math. I am currently scheduled to attend a "Managing Conflict" course in August 2007 and "Working with Difficult People" in September 2007.

Certification in Grants Management and NBS Travel System for domestic and international travel, 6/2003. My training in the NBS Travel System helped me to develop advanced skills in use of the system and enhances my ability to advise and guide the administrative team I manage to improve their abilities to use the system.

Federal Human Resources Management, Business Communications Writing; and Federal Administrative Support, 2002. This is a comprehensive course that covered customer service, organization, office equipment, office administration, and other core administrative functions.

Basics of Federal Human Resources Management, 1/2002. I gained valuable knowledge of position classifications, employee relations, training and career development, recruitment and placement, and labor management relations through a course. A final team project gave me the opportunity to practice recruitment, including writing a position description and a federal vacancy announcement for USAJOBS posting.

Administrative Assistant for Federal Personnel Management, 2002. Provided me with a comprehensive knowledge base on how individual agencies design and operate programs to fit their own respective needs. This training included position and pay management, staff and placement, training and career development, employee relations, operations, and labor management skills. (9/2002)

STAFF TRAINING: As a supervisor at NIH, I am aware of important training programs available for employees to mentor and motivate staff development. While training is widely accepted as an employee benefit and a method of improving employee morale, enhancing employee skills has become imperative. As a Task Leader, I constantly monitor my staff's work performance and encourage them to take advantage of the many training opportunities afforded by the federal government.

An In-Depth Look at KSAs and Essays

Whether you write a CCAR Narrative, Example, or List KSAs and Essays, you should provide specific examples of paid and nonpaid work experience, education, training, awards, and honors that support each major work area of an announced position. Announcements can require as many as 12 (or more) questionnaire essays. There can be as many as four to six KSAs listed in each announcement.

KSAs and Essays Are a Writing Test

You can also think of your KSAs and Essays as a writing test. KSAs are initially graded, or "rated," by first-level personnel reviewers. Or they could be reviewed by a panel of subject-matter experts. You have to pass this first level for your application to go on to the hiring panel or hiring manager. Your answers will demonstrate whether you can analyze a question and answer it, understand the agency's mission, and write a narrative that relates your experience to the special needs of the position and organization. The reviewers are also looking to see whether you can follow directions closely, and apply good computer and writing skills in developing a document that clearly articulates your job knowledge, skills, and abilities.

Ideally, the KSA or Essay will be a good example that is also interesting to the reader. The hiring manager may have a stack of 30 qualified candidates to consider. Including memorable examples written in clear and easy-to-read text will go a long way toward getting your application into the list of Best Qualified candidates.

> **Note:** KSAs are written in the first person ("*I did this and that*") and are typically one-half to one full page each.

The Office of Personnel Management's (OPM's) Definition of Knowledge, Skills, and Abilities

Here's how the government defines knowledge, skills, and abilities:

* **Knowledge:** An organized body of information, usually of a factual or procedural nature, which, if applied, makes adequate performance on the job possible.
* **Skills:** The proficient manual, verbal, or mental manipulation of data, people, or things. Observable, quantifiable, measurable.
* **Abilities:** The power to perform an activity at the present time. Implied is a lack of discernible barriers, either physical or mental, to performing the activity.

How Agencies Grade KSAs

For the paper KSAs, the federal personnel staffing specialists have a "rating and ranking" system for each KSA statement, called a *crediting plan.* The crediting plans vary per job opening and are used by the reviewer as an objective tool to rate your submission. Your statements will be rated as Best Qualified or Minimally Qualified. With an effective presentation and sufficient detail so that the reviewer can determine the level of your knowledge, skill, or ability, you will have a better chance of convincing the hiring staff to rank you as Best Qualified.

Example of KSA Crediting Plan

Here is an example of what a crediting plan might look like for a GS-7 secretary position. The points you earn for each item can range from 1 to 5, depending on the importance of the desired skill. The goal is to achieve 5 points for each Knowledge, Skill, and Ability area listed. You can obtain a score of 5 by writing an excellent example demonstrating your highest level of skill.

1. Ability to maintain and plan schedules, respond to changes in scheduling in order to maintain supervisor's calendar, and ensure smooth flow of office operation. _____ **points**

2. Skill in utilizing word-processing programs and other automated programs in order to prepare correspondence and reports and to track the status of such documents. _____ **points**

3. Ability to communicate orally in order to receive and direct calls and to give technical assistance. _____ **points**

4. Ability to independently plan and carry out multiple assignments under short deadlines and to provide substantive support on special projects. _____ **points**

5. Ability to acquire and apply knowledge of the responsibility of various administrative and program offices in order to refer calls and correspondence to appropriate offices and to coordinate and review the format, grammar, and organization of various work products from these offices. _____ **points**

Because the crediting plans are a confidential rating assessment, they are not public information. So you probably won't know which KSAs the hiring managers consider to be the most important. Just remember when you're writing the KSAs that you are being graded and that you want to achieve maximum points for each KSA.

How to Write Narrative CCAR KSAs

Remember that your KSAs and essays have two goals. First, you want to present convincing evidence that your knowledge, skills, and abilities are a close match to those that the advertised position requires. Second, you want to tell an engaging story or relevant example that rings true to the reader and presents you as a person of depth and character. Therefore, your KSA should include the elements of a good story.

The basic outline for the Narrative CCAR KSA is as follows:

1. A good opening that makes some general statement about you, your experience, your opinions, or what you think is important about this KSA.

2. One or two strong examples that follow the CCAR (Context, Challenge, Actions, Result—*hold on, I'll get to that in a moment*) format. One good example could also be effective, if the example is excellent and demonstrates the KSA.

3. A closing that draws it all together.

OPM recommends that if you are writing a narrative KSA, you should include the *Context,* the *Challenge,* your *Actions,* and the *Result* (CCAR) for each example that you cite. Here are more details on each of these elements:

★ **Context:** What was the specific circumstance that led to the task or challenge you are going to describe? Where were you working? Had you just started the job, or had you been there for quite a while? Were you assigned the task, or did you show initiative by identifying a problem yourself that you felt needed resolution? What was the situation that made this issue critical to the organization?

★ **Challenge:** What was the specific task you had to resolve? What obstacles did you have to over-come? What made completing this example a challenge? Short timeframe? Gaining cooperation from others? First-time project? The challenge(s) of your project can earn more points because it shows *why* you were working on the project.

★ **Actions:** What were the detailed steps that you took to resolve the challenge? These do not have to be earth-shaking. The fact that you met with your team or management, pulled together a plan, and then executed it is just fine. By providing details, you bring the situation to life and set yourself apart from the competition. The reader will know that you really were there and lived through this—that you are not just recounting a general circumstance that any-one might conjure up.

★ **Result:** What happened? In some cases, you might be able to provide quantitative results (for example, your actions resulted in saving significant costs or time for the government). In other cases, you might have received an award or at least a personal thank-you from your supervisor or another party. You might even be able to use an example in which the resolution was not ideal, but in which you made the best decision in a difficult scenario and at least mitigated the outcome.

> ★ **Note:** You can use this same CCAR model for writing SES Executive Core Qualifications (see chapter 19 for more on applying for SES positions).

Essay and KSA Samples

The remainder of this chapter is a collection of example KSAs and Essays in the three formats: KSA CCAR Narrative, Example, and List Style. Choose the style that best fits your experience and writing skill.

Sample 1: Narrative CCAR KSA for Military Senior Instructor seeking Federal Air Marshal position.

> Ability to communicate effectively in curriculum design that means changing missions.
>
> Introduction: Throughout my career, I have created and updated curriculum, assessed the need to change and streamline training, and implemented new training curriculum on at least five occasions in the last ten years.
>
> Context: In my last position with USMC, as Senior Marine Instructor/Operations Chief, I directed a staff of 21 instructors and reported to the Commanding Officer, Executive Officer, Chief Instructor, and Curriculum Development Officer.
>
> Challenge: My predecessor had been relieved of his duty for performance issues and the training schools were not meeting training objectives with growing mission/theater needs in Iraq. The department had failed an inspection. I was tasked with restructuring the train-ing schools, ensuring that students received the necessary information and the curriculum supported that objective.
>
> Actions: The two schools I managed were the military occupational specialties of the small arms technician and electro-optical ordnance repairer. Although I was experienced in the former, I was not familiar with the latter. Given that, I needed to learn the subject matter quickly, analyze the relevant training, and recommend and implement reforms as needed.

(continued)

(continued)

This was a major change for the instructors who had been inadequately managed, so my communications with them and senior management were crucial.

One significant issue I uncovered was that the electro-optical ordnance class was overly long, taking three weeks to teach one week of material. This was a significant waste of instructor resources, as well as poor use of student time—the faster students were trained, the faster they could begin working in new jobs.

RESULTS: The new curriculum was restructured to a highly efficient and effective one-week program with 20 hours of classroom time and 20 hours of bench practice. I saved two weeks and produced trained Specialty Electronics Technicians in one-third the time. More than 750 Marines have completed the program with high performance reviews in the field. The Commander has been briefed and has given wide approval for the more efficient training programs.

Sample 2: Narrative CCAR KSA for Veterans Rehabilitation Counselor seeking lateral promotion with the Veterans Administration.

Knowledge of vocational rehabilitation counseling and case management techniques.

Intro Paragraph: I have over 18 years of experience in vocational rehabilitation counseling and case management. My current position as a Vocational Rehabilitation Counselor for the Miami Veterans Health Administration Hospital has built on the skills and experience I developed at the Seattle Veterans Benefits Administration (2000–2005).

I am experienced with counseling and case management, as well as with the more personal aspects of dealing with a diverse population of clients, who are in almost all cases struggling with significant life issues. The counseling process requires participation by both parties, so I create a working alliance with them by really listening to their story and asking questions to get a better understanding of their current situation. I offer compassion, understanding, and empathy integrated with advice and concrete options that empower and motivate them to choose the right course of action for themselves.

Context and challenge: My position with the Seattle Veterans Benefits Administration required me to manage a case load that averaged 200 concurrent clients.

Actions: In that position, I worked one-on-one with veterans with a wide range of physical, mental, and social disabilities. My duties included conducting a comprehensive intake assessment that included administering and evaluating a suite of vocational and aptitude test results, reviewing medical and psychological records, developing a rehabilitation plan, and then providing highly customized individual and group counseling.

I successfully utilized multiple online tools. This included state and VA computer databases such as WOIS/The Career Information System in the State of Washington, C/WINRS, the Benefits Delivery Network (BDN), the Bureau of Labor Statistics' *Occupational Outlook Handbook* and O*NET system, the Department of Labor database that provides comprehensive information for over 950 occupations that are key to the economy.

Results: With over 200 veteran cases in progress, I consistently managed approximately 50 in an active education and employment basis. Weekly I received notice from an average of two to three veterans who were successfully hired into business, government, and nonprofit organizations.

Sample 3: List KSA for Veterans Rehabilitation Counselor seeking lateral promotion with the Veterans Administration.

Knowledge of vocational rehabilitation counseling and case management techniques.

Over 18 years of experience in vocational rehabilitation counseling and case management.

- Current position: Vocational Rehabilitation Counselor, Miami Veterans Health Administration Hospital
- State of Florida Division of Blind Services (1988–2000)
- Seattle Veterans Benefits Administration (2000–2005)
- BA in Psychology from Louisiana State University
- MS in Visual Disabilities from Florida State University
- Postgraduate coursework in Counseling Theories and Techniques at Florida Atlantic University.

TECHNICAL COUNSELING, ASSESSMENT, AND CASE MANAGEMENT:

Experienced with a diverse population of clients with significant life issues.

As a Counselor with Seattle Veterans Benefits Administration, I managed a case load that averaged 200 concurrent clients.

Conducted a comprehensive intake assessment that included administering and evaluating a suite of vocational and aptitude test results, reviewing medical and psychological records, developing a rehabilitation plan, and then providing highly customized individual and group counseling.

RESOURCE MANAGEMENT:

Develop and utilize a wide range of VA, educational, and vocational resources to assist each veteran in setting and achieving their goals.

TRAINING AND TRANSITION COUNSELING:

Advise veterans toward improving their basic living conditions by completing training and education to transition to a paid career.

SPECIALIZED KNOWLEDGE AND REGULATIONS:

Maintain a high volume of case records in compliance with federal regulations, policies, and guidelines.

Utilize multiple online tools: state and VA computer databases such as WOIS/The Career Information System in the State of Washington, C/WINRS, the Benefits Delivery Network (BDN), the Bureau of Labor Statistics' Occupational Outlook Handbook and O*NET system, the Department of Labor database that provides comprehensive information for over 950 occupations that are key to the economy.

Sample 4: List KSA for Administrative Assistant (OA) seeking IT Specialist position.

ESSAY QUESTION: Please describe examples of work performed in software applications and data-bases.

POWERPOINT TRAINING CURRICULUM:

As a Lead Extramural Support Assistant (Task Leader) for the NIH, manipulated data for training, conferences, meetings, or special projects. I designed a PowerPoint presentation to teach the DEAS staff. Designed a PowerPoint that included curriculum lessons for proper protocol for e-mail and voice-mail etiquette using text and animated graphics in an electronic version. I also created a PowerPoint presentation to train staff in use of the AMBIS system.

EXCEL TABLES:

I designed and managed Excel tables for logging my travel reviews. Created a matrix to track the program or branch to which the DEAS support staff was assigned. Created and merged letters, mailing labels, tent cards, and name badges using the Microsoft Excel database in a text-file format for meetings and conferences. Merged data directly from our Excel database into letter format in MS Word; created mailing labels in a script font. Efficient in using Word and PowerPoint for letters, forms, and envelopes.

MICROSOFT PUBLISHER LOGO AND GRAPHIC DESIGNS:

Skilled with Microsoft Publisher for desktop publishing and to create specialized graphics. As a federal contractor with Hi-Tech International (HTI), I designed the official business stationery (such as a fax cover sheet, letterhead, envelopes, labels, and business cards). I also helped rewrite the text. The President and Executive Vice President were very pleased with the professionalism of their new business communications and professional logo design.

MICROSOFT ACCESS DATABASE DATA AND WINFAX:

With the Management Assistance Corporation (1999-2001), I administered a Microsoft Access database for the National Institute on Drug Abuse. The database included infor-mation for over 140 organizations and 400 individuals. I coordinated all database activi-ties, including merged data, files with letters, mailing labels, and a monthly newsletter that I distributed using broadcast fax technology (WinFax Pro).

GRAPHIC DESIGN SOFTWARE FOR SPECIAL PROJECTS:

Create specialized documents for friends and family and also work with small businesses. I have advanced skills using CorelDRAW, PhotoShop, Adobe Acrobat, Paint Shop Pro, and other desktop-publishing software.

Sample 5: Narrative CCAR KSA for Lead Transportation Security Specialist seeking a promotion to Supervisory Transportation Security Specialist.

Ability to communicate effectively, orally and in writing, to deliver high-visibility presentations and briefings and a wide array of technically written documents on a program or project.

I effectively communicate with stakeholders internal and external to the Transportation Safety Administration (TSA), which is critical to the success of our strategies in protecting the nation's aviation and other modes of transport.

Context:

As a TRANSPORTATION SECURITY SPECIALIST, Office of Law Enforcement for Security Assessment (2003 to present), I lead on-site security vulnerability assessments, including the Man Portable Defense Systems (MANPADS) mitigation system at LaGuardia International Airport, Sept. 2005.

Challenge:

During the initial meeting, I detected concerns about our methodologies and the impact of our final findings. Throughout the week, in addition to my physical inspection activities, I spoke informally with a wide range of personnel, reviewed documentation, and kept a careful log of everything we noted and discussed.

Actions:

- I arrived with a team of four assessment officials representing the TSA, the FBI, and the Assistant Federal Security Directors for Law Enforcement (AFSDLEs), as part of a routine, scheduled assessment activity.
- Our first action was to participate in an in-briefing that involved the local Federal Security Director, local airport law enforcement officials, state police, Department of Homeland Security representatives, and management from the airport's traffic control tower.
- I presented our plan for the coming week, which would include a physical inspection focusing on the airport's perimeter, personal interviews with key airport and law enforcement personnel, and evaluation of their MANPADS mitigation plan.

Results:

What started out as a tense, 30-person event gradually evolved into a discussion among peers that was ultimately more successful. After my return to Washington, I completed the final 25-page document, which was reviewed and approved well before our deadline, including detailed notes from our inspections and interviews. I wrote 10 recommendations to improve our methodologies for security assessment in the future that would streamline the analysis at all major U.S. airports. My narrative report was further analyzed for style and content and has been used as a template for subsequent Security Assessment Analysis Reports.

Sample 6: List KSA for FEMA Mobile Home Support Specialist, temporary position seeking Core position as GS-0301-09.

Ability to gather, analyze, and evaluate methods and techniques, and recommend changes in policy and procedures to enhance the success of the direct housing program.

I have recommended changes in policies and procedures on numerous occasions to improve the efficiency of the direct housing program.

A. I provided contractors with guidelines and procedures for developing quality work packets for quick processing.

Upon receiving incoming work-order packets from county contractors, I reviewed documents requesting a specific action involving the installation, swap, deactivation, or maintenance of a travel trailer or mobile home. I read site maps created by contractors, as well as various forms used to show the condition of housing units and information requested by myself and others in the department.

(continued)

(continued)

B. I analyzed 70 direct housing program packets per week, containing requests and information from applicants, and determined current housing needs. Expedited requests as much as possible.

All of these packets contained information for applicants across the lower six counties of South Mississippi, as well as applicants from Louisiana who are being housed in Mississippi.

C. I provided contractors with a new version of the information update (IU) form to use when on site in order to improve consistency of on-site information.

These are used to summarize the site assessment in order to provide consistent information on the site. Explained how to document applicant information and make recommendations for fulfilling the request because the contractor is the only one physically viewing the applicant and the site.

D. I made recommendations on how to expedite requests by communicating with lead supervisors on where information was not flowing properly from site inspectors to the mobile homes operations department.

Sample 7: Example KSA for Defense Finance and Accounting Service Accountant, GS-9, seeking a promotion to an Accountant, GS-11, position. The Columbus Headquarters for DFAS is expanding with 3,000 new positions.

In 500 words or less, provide specific examples that describe your level of experience in applying financial management theories, concepts, principles, and methods to the financial management functions you have performed.

422 words:

During my 20-plus-year federal career as an Accountant, I have gained and utilized knowledge and skill in applying financial management theories, concepts, principles, and methods to a variety of financial management functions. I have held positions in accounting and payroll and have learned specialized job procedures, problem solving discipline, and proficiency in applying statistical theories, practical concepts, and policies for administrative program operations and business line objectives.

Example 1. In my present DFAS Accountant position, one of my critical tasks is to prepare a monthly management tool for the Treasury Index 97 and 21 appropriations Suspense Account Report (SAR), which summarizes and captures pending clearing accounts of receipts, collections, remittance, and disbursements suspense accounts. I monitor, reconcile, prepare, report, and populate the numerical data into spreadsheets and ensure it is accurate and timely to cover the number, amount, and age of suspense accounting transactions for upper management. Once the data is compiled, I reconcile and balance the information on a collective spreadsheet that compares current month and prior month data. The data is applied to various reports and forwarded to headquarters for further comparison. My reports help to assess suspended accounting transactions and whether the organization is in compliance with various government accounting regulations.

Example 2. In my prior accounting position, I monitored problem disbursements to prevent negative unliquidated obligations (NULO) and unliquidated obligations that were overdisbursed. I ran daily queries in Database Accounting Reconciliation System (DARS) and created a spreadsheet separated by program codes. After compiling the information, I distributed the spreadsheets to the accounting technicians that handled that particular program code and requested actions to clear over-disbursed funds of 30 days or more. Using careful review, I ensured that none exceeded 120 days. If any were identified, I reported them on the monthly Customer Index and Balance Scorecard with explanations for the causes and what actions needed to be taken to resolve the problems. I would also notify my supervisor of any accounting transactions that were over 60 days and exceeded $100,000.

Example 3. Another of my responsibilities was to plan, organize, and conduct a Joint Review three times a year to reconcile U.S. Army accounting appropriations. I prepared an obligation report organized by program codes and reviewed each line with program managers and budget analysts, determining whether each obligation and accounting line needed to remain open, be adjusted, be de-obligated, or needed further research for action to be taken. The Joint Reviews helped our customer be better prepared for fiscal year-end closeout on various contracts, travel vouchers, and obligations.

Summary

This second or Assessment part of most federal applications is critical. Writing your KSAs and Essays can take time, concentration, and effort to write great examples that demonstrate your performance on the job. Both KSAs and essays are really pre-interview questions, so they are a great opportunity to give examples. In fact, your answers and examples could result in an interview. So, this is your chance to impress by writing about your best experiences and results of your efforts.

The next chapter reviews the Questions in more detail. The questions can be multiple choice, or can result in an essay or example demonstrating your performance. Usually, you can't get away from KSAs and Essays on your federal application.

CHAPTER 10

Questions and Self-Assessment Essays

This chapter focuses on KSA questions, including the styles of questions that you will be expected to answer as part of your application. The questions are a portion of a three-part job application system that includes the following:

1. Your personal profile (personnel-type questions) and an electronic resume copied and pasted into a resume builder

2. Job-Related or Core Questions with self-assessment lists and/or essays

3. Additional information to fax

> ⭐ **Note:** Coverage of KSA questions is all new for this edition of the *Federal Resume Guidebook.* When the Third Edition was published, the popular application formats were paper federal resumes and KSAs, plus Resumix for DOD agencies.

More than 100 federal agencies are using the Electronic Resume + Questionnaire format as their application style. Get ready for multiple-choice, true/false, yes/no, check all that apply, and essay questions. The assessment questions are written by human resources specialists and managers to enable them to find the best candidates for their position. The questionnaire serves as an examination to determine your level of knowledge, skills, abilities, and competencies for the job. The questionnaire will ask you what your skill level is. If you check the box that states you are the "office expert—train others, consult with others," you may be asked for a short essay to demonstrate this level of experience.

Responding to Questions and Essays

The essays you write and the examples you provide for the questions should demonstrate your performance level. When writing your essays and giving examples, also consider the "Duties," "Specialized Experience," and questions. If you can provide examples that are relevant to the target agency and position, the HR specialist will appreciate your skills even more.

The writing style for essays can be any of the styles covered in chapter 9: narrative CCAR KSA, example, or list style essays. Be sure to follow the character- or word-limitation instructions carefully.

Human resources offices will rate and rank you based on your self-assessment. The HR specialist will *not* rate and rank your narrative examples. The examples you write will demonstrate and support your skill level.

The questionnaire is a mandatory part of the application. Some people who apply to the Resume + Questionnaire + Fax applications lose consideration for a job because they do not complete one of the components of the application. If you are a serious candidate for a certain job, you must follow the directions, answer the questions, submit your essay answers, and fax your additional information.

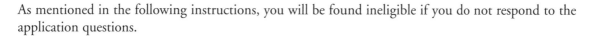

As mentioned in the following instructions, you will be found ineligible if you do not respond to the application questions.

Sample Instructions for Responding to Questions and Essays

The following two paragraphs are instructions written by the human resources specialist about rating the applicant's qualifications. You can see that eligible applicants will receive a rating based on their responses. Also please see the warning. They will review your resume against your questionnaire assessment. You should use the questions to update your resume.

BASIS OF RATING

Applicants will be rated on the extent and quality of experience, education, and training relevant to the duties of the position. Eligible applicants will receive a numerical rating based on their responses to the application questions for this position submitted online via EZHire@EPA. These responses must be substantiated by your online resume (passing scores range from 70 to 100 before the addition of Veterans Preference points). Applicants who do not respond to the application questions may be rated ineligible.

WARNING! Your answers will be verified against information provided in your online resume. Be sure that your resume clearly supports your responses to all the questions by addressing experience and education relevant to this position. If you exaggerate or falsify your experience and/or education, you may be removed from employment consideration. You should make a fair and accurate assessment of your qualifications.

The Many Forms of Questions and Self-Assessment Answers

The following questionnaire styles are popular on federal applications. Get ready to check all that apply, select your skill level, and back it up with examples. Very important: You should not exaggerate your qualifications.

⭐ **Tip:** Be sure to be truthful with your self-assessment. But also be sure to consider carefully your skills and abilities. If you can do this job, think about your skills from all of your past history, not just your current position.

---

1. Standard Self-Assessment Question

The best answer to this question would be number 5.

Conducts on-site visits to assess the condition of institutions which have closed or which are in imminent danger of closing in order to take action to secure agency interest by seizing records, promissory notes, and other assets.

1. I have not had education, training, or experience in performing this task.

2. I have had education or training in performing this task, but have not yet performed it on the job.

3. I have performed this task on the job, with close supervision from supervisor or senior employee.

(continued)

(continued)

> 4. I have performed this task as a regular part of the job, independently and usually without review by supervisor or senior employee.
>
> 5. This task has been a central or major part of my work. I have performed it myself routinely, and I have trained others in performance of this task and/or others have consulted me as an expert for assistance in performing this task.

2. Check All That Apply

The best answer for both of these questions would be all of them.

> Which of the following types of documents have you written?
>
> > Check all that apply:
> >
> > > Correspondence
> > >
> > > Technical reports
> > >
> > > Regulatory/statutory material
> > >
> > > Policy or procedures
> > >
> > > Analyses of proposed policy, legislative, or management initiatives
> > >
> > > Memos
> > >
> > > Newsletters
> > >
> > > Training materials
>
> Select the statements that describe your experience communicating project information to senior management officials.
>
> > Check all that apply
> >
> > 1. I have met with policy officials on a continuing basis to discuss policy proposals.
> >
> > 2. I have met with policy officials to brief them on current project status.
> >
> > 3. I have briefed key leadership on costs, impact, feasibility, alternatives, issues and recommendations, and status of projects.
> >
> > 4. I have developed policies, regulations, procedures, or analyses for senior management.
> >
> > 5. I have presented policies, regulations, procedures, analyses, and recommendations to key leadership.
> >
> > 6. I have assisted in the preparation of policy recommendations, procedures, or analyses, providing data and background information to senior officials as requested.
> >
> > 7. I have developed comprehensive materials for reports, briefings, and meetings.
> >
> > 8. I have communicated program strategies, goals, objectives, and priorities to program personnel.
> >
> > 9. I have prepared briefing materials for use by or presentation to senior management officials.
> >
> > 10. I have contributed to Office of Management and Budget (OMB) 300 exhibits.
> >
> > 11. None of the above.

3. Specific to the Job Skill Self-Assessment Questions

Read the answers carefully. Try to find the most complex answer.

Please indicate which of the following describe your experience in providing support to the security adjudication process:

Check all that apply

1. Initiated appropriate Bureau indices checks, arrest record checks, Central Intelligence Agency (CIA) information checks, ELSUR checks, and the like, in attempting to obtain pertinent identifying information relative to subject involved in each individual case.

2. Received and reviewed incoming material such as applications, Changes in Marital Status forms, Personnel Status Forms, and the like, for the purpose of discerning merit for granting, continuing, and/or revoking security clearance and access authorizations.

3. Assisted supervisor and/or coworkers with a segment of typical security clearance adjudications.

4. None of the above.

In the text box below, provide a brief summary of your experience providing support to the security adjudication process:

(Essay Question)

Select the statement that best describes your highest level of experience in planning and implementing space renovations for and relocations of an entire organizational unit.

1. I have education, training, or experience in planning relocations and space renovations.

2. I have training or education in planning space renovations and relocations, but have not applied it on the job.

3. I have performed this task at an organization's headquarters level.

4. I have performed this task at an organization's field office.

5. I have performed this task among several field offices.

6. I have performed this task at both a field office and the headquarters level.

7. I have performed this task among several large organizational/departmental offices.

8. None of the above.

---

4. General Self-Assessment Questions with Essays

Number 5 is the best answer.

Select the statement that best describes your level of experience applying analytical and evaluative methods and techniques to issues or studies concerning the management of space.

1. I have not had education, training, or experience administering, working with, or performing this task or function.

2. I have had education or training administering, working with, or performing this task or function, but have not yet used it on the job.

3. I have administered, worked with, or performed this task or function with close review and assistance from a supervisor, a senior employee, or a senior consultant.

(continued)

(continued)

4. I have administered, worked with, or performed this task or function as a regular part of a job and only in unique or unusual situations did I require assistance or review by a supervisor, senior employee, or senior consultant.

5. I have administered, worked with, or performed this task or function as a regular part of a job, even in unique or unusual situations. I do not require assistance or review by a supervisor, senior employee, or senior consultant.

Please describe your experience in space management to include space programming and your ability to efficiently move an organization from one location to another.

(Essay Question)

In 1,000 words or less, please describe an analysis of a program that you have conducted, including the methodology and tools used to conduct the analysis, alternative courses of action, and the result of your analysis.

(Essay Question)

In 300 words or less, describe a situation where you had technical authority to authorize or disapprove funding requests, obligations, and expenditures of funds based on your interpretation of relevant law, regulation, or policy.

(Essay Question)

Select the response that best reflects your highest level of experience in processing administrative employment discrimination complaints in the federal sector with regard to Disciplinary Actions (counseling, reprimand, warning, suspension, demotion, leave restriction, removal).

1. I have not had the education, training, or experience in performing this task.

2. I have had specific training or education directly related to this task, although I have not performed this task on the job.

3. I have performed this task on the job with assistance from a team leader, supervisor, or other employee to ensure compliance with proper procedures.

4. I have performed this task on the job independently with approval of the final product by a team leader or a supervisor.

5. I have served as technical expert authority on this task, providing guidance or supervision to others because of my background.

If you selected choice 4 or 5, please provide a narrative supporting your answer to the above question, including information on the circumstances, the complexity of the work performed, the length of time, and the organization where the work was performed. Please limit response to 1/2 page (1,500 characters).

(Essay Question)

5. Yes/No, Plus Essay

"Yes" is the best answer.

Do you have work experience that provided you with a comprehensive knowledge and application of legislation, regulations, policies, and procedures governing the Student Financial Assistance Title IV Family Federal Education Loan (FFEL) Program and the current policies and requirements relating to the administration of the Title IV FFEL program?

Yes   No

If you answer "Yes," you will be asked the following question(s):

> Please elaborate.
>
> *(Essay Question)*

6. Tricky Question

Answer number 4 is okay, but 5 is better.

> Select the response that best describes your experience applying analytical and evaluative methods and techniques to assess program development or execution in order to improve organizational effectiveness and efficiency.
>
> 1. I have not had experience applying analytical and evaluative methods and techniques to assess program development or execution in order to improve organizational effectiveness and efficiency.
>
> 2. I have completed education or training in applying analytical and evaluative methods and techniques to assess program development or execution in order to improve organizational effectiveness and efficiency, but have not yet performed this task on the job.
>
> 3. I have applied analytical and evaluative methods and techniques to assess program development or execution in order to improve organizational effectiveness and efficiency under close supervision by a supervisor or senior employee.
>
> 4. I have applied analytical and evaluative methods and techniques to assess program development or execution in order to improve organizational effectiveness and efficiency as a regular part of a job, independently and usually without review by a supervisor or senior employee.
>
> 5. I have applied analytical and evaluative methods and techniques to assess program development or execution in order to improve organizational effectiveness and efficiency routinely as a major part of my work. I have supervised or trained others in performing this task and/or others have consulted me for expert assistance in performing this task.

Write Your Questions and Essay Answers in Word Offline Ahead of Time

The best way to study the questionnaire, write your answers, and prepare to submit your online application is to copy and paste the entire questionnaire into a Word file. This method makes it easier to check off your answers and write your essays ahead of time. Then you can go back online and answer the questions and copy and paste your essays fairly quickly.

Be sure to leave enough time before the application deadline to copy and paste the answers and information online. Some electronic submission systems take up to 48 hours to register your submission.

Case Study: TSA Supervisory Screener

The following case study is a real questionnaire and essay for a promotion at TSA. The questionnaire and essays take several hours to write, so find your questions ahead of time and begin to write them offline. Then copy and paste the text into the online form. Try to set aside several hours for submitting online.

Here is an example of a TSA Supervisory Screener questionnaire and answers that were copied and pasted online. There were a total of 33 questions and 10 essays. The 10 essays support the important competencies for TSA (these are covered in chapter 8). This particular application took three hours to submit online and five or six hours to write prior to submission. What happened? This applicant was rated as Highly Qualified and referred for an interview.

The 10 Essays Requested Are Also the TSA's Core Competencies

1. In the space provided, please describe briefly an example of your **conflict management** skills.
2. In the space provided, please support your choice by briefly describing an example of your **customer service skills.**
3. Please provide a specific example of how you **obtained facts,** information, or data relevant to a particular **problem, question, or issue.**
4. In the space provided, please support your answer by providing a brief example of your experience in **problem-solving.**
5. Please provide two detailed examples of how you handled **unexpected or stressful situations** in the workplace.
6. Briefly describe a **team** that you worked on, including the nature and purpose of the team and your responsibilities for the team.
7. In the space provided, please describe two specific examples of documents you have **written.**
8. Please provide a specific example of a situation where you have issued **instructions** and made requests to individuals.
9. In the space provided, please describe an example of a time when you had to **balance workloads and tasks** among yourself and others.
10. Please provide a specific example of a situation where you had to complete **safety logs, incident reports,** and other records as part of your job.

⭐ **Tip**: Be sure to have your Questions and Answers e-mailed to you from the last page of your online announcement.

The following text is an e-mail from the TSA Recruitment office that contained copies of this job seeker's questions and answers. Be sure to check off that you want to receive an e-mail copy of your questions and answers (if you get this opportunity in the online application system).

Following is a sample e-mail received with TSA Questions and Answers:

Thank you for applying to the position TSA-BWI-2006-0005, Supervisory Transportation Security Officer (Screener) at Transportation Security Administration.

Your responses, as listed below, are being reviewed. You may revise your answers until this vacancy announcement closes by logging into TSA Online and reapplying for the same position.

Band G responses:

1. Do you have at least six months of full-time equivalent work experience as a Lead Transportation Security Officer (Screener), SV-1802-F (formerly SV-0019-F, GS-9 level) OR six months of full-time equivalent or higher security experience in the federal government or private sector? Full-time experience is based on a 40-hour work week. Part-time experience is credited proportionately.

    Answer: Yes

2. I am a current TSA employee at Baltimore/Washington International Airport (BWI).

    Answer: True

All Bands Responses:

1. From the following activities that involve conflict management, please identify those you have performed.

    Answer: I have applied TSA guidance to resolve complaints of Screeners.

    I have resolved conflicts arising among screeners.

    I have resolved conflicts over the enforcement of security rules with the traveling public.

    I have resolved conflicts with other employees or team members that required cooperation, coordination of activities, and reaching consensus.

2. In the space provided, please describe briefly an example of your conflict management skills.

    (Narrative CCAR Essay)

    Answer: (context) I negotiated a solution with an irate passenger recently, as a Lead Screener. (challenge) The passenger was highly irate due to the fact he could not take a special garden cutting tool to his mother for Mother's Day. When the TSO originally presented the passenger with his options he quickly escalated to the point where he was intimidating the female officer. (actions) I was presently on another lane and quickly went over to the location, where I quickly assumed control of the situation and again in a calm, firm, clear, and precise manner explained all of the passenger's options. (results) After the passenger took the information in, he decided to relinquish the item and then apologized to the female TSO and to me for his actions.

3. Which of the following best reflects how you routinely use equipment, supplies, and resources in your work?

    Answer: I plan, monitor, and make necessary adjustments for the efficient use of equipment, supplies, and resources.

4. Which best describes your skills in providing customer service to the traveling public?

    Answer: I help customers understand the security-screening policies and procedures.

5. In the space provided, please support your choice by briefly describing an example of your customer service skills.

    (Example Answer)

    Answer: When in doubt or uncertainty, always take the safest course, be sure to rely on our SOP and your training; they are the best tools we have; and two, treat others as you would like to be treated. With these two mottos, there is never room for failure,

(continued)

(continued)

and my customer service skills are very well developed from years of servicing business and individual customers. I realize that the passengers are busy and concerned about lines, getting to the gate, and all of their personal items being safely sent through the x-ray equipment. I am aware of the special needs for the parents of small children, seniors, and individuals with assistive devices. I am particularly aware of special needs as I see these passengers coming through the line. I am attentive, watching the screeners and their communications skills in giving directions and giving special instructions in a nonthreatening way. With many customers having hip and knee implants, I ensure that my team members are efficient in wanding and giving special services to ensure the safety of our aircraft, facilities, and passengers. I emphasize courteous, informative support, as well as eye contact and a smile if possible to all passengers in the screening area.

6. From the following list please identify those situations where you have adapted your behavior or work methods to adjust to other people or to changing situations or work schedules.

   Answer:

   To facilitate the amicable resolution of competing or conflicting interests among parties whose cooperation is needed to meet an objective.

   To interact effectively in situations where frequent changes, delays, or unexpected events arise that cause major shifts in priorities, timetables, or work assignments.

   To provide direction, guidance, or instruction to staff.

   To persuade and/or inspire others to adopt new methods, procedures, or techniques to improve operations.

   To defuse confrontational situations with people who are difficult, hostile, or distressed.

   To develop trusting, productive working relationships with subordinates, colleagues, and supervisors to achieve goals and objectives.

   To work cooperatively with others as a team to achieve a project or program goal.

7. Select one description that best represents your highest level of experience in interacting with various groups and individuals.

   Answer: Experience that involves routinely working with managers to resolve issues and problems that arise on a daily basis.

8. Please select the response that best describes your experience or training interpreting verbal communications and directions.

   Answer: I have trained others in interpreting verbal communications and directions and (or) others have consulted me as an expert for assistance in performing this area.

9. From the list below, please identify the ways you have obtained facts, information, or data relevant to a particular problem, question, or issue.

   Answer:

   Observation of events or situations

   Discussion with others

   Research or retrieval from written electronic sources

10. Please provide a specific example of how you obtained facts, information, or data relevant to a particular problem, question, or issue.

    (Narrative CCAR Essay Answer)

    Answer: (context and challenge) As the Lead Screener, I have created a new customer service survey to improve information about customer services. (actions) I have taken the responsibility to train others to administer the survey to the passengers as well as compile the data. Additionally, I have set up an MS Excel spreadsheet to keep track of the data and daily operations. These surveys have proven to be a valuable two-way tool

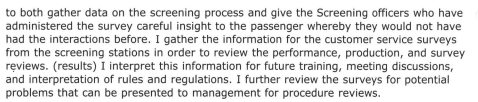

to both gather data on the screening process and give the Screening officers who have administered the survey careful insight to the passenger whereby they would not have had the interactions before. I gather the information for the customer service surveys from the screening stations in order to review the performance, production, and survey reviews. (results) I interpret this information for future training, meeting discussions, and interpretation of rules and regulations. I further review the surveys for potential problems that can be presented to management for procedure reviews.

11. In which of the following events have you communicated orally or made oral presentations?

Answer:

Speeches

Conferences

Meetings

One-on-one discussions

Telephone inquiries

Training

Technical assistance

Interviews

Briefings

12. In the space provided, please support your answer by providing a brief example of your experience in problem-solving.

(Short CCAR Example)

Answer: (challenge) As we began to work the international pier on our new rotation, I noted that some of our foreign travelers were taking a longer than usual time gathering up their items after going through the X-ray. This reduced productivity in busy times. (actions) After doing some measurements I determined we could place an extra table after the initial one, allowing more space and time for the passengers. (results) This has worked so well that the table has quietly now become part of the everyday fixtures as it seems everyone uses it now.

13. From the list below, please identify those situations you have encountered on the job.

Answer:

Pressure

Stress

Emergencies

Hostile individuals

Setbacks

Personal problems

Work-related problems

14. Please provide two detailed examples of how you handled unexpected or stressful situations in the workplace.

(Two Short CCAR Answers/Examples)

Answer:

1. (context) On May 14th, while working as Acting Supervisor on D Pier. I managed the floor while fully integrating the new procedures to Pier NSF workforce. (challenge) Immediately after they arrived, it was clear they were only processing 20 passengers at the most per half hour. (actions) I immediately began an integration plan whereby I

(continued)

(continued)

mixed the NSF staff for the day with regular BWI workers. The work volume increased and I requested the trainers step up and perform the work functions while the OJT officers assisted. (results) These actions allowed me to receive an accommodation from management for quick, responsive handling of all situations in a calm and firm manner.

   2. (context and challenge) While in the acting role of supervising D Pier, the largest at BWI, we had a situation whereby an additional crew was required at the International pier. (actions) D Pier was very busy and I was just about to send a crew to their first break when I took the call from the International Pier. I went to the Team Lead and explained the situation in detail and that I wanted them to forgo the break initially until they could break free from duties on the International Pier. (Results) Everyone was unhappy, so I negotiated a solution. I determined that they would be needed as a full team for only 30 minutes and negotiated a self break while the crew was on E Pier. All were satisfied with the extra communication and solution, and the once tense situation was abated.

15. Which of the following best describes your work experience in a team environment?

   Answer: I regularly work in team settings and frequently lead teams in work-related projects.

16. Briefly describe a team that you worked on, including the nature and purpose of the team and your responsibilities for the team.

   (Short List Answer)

   Answer: (context) I am the team lead for 6 direct reports and up to 10 subordinate screeners who provide security screening at BWI Airport. (actions) I set the workload priorities based on the aircraft schedules and available screener staff. The team is trained in policies and procedures and I rotate the new employees with senior employees to gain a balance of knowledge. In fact, the team members provide informal on-the-job training on customer services, policies and procedures, and daily operations. We are a communicative and cooperative team; we recognize strengths and assist with special passenger situations. I communicate needed direction and give disciplinary warnings as needed. But I strive to monitor performance, cooperation, and work attitude to increase customer satisfaction.

17. Which of the following types of documents have you written?

   Answer:

   Correspondence

   Technical reports

   Regulatory/statutory material

   Policy or procedures

   Analyses of proposed policy, legislative, or management initiatives

   Memos

   Newsletters

   Training materials

18. In the space provided, please describe two specific examples of documents you have written.

   (List Answer)

   Answer: At TSA, my written works include employee evaluations, performance reports, production narratives, and case reports on incidents, including recommendations.

   PUBLICATIONS AUTHORED

   Active 99 "Installation of ANC on Combined Heat/Power Plant. Holland"; 1999

   Prime Power Magazine "Noise Control for Neighborhood Gensets"; 1999

Bulk and Powder Solids Tech. "Successful Use of Active Noise Control on the Rotary PD Blower"; 1995

TECHNICAL PAPERS AUTHORED AND PRESENTED

Maryland Department of Environment (Technical presentation); Baltimore, MD; 2003

Institute Noise Control Engineers Active Conference; Ft. Lauderdale, FL; 1999

Society of Automotive Engineers Conference; Eugene, OR; 1997

American Industrial Hygiene Association Conference; Washington, D.C.; 1996

South American Petroleum Symposium; Colombia, S.A.; 1996

Alberta Energy/Utilities Commission Noise Control Power Energy Industry; Alberta, Canada; 1996

University of Pretoria; Republic of South Africa; 1995

19. Please select the response that best describes your experience issuing instructions and making requests to individuals.

   Answer: I have trained others in issuing instructions and making requests to individuals and (or) others have consulted me as an expert for assistance in performing this area.

20. Please provide a specific example of a situation where you have issued instructions and made requests to individuals.

   (List Answer)

   Answer: As a Lead Screener at TSA, I am continually training officers on the latest procedures and processes based on volume of activity, threat alerts, security concerns, and workforce availability. I have consulted with other lead officers in policies and procedures and discussed efficiency and customer service concerns. While in the role of Chief Environmental Safety Officer for CSX Railroad, I routinely issued operating and safety instructions for the safe and secure transport of commodities that move on both railcars and over-the-highway trucks. One such instruction required all loader personnel to wear both safety gloves and the proper respirators while transloading hazardous chemicals from the railcar to the truck.

21. Which of the following have you done as a routine part of your professional work experience?

   Answer:

   Identify needed tasks to be performed

   Assign tasks and monitor performance

   Schedule adequate personnel

   Monitor flow and make necessary adjustments

   Distribute tasks among employees according to skill level

   Make resource decisions for periods of high demand

   Anticipate and resolve problems

22. In the space provided, please describe an example of a time when you had to balance workloads and tasks among yourself and others.

   (Short CCAR Answer)

   Answer: (context) I balance the workloads and tasks among my team members on a daily and weekly basis, depending on the pier operations, availability of crew members, and security concerns. I balanced the workload and work flow carefully when I was tasked with Acting Supervisor on the D Pier. I managed the floor while integrating the new NSF workforce. (challenge and actions) Recognized problems with efficiency and advised the trainees to increase volume and communication with the passengers. I recognized logistical problems and decided the additional space was needed for passengers

(continued)

(continued)

to manage bags and personal property. (results) Was responsive to the new pier operations flow and received an accommodation for the handling of the situation.

23. Please select the response that best describes your experience completing safety logs, incident reports, and other records.

     Answer: I have trained others in completing safety logs, incident reports, and other records and (or) others have consulted me as an expert for assistance in performing this area.

24. Please provide a specific example of a situation where you had to complete safety logs, incident reports, and other records as part of your job.

     (Short Narrative Answer)

     Answer: While in the role of Operations Manager at CSX Railroad, I was responsible for oversight and reporting of all major incidents to the Federal Railroad Administration. I compiled accident investigation reports, interviews, photographs, and expert analyses into an accident report for formal review and findings. These accident reports were reviewed by media, government oversight, and safety agencies. The quality and detail of the incident reports was expert and took up to 6 months to complete, depending on the severity of the incident.

25. Please select the response that best describes your experience or training with security screening equipment.

     Answer: I have trained others in using security screening equipment and (or) others have consulted me as an expert for assistance in performing this area.

26. Please select the response that best describes your experience overseeing screening operations and ensuring the correct application of screening procedures.

     Answer: I have trained others in overseeing screening operations and ensuring the correct application of screening procedures and (or) others have consulted me as an expert for assistance in performing this area.

27. Please select the response that best describes your experience providing on-the-job correction and instruction on screening procedures.

     Answer: I have trained others in providing on-the-job correction and instruction on screening procedures and (or) others have consulted me as an expert for assistance in performing this area.

28. Please select the response that best describes your experience or training distinguishing between relevant visual cues or information and irrelevant or distracting information.

     Answer: I have trained others in distinguishing between relevant visual cues or information and irrelevant or distracting information and (or) others have consulted me as an expert for assistance in performing this area.

29. Please select the response that best describes your experience or training visually inspecting persons, property, or equipment.

     Answer: I have trained others in visually inspecting persons, property, or equipment and (or) others have consulted me as an expert for assistance in performing this area.

30. Please select the response that best describes your experience or training recognizing differences, similarities, or patterns in circumstances or events.

     Answer: I have trained others in recognizing differences, similarities, or patterns in circumstances or events and (or) others have consulted me as an expert for assistance in performing this area.

Locations:

Anne Arundel County, MD

Please make sure that you have entered your resume. You will be disqualified from consideration if your resume has not been entered before this vacancy closes.

Please remember to send all supporting documentation to the HR office for proper consideration.

Thank you for using the TSA Online!

Summary

The questions that accompany federal applications can be challenging. You can never tell how many questions, or what kind of questions, will be asked. They can be multiple-choice, yes/no, or true/false. They can be essay questions or self-assessment questions. It's important to review the "how to apply" instructions when you are planning your time to apply for the position. Find out how many essays are required for the application right away and get ready to write your examples. The examples will demonstrate your performance level and your experience. The examples might result in your referral to the supervisor, so take your time and give compelling and relevant ones.

Navigating USAJOBS and Announcement Analysis Strategies

CHAPTER 11

Vacancy Announcement Analysis Techniques

At a Peace Corps Federal Career Conference last week, I told 75 returning Peace Corps Volunteers that they could not write a federal resume until they found two or three vacancy announcements that were a correct fit for their qualifications and interest. Why? Because the information in the vacancy announcement will help them write work experience descriptions that are focused toward the future job.

Serious federal job seekers look for great announcements almost every day. Using the Internet through any computer at home, at work, or in a library or career center, you can find federal jobs within minutes of them being posted. To save time, you can sign up for automatic e-mail notifications from some Web sites by setting up a specific profile of the job you are seeking.

You can't begin a federal job search without studying vacancy announcements. This research will give you information about the jobs, duties, salaries, locations, agencies, and what is needed to apply. The Duties and Qualifications sections of the announcements clearly show the top skills needed for the Best Qualified status. In the "duties" section of the announcements, I marked each sentence with a number, so that you can analyze each sentence in the announcement for keywords.

By carefully analyzing the target announcement—the duties, qualifications, KSAs and questions—you will find language that can fit into your resume. Use some of the hiring agency's own words in your resume to carefully match your resume to the position. The specialized language in the resume should also include keywords that are relevant to the position. If you are submitting your resume to a Resumix system, you should also include searchable terms. The Resumix agencies (Navy, Army, Air Force, and DOD agencies) search for qualified candidates using keywords found in the vacancy announcements and position descriptions. Check out the three sample announcements later in this chapter, especially for the critical skills, qualifications, and keywords.

Step 1: Find Vacancy Announcements

You can find most federal vacancy announcements at the following Web sites. All jobs are posted on these Web sites, including jobs for the Army, Navy, and Air Force, which also have their own Web sites and job listings.

- ★ **www.usajobs.gov:** The official Office of Personnel Management Web site
- ★ **www.avuecentral.com:** Federal agency jobs Web site

In addition, you can find vacancy announcements through several other sources, which are detailed in the following sections.

Agency Web Sites

Most agencies list their jobs at their own Web sites, as well as at www.usajobs.gov. If you have targeted a specific agency, such as the Federal Bureau of Investigation, it would be much faster to search for jobs at www.fbijobs.gov than at the OPM's main site. Or if you wanted a job at the National Institutes of Health, you could go directly to www.hhs.gov.

Private-Industry Federal Job Sites

You can find federal jobs at privately owned and operated databases as well. These cost a few dollars for membership and access, but the databases are nicely managed, so you might be able to find specific jobs faster than on other Web sites. Here are a few examples of these types of sites:

- ★ www.fedjobs.com
- ★ www.federaljobsearch.com

Civilian Job Listings with Defense and Military Agencies

Looking for a job as a civilian on a military base? You don't have to join the military service to work as a civilian in a Department of Defense agency. You can look for job announcements at the following Web pages:

- ★ **Navy/Marines:** https://www.donhr.navy.mil/
- ★ **Army:** www.cpol.army.mil
- ★ **Air Force:** https://ww2.afpc.randolph.af.mil/resweb/
- ★ **Department of Defense:** www.defenselink.mil/sites/c.html#CivilianJobOpportunities
- ★ **Department of Homeland Security:** www.dhs.gov/xabout/careers/index.shtm

Your Network

Do you know someone who works in government? What agency does this person work for? What is this person's job? Is this individual's agency growing or downsizing? Is it hiring? What kinds of people does the agency hire? How can you apply? Does the person you know have any clout with hiring managers? These are the questions you should ask your neighbor, golf partner, and fellow churchgoer. This person's agency might be adding a new program and needs to hire more program managers, contract specialists, and computer specialists. This person might not know that you would like to work for the government and that you have expertise in a particular area. Network. Meet and talk with as many people as you can. You never know where you'll find a good lead.

Federal employees and others will tell you that your network is very important. Think long range. Listen for new programs and initiatives, especially those that will require specialized technical skills.

Reading, Listening to the News, and Keeping Your Eyes Open

Read federal newspapers, union newsletters, the federal page in your newspaper if it has one, the federal pages in the *Washington Post* (available online at www.washingtonpost.com), and *Government Executive Magazine* (also available online at www.govexec.com) to stay on top of what's going on in government.

Step 2: Analyze the Vacancy Announcement and "How to Apply" Instructions

Once you have found a job opportunity that interests you, save or print the vacancy announcement for thorough study. Don't be intimidated by the length and look of the announcement. We'll teach you how to discover the important information in the announcement and what the various sections mean. On USAJOBS announcements, scroll down to Print Preview. You can click on this and the entire announcement can be printed and saved for future analysis and documentation.

> ⭐ **Tip:** Save announcements that you apply to. You will need the announcement to prepare for an interview.

Get ready for a challenge—and read the directions. Federal agency human resources offices choose the announcement format, writing style, instructions on "how to apply," and what to submit as an application. Announcements from different agencies may have different application instructions.

This chapter gives examples of and analyzes three of the most typical announcement formats:

1. A USAJOBS announcement that requires you to set up a profile and a My USAJOBS account. Then you create your resume in the USAJOBS Resume Builder. The USAJOBS announcement format also asks for answers to an in-depth questionnaire.

2. A "paper federal resume and KSA announcement" from an agency that is not automated. Some agencies do not yet have an electronic database; however, more and more agencies are converting to electronic databases. This format might disappear in the next two to five years.

3. A Resumix announcement with a supplemental data sheet from the Army. The Army, Navy, Marines, and Air Force use Resumix announcements.

A USAJOBS/OPM Questionnaire Announcement

You can use your USAJOBS resume to apply for many positions online. This announcement is for an Administrative/Mission Support position. It's important to have a My USAJOBS account set up ahead of time so that you can follow the "how to apply" instructions and complete the online questionnaire.

Figure 11.1: A sample of a USAJOBS vacancy announcement.

Here are the important elements of a USAJOBS recruitment announcement. This is an excellent announcement because you could take this job as a GS-7 and eventually be promoted to a GS-11.

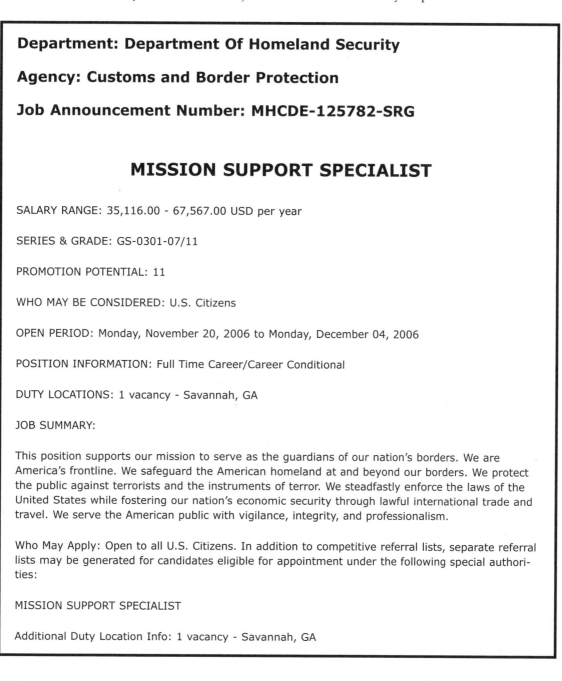

Department: Department Of Homeland Security

Agency: Customs and Border Protection

Job Announcement Number: MHCDE-125782-SRG

MISSION SUPPORT SPECIALIST

SALARY RANGE: 35,116.00 - 67,567.00 USD per year

SERIES & GRADE: GS-0301-07/11

PROMOTION POTENTIAL: 11

WHO MAY BE CONSIDERED: U.S. Citizens

OPEN PERIOD: Monday, November 20, 2006 to Monday, December 04, 2006

POSITION INFORMATION: Full Time Career/Career Conditional

DUTY LOCATIONS: 1 vacancy - Savannah, GA

JOB SUMMARY:

This position supports our mission to serve as the guardians of our nation's borders. We are America's frontline. We safeguard the American homeland at and beyond our borders. We protect the public against terrorists and the instruments of terror. We steadfastly enforce the laws of the United States while fostering our nation's economic security through lawful international trade and travel. We serve the American public with vigilance, integrity, and professionalism.

Who May Apply: Open to all U.S. Citizens. In addition to competitive referral lists, separate referral lists may be generated for candidates eligible for appointment under the following special authorities:

MISSION SUPPORT SPECIALIST

Additional Duty Location Info: 1 vacancy - Savannah, GA

Note: You will need to cover the following top seven skills in your resume for this job. There will be a lot of problem-solving and adjustment to change in this administrative position.

MAJOR DUTIES:

1. You will independently complete a wide variety of assignments requiring the application of fundamental principles, concepts, techniques, and **guidelines in an administrative specialty area.**

2. You will participate in complex studies and projects designed to develop broader expertise.

3. You will also **conduct detailed planning to gather and interpret information** and data for singular complex problems, issues, and unusual circumstances and determine the most effective approach at solving customer requirements. **(interpret customer needs)**

4. Additionally, you will **improve or enhance current services** to ensure that such services meet management's business objectives.

5. You will assess situations that are complicated by ambiguous, disputed, conflicting and/or incomplete data, requiring significant reconstruction to isolate issues and/or problems. **(situation problem-solving)**

6. You will analyze the effects of changes in laws and regulations as they pertain to **management services** and identify and extract additional pertinent information. **(improve services based on changes)**

7. You will define issues or problems in terms that are compatible with appropriate laws, policies, or regulations and weigh pertinent facts in formulating a legal and/or factually supportable position. **(more problem-solving having to do with laws, policies, and regulations)**

Qualifications and Specialized Experience:

Note: This description is more down to earth in terms of the job tasks. Make sure you give examples of the following in your resume in order to qualify for this position. They are going to give the candidate developmental assignments to develop skills. That's great!

GS-7: You qualify at the GS-7 level if you possess one year of specialized experience that equipped you with the skills needed to perform the job duties. This experience must have been equivalent to at least the GS-5 grade level. Examples include performing developmental assignments under the close guidance of a higher-level specialist that provided exposure to a wide variety of management and administrative methods, techniques, and practices such as updating budget data on spreadsheets; compiling data for budget requests; preparing requests for personnel action; providing orientation to new employees; coordinating office moves and telephone service requirements; monitoring usage of government motor vehicles; collecting and analyzing information related to workflow, office procedures, and control systems in support of program evaluations; and responding to routine questions concerning administrative procedures and requirements.

3. How You Will Be Evaluated and Questionnaire:

Note: You will submit your resume and answer questions for this position. Your answers to the questions should match your resume content.

You will be evaluated based upon the responses you provide on the job-specific questionnaire that is required as part of the application process for this position. You will be rated based on your responses and assigned a score ranging from 70 to 100 points.

All the information you provide may be verified by a review of the work experience and/or education as shown on your application forms, by checking references and through other means, such as the interview process. This verification could occur at any stage of the application process. Any exaggeration of your experience, false statements, or attempts to conceal information may be grounds for rating you ineligible, not hiring you, or for firing you after you begin work.

4. How to Apply:

Note: This is a USAJOBS resume plus Job-Specific Questionnaire. The questionnaire is located on the OPM site. The questionnaire is very important. You will also need to fax other information based on the announcement instructions.

You must complete the online occupational questionnaire and submit a resume to receive consideration for this vacancy announcement. Please be sure to respond to all questions in the online questionnaire. Omissions or errors may affect your rating or result in your being rated ineligible.

To start a new occupational questionnaire, click the link below. Once you have completed the occupational questionnaire, select the "Finish" button. At the next screen, click the "Submit" button.

https://www.hr-services.org/usasonlineapp/usasonlineapp.aspx

A Paper Federal Resume and KSA Announcement

The Transportation Security Agency is an agency that still receives applications via paper, mail, and fax. The application asks for both federal resume and KSAs. You should send your paper applications by registered or certified mail, so that you can ensure they are received.

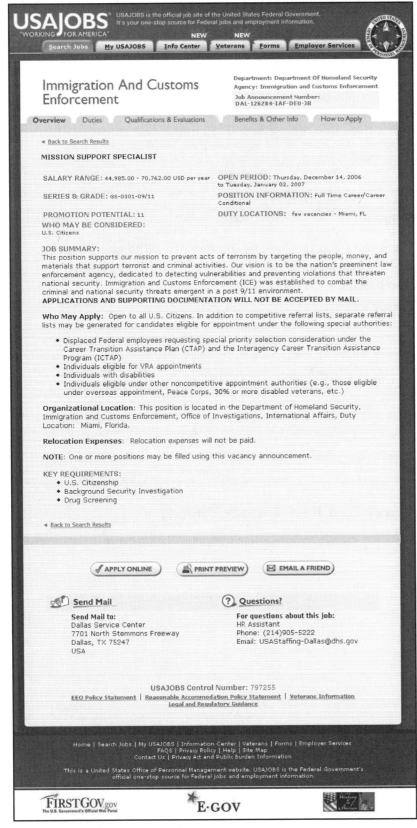

Figure 11.2: A sample paper federal resume and KSA announcement.

1. Major Duties:

Note: You will need to cover these top five skills in your resume for this job.

1. He or she will assist in **analyzing and reviewing flight crew information data** received from air carriers and cargo operators and ensuring that the information received is accurate and complete.

2. The incumbent will also **analyze transportation vetting results** for possible threats to national security.

3. Specific responsibilities will include **research and analysis of web-based applications** and other data sources. Will assist in compiling daily compliance reports, communicate with industry, TSA Principal Security Inspectors, assist in resolving flight crew manifest problems, and conduct terrorist-related security reviews of personnel involved in all aspects of the National Transportation schema.

4. Also, will work closely with DHS agencies and the intelligence community.

5. Assists the lead analyst in identifying problems and seeking ways to improve the process.

2. Qualifications and Specialized Experience:

Note: To qualify for this job, you need one year of specialized experience in analyzing transportation security intelligence information for possible threats to national security.

Candidates must meet the qualification requirements of this position no later than the closing date of the vacancy announcement. All applicants must demonstrate one year of specialized experience equivalent to that of the next lower pay band/grade level in the Federal Service or private sector. This will be an F or G band position with potential for advancement to the H Pay Band. For the SV-F pay band, applicants must have one year of specialized experience equivalent to the GS-5/7 grade level. For the SV-G pay band, applicants must have one year of specialized experience equivalent to the SV-F pay band or the GS-9 grade level.

SPECIALIZED EXPERIENCE is defined as experience that has equipped the applicant with the particular knowledge, skills, and abilities to successfully perform the duties of the position, and is typically in or related to the work of the position to be filled. Such experience will include analyzing transportation security intelligence information for possible threats to national security.

3. How You Will Be Evaluated and KSAs:

Note: This announcement requires KSAs that demonstrate your experience in these areas. This is a specific announcement. KSA 1 is very technical. You should write examples that cover this requirement: "Your description may include one or more examples of accomplishments, problems resolved, risks/threats averted, or processes improved as a result of your efforts."

Applicants will be evaluated on their total background including experience, education, awards, training, and self-development as it relates to the position.

Responses to the evaluation criteria may be ranked according to relative merit for this position and identified as being "qualified" or "best qualified." Selection for this position will be made only from among candidates possessing the best qualifications.

Your description should explain the nature of experience, accomplishments, education, and training opportunities that best illustrate how, to what degree, and with what impact you have applied/used each of the knowledge, skills, and abilities needed for successful performance in this position. Your description may include one or more examples of accomplishments, problems resolved, risks/threats averted, or processes improved as a result of your efforts.

KSAs:

1. Knowledge of relevant federal regulations, security directives, and emergency amendments as they pertain to the aviation regulatory requirements to include 49 CPR Ports 1544, 1546, and 1550.

2. **Oral Communication:** Makes clear and convincing oral presentations to individuals or groups; listens effectively and clarifies information as needed; facilitates an open exchange of ideas and fosters an atmosphere of open communication.

3. Ability to work in a dynamic team environment with continuous challenges and changing priorities.

4. **Planning and Evaluating:** Determines objectives and strategies; organizes work; sets priorities; determines resource requirements; coordinates with other parts of the organization to accomplish goals; monitors and evaluates the progress and outcomes of operational plans; anticipates potential threats or opportunities.

5. **Problem Solving:** Identities and analyzes problems; distinguishes between relevant and irrelevant information to make logical decisions; provides solutions to individual and organizational problems.

6. Knowledge and understanding of the Treasury Enforcement Communication System (TECS) used in the **vetting process.**

4. How to Apply:

Note: This is a paper, fax, or hand-deliver application. If you mail it, you should send by FedEx, UPS, or another mail system that enables you to track the package.

You may mail your application to: TSA Recruitment Center, 2711 Jefferson Davis Highway, Suite 601, Code FPMI, Arlington, VA 22202. You may also fax your application to 1-888-275-5116. To verify receipt of your faxed application, please call 1-800-887-1895. If you need assistance or have questions, please contact Ben Elliott, HR Specialist, at (703) 415-7501, Ext. 324. Applicants who have a hearing impairment may contact TTY 1-800-887-5506 for further assistance. Application MUST BE RECEIVED by fax, mail, or delivered to the above address no later than the close of business on the closing date of this vacancy announcement.

Navy Resumix Announcement

This Navy announcement has a closing date. Some Navy announcements have an Open Continuous closing date (usually within 6 to 12 months). This is a resume-only announcement.

Department of the Navy
CIVILIAN HUMAN RESOURCES

No Limits, No Bounds

Civilian jobs that make a difference to our country and the world

Job Announcement Detail
To print this announcement, select your browser print button or click on your right mouse key and select the Print function.

To apply for this job announcement on-line, you must login to your account first.

You may do so by: (1) clicking the 'Login to CHART' button at the bottom of this page and (2) entering your account information in the submit form.

If you do not have an account, please return to the Homepage by clicking the 'Go to Homepage' button at the bottom of this page and complete the 'Create Account' process.

EDUCATION SERVICES SPECIALIST

GS-1740 -05, 09, 11, 12, 13, 14, 15
YA-1740-1, 2, 3
YC-1740-1, 2, 3
$24,075 - $133,988 per Annum

Announcement Number: DON1740   Open Date: 03/20/2006

Closing Date: OPEN CONTINUOUS

The Department of the Navy recruits talented people for a variety of occupations and grade levels throughout the world. We anticipate numerous vacancies for this position and we will maintain an inventory of high-caliber applicants to be referred when a vacancy occurs. When you apply under this announcement, your application will be placed in our candidate inventory and considered as vacancies become available. Because this announcement may be used to fill vacancies at various grade/pay levels and locations, be sure you clearly state your skills, all acceptable grade/pay level, and desired job locations when you apply.

Salary Range
$24,075 - $133,988 per Annum Based on the position

Job Location(s)

CA, Camp Pendleton ; CA, San Diego ; CT, Groton ; DC, Washington ; FL, Jacksonville ; FL, Mayport ; FL, Pensacola ; HI, Pearl Harbor ; IL, Great Lakes ; MA, Boston ; TN, Millington ; VA, Norfolk

About the Job

Apply your knowledge to benefit others. In this occupation you may supervise, lead or perform various professional educational duties to administer, promote, conduct, or evaluate programs and activities designed to provide individualized career-related or self-development education plans. You may also provide student-counseling services to establish educational and occupational objectives. Make a real difference in people's lives--apply now.

About Us

Want to know how the different Department of the Navy organizations work together to support our Nation's defense? Click on Major Claimants.

Job Benefits

The Department of the Navy offers a comprehensive benefits package that includes, in part, paid vacation, sick leave, holidays and a 401K-type retirement plan. Click here for additional details.

Who May Apply

You! If you are a current or former permanent Federal employee, are eligible for a Veterans' Employment Opportunity Act (VEOA), or a non-competitive hiring authority as defined on the Common Hiring Program Category Definitions, apply now.

How to Apply

It's easy! You can apply for this announcement on-line by simply clicking on the "Apply Now" button.

If you submit your resume through "Apply Now", it will normally be processed and available for vacancies filled by this announcement within two business days from receipt. You can verify that the processing is complete by viewing the "My Job Interests" area of your CHART account.

Department of the Navy is an equal employment opportunity employer.

Click here for other information and qualifications requirements for this job.

To apply for this job announcement on-line, you must login to your account first.

You may do so by: (1) clicking the 'Login to CHART' button below and (2) entering your account information in the submit form.

If you do not have an account, please return to the Homepage by clicking the 'Go to Homepage' button below and complete the 'Create Account' process.

[Login to CHART]   [Go to Homepage]   [Email to a Friend]

Deputy Assistant Secretary of the Navy (Civilian Human Resources)
This is an Official U.S. Navy Web Site

Figure 11.3: A sample Navy Resumix announcement.

EDUCATION SERVICES SPECIALIST

GS-1740-11

$54,272 - $70,558 per Annum

Announcement Number: SE6-1740-119612-DE

Open: 11/27/06

Closing Date: 12/01/2006

Salary Range: $54,272 - $70,558 per Annum

1. Major Duties:

⭐ **Note:** This position has seven major job responsibilities. To be Best Qualified for the job, make sure these seven skills are also covered in your Resumix.

---

1. The incumbent **supervises, directs and coordinates a staff of professional and para-professional support personnel** and provides the leadership necessary to maintain an effective and productive work force.

2. The incumbent serves as an **Education Services Officer** with the responsibility for **planning and developing** an installation-level Navy Voluntary Education Program at the National Naval Medical Center.

3. The incumbent directs the **development of programs** to meet installation educational needs; coordinates and negotiates with various civilian universities and educational institutions to **establish and conduct** educational programs within installation facilities and arranges off-base tuition assistance programs with local universities, colleges or educational institutions.

4. **Conducts assessments** of contract education delivery when directed. Provides academic and vocational counseling to active duty military personnel, and on a space available basis to their dependents.

5. **Evaluates logistical and personnel requirements** and **makes recommendations** to Area Manager.

6. **Manages the site Tuition Assistance system** and authorizes tuition assistance funds for eligible personnel. Serves as Test Control Officer or Alternate Test Control Officer with the responsibility for procurement, issue, control, use, inspection, disposition and security of all test items.

7. The incumbent must be able and willing to **in port** and **at sea** for periods of several days, including overnight stays away form homeport, when the need arises.

2. Qualifications and Specialized Experience:

Note: This section was not in this announcement.

3. How You Will Be Evaluated and KSAs:

Note: These KSAs should be covered in the text of your resume. These KSAs are very similar to the duties above.

Applicants should include sufficient information in their resume/application that demonstrates their experience, knowledge, skills, training, and/or education in the following:

1. Skill in developing and implementing educational programs.

2. Ability to manage educational programs and contracts.

3. Ability to lead, manage, and supervise paraprofessional employees.

4. Ability to communicate both orally and in writing.

5. Skill in applying academic counseling techniques/practices and knowledge of educational opportunities.

Hiring Organization

Naval Education and Training Professional

Voluntary Education Department, Northeastern Area Manager, NCEC National Naval Medical Center

4. How to Apply:

Note: To apply for this position, you will need a profile set up in the Navy CHART Resumix system. Then you can follow the directions to "self-nominate" for this position. It's pretty easy.

It's easy! You can apply for this announcement online by simply clicking on the "Apply Now" button. For hardcopy job application instructions, click here. Your job application must be received by the closing date.

Summary

Federal vacancy announcements are fairly long, but if you take your time and analyze critical sections, you can find the information you need to write the best possible federal resume for the position. The human resources specialists write detailed announcements to help you understand the job. You can use this information to your benefit. You can easily analyze the three announcements in this chapter by just carefully reviewing each duty, qualification, KSA, and question contained in the announcement. Take your time, focus, update your resume with keywords and skills, and you will stand a chance of being Best Qualified for your target position.

CHAPTER 12

Applying for Jobs with USAJOBS and Other Federal Resume Builders

The first 11 chapters of this book were focused on writing great content in your federal resume. Now it's time to structure that great content into the resume builder for your agency.

This chapter is dedicated to giving you an overview of the resume builders you will find during your federal job search and application process. The good news is that once you have one good federal resume, you can use that resume for all the resume builders—with some editing to fit the maximum character count of the builders' headings/fields.

> ⭐ **Tip:** Once you have a universal electronic resume written in your favorite software, you are ready to copy and paste into any resume builder (with some editing).

The resume builder headings lists for six resume builders will help you analyze your resume sections and fit your content into the builders. You can count your characters using Microsoft Word. Highlight the content that you would like counted. Select Tools, Word Count from the menu. You can count your characters with and without spaces.

These builder lists were designed to warn you that there is more than one resume builder and online application system. You will see that the federal agencies are using a variety of "how to apply" instructions, resume builder formats, character lengths, page lengths, and resume fields. You will be mixing and matching your resume sections into the resume builders. The important thing is to read the directions. The total application process beyond the resume builder might involve a Questionnaire, Supplemental Data Sheet, Core Questions, and faxing information to the HR office.

> ⭐ **Tip:** Read the directions for the Profile, Resume Builder, Questions, Supplemental Data Sheet, Fax Information, and Submit sections.

Maximize Your Use of the Resume Builders

Even though the resume builders are inflexible in terms of organization of resume information (the old paper federal resumes were much more flexible), they are the door to the supervisor and you should take time and effort to make your online resume look good. The samples in this book will show you techniques for improving content and readability of the words in your resume—even if the application is just a small field on a Web page.

Once you have your federal resume written, formatted like the samples in the book, and focused toward one or two occupational series, you are about 80 percent ready to apply for any job. The resume builder lists at the end of the chapter give an overview of the builders agencies are using today. This chart will be changing frequently, so don't be surprised if an agency has different instructions than published in this book. The QuickHire builders are changing to USAJOBS builders all the time. That's the most typical change the agencies are making right now. The QuickHire resume is a five-page resume, as is the USAJOBS resume. So the content will match. But the builder format is changing a lot.

If you count the characters of your Work Experience, Training, Awards, Additional Information, and other sections, you will be ready to edit slightly and copy and paste your content into the builders.

The USAJOBS Work Experience field is 3,000 characters. If your work experience description is 5,500 characters and you can't bear to delete anything, you can use two job blocks for job 1 in USAJOBS. Just type *continued in job block 2*. And then type: *CONTINUED-BUDGET ANALYST* in the job title section. This way the supervisor will know that the description in job 2 is a continuation of job 1.

The Most Popular Federal Resume Builders and Their Resume Headings

The most popular federal resume builders are listed in the following sections. We have collected the names of each of their resume sections and the number of characters that you can insert into each field. This is a handy guide for copying and pasting into many builders.

The Work Experience section is very important to the success of your federal resume. If you need more space than the characters allow, you can always continue your job description into the next job. Just type *CONTINUED* in front of the job title for the next job entry.

USAJOBS Resume Builder

USAJOBS is managed by Monster.com and is getting better all the time. The USAJOBS resume builder is almost mandatory for any federal job seeker. It's good to set up a My USAJOBS profile and submit a starter resume into the system. This way you can access questionnaires and further information easily.

The sections of the USAJOBS resume builder are the following:

1. Candidate Information.
2. Work Experience: You are allowed 3,000 characters per job block and can list an unlimited number of jobs.
3. Education.
4. Relevant Coursework, Licensures, and Certifications: 2,000 characters.
5. Job Related Training: 2,000 characters.
6. References.
7. Additional Language Skills.
8. Affiliations.
9. Professional Publications: 2,000 characters.
10. Additional Information: Job-related honors, awards, leadership activities, skills (such as computer software proficiency or typing speed), or any other information requested by a specific job announcement. You are allowed 22,000 characters (because some agencies will have you paste your KSAs here).

ability: Be sure to check off all your preferences.

ed Locations.

> **Tip:** Remember that when you update your current resume in any of the Resumix builders, it will overlay the old resume on file. The only builder that allows more than one resume version is USAJOBS.

QuickHire

QuickHire is owned by Monster.com and is located in Alexandria, Virginia. QuickHire manages recruitment, resume collection, and assessment of candidates for hundreds of federal agencies. You can recognize a QuickHire announcement and questionnaire by the word QuickHire in the Web address (URL). QuickHire applications are known for including both a resume and a questionnaire. The resume could be submitted into USAJOBS, or it could be submitted into the QuickHire database, depending on the agency announcement instructions. Just click on the Apply Now link and it will take you to either the QuickHire builder or the USAJOBS builder.

The sections of the QuickHire builder are the following:

1. User Information
2. Citizenship
3. Military Information
4. Work Experience: a total of 16,000 characters for all jobs
5. 25 yes/no questions about working for the federal government

After inserting your information into the resume builder, you answer the questions.

Avue Central

Avue Central is owned and operated Avue Digital Services. More than 25 federal agencies use the Avue system to collect resumes, assess candidates, and manage recruitment. If you submit your resume into Avue Central's resume builder, you can apply for jobs with any of its customer agencies. You can see the agency names by looking at the homepage: www.avuecentral.com. One of the best features of Avue Central's announcements is the position description that is also developed for the job.

Following are the headings for the Avue Central resume builder:

1. Personal Information.
2. Applicant Information.
3. Work History: 4,000 characters.
4. Eligibilities.
5. References.
6. Educational Background.
7. Relevant Information.
8. Awards, Community Service, Training, Certifications, Collateral Duties, Significant Details.
9. Other Considerations: Military Details.
10. Additional Information (no maximum character space is indicated).

11. Supporting Documentation: You can add files by browsing and uploading.

12. "Prepare a hard copy of my resume."

Resumix

Resumix is owned by Yahoo! HotJobs and is the only system where the HR specialist and supervisor search for the Best Qualified candidates with a set of keywords and skills for the position. This system is a keyword system, and you should carefully study the language in your resume to make sure you have included the correct keywords (see chapter 6 for more on keywords).

We describe the headings and characters for three Resumix builders in the following sections. These are the three largest DOD hiring agencies.

CPOL Resume Builder Headings

You can access the CPOL builder at www.cpol.army.mil. Headings for the builder are the following:

1. Contact Information.

2. Work Experience: 12,000 characters for all jobs.

3. Education: 2,000 characters for all education entries.

4. Additional Information (training, licenses, certifications, performance appraisals/ratings, awards, and so on): 6,000 characters for all information.

5. "Click here for worksheets:" You can click for worksheets, or simply copy and paste your content into the three fields above (that's much easier).

CHART Resume Builder Headings

You can access the CHART builder at https://chart.donhr.navy.mil/. Headings for this builder are the following:

1. Contact Information

2. Eligibility

3. Education

4. Work History: 7,500 characters

5. Other Work-Related History: Training, Licenses, and Certificates

6. Performance Ratings, Awards, Honors, and Recognitions: 1,500 characters

7. Other Information: 7,000 characters

8. U.S. Military Service

9. Additional Data Sheet

Air Force Personnel Center Resume Builder Headings

You can access the AFPC builder at https://ww2.afpc.randolph.af.mil/resweb/. Headings for this builder are the following:

1. Personal Information.

2. Summary of Skills: Enter all the actual skills you possess; for example, filing, Flash programming, budget preparations, spreadsheets, aircraft engine assemblies, T-38 engine repair, electrical motor fabrication, and so on. Limited to 1,500 characters, including spaces. Avoid using the Enter key, use Shift and Enter to begin the next text line.

3. Experience and Employment History: 1,500 characters, 6 jobs.

4. Licenses/Certificates: 300 characters.

5. Awards: 300 characters.

6. Other Information: 300 characters.

7. Education Requirements.

8. Supplemental Information.

Air Force Civilian Personnel System: Using Its Resume Writer Program

By Captain Donna L. de Wildt, President & Protocol Officer, Diplomatics, Inc.

The purpose of this article is to arm you with the hands-on facts you need in order to successfully and skillfully use the AF Resume Writer.

> **Note:** Only resumes submitted *electronically* using the AF Resume Writer may be updated online; mailed applications must be resubmitted each time a change is necessary. For mailed applications, allow seven business days **from the date of receipt at the AF Personnel center** for your data to be entered into the system for it to be effective. Resumes submitted electronically using the AF Resume Writer are normally available for updating within 24 hours. Updating is currently permitted once per day, but this is in the process of being changed to "anytime."

When exploring a civilian position with the United States Air Force, be forewarned that its application process using its preferred AF Resume Writer is the most restrictive of all the federal jobs application programs. You are very limited as to the amount and type of data you can submit. A predeveloped resume is prohibited from electronic submission through this program. You still have the option of mailing in your data, but it must follow the outline described in the AF Resume Writer Job Kit. The Kit can be found by entering https://ww2.afpc.randolph.af.mil/resweb/ in your browser; then click on the Job Kit link in the upper-left corner of the site. Study the Kit before beginning data entry.

> **Note:** You cannot Self-Nominate for a position until your resume has been accepted and entered into the AF Civilian Personnel system.

Each Work History block permits you to enter *only* 1,500 characters, meaning approximately one paragraph of data. If you exceed the 1,500-character limit, the system automatically truncates what you have written to meet the 1,500 character ceiling. There is no way to exceed it. How do we know this? We've used the system and tried circumventing its restrictions using every conceivable formula.

> ⭐ Tip: Prepare your Work History statements in Word, then save the file as a text document before transferring the data to its respective blocks in the Resume Writer. This gives you the opportunity to check the character count, spelling, and grammar in Word before making the data transfer. Be advised, though, that there is a varying discrepancy between the Word character count and the one in the Resume Writer. I don't need to tell you which one is less liberal!

Once you've entered your data for a specific block, it is imperative to place your cursor flush with the very last character of your written work for each entry and then press Delete. This will cancel out any stray characters outside of your 1,500-character paragraph. If you do not do this, it will cost you with the loss of usable character space.

> ⭐ Note: Until you get comfortable using the AF Resume Writer always save a copy of your data in Word before pressing the Delete key to cancel out stray characters and spaces. Yes, spaces count as characters.

Another caveat is the fact that you may have to justify up to nine, yes, nine KSAs (Knowledge, Skills, and Abilities) statements within the data. It is a difficult task given that you have the 1,500-character limitation per job. This is clearly spelled out in the Air Force Resume Writer Job Kit. By not following the Kit's instructions, you run the risk of not being considered for the vacancy you're applying for. Write your material as if you were writing a normal paragraph; bullet statements are not acceptable. Similarly, the blocks for Licenses/Certificates, Special Training, and Awards are limited to 300 characters each. Select your most relevant and important data for entry into these blocks.

This job applicant wrote to an HR specialist at the AF Personnel Center asking for any information about integrating the nine KSAs into the 1,500-character space for each job. This is the response she received:

> Each KSA question is not required to be written in your resume. We are aware of the KSA questions. Just the information relevant to the position is required to be referenced/covered in your work experience. Resumes should not be written to address a particular career field, unless that is the only career field you intend to apply for. Your resume should be all-inclusive and describe significant experience, education, and training.

Three Last Tips Concerning Deadlines and Apostrophes

I don't know the mechanics as to why the apostrophes in my defense document were converting to question marks in the final product, but they were. In addition, the accent marks in foreign words were completely eliminated from the document. What I finally did, that worked, was writing my material in Word and then saving it as a text document. I cut and pasted it from there into the official product.

It's also very important for interested candidates using the site to **not** wait until the closing date to finish their application; 48 hours prior is my suggestion for two primary reasons:

★ The site may go down for upgrades without notice at any time.

★ It takes at least 24 hours for an application to be fully processed once submitted.

Summary of Resume Builder Headings

As you can see from the preceding heading listings, the builders are similar but not the same. The only builder that gives space for a Summary at the beginning of the resume is the AF builder. The USAJOBS builder gives you 22,000 characters for Additional Information. We have reviewed six resume builders, but there are many more. When applying for jobs on USAJOBS, you will simply go to the Apply Now button and follow the directions.

Table 12.1: Federal Resume Builder Chart

Name of Agency Builder	Agency Jobs Web Site	Recruitment Name	Assessment	Questions?
Agriculture	www.usda.gov/da/ employ/director.htm	USAJOBS	Yes	Yes
Air Force	www.afpc.randolph.af.mil/resweb	AFPC/Resumix	No	KSAs in the res.
Army Civilian Personnel	www.cpol.army.mil	CPOL/Resumix	No	No
Avue Central	www.avuecentral.com	Avue Central	Yes	Yes
Bureau of Land Management	www.blm.gov/jobs/	BLM Jobs QuickHire	Yes	Yes
Central Intelligence Agency	www.cia.gov https://www.cia.gov/careers/index.html	CIA Builder	No	No
Citizenship	www.uscis.gov/	USAJOBS	Yes	No
Commerce	www.usajobs.gov	ACES QuickHire	Yes	Yes
Customs & Border Protection	www.cbp.gov/xp/cgov/careers/jobs/ entry_level_status.xml	CASS	Yes	Yes
Defense Contract Management Agency	www.dcma.mil/careers.htm	DCMA Careers/Resumix	No	No
Defense Finance & Accounting	www.dod.mil/dfas/careers.html	DFAS Careers/Resumix	No	No
Defense Logistics Agency	www.dla.mil https://sec.hr.dla.mil/apply/	Automated Staffing Prog. (ASP) Resumix	No	No
Defense Supply Agency	https://storm.psd.whs.mil/cgi-bin/apply.pl	HRSC Resumix	No	No
Education	https://storm.psd.whs.mil/cgi-bin/ apply.pl?action=PrepRes http://jobsearch.edhires.ed.gov	EdHIRESQuickHire	Yes	Yes

(conti

(continued)

Name of Agency Builder	Agency Jobs Web Site	Recruitment Name	Assessment	Resume Builders
Energy (National Security)	www.energy.gov/careers@energy.htm www.doe.gov/nationalsecurity/index.htm	DOEJOBS Paper	Yes	Yes
Environmental Protection Agency	www.epa.gov/ezhire/	EZ Hire, QuickHire	Yes	Yes
FAA	http://jobs.faa.gov/OnlineApplications.htm https://jobs.faa.gov/asap/	ASAP	Yes	Yes
FBI	www.fbijobs.gov www.fbijobs.gov/03.asp https://jobs1.quickhire.com/scripts/fbi.exe	FBIJOBS, QuickHire	Yes	Yes
FEMA	www.fema.gov/career	Paper	No	Yes
Forest Service	www.fs.fed.us/fsjobs/openings.html http://jobsearch.usajobs.opm.gov/a9fs.asp	Avue Central	Yes	Yes
General Accountability Office	www.gao.gov/jobopp.htm https://jobs.quickhire.com/scripts/gao.exe	GAO Careers/QuickHire	Yes	Yes
General Services Administration	www.gsa.gov (GSA Jobs link on right)	GSA Jobs/QuickHire	Yes	Yes
HHS Careers at Rockville	https://jobs.quickhire.com/scripts/hhs-rhrc.exe	USAJOBS/QuickHire	Yes	Yes
HHS National	www.usajobs.gov			
Homeland Security	www.dhs.gov/xabout/careers/	USAJOBS	Yes	Yes
Housing and Urban Development	www.hud.gov/jobs/index.cfm http://jobsearch.usajobs.opm.gov/a9hudp.asp	Paper	No	Yes
Interior	https://jobs1.quickhire.com/scripts/blm.exe	DOIJOBS/QuickHire	Yes	Yes

Name of Agency Builder	Agency Jobs Web Site	Recruitment Name	Assessment	Questions?
Justice	www.usdoj.gov www.avuecentral.com	Avue Central	Yes	Yes
Labor	www.dol.gov/dol/jobs.htm (read questions on Qualifications page, scroll down)	DOORS/USAJOBS	Yes	Yes
National Aeronautics and Space Administration	www.nasajobs.nasa.gov/	USAJOBS	Yes	Yes
National Security Agency	www.nsa.gov/home_ html.cfm (choose Careers)	NSA Careers	No	No
Navy CHART	https://www.donhr.navy.mil/	Navy CHART/Resumix	No	No
Office of Secretary of Defense	www.defenselink.mil/sites/ c.html#CivilianJobOpportunities	HRD Resumix	No	No
Peace Corps	www.avuecentral.com	Avue Central	Yes	Yes
Small Business Administration	www.usajobs.gov	Paper	No	No
State Department	http://careers.state.gov/	Gateway to State	Yes	Yes
Transportation	http://careers.dot.gov/	USAJOBS/QuickHire	Yes	Yes
Transportation Security Agency	www.usajobs.gov	Paper	No	Yes
U.S. Marshals Service	www.avuecentral.com	Avue Central	Yes	Yes
Veterans Administration	www.va.gov/jobs/Career_Search.asp www.va.gov/JOBS/hiring/apply/ vacancy.asp	Paper	KSAs	Yes

Disclaimer: Research for this spreadsheet was completed on December 2, 2006. Please know that resume builders, Web site addresses, methods of collecting resumes, and other information may change from week to week. We will attempt to stay up-to-date by posting this spreadsheet at www.resume-place.com/jsguide/resumebuilder. Please write Mark Hoyer with any new information that you may learn: resumebuilder@resume-place.com.

Summary

If you write your resume in Word, save it, date it, and count the characters, you will be ready to copy and paste it into federal resume builders and apply for federal jobs. Remember that there usually are two, three, or four steps to actually applying for the job: creating your profile, submitting your resume, answering questions, and faxing other information. Be sure to follow the directions. After the resume is in the resume builder, you can keep reading and find the Occupational Questions or other instructions. And at the end, don't forget to actually APPLY, SUBMIT, or SELF-NOMINATE for your job!

Part 5

Special Insight for Targeting Occupational Series

Science, Medicine, and Health Policy: Converting a Curriculum Vitae into a Federal Resume

By David Raikow, Ph.D.

This chapter examines the differences between a Curriculum Vitae (CV) and a federal resume. Then it gives step-by-step instructions for converting your CV to a federal resume. Then it gives other hints for crafting your federal resume and shows an example.

The Difference Between a CV and a Federal Resume

Although scientists and graduate students are very familiar with the Curriculum Vitae (CV), business resumes and federal resumes differ substantially from the CV. Whereas a business resume is usually limited to two pages and is highly focused or tailored to a job ad, the CV has no length limit and is meant to catalog the sum total of your experience. You can add a description of yourself in the form of a tagline or brief profile statement to a business resume; however, that type of information is usually included in the cover letter when you're using a CV to apply for scientific jobs outside of government. Business resumes are meant to be quickly scanned, whereas CVs are meant to be studied.

Both the format and actual information presented in a business resume vary widely. CVs in general have standard sections; additionally, discipline-specific CVs have their own standard sections. Federal resumes fall between these two extremes.

As a scientist or graduate student, you should already have a CV. Indeed, it's a good idea to update your CV every time you do something new such as publish, get a grant, or present a paper at a meeting. Some things never leave your CV (such as your publications); however, you might decide that other things are too old or are no longer relevant to include on your CV as you advance professionally (such as the committees you served on as a graduate student). Even then, it's a good idea to save those deleted items in a separate file because you never know when you'll need to remind yourself of what you actually did in the past (such as now, as you write a federal resume!). Building a CV is a continual process and should be taken seriously; that's why spending a few minutes to update it whenever necessary is important.

The good news is that it's easy to adapt your CV into a federal resume. CVs have standard sections, including contact information and affiliation, education, professional experience, publications, and so on. Some of these sections can go by different names. Whether you use a section labeled Professional

Activities or Academic Service; Teaching Experience or Courses Taught; Grants, Grants and Funding, Selected Grants, or Competitive Grants is not important here. You might even have sections that are not discussed here or sections that are particular to your field of study. Just match the sections discussed here with your own and follow the examples for sections with similar kinds of information in lieu of an exact match.

The following table is a quick comparison between what sections a typical CV contains and what a generic federal resume contains. However, in practice, scientists applying to science jobs can actually bend these rules to create a hybrid CV/federal resume (see "Why Scientific Federal Resumes Are Different," later in this chapter).

Curriculum Vitae	Generic Federal Resume
No length limit	Maximum of five pages
Contact information and affiliation	✔ + additional information
No objective	Objective
Research interests	Profile statement
Education	✔ + high school
Honors	✔
Grants	✔ (or incorporated into project descriptions)
Employment	✔ (combined with job or project descriptions)
Research experience	Project experience descriptions
Teaching experience	Usually incorporated into skills
Professional activities/academic service	Usually incorporated into skills
Extension and outreach/community service	Usually incorporated into skills
Current/professional memberships	✔
Certifications	✔
Contributed papers/presentations at meetings	✔
Collaborators	No, incorporated into project descriptions
Students advised	No, incorporated into skills if relevant
References	No, usually asked for separately
Book reviews/other publications	✔ (or incorporated in skills)
Scientific publications	✔ (or a summary)
Skill lists by class	✔

Section-by-Section Conversion Instructions

The following sections step you through converting each section of your CV to a federal resume.

Contact Information and Affiliation

Use your name, affiliation, and contact information as you would on a CV, but add your citizenship, Social Security number, Veterans' Preference, and federal civilian status (they're required as "compliance" information).

Objective

State the position for which you are applying, including title and job application reference number, just below your contact information.

Profile Statement

Include a Profile statement just below your objective. State what kind of scientist you are; in other words, your fields of expertise and the kind of experience you have. This is your first opportunity to include keywords from the announcement (See chapter 5, "Focusing Strategies: Top Skills, Profile Statements, and Specialized Qualifications.") Also state how many years of hands-on experience you have, if it is over four years.

Education

List your degrees, majors, and school name as you would on a CV, but add the school city, state, and ZIP code.

Honors

List your fellowships, awards, and honors as you would on a CV.

Grants

These can be listed as you would on a CV if you want to highlight them. Otherwise, you can incorporate grants into the project descriptions (see "Project Experience Descriptions" later in this chapter) if you don't have many or are a graduate student.

Employment

List your positions but add descriptions of your duties. This is where you must add keywords or phrases from the job announcement. You shouldn't need to embellish here; after all, you should be applying for jobs for which you have relevant experience. You will, however, need to phrase your descriptions so that the human resources personnel who are grading your application can see that you are indeed qualified. (See chapter 2 for more on writing work experience descriptions.) Working on expanding job duties can also help to identify roles you've played during your career that can also be summarized in the Profile section.

If you're a graduate student or a recent graduate, delete the Employment section and highlight your experience under the Project Descriptions section.

Research Experience

It can be useful to organize your scientific or technical experience in terms of the major projects you have undertaken. Many scientists early in their careers do this in their CVs. In federal resumes, project experience descriptions can substitute for a series of specific jobs or job titles that you don't have. The concept is the same as describing previous jobs. You need to name the project, state where you conducted it, state when you conducted it, state the number of hours a week you spent on it, and describe what you did. (See chapter 2, "Work Experience: The Most Important Section of Your Resume.") You might also have other relevant experience, such as a college internship, which could have its own separate section and short description.

Teaching Experience

Unless the job is a teaching position or contains a major teaching component, you can incorporate teaching experience into your skill lists (see "Skill Lists by Class" later in this chapter).

Professional Activities or Service

Professional Activities can be incorporated into skill lists or job descriptions. However, if you have a lot of experience here, you can use a section much like a CV (see "Why Scientific Federal Resumes Are Different," later in this chapter. If the advertised position is administrative, you can include a specific Administrative Skill List (see "Skill Lists by Class" later in this chapter).

Extension and Outreach

Extension and Outreach or Community Service can be incorporated into skill lists or job descriptions. If you have a lot of experience, however, you can create a separate section.

Current Memberships in Societies or Professional Organizations

List your memberships as you would on a CV.

Certifications

List your certifications as you would on a CV.

Presentations Given at Meetings or Conferences

Some people list all of their presentations by title complete with authors, formatted like a bibliographic reference on their CV. I don't recommend this because it takes up a lot of space, especially if you have given many presentations, and is difficult to glean information from. I recommend a two-part listing. First, list the name of the society or meeting followed by the years in which you have given presentations. Then create a short listing of talks with titles, meetings, years, and coauthors. The trick is to format the listing so that it can be quickly scanned.

Collaborators

You can name collaborators if relevant within job or project descriptions, or create a separate list. Lists of collaborators are now commonly seen in CVs.

Students Advised or Mentored

You can list your students in a separate section, or summarize your mentoring activities within a skill list.

References

Some people include a list of references in their CVs. Employers usually ask for lists of references separate from the resume. This is often the case for government positions, but you can include a list of professional references.

Book Reviews, Non-scientific, or Non-peer-reviewed Publications

You might want to list such publications on your federal resume as you would on your CV. Use your field's standard notational format. You could alternatively summarize this type of writing within skill lists, unless the job description specifically calls for this kind of experience.

Scientific or Peer-Reviewed Publications

List your peer-reviewed publications as you would on a CV, in standard format. Include papers in review.

Skill Lists by Class

As a scientist, you have amassed many skills. Chances are, though, you've never had to actually think about it and list them all. Listing your skills can take some time, but it is extremely important in the federal resume. These skill lists can be presented in the federal resume as either individual top-level sections or subsections within a section labeled "Skills." Skill lists are very useful for graduate students and those who are at an early stage in their career.

I recommend grouping your skills into classes that are relevant to your field of study and the job announcement. For example, you might have laboratory skills, field-data-collection skills, and computer skills. You might want to group specific types of computer skills together. It's up to you. The different skill sets you organize give you a chance to creatively customize your federal resume to yourself and the job announcement.

To figure out exactly what skills you have, I recommend walking through the steps of the various projects that you have done and cataloging the skills necessary to do each step. For example, an ecologist might have studied the ecosystem of a stream. In order to do this, she took water samples, measured temperature and other parameters, collected organisms, and brought them back to the lab for analysis. Later she compiled her data and analyzed it. What specific skills were necessary to do all this? She had to collect water samples without contaminating them. She had to run specific chemical tests in the lab. She had to know how to collect specific organisms, handle them, identify them, and preserve them. She had to manage her data in spreadsheets or databases and then analyze them statistically. The skill set derived from this project and listed on the federal resume will be specific and lengthy, and perhaps will contain discipline-specific terminology (more on jargon in the next section). Be careful not to lump different skills under general titles. For example, "microscopy" is too vague. Instead, do you know how to prepare samples for microscopy, operate specific types of microscopes, identify microscopic organisms or tissues, or all of these things?

You should also include a section or sections that describe your communication skills and experience. In this section, include your writing skills (grants, reports, protocols, papers, and so on); oral presentation skills (workshops, presentations at national meetings or conferences, guest lectures, and so on); teaching (unless it's in a separate section); and interactions with the public, the media, and students.

Other Hints for Crafting Your Federal Resume

There are a few other considerations to keep in mind as you convert your CV into a federal resume. These include tailoring the writing to your audience and compensating for a lack of formal experience outside of college.

Balancing Jargon and Clarity

Scientists are used to speaking in their own technical language. The problem is that the people who evaluate applications are not scientists. Indeed, your application will be evaluated by human resources personnel who will not have technical training in your discipline. If the HR personnel cannot understand the language you use, you might not be rated as highly as you could be. So, make it easy for them to understand your qualifications. At the same time, it is probably impossible to adequately describe your experience without some degree of technical specificity. Also, once you get past the first cut, your federal resume will be evaluated by someone with scientific or technical training. Additionally, resumes might be scanned for technical keywords. Thus, it is important to balance technical language or jargon with clarity for non-scientists.

You can achieve balance between jargon and clarity in several ways.

★ First, scan the job announcement for keywords and phrases, and use them to describe your experience. Again, you don't need to embellish if you are applying for a job for which you have relevant experience and which is at the appropriate GS-level. You're simply choosing to phrase your experience so that the HR personnel can recognize it.

★ Second, simplify the titles of projects if they are very technical. If you are using project descriptions, title the projects descriptively, but more simply than publication titles. For example, a project entitled "Cellular mechanisms of protein transport" can be better than "Binding homologue identification using affinity purification in lymphocytes." You can then be more detailed and technical in the description as well as in your KSAs. The exception would be if technical keywords are present in the announcement.

★ Third, if the job announcement calls for knowledge of something specific, such as statistics, do not simply list the statistical tests with which you have experience. Instead, say "statistical analysis" in a skill list, and then briefly list the tests you have performed, grouped, and identified by type.

★ Fourth, be sure to expand all acronyms at their first use. Each discipline, region, department, and lab has its own "alphabet soup," so don't assume others will understand it.

Graduate Students and Recent Grads Versus Established Scientists

Graduate students or recent graduates face some issues that established scientists do not. Foremost is the fact that you have spent all your time in graduate school and not in different jobs with separate titles. To deal with this, list your experience as specific projects you've undertaken. If you don't have many grants, you can delete the Grants section and incorporate the grants you have into project descriptions to deemphasize having few grants. Another issue is how to quantify your hands-on experience. The human resources personnel who will evaluate your application have strict guidelines concerning the calculation of time spent on the job. If you've just graduated, how do you quantify your experience in terms of hours spent per week? The solution is to count the semesters that you have been earning graduate-level credits for research and total them into years. You can count this as full-time work experience (40 hours per week) and your statements are supported by your transcripts.

All federal resumes should include narrative descriptions of past jobs or projects. But as scientists advance and gain experience, their skill sets increase, and established scientists might find that listing all their skills is redundant with detailed job or project descriptions. Because you should avoid redundancy in your federal resume, I recommend that you reach a balance between skill lists and narrative descriptions. Scientists early in their careers should certainly have narrative descriptions, but they should stress skill lists. As you advance, the number and size of narrative descriptions should increase while skill lists become smaller and more general. Established scientists should have a minimum of skill lists, if any. In addition, the Major Accomplishments section is best used by more senior-level scientists. If you include a Major Accomplishments section early in your career, it might backfire by implying that, for example, all you've done is get your degree.

Why Scientific Federal Resumes Are Different

Many federal scientific job and post-doctoral announcements specifically call for CVs. Moreover, you might cringe at the thought of having to pare down your experience and accomplishments into five pages or so, especially if you are at a senior level. If that weren't enough, you're probably also applying for academic positions and do not relish having to continually update and adapt two documents. Don't sweat it; there is a solution.

Scientific federal resumes are different because common practices in science are not present in other careers. All federal scientists started in academia in order to obtain advanced degrees. As such, all federal scientists are familiar with CVs, just like you. In fact, some permanent scientific jobs, term-positions, and post-docs in the federal government are evaluated as academic jobs are, complete with giving a seminar, meeting the primary investigators of a lab, interviews, and comments concerning applicants solicited from the scientific staff. Such a gauntlet usually follows evaluation and ranking by HR personnel, of course. Such rigorous interviews are allowable because many of these jobs are in the Excepted Service, which allows nonstandard selection procedures. Some jobs like post-docs in the Excepted Service have simple procedures, such as submitting a CV or resume and cover letter. Selecting officials are usually the scientists you will be working with, and hence are not expecting you to limit your resume to five pages or so. Indeed, for those with more experience, limiting your resume to five pages will be detrimental to your application.

The solution is to create a hybrid CV/federal resume. This document allows you more freedom than a generic federal resume, and can be used for federal and academic job applications. Hybrids look like federal resumes in that they have a summarizing first page (see chapter 4, "Additional Information"). Hybrids also have detailed descriptions of job duties and roles, and contain all the sections a generic federal resume would. But hybrids also contain any section you would normally include in a CV (without repeating information), and can be as long as you like. It is still vital, however, that you include all required compliance information and make other information easy to glean.

Example Federal Resume/Curriculum Vitae

Here is real example of a hybrid CV/federal resume.

This CV/federal resume contains more work experience than a traditional CV. Shortening it into a generic federal resume would reduce your chances of landing a job. Note the Profile section, which has been subdivided by roles. The Professional Experience section is organized by job and then project. Note the use of sentence fragments in active voice. Previous experience still contains a skill list. Papers Contributed as Primary Author is an example of the two-part format. Other sections are formatted for the federal resume, but there are more than would be typical of a generic federal resume. The length, at 10 pages, makes it more like a CV.

Target Job: Aquatic Ecologist, GS-0408-12 from current position as Research Aquatic Biologist, GS-0401-11.
Resume Format: Federal Paper resume/CV hybrid.
Federal to federal career promotion.

David F. Raikow, Ph.D.

123 Plymouth Rd, Ann Arbor, MI 48123
(123) 456-7890 (Cell), david.raikow@email.gov
Citizenship: U.S., SSN: 000-00-0000, Veteran's Preference: N/A
Federal Civilian Status: Research Aquatic Biologist, GS-0401-11, November 2003-present
Position: Aquatic Ecologist/Ecologist

PROFILE

Research Aquatic Biologist: ESA Certified Ecologist; invasion biology, stream ecology, ecosystem ecology, aquatic biology, limnology, landscape ecology, community ecology, stable isotopes, food webs, biogeochemistry, ecotoxicology.

Scientific Primary Investigator (PI): Initiate, design, and lead biological research programs; write grant proposals; create new methodologies and adapt existing methodologies to test new hypotheses; hire and supervise support staff; implement QA/QC measures; manage and explore data using spreadsheets and databases; statistically analyze data using standard, multivariate, and geospatial statistics; publish results in peer-reviewed primary scientific journals, present results at conferences.

Agency Representative: Represent NOAA, GLERL, and the NOAA National Center for Research on Aquatic Invasive Species at scientific and regulatory workshops, meetings, and conferences; confer and build new relationships with federal and state agencies and organizations; critique scientific merit of proposed federal regulations.

Writer and Speaker: Write budgets, protocols, status reports, book reviews, book proposals, book chapters, and books; critique scientific manuscripts; critique grant proposals; present complex scientific concepts to scientists, untrained audiences, congressional delegates, and the media; teach students; create and present seminars and workshops for lay people.

EDUCATION

Ph.D.	2002	Ecology, Evolutionary Biology and Behavior (EEBB) and Zoology (dual degree), Department of Zoology and W. K. Kellogg Biological Station, Michigan State University, East Lansing, MI 48824; Advisor: Stephen K. Hamilton; Dissertation: "How the Feeding Ecology of Native and Exotic Mussels Affects Freshwater Ecosystems."
M.S.	1996	Biological Sciences, Ecology and Evolution Program, Department of Biological Sciences, University of Pittsburgh, Pittsburgh, PA 15260; Advisor: William Coffman; Thesis: "Macroinvertebrate Diversity and Substrate Heterogeneity in Linesville Creek."
B.S.	1993	Biological Sciences, Department of Biological Sciences, University of Pittsburgh; Advisor: Kenneth W. Cummins; Senior Thesis: "Factors That Affect Coarse Particulate Organic Matter Retention in an Appalachian Mountain Stream."
B.A.	1993	History and Philosophy of Science (HPS), University of Pittsburgh.
Diploma	1988	Center for Advanced Study, Peabody High School, Pittsburgh, PA 15206.

PROFESSIONAL CERTIFICATIONS

Certified Ecologist, Ecological Society of America	2003
Certified in Teaching College Science and Mathematics, Michigan State University	2002

1

(continued)

(continued)

David F. Raikow, Ph.D.

PROFESSIONAL EXPERIENCE

RESEARCH AQUATIC BIOLOGIST, *GS-0401-11, step 3*   45 hrs. per week
November 2003 to Present $59,615
Great Lakes Environmental Research Laboratory (GLERL)   Supervisor: Dr. Peter F. Landrum
National Oceanic and Atmospheric Administration (NOAA)   Contact supervisor? Yes
2205 Commonwealth Blvd., Ann Arbor, MI 48105-2945   (123) 456-7890

Primary Investigator (PI)
- Apply knowledge as subject matter expert in aquatic ecology.
- Create and manage research programs.
- Collect, explore, manage, and analyze data; present and publish results.

Assigned Projects:

"Resting Eggs in Ship Ballast Tanks—An Unaddressed Secondary Invasion Vector"
- Learn ecotoxicological methodology and then design and implement a research program.
- Analyze the dose-response of aquatic invertebrate resting eggs to biocides using bioassays.
- Evaluate efficacy of treating commercial ship ballast tanks to prevent new biological invasions.
- Accomplishments: Created new methods for the scientific evaluation of the effect of stressors on aquatic invertebrate resting eggs; published results in a peer-reviewed scientific journal.

"NOBOB-2: Identifying, Verifying, and Establishing Options for Best Management Practices"
- Sample ship ballast tanks in the field.
- Conduct laboratory experiments.

"National Center for Research on Aquatic Invasive Species (NCRAIS)"
- Represent NCRAIS, GLERL, and NOAA at scientific and regulatory meetings.
- Evaluate, prioritize, and recommend invasive species research priorities.
- Analyze and critique scientific merit of proposed federal regulations.
- Interact with federal agencies (USGS, EPA, NASA, FWS, Sea Grant, Coast Guard), universities (Michigan, Michigan State, Windsor, Toledo, Purdue), non-gov't. orgs (Great Lakes Commission).

"Great Lakes Aquatic Nonindigenous Species Information System (GLANSIS)"
- Develop, plan, and create the first "one-stop" resource of biological information on Great Lakes exotic species by using advanced distributed database technology.
- Obtained $35K grant from the Great Lakes Fisheries Trust.

Original Projects:

"Forecasting Resource Sheds in Lake Erie"
- Create original research thrust; initiate new interdisciplinary collaboration.
- Model geographic extent of the areas providing resources to point locations (resource sheds) using novel hindcasting applications of circulation (particle tracking) models (Dr. Joseph Atkinson, University at Buffalo) and novel applications of watershed flow models (Dr. Tom Croley, GLERL).

"Spatial Patterns of Stable Isotope Signatures in Sediments of Lake Erie"
- Collaborator, Erie Comprehensive Collaborative Study (ECCS).
- Conduct spatial analysis of stable isotope distribution in Lake Erie sediments.

"Spatio-Temporal Patterns of Zooplankton Community Structure in Lake Erie"
- New research thrust as Co-PI of the International Field Years on Lake Erie (IFYLE).

"Expansion of Great Lakes Summer Student Fellowship Program"
- Initiated enhancement of the 28-student intern program to include a four-part seminar series (2005).
- Created and occupy role as ombudsman.

2

David F. Raikow, Ph.D.

PROFESSIONAL SERVICE

Panels and Symposia:
- Alternate NOAA Representative to the Great Lakes Aquatic Nuisance Species Panel, 2005.
- Invited Panelist and Speaker on Invasive Species Research Priorities: IAGLR conference forum "Great Lakes Research Needs," sponsored by MI Department of Environmental Quality, 2005.
- Invited Participant: "Aquatic Nuisance Species and the Disruption of the Great Lakes Food Web Symposium," sponsored by the National Wildlife Federation, 2005.
- Invited Participant: "Aquatic Invasive Species Database Summit," 2005.
- Invited Participant: "NOAA Aquatic Invasive Species Retreat," 2005.
- Participant: "AIS Rapid Response Workshop," Great Lakes Commission, 2004.
- Participant: "Lake Erie Science Planning Workshop," GLERL, 2004.
- Participant: "National Ecological Observation Network Workshop," Kellogg Biological Station, 2004.
- Attendee: "Great Lakes—Baltic Sea Invasive Species Symposium," 2004.
- Attendee: "Great Lakes Aquatic Nuisance Species Panel Meeting," 2004.
- Attendee: "Lake Erie Center Research Coordination Workshop," 2004.

Written Contributions:
- NOAA Aquatic Invasive Species Program Five-Year Strategic Plan, 2006.
- Aquatic Invasive Species Research Priorities, Great Lakes ANS Panel, 2004.
- Control and Management Research Priorities, NOAA AIS Research Strategy Workshop, 2004.
- International Maritime Organization (IMO) Ballast Water Organism Mitigation Standards, Ballast Water Technology Type Testing Regulations, and Draft Guidelines for Ranking Invasive Species Projects in Natural Areas. Technologies, U.S. Coast Guard, 2004.

Invited Seminars:
- "Biological Invasions in the Great Lakes: Science, Policy, and Management," Great Lakes Research Planning Workshop, Purdue University, 2004.
- "Biological Invasions in the Great Lakes: Science, Policy, and Management," NOAA Great Lakes Seminar Series, GLERL, 2004.
- "Newly Discovered and Corroborated Deleterious Effects of Zebra Mussels on Lake Ecosystems," GLERL, 2003.
- "The Lotic Intersite Nitrogen eXperiment (LINX)," Department of Biological Sciences, University of Pittsburgh, 2001.

Manuscript Review:
- *Limnology and Oceanography, Journal of the North American Benthological Society, Wetlands, Hydrobiologia, Marine Biology, Journal of Great Lakes Research, Marine Ecology Progress Series.*

Proposal Review:
- NOAA Sea Grant, NOAA Great Lakes Ecosystem Research, Cooperative Institute for Coastal and Estuarine Environmental Technology, GLERL International Field Years on Lake Erie.

Symposium and Workshop Organization:
- Environmental Science Careers Seminar Series. Created and presented a four-part seminar series for college and graduate students, GLERL, 2005.
- NOAA Aquatic Invasive Species Research Strategy Workshop. Lead the Control and Management breakout workgroup, 2004.
- Stable Isotopes in Aquatic Food Web Research: Pitfalls and Potentials. Proposed, created, and led a workshop at the LTER All-Scientist Meeting, 2001.
- First Biennial Western Pennsylvania Symposium of Ecologists, Evolutionary Biologists, and Systematists. Co-organized and co-hosted meeting at the Carnegie Powdermill Nature Reserve, 1995.

University Service:
- Student representative to faculty, Kellogg Biological Station, 2001-2002.
- Lecturer to Congressional delegates on biological invasion during a site review, 2000.

3

(continued)

(continued)

David F. Raikow, Ph.D.

PREVIOUS EXPERIENCE

RESEARCH ASSISTANT / GRADUATE STUDENT, August 1996 to August 2002, 50–60 hrs. per week, $17,000, Supervisor: Dr. Stephen Hamilton, Contact Supervisor? Yes: (123) 456-7890, Michigan State University (MSU), Kellogg Biological Station (KBS), 3700 East Gull Lake Rd., Hickory Corners, MI 49060

Aquatic Ecologist
- Applied knowledge of community ecology, ecosystem ecology, biogeochemistry, and landscape ecology.
- Designed, executed, analyzed, documented, presented, and published aquatic ecological research studies.
- Designed laboratory and field experiments including environmental monitoring of aquatic ecosystems.
- Wrote grant proposals and budgets.
- Organized data in spreadsheets; extracted data from databases using queries.
- Applied basic, multivariate, and geospatial statistics using SAS, SPSS, Systat, and GS+.
- Measured physical ecosystem parameters of streams, lakes, and wetlands.
- Sampled water, organic matter, suspended sediment, sediment cores, and sediment traps.
- Conducted in-situ tracer additions in aquatic ecosystems.
- Collected and analyzed stable isotopes.
- Collected fish, benthic macroinvertebrates, mussels, zooplankton, periphyton, and phytoplankton.
- Identified benthic macroinvertebrates, mussels, zooplankton, and phytoplankton.
- Analyzed chlorophyll, dissolved and particulate carbon, nitrogen, and phosphorus nutrient species.
- Used HPLC, GC, IC, CHN Analyzer, Spectrophotometer, and Mass Spectrometer.

Projects:
"How the Feeding Ecology of Native and Exotic Mussels Affects Freshwater Ecosystems"
- Ph.D. dissertation.
- Discovered dominance of the toxic alga *Microcystis aeruginosa* in zebra mussel-invaded lakes.
- Identified competitive interactions between zebra mussels and larval fish.

"The Lotic Intersite Nitrogen eXperiment (LINX)"
- Supported stream food web and nutrient cycling experiments and created three new experiments.
- Identified organic matter subsidy to stream mussels from wetlands in complex watershed.

"Long-Term Ecological Research (LTER)"
- Collected samples and measured parameters for long-term monitoring of aquatic ecosystems.

GRADUATE STUDENT, August 1994 to July 1996, 50-60 hrs. per week, $15,000, Supervisor: Dr. William Coffman, Contact Supervisor? Yes: (123) 456-7890, Department of Biological Sciences, University of Pittsburgh, Pittsburgh, PA 15260

Aquatic Ecologist

Project:
"Stream Macroinvertebrate Diversity and Substrate Heterogeneity"
- M.S. Thesis.
- Designed, executed, analyzed, documented, and presented ecological study; supervised assistants.

WRITER, November 2002 to August 2004, 5-20 hrs. per week, $40 per hr. (commission), Supervisor: Kathryn Troutman, Contact Supervisor? Yes: (888) 480-8265, The Resume Place, 89 Mellor Ave., Baltimore, MD 21228

Certified Federal Job Search Trainer and Resume Writer
- Wrote federal resumes, business resumes, KSAs, SES ECQs, etc.
- Organized and ran public seminar and workshop at the Carnegie Library of Pittsburgh.

4

David F. Raikow, Ph.D.

PAPERS CONTRIBUTED AS PRIMARY AUTHOR

International Association for Great Lakes Research (IAGLR) Conference	2005, 2006
International Conference on Aquatic Invasive Species (ICAIS)	2004, 2006
Great Lakes Regional Data Exchange (RDX) Conference	2004
Ecological Society of America (ESA) Annual Conference	1997, 2000, 2002
North American Benthological Society (NABS) Annual Conference	1993, 1997, 1999, 2000, 2001
Long-Term Ecological Research (LTER) All Scientist Meeting	2000
Freshwater Mollusk Conservation Society (FMCS) Symposium	1999

"Resource Shed Delineation in Lake Erie"
    2006   IAGLR   Poster   D.F. Raikow, J.F. Atkinson, T.E. Croley

"Sensitivity of Aquatic and Invertebrate Resting Eggs to Proposed Ballast Tank Treatment Methods"
    2006   ICAIS   Poster   D.F. Raikow, D.F. Reid, P. Landrum

"Great Lakes Aquatic Invasive Species Research Priorities"
    2005   IAGLR   Invited Presentation D.F. Raikow

"Great Lakes Aquatic Nonindigenous Species Information System"
    2004   RDX   Presentation   D.F. Raikow

"Acute Toxicity of SeaKleen (Menadione) to Zooplankton Diapausing Eggs"
    2004   ICAIS   Presentation   D.F. Raikow, D.F. Reid, P. Landrum, H. Vanderploeg, S. Constant

"Dominance of the Cyanobacterium *M. aeruginosa* in Low-Nutrient Lakes as Associated with Zebra Mussels"
    2004   ICAIS   Presentation   D.F. Raikow, O. Sarnelle, A.E. Wilson, S.K. Hamilton

"Zebra Mussel Impacts on Phytoplankton Across a Productivity Gradient in Michigan Lakes"
    2002   ESA   Presentation   D.F. Raikow, O. Sarnelle, S.K. Hamilton, A.E. Wilson

"The Promises and Problems of Using Stable Isotopes to Study Unionid Diets"
    2001   NABS   Poster   D.F. Raikow, S.K. Hamilton

"Competition for Food Between Zebra Mussels and Larval Bluegill"
    2000   ESA   Poster   D.F. Raikow

"An Examination of Stream Bivalves and Their Food Resources Using Stable Isotopes"
    2000   NABS   Poster   D.F. Raikow, S.K. Hamilton

"Nitrogen Uptake in Newly Conditioned Stream Organic Matter"
    2000   LTER   Poster   D.F. Raikow

"Nitrogen Uptake in Newly Conditioned Stream Organic Matter"
    1999   NABS   Poster   D.F. Raikow

"The Contribution of Unionids to Nitrogen Cycling in a Stream Ecosystem"
    1999   FMCS   Poster   D.F. Raikow

"Macroinvertebrate Diversity and Substrate Heterogeneity in Stream Riffles"
    1997   ESA   Poster   D.F. Raikow

"Macroinvertebrate Diversity and Substrate Heterogeneity in Stream Riffles"
    1997   NABS   Presentation   D.F. Raikow

"Coarse Particulate Organic Matter Retention in an Appalachian Mountain Stream"
    1993   NABS   Poster   D.F. Raikow, S.A. Grubbs, K.W. Cummins

5

(continued)

(continued)

David F. Raikow, Ph.D.

TEACHING EXPERIENCE

Teaching College Science and Mathematics Certificate Program, MSU, 2002:
- Class: Teaching College Science, NSC 870.
- 10 Workshops: Planning a Course, Pedagogical Changes, A Model for the Systematic Introduction of Ethics, Designing Group Experiences, Academic Myths We Live By, Finding a Job, Grading Papers, Choosing Tools, Online Cheating, Web Site Building
- Mentored Teaching Project: "Improving Links Between the Elements of a Field Ecology Course."

Guest lecture: "The Ecology of Biological Invasions," for the graduate course Community and Ecosystem Ecology, Michigan State University, 2000–2004.

Classes Taught:
- Genetics: Recitation instructor.
      Led discussions, answered questions, wrote and evaluated quizzes, graded tests, 2000–2002.
- Ecology Lab: Michigan State University and University of Pittsburgh.
      Ran campus-based labs, assisted in field-based courses, 1995, 2001.
- Ecology: Michigan State University and University of Pittsburgh field stations.
      Assisted lecture classes, wrote and evaluated tests, 1995, 2001.
- Ecology of Fishes: Assisted University of Pittsburgh field course, 1996.
- Introductory Biology Lab: Michigan State University and University of Pittsburgh.
      Ran labs, created tests, evaluated student presentations, 1994–1997.

HONORS

Fellowship, Graduate Research Training Group (RTG), Michigan State University.	1997–1999
Graduation Cum Laude, University of Pittsburgh	1993
Departmental Honors, Biological Sciences, University of Pittsburgh	1993
Departmental Honors, History and Philosophy of Science, University of Pittsburgh	1993

PROFESSIONAL MEMBERSHIPS

International Association for Great Lakes Research	joined in 2005
American Society of Limnology and Oceanography	joined in 2000
Ecological Society of America	joined in 1997
North American Benthological Society	joined in 1993

CONTINUING EDUCATION

Advanced Conservation GIS	32 hrs.	Smithsonian Conservation and Research Center	2006
Introduction to ArcGIS I	16 hrs.	ESRI	2005
Introduction to ArcGIS II	24 hrs.	ESRI	2005
Microsoft Access I	8 hrs.	Washtenaw Community College	2004
Microsoft Access II	8 hrs.	Washtenaw Community College	2004

OUTREACH and COMMUNITY SERVICE

National Ocean Science Bowl, Moderator, Science Judge	2004–2006
International Science and Engineering Fair, Grand Awards Judge	2000–2006
Interviewee for newspapers, television, and radio concerning biological invasion	2000–2005
Invited Speaker, Lego Robotics Teams, Women in Science Program, University of Michigan	2005
Consultant for *Minneapolis Star Tribune* invasive species list	2004
Volunteer in the NOAA booth at the Detroit International Boat Show	2004
Lecturer on biological invasion at local community groups such as the Rotary Club	2000–2001
Mentor to 7th grader with school project: "Will Turtles Eat Zebra Mussels?"	1998
Emergency Medical Technician, Medical Supply Officer, Secretary: Foxwall EMS	1989–1992

6

David F. Raikow, Ph.D.

GRANTS AS PROJECT LEADER

Pending:

$ 2,499,620	Submitted	NOAA Ecofore Program "Forecasting Potential Spread of Introduced Species"
$ 284,218	Submitted	NOAA Ecofore Program "Forecasting Resource Sheds"
$ 500,000	Pre-proposal	Great Lakes Protection Fund "Using Ecological Forecasting to Prioritize Aquatic Invasive Species Prevention Efforts and Inform Policy"
$ 150,000	Pre-proposal	NY Sea Grant "Resource Shed Delineation in Lake Ontario and Lake Erie"
$ 120,000	Pre-proposal	Great Lakes Fishery Commission "Role of Artificial Waterways as Pathways for AIS"
$ 103,550	Pre-proposal	Great Lakes Fishery Commission "Mapping Resource Sheds in Lake Erie"

External:

$ 35,000	Funded 2005	Great Lakes Fisheries Trust "Great Lakes Aquatic Nonindigenous Species Information System"
$ 21,650	Funded 1999	Kalamazoo Community Foundation "Can the Zebra Mussel Suppress Bluegill and Promote Microcystis?"

GLERL Internal (excludes pay, benefits, overhead, and vessel expenses):

$ 18,800	2006	Resting Egg, GLANSIS, Resource Sheds, IFYLE Continuation
$ 11,500	2005	Stable Isotope Analysis of the Lake Erie Food Web, IFYLE
$ 7,000	2004	Resting Egg and GLANSIS Continuation

Student:

$ 600	1997	Sigma-Xi, "Migration Patterns of Emergent Stream Insects"
$ ~ 6,000	1996-2002	MSU: EEBB, RTG, Zoology Dept., Lauff Research Award, etc.
$ 900	1995	McKinley Research Fund, University of Pittsburgh
$ 1,000	1993	Howard Hughes Medical Institute, University of Pittsburgh

7

(continued)

(continued)

David F. Raikow, Ph.D.

COLLABORATORS

Al-asam, Ihsan	Dept. of Earth Sciences, University of Windsor
Alexandrov, Borys	Odessa Branch, Institute of Biology of the Southern Seas, Ukraine
Atkinson, Joseph	Great Lakes Program, University at Buffalo
Ciborowski, Jan	Dept. of Biological Sciences, University of Windsor
Croley, Tom	NOAA Great Lakes Environmental Research Laboratory
Fuller, Pam	USGS Center for Aquatic Resources Studies
Gollasch, Stephan	Gollasch Consulting, Hamburg, Germany
Hamilton, Stephen	Dept. of Zoology, Michigan State University
Johannsson, Ora	Fisheries and Oceans Canada
Kolar, Cynthia	USGS Invasive Species Program
Krause, Ann	Center for Systems Int. and Sustainability, Michigan State University
Landrum, Peter	NOAA Great Lakes Environmental Research Laboratory
Lodge, David	University of Notre Dame
Lohman, Kirk	USGS Upper Midwest Environmental Sciences Center
Ludsin, Stuart	NOAA Great Lakes Environmental Research Laboratory
Olenin, Sergej	Klaipeda University, Lithuania
Reid, David	NOAA Great Lakes Environmental Research Laboratory
Ricciardi, Tony	Redpath Museum, McGill University
Sarnelle, Orlando	Dept. of Fisheries and Wildlife, Michigan State University
Schwab, David	NOAA Great Lakes Environmental Research Laboratory
Stockwell, David	University of San Diego Supercomputer Center
Wilson, Alan	School of Biology, Georgia Institute of Technology

NONFICTION PUBLICATIONS

Contributing author to *The Student's Federal Career Guide* by Kathryn Troutman. Wrote initial draft, 2004.

Contributing author to *Federal Resume Guidebook*, Fourth Edition, by Kathryn Troutman. Wrote chapter: "Science, Medicine, and Health Policy: Converting a Curriculum Vitae into a Federal Resume," 2006.

NON PEER-REVIEWED SCIENTIFIC PUBLICATIONS

Stevens, M.H.H., D.F. **Raikow**, M.R. Servedio, R.J. Collins, T.L. Schumann, A.N. Tipper, and W.P. Carson. 1996. "Hutchinson's Chariot: A Review of Species Diversity in Space and Time, by M.L. Rosenzweig." *Plant Science Bulletin.*

SCIENTIFIC MANUSCRIPTS IN PREPARATION

Raikow, D.F., D.F. Reid, and P.F. Landrum. In preparation, "Effect of Heat, Ultraviolet Light, and Low Oxygen on Aquatic Invertebrate Resting Eggs: A Test of Non-Chemical Ballast Tank Treatment Options." For *Environmental Toxicology and Chemistry.*

Reid, D.F., and D.F. **Raikow.** In preparation, "Aquatic Invasive Species: Where Science, Policy, and Economics Meet Head-On." For *Integrated Environmental Assessment and Management.*

Reid, D.F., T.H. Johengen, S.A. Constant, D.F. **Raikow**, S.A. Bailey, and H.J. MacIsaac. In preparation, "Design and Evaluation of Incubator-Emergence Traps (IETraps) for Use in Hatching Studies in Ballast Tanks." For *Limnology and Oceanography Methods.*

Raikow, D.F., J.F. Atkinson, and T.E. Croley. In preparation, "Resource Shed Modeling in the Great Lakes." For *Limnology and Oceanography.*

Croley, T.E., D.F. **Raikow**, J.F. Atkinson, and C. He. In preparation, "Hydrological Resource Sheds." For *Journal of Hydrologic Engineering.*

8

David F. Raikow, Ph.D.

PEER-REVIEWED SCIENTIFIC PUBLICATIONS

Raikow, D.F., D.F. Reid, E.E. Maynard, and P.F. Landrum. 2006. "Sensitivity of Aquatic Invertebrate Resting Eggs to SeaKleen® (Menadione): A Test of Potential Ballast Tank Treatment Options." *Environmental Toxicology and Chemistry* 25: 552-559.

Sarnelle, O., A.E. Wilson, S.K. Hamilton, L.B. Knoll, and D.F. **Raikow.** 2005. "Complex Interactions Between the Zebra Mussel, *Dreissena polymorpha,* and the Noxious Phytoplankter, *Microcystis aeruginosa." Limnology and Oceanography* 50: 896-904.

Hamilton, S.K., J.L. Tank, D.F. **Raikow,** E. Siler, N. Dorn, and N. Leonard. 2004. "Using Stable Isotope Tracer Additions to Study Food Webs: A Model to Interpret Results from a Woodland Stream." *Journal of the North American Benthological Society* 23: 429-448.

Raikow, D.F. 2004. "Food Web Interactions Between Larval Bluegill Sunfish (*Lepomis macrochirus*) and Exotic Zebra Mussels *(Dreissena polymorpha)." Canadian Journal of Fisheries and Aquatic Sciences* 61: 497-504.

Raikow, D.F., O. Sarnelle, A.E. Wilson, and S.K. Hamilton. 2004. "Dominance of the Noxious Cyanobacterium *Microcystis aeruginosa* in Low-Nutrient Lakes as Associated with Exotic Zebra Mussels." *Limnology and Oceanography* 49: 482-487.

Raikow, D.F., and S. K. Hamilton. 2001. "Bivalve Diets in a Midwestern U.S. Stream: A Stable Isotope Enrichment Study." *Limnology and Oceanography* 46: 514-522.

Hamilton, S.K., J.L. Tank, D.F. **Raikow,** W.M. Wollheim, B.J. Peterson, and J.R. Webster. 2001. "Nitrogen Uptake and Transformation in a Midwestern U.S. Stream: A Stable Isotope Enrichment Study." *Biogeochemistry* 54: 297-340.

Raikow, D.F., S.A. Grubbs, and K.W. Cummins. 1995. "Debris Dam Dynamics and Coarse Particulate Organic Matter Retention in an Appalachian Mountain Stream." *Journal of the North American Benthological Society* 14: 535-546.

Searcy, W.A., S. Coffman, and D.F. **Raikow.** 1994. "Habituation, Recovery, and the Similarity of Song Types Within Repertories in Red-Winged Blackbirds *(Agelaius phoeniceus)." Ethology* 98: 38-49.

9

(continued)

(continued)

David F. Raikow, Ph.D.

REFERENCES

Dr. Peter F. Landrum
Science Branch Chief
Senior Research Chemist
Great Lakes Environmental Research Laboratory (GLERL)
National Oceanic and Atmospheric Administration (NOAA)
2205 Commonwealth Blvd.
Ann Arbor, MI 48105-2945
(123) 456-7890
peter.landrum@email.gov

Dr. David F. Reid
Director, NOAA National Center for Research on Aquatic Invasive Species
Senior Research Physical Scientist
Great Lakes Environmental Research Laboratory (GLERL)
National Oceanic and Atmospheric Administration (NOAA)
2205 Commonwealth Blvd.
Ann Arbor, MI 48105-2945
(123) 456-7890
david.reid@email.gov

Dr. Stephen K. Hamilton
Associate Professor
Kellogg Biological Station
Michigan State University
3700 East Gull Lake Dr.
Hickory Corners, MI 49060
(123) 456-7890
hamilton@email.edu

Dr. Gary Mittelbach
Professor
Kellogg Biological Station
Michigan State University
3700 East Gull Lake Dr.
Hickory Corners, MI 49060
(123) 456-7890
mittelbach@email.edu

10

Figure 13.1: Sample Aquatic Ecologist resume.

Summary

The federal CV focuses on education, experience, and specialized qualifications. Your federal resume/CV is an important document to demonstrate that you are a subject-matter expert. And the resume can result in higher earnings because salaries are negotiable. Your federal resume is your application and examination. If your resume is not detailed enough, the interview might not occur.

CHAPTER 14

Information Technology Resumes

W riting a resume for the IT world has some interesting challenges, whether the resume targets a job in private industry or the federal government. On the one hand, you want to impress the reader with your technical expertise, and what better way to do that than to use lots of technical jargon (appropriately, of course!)? On the other hand, your resume will likely also be read by a variety of nontechnical personnel, from the junior human resources specialist logging in the resume or performing an initial screening, all the way to the hiring manager, who may or may not have a technical background. How can you satisfy both of these audiences, plus position yourself as the "Best Qualified" for the position you want?

That's the purpose of this chapter, to help you first of all to understand the types of IT jobs available in the federal world so that you can do a good job of the most important step—selecting those positions that are the best matches for your career aspirations and experience—and then knowing how to present your IT education, training, and job experience in an effective marketing format that produces results.

Government IT Jobs in the 21st Century

The most interesting trend in federal IT jobs is that more and more, the government is taking its lead from industry. In all areas, government managers are challenged to think like entrepreneurs, to focus on the bottom line, and to build standard, repeatable business processes based on industry-wide best practices. Always remember in developing your federal resume, your KSAs, your cover letter, and any other component of your application package that IT systems and software are *never* the end goal; they are merely the tools to build successful, mission-driven business systems. Every job duty and accomplishment you describe should maintain that focus.

What does this mean in the IT arena? First of all, look to the key business drivers in the IT industry and you will find the federal government in lock step.

Industry Certifications

IT positions in both the government and industry increasingly require industry certifications. Those most in demand include the following:

★ **Microsoft:** Microsoft Certified Systems Engineer (MCSE) is probably the most in demand, but Microsoft certifications of any type (and there are many) are highly valued. Search for "certifications" at www.microsoft.com for descriptions of the current Microsoft certifications (www.microsoft.com/learning/mcp/certifications.asp as of the publication date of this guide).

★ **Cisco:** Like Microsoft, Cisco has a wide range of certifications, from Cisco Certified Network Associate (CCNA) and Cisco Certified Network Professional (CCNP) to Cisco Certified Network Design Associate (CCDA) and Cisco Certified Network Design Professional (CCDP). Search for "certifications" at www.cisco.com for a description of the current Cisco certifications (www.cisco.com/web/learning/le3/learning_career_certifications_and_learning_ paths_home.html as of the publication date of this guide).

★ **PMI:** The Project Management Institute (PMI) has become the standard for project management best practices for the federal government as well as for private industry. Increasingly, government contracts are requiring that the Project Manager be either PMI certified as a Project Management Professional (PMP) or have a Defense Acquisition Workforce Improvement Act (DAWIA) certification (available only as a government employee), particularly for any IT position that includes IT acquisitions. With the government under continued pressure to outsource all work not "inherently governmental," many government IT positions have core responsibilities centered on managing outsourced work products. Related disciplines that you should stress in your resume and KSAs include Risk Management, Configuration Management, Earned Value Management, Quality Assurance, and Communications Management.

★ **ITIL:** Information Technology Infrastructure Library. This is actually an IT service delivery standard derived from the British government. As PMI focuses generically on project management issues across any industry, this is increasingly becoming PMI's IT companion. ITIL brings together many of the disciplines you have come to know in the IT world: Problem Management, Configuration Management, Release Management, and so forth. Check out www.itil.co.uk for further details on this IT service management approach and its associated certifications. Any and all of these disciplines and terms, if you have this type of experience, should be referenced in your resume materials.

★ **IT Security Certifications:** CISSP (Certified Information Systems Security Professional) is probably the most in demand ("gold standard") certification in the market. Given the ever-present security threat to enterprise systems and data assets, if you have this or other IT security credentials, you probably will have a job!

★ **IT Planning Certifications:** There are many opportunities as well for Enterprise Architecture (EA) and even Chief Information Officer (CIO) certifications. Take a look at the GSA CIO University for one example of a CIO certification widely respected in the federal government (www.cio.gov/index.cfm?function=cio_university) and at the EA certification provided by the Institute for Enterprise Architecture Developments (www.enterprise-architecture.info/EA_Certification.htm).

★ **CMM/CMMI:** Capability Maturity Model and Capability Maturity Model Integration (CMMI) are process-improvement standards developed and fostered by the Carnegie Mellon Software Engineering Institute (SEI). The federal government is increasingly pushing for both its own organizations and contractors to implement best practices for process management that are validated in a CMM or CMMI rating. Although this is really an organizational certification, any training or experience you have in assisting your firm or client to gain a CMM/CMMI rating should be highlighted. Read more at www.sei.cmu.edu/sei-home.html, www.sei.cmu.edu/news-at-sei/whats-new/contract-renewal.htm, www.sei.cmu.edu/cmmi/cmmi.html, and www.sei.cmu.edu/cmm/.

If you have one of these or other certifications, you definitely will want to highlight this in the first half of the first page of your federal resume. If you do not have any certifications, there is no time like the present to get started. Although formal training is important, you can get started on many of these certifications through self-study, and the time and cost invested will be well paid back.

Enterprise Architectures

Both industry and government have realized that reinventing the wheel again and again is neither fiscally nor mission responsible. Many job positions posted by the federal government are derived from federal-wide initiatives to design "reusable," "interoperable," "accessible," "scaleable," "enterprise" systems and solutions. Start by taking a look at the President's Management Agenda from 2001 (www.whitehouse.gov/omb/egov/), which underscores the wider **E-Gov** initiative to improve services to citizens through the use of technology and includes such initiatives as **Enterprise Architectures, Electronic Document Interchange (EDI), E-Commerce,** and **System Development Life Cycles (SDLC).**

Systems Development Life Cycle (SDLC)

The government has learned the lesson that the real cost for a system is the total life-cycle cost—from product or system inception through development, testing, acceptance, implementation, and then life-cycle support and even decommissioning. If you are a software developer or even plan, acquire, and then implement new systems, you have had to consider all of these life-cycle aspects. Again, incorporating the appropriate and accepted term for this experience into your resume demonstrates your expertise and awareness of the imperatives on the IT industry and federal IT initiatives.

Continuity of Operations (COOP)

Continuity of Operations (COOP) and Disaster Recovery Planning have been high on the federal government's to-do list since 9/11. One place to start is by consulting FEMA's Federal Preparedness Circular (FPC) 65 (www.fas.org/irp/offdocs/pdd/fpc-65.htm). It is very likely that you will have played some role in disaster preparedness in any IT position in which you have served. Highlighting this experience and relating it to the term "COOP" will ring true to the hiring manager for almost all positions.

Business Process Reengineering (BPR)

Remember the focus on documented, repeatable business processes? The buzzword in the business world for developing these is Business Process Reengineering (BPR). If you have been around awhile in the IT world, you have at some point had to think about how you currently manage a process (the "as-is" scenario) and how you could improve it in the future (the "to-be" process). If you have led or participated on projects to map processes like this, you have essentially been involved in BPR (and should take credit for it and use the correct term).

IT Planning

Whether you have formally served as a Contracting Officer's Technical Representative (COTR) in the federal government or at a minimum researched, recommended, and documented requirements for IT items or services to be procured, this is one area that you should definitely highlight. Become familiar with terms such as Statement of Work (SOW), Statement of Objectives (SOO), and Request for Proposals (RFP). Even for private-industry experience, try to cast your expertise in these terms. There are a number of initiatives, standards, and regulations related to IT Strategic Planning, Capital Planning, and Portfolio/Project Management (PPM) that you should be aware of, including the following:

★ **IT Capital Planning and Investment Control (CPIC), OMB Exhibit 300s,** and **OMB Circular A-11,** which provides guidance on preparing the federal budget (www.whitehouse.gov/omb/circulars/a11/03toc.html). A few other interesting links include www.osec.doc.gov/cio/oipr/Ex300_instructions.htm and www.doi.gov/pam/cpic/IT.pdf.

★ **OMB Circular A-130,** which establishes policies for the management of federal information resources (www.whitehouse.gov/omb/circulars/a130/a130trans4.pdf).

★ **Security Federal Information Security Management Act of 2002 (FISMA),** which was designed to enhance computer and network security within the federal government by implementing regular security audits (http://csrc.nist.gov/policies/FISMA-final.pdf).

★ **Clinger-Cohen Act of 1996** or the Information Technology Management Reform Act, which requires the federal government to use performance-based management principles for acquiring information technology (http://govinfo.library.unt.edu/npr/library/misc/itref.html).

Data Management

Another key area for industry and government is managing critical "data assets." It is no exaggeration that after its personnel, the second most critical asset for any organization is its data. The imperative in industry and government is to define and implement systems and processes that ensure that the right data items are identified, managed, and made accessible to business processes. Think about any initiative in which you assisted your organization or client to identify key data items to be collected, stored, and published, and correctly identify this as Data Management. A close discipline to this is **Records Management**—managing as Controlled Items (CIs) the key personnel and business records and documents for the organization. Include references to any records-management systems you have used in your current or recent positions.

IT Job Series: How the Federal Government Has Organized IT Positions

The first step in conducting an effective job search for IT positions in the federal government is to understand the various job series that apply to IT-related positions (see www.opm.gov/fedclass and select Position Classification Standards under White Collar Positions; see www.opm.gov/fedclass/html/gsseries.asp to find detailed descriptions for each job series). Note that on USAJOBS (www.usajobs.gov) you can search for IT jobs first of all on the Basic Search tab by selecting Information Technology under the Job Category Search field. There is also a Series Search tab that allows you to select job announcements based on the target job series.

Jobs in Series GS-2210 and Beyond

The primary job series for most IT professionals is GS-2210, Information Technology Management. Although most IT-related positions are classified under this category, there are a few others of interest if you have very specific skills. The distinctions between these categories are as follows:[1]

★ **GS-2210, Information Technology Management:** These jobs are characterized as "administrative IT technology work" and are positions that "manage, supervise, lead, administer, develop, deliver, and support information technology (IT) systems and services. Whereas many positions may require the skilled use of Automated Information Systems (AIS), the distinction is that these positions have Information Technology as their primary focus. (See the following section for more details.)

★ **GS-2299, Information Technology Student Trainee:** These positions do not refer to the temporary, summer job types of employment, but for "student trainee positions made under career-conditional or career appointments in the competitive service. A student may be appointed to any position that leads to qualification in a two-grade interval professional, administrative, or technical occupational series and that provides an opportunity for the student's growth and development toward the target position."

---

[1]Definitions adapted from position descriptions found on www.opm.gov/fedclass/html/gsseries.asp.

★ GS-0332, **Computer Operations Series:** This series covers positions where the primary duties involve "operating or supervising the operations of the controls of the digital computer system." If you have experience as a Computer Operator, you might want to check positions in this category as well as in GS-2210.

★ GS-0335, **Computer Clerk and Assistant Series:** This series is closely aligned with GS-0335 in that it focuses on providing a clerical level of data-processing support. Example duties as a Computer Assistant might be installing new desktop systems, issuing data media, maintaining system documentation, and receiving and resolving routine user trouble calls.

★ GS-0854, **Computer Engineering Series:** These Computer Engineering positions are characterized as "professional" positions requiring extensive academic qualifications in computer hardware, software, and system architectures. The work revolves around the "research, design, development, testing, evaluation, and maintenance of computer hardware and systems software in an integrated manner." Example positions might involve developing computer simulations or leading the design and integration of complex IT systems.

★ GS-1550, **Computer Science Series:** This is the most scientifically oriented type of IT work and would typically require advanced degrees and skills in computer science, engineering, statistics, and mathematics, and involve "research into computer science methods and techniques."

More Details on the 2210 Series

The Office of Personnel Management (OPM) *Job Family Classification Standard for Administrative Work in the Information Technology Group, GS-2200* (www.opm.gov/fedclass/gs2200a.pdf), notes that the GS-2210 series covers the following:

> Two grade-interval administrative positions that manage, supervise, lead, administer, develop, deliver, and support information technology (IT) systems and services. This series covers only those positions for which the paramount requirement is knowledge of IT principles, concepts, and methods; for example, data storage, software applications, and networking.
>
> Information technology refers to systems and services used in the automated acquisition, storage, manipulation, management, movement, control, display, switching, interchange, transmission, assurance, or reception of information. Information technology equipment includes computers, network components, peripheral equipment, software, firmware, services, and related resources.

The GS-2210 series is considered an administrative position as opposed to a "clerical or professional" position. Usually a professional series requires education. For example, GS-1550 (Computer Science) and GS-0854 (Computer Engineer) are considered professional series because they require a body of knowledge related to math and science (essentially a college degree with courses taken in math, engineering, statistics, or computer science). Because the 2210 is an administrative series, people who come in as a GS-2210-5 and have position potential to GS-2210-11 have the possibility of being promoted to GS-7/9/11 (two grades at a time). After you reach GS-11, you can be promoted only one grade at a time (to GS-12/13/14/15).

The GS-2210 series includes, but is not limited to, the specialties included in table 14.1. Note the specialty abbreviation that is often included in the job title in the position description.

Table 14.1: Descriptions for the GS-2200 Occupational Series[2]

GS-2200 Specialty	Description
Policy and Planning (PLCYPLN)	Work that involves a wide range of IT management activities that typically extend and apply to an entire organization or major components of an organization. This includes strategic planning, capital planning and investment control, workforce planning, policy and standards development, resource management, knowledge management, architecture and infrastructure planning and management, auditing, and information security management.
Security (INFOSEC)	Work that involves ensuring the confidentiality, integrity, and availability of systems, networks, and data through the planning, analysis, development, implementation, maintenance, and enhancement of information systems security programs, policies, procedures, and tools.
Systems Analysis (SYSANALYSIS)	Work that involves applying analytical processes to the planning, design, and implementation of new and improved information systems to meet the business requirements of customer organizations.
Applications Software (APPSW)	Work that involves the design, documentation, development, modification, testing, installation, implementation, and support of new or existing applications software.
Operating Systems (OS)	Work that involves the planning, installation, configuration, testing, implementation, and management of the systems environment in support of the organization's IT architecture and business needs.
Network Services (NETWORK)	Work that involves the planning, analysis, design, development, testing, quality assurance, configuration, installation, implementation, integration, maintenance, and/or management of networked systems used for the transmission of information in voice, data, and/or video formats.
Data Management (DATAMGT)	Work that involves the planning, development, implementation, and administration of systems for the acquisition, storage, and retrieval of data.
Internet (INET)	Work that involves the technical planning, design, development, testing, implementation, and management of Internet, intranet, and extranet activities, including systems/applications development and technical management of Web sites. This specialty includes only positions that require the application of technical knowledge of Internet systems, services, and technologies.

(continued)

[2]*Descriptions taken from Descriptions for the GS-2200 Occupational Series, www.opm.gov/fedclass/gs2200a.pdf.*

(continued)

GS-2200 Specialty	Description
Systems Administration (SYSADMIN)	Work that involves planning and coordinating the installation, testing, operation, troubleshooting, and maintenance of hardware and software systems.
Customer Support (CUSTSPT)	Work that involves the planning and delivery of customer support services, including installation, configuration, troubleshooting, customer assistance, and/or training, in response to customer requirements.

Selecting the Right Job Announcement for You

Selecting the right job announcement in the first place is just as critical for IT positions as for any other job search. No matter how good your resume and KSA materials are, if you truly do not have the credentials required by the hiring manager, it is close to certain that you will not be in the Best Qualified range. So how can you tell from reading an IT job announcement whether you might be minimally qualified or seriously at the top of the pack?

Analyzing an Example Announcement

Let's take an example IT job announcement and really look at it. Here is an actual job announcement for an Information Security Specialist at the GS-11/12 level. Table 14.2 presents each sentence from the vacancy announcement and the skills required for the job, and an interpretation of the requirement for this skill.

The first thing you should do is to reduce the job announcement to bullets and highlight the key requirement expressed in each bullet. Then, for each bullet, you need to make a judgment call on whether the requirement is a clear, hard requirement (e.g., you must have experience in this very explicit application or system in order to qualify) or a more generalized skill that could be satisfied from a fairly different context.

Looking at the IT Specialist (INFOSEC) position, let's categorize the bullets (see table 14.2).

Table 14.2: Analyzing Required Skills for an IT Specialist Position

Job Requirement	Skills and/or Experience You Must have	Interpretation
The incumbent acts as the subject matter expert for the Information Assurance Group within the Network Security (NETSEC) Division and is responsible for ensuring that the DoD, OIG automated information systems (AISs), and networks are in compliance with the DoD Information Assurance (IA) policies, guidance, and standards.	• Have fairly senior technical knowledge of Information Security practices and principles • Ensure that IT systems comply with DoD Information Assurance policies	This is a fairly general statement. Good, solid experience in any technical IT security specialist role would probably meet this qualification. (But note that you must have specific knowledge of federal security laws!)
The incumbent is responsible for developing, implementing, maintaining, and reviewing an information security program to ensure compliance for all centrally maintained AIS and networks at all levels.	• Actual experience developing an IT security program and plan.	Again, if you have experience, even in private industry, with evaluating IT security risks and vulnerabilities and designing and implementing a formal security plan, you would probably qualify here. Just implementing standard security measures on systems would likely not be sufficient.
Ensures the integrity, availability, confidentiality, non-repudiation, and authentication of DoD, OIG AISs, and networks via reviews and the use of auditing and security policy enforcement tools.	• Technical skills with IT security policy applications and tools. • Experience actually defining and implementing security audits.	Although they are not requiring experience with a specific set of security tools, you should have real experience with at least one tools suite. Just reading about them is not enough.
Interprets current department and federal AIS security laws, regulations, policies, standards, and guidelines.	• Specific knowledge of federal security laws, policies, and actual experience interpreting them.	You would need actual demonstrated evidence that you have applied a knowledge of federal security laws, regulations, policies, and so on.

(continued)

(continued)

Job Requirement	Skills and/or Experience You Must Have	Interpretation
Coordinates with the Office of Security in the certification and accreditations of centrally managed AISs and networks; communicates security-related IA issues or items of interest affecting the DoD, OIG; and tests, verifies, and ensures that adequate security controls exist with the AISs and networks.	• Experience guiding an organization through the C&A of a government computer system or network. • Identifying and mitigating IT security vulnerabilities. • You should at a minimum have actual experience participating in or leading a C&A process for a system or network.	This second bullet could probably be satisfied with either hands-on technical experience or more IT security management experience.

Summarizing table 14.2, if you were applying for this position, you would want to ensure that you have clear bullets and accomplishments highlighting your experience in the following areas:

1. Leading formal C&A efforts to certify new computer systems or networks.
2. Developing and implementing formal System Security Plans (SSPs) and other formal IT security plans.
3. Using security application suites, auditing tools, and so on.
4. Interpreting and applying federal security laws, policies, and so on.

Coupled with a general discussion of your IT security roles, responsibilities, and accomplishments in current and past positions, you would have a very competitive resume. You can see how critical this process is in selecting a position that is genuinely a good match for your skills and experience. If after this type of analysis, you find that you really do not have one of the key required skills, it is highly unlikely that you would ultimately be selected for the position.

When You Don't Match the Requirements Exactly

The toughest call is when the announcement mentions a specific government application or system that you could have used only if you were already in that job or agency. In this case, consider several factors, including the exact language used (is this *required*, or *desirable*?) as well as the overall announcement itself. If there is one position and the posting time is short, the requirement is probably very firm. If there are multiple positions available, you might have a better chance of gaining an interview even if your experience is missing one of the requirements.

The real danger, especially for the applicant coming in from outside the federal government, is that you might assume that an unfamiliar term such as "certification and accreditation" is just a generic description of the process of putting into place a robust plan to manage information technology security threats. In actuality, Certification and Accreditation (C&A) usually is capitalized (it was *not* in this actual job announcement) and refers to a very formalized process within the federal government of identifying, prioritizing, and putting into place appropriate controls for all of the potential risks associated with bringing a new system or network into production. Although different federal agencies may follow different standards and processes (look into the Defense Information Technology Security Certification and Accreditation Process [DITSCAP], the National Information Assurance Certification and Accreditation Process [NIACAP], and the National Industrial Security Program [NISP]), it is generally safe to say that agencies as a general rule have fairly formalized requirements in this area.

The ideal approach, of course, would be to speak with someone in a similar technical environment to ensure that you fully understand the requirements. Don't hesitate to use any technical contacts you have to look over the job announcement with you if you see any terms that you are not 100 percent certain you understand. As with any position, you can also call the Point of Contact provided with the announcement to better understand what they are looking for.

Frequently Asked Questions About IT Federal Resumes

This chapter assumes that you already know the basics of putting together your federal resume (see chapters 2, 3, 4, and 5) and you have done the job analysis (see chapter 13) to identify those key knowledge, skills, abilities, and experience you need to highlight to be fully qualified for the target positions. Here then are some recommendations and answers to common questions about putting together a really effective IT resume.

Remember that every IT job seeker's specific experience and situation will be different, and this, plus the specifics of the job you are applying for, need to be taken into account in the final format, organization, and content of your resume. So take these as good rules of thumb, but also feel free to apply a different strategy if it makes sense for your particular situation.

Table 14.3: Frequently Asked Questions (FAQs) for IT Federal Resumes

IT Resume FAQ	Rule of Thumb
Where should I put my certification?	Certifications are as important for federal IT positions as they are increasingly in private industry. Don't bury them on the last page (unless you have to, as in a Resumix resume). These belong near the top of the first page. See figure 14.1, which places these after the PROFILE and any CLEARANCE you may have.
Where should I put my clearance(s)?	Security clearances are tremendously important in the current job environment. If you have or have ever had a clearance, you should note this right after your PROFILE. Include dates and whether the clearance is still current. Even the fact that you have an expired clearance could be an asset in that the hiring manager might feel you would pass a new background investigation.

(continued)

(continued)

IT Resume FAQ	Rule of Thumb
Where and how should I list all of the hardware/ software I have worked with?	This is a tough one and it really depends on just how "hands-on" the target position is and whether you have really impressive achievements that will take up lots of real estate on the first page of the resume. The rule of thumb here: If you are very hands-on in your position—a system administrator, software developer, or systems integrator—you should probably provide a categorized list of your key technical skill areas at the bottom of page 1. If you currently work more as a project manager or supervisor, devote the first page more to your expertise section and accomplishments and save the technical skills for the last page. Secondly, wipe out all the outdated technologies from your resume. Nothing looks more dated than including references to Wang, Windows for Workgroups, and COBOL (unless, of course, you are actually applying for a COBOL position if there is one still lurking out there somewhere). Even "client/server" at this point sounds pretty out-of-date in a Web-centric world. One more note: Avoid the obvious. Don't drill down to the point that you are listing every single version of software you have ever used or every printer you ever touched. Suffice it to say that you have worked on Tektronix printers, Cisco routers, or Dell servers. You can always mention specific models in your achievements or KSAs, but don't trivialize your experience by listing everything you ever touched. Also, do not include applications, programming languages, or systems that you just studied in college or training courses (although it is okay to include these if you specifically mention the fact that this was through academic study only).
I am a contractor to a specific federal agency. How do I indicate that in my resume?	Be very careful here. As a contractor, you need to carefully list your employer as your contracting firm. Never imply that you worked for an agency if you were not a federal employee. Instead, include the agency's name either in your job description ("Provided contracted system administration support for XYZ Agency…") and/or in your job accomplishments. A neat way that works in some circumstances is to provide a general job description first and then show KEY CUSTOMERS AND PROJECTS (See figure 14.1).
What is the best way to describe my current and past positions?	See figures 14.1 and 14.2 for two completely different resume formats. There are two key ideas to consider. First of all, start by explaining something about the company or organization you work for. Instead of just providing your employer's name, include at least a one-line description of what the firm or agency does. At some level, you can "ride on the coattails" of your employer. Including the fact that your employer is an "industry-leading provider of…" or "serves over 10,000 clients…" will enhance your personal role.

IT Resume FAQ	Rule of Thumb
	Next, be sure to provide some idea of the scope and responsibilities of each position. Although accomplishments are very important, it is still important to answer the question, "What do I do?" Include numbers. If you managed an IT budget, for example, say so and provide the amount. The same applies to any projects that you describe.
How do I select and then properly describe my accomplishments?	The most important rule of thumb is to "name every accomplishment." If the project never really had a formal name, make one up. Instead of just saying that you implemented a tracking system for all system changes, at least call it a System Change Log (capitalized). Instead of just saying that you implemented a process to deploy system patches, call it an Enterprise Patch Management System. This gives the impression that you developed something of lasting importance (which you probably did). As far as selecting the accomplishments, do not worry that every accomplishment has to be prize winning. The key is to look for specific milestones and ways that you improved your current working environment. These could be as significant as designing and implementing a new system or as concrete as developing a Standard Operating Procedure (SOP), representing your group at a conference, or researching and recommending a new product. Whenever possible, include *numbers* (numbers of systems or users, cost of a new system, percent improvement in system uptime, and so on).
Should I include *all* of my IT training courses?	That depends on how long you have been in the workforce and how many training courses you have. If you are new to the IT workforce and have only a few training courses, include every one! If you have been around for a while and have lots and lots of training courses, include only those in the last 10 years and pick out of those the ones that are the most impressive and most applicable to the job you are applying for. If there is a certain course you know they are looking for, include it regardless of how long ago it was.
How many courses should I include?	Never more than 10 to 15, and consider the final length of the resume.
Do I have to write a new resume for each position I apply to?	No. Go through the position analysis presented in chapter 11 and make sure that you have a clear reference somewhere in your resume to every one of the final key requirements for the position. After that, look through the job position description, pick out five to eight of the phrases used in their job description, and try to insert these someplace in your resume. Don't be too obvious—vary them a little. Once you have a really solid resume, this should take no more than 15 to 20 minutes.

(continued)

(continued)

IT Resume FAQ	Rule of Thumb
Do I have to spell out really common IT terms?	Yes. Even spell out Information Technology (IT) the first time you use it. Never assume that your reader understands any acronym. Beyond this, it is critically important that you start by explaining any system or project in a clear, simple fashion that any reasonably informed reader could understand. Even if the target hiring manager is an expert, he or she will be impressed that you understand the technology well enough to explain it to a lay reader.
What do I do if my job is classified?	First of all, follow the classification guidelines provided by the institution or agency that you serve. Remember that the hiring agency is not as interested in the specifics as they are in the key skills and experiences you have developed. It is perfectly acceptable, in fact in some cases mandatory, to show the name of your agency or organization as CLASSIFIED, and then to provide only a generalized, high-level description of your job duties. Coupled with your security classification, this will be interpreted as an asset.

Focusing on Your IT Career

Remember that there is no substitute for experience and qualifications. Although an effective IT resume is a great tool to assist you in getting the positions and career to which you aspire, hiring managers inside and outside the government ultimately are looking for well-qualified and experienced employees. Consider that carefully as you evaluate and pursue both academic training and job opportunities. Getting a firm grounding in your field is paramount, and nothing will make you stand out more than good, solid experience in the key functions of your trade. Beyond that, a formal education is the best bet for future promotion potential. To get to senior positions inside or outside Information Technology, nothing beats a college education.

Example Federal Resumes for IT Positions

Here are two fairly different examples of effective IT resumes. Note that although there are several "must haves" for any federal resume, you still have a lot of latitude in how you present the information. The most important point to remember is to carefully read the job announcement. Read every line and make sure that you have not omitted any detail they require. Plus be sure to have the resume in the format requested.

Target Job: Information Technology Specialist, GS-2210-07, from current position as Lead Computer Technician.
Resume Format: Paper federal resume.
Private industry to federal career transition.

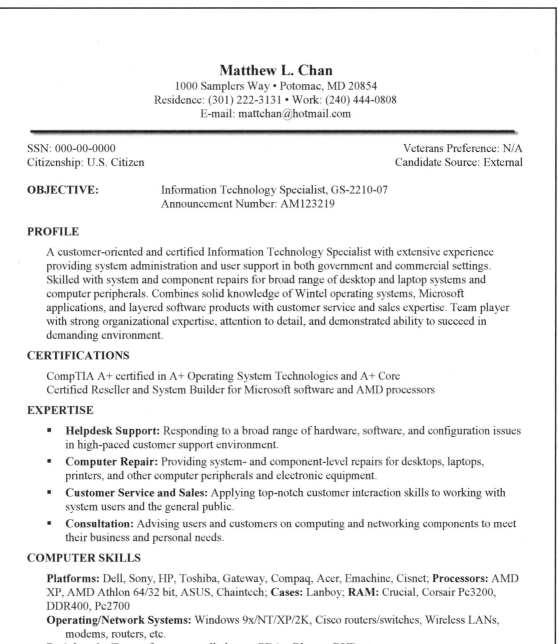

Matthew L. Chan
1000 Samplers Way • Potomac, MD 20854
Residence: (301) 222-3131 • Work: (240) 444-0808
E-mail: mattchan@hotmail.com

SSN: 000-00-0000   Veterans Preference: N/A
Citizenship: U.S. Citizen   Candidate Source: External

OBJECTIVE: Information Technology Specialist, GS-2210-07
                        Announcement Number: AM123219

PROFILE

A customer-oriented and certified Information Technology Specialist with extensive experience
providing system administration and user support in both government and commercial settings.
Skilled with system and component repairs for broad range of desktop and laptop systems and
computer peripherals. Combines solid knowledge of Wintel operating systems, Microsoft
applications, and layered software products with customer service and sales expertise. Team player
with strong organizational expertise, attention to detail, and demonstrated ability to succeed in
demanding environment.

CERTIFICATIONS

CompTIA A+ certified in A+ Operating System Technologies and A+ Core
Certified Reseller and System Builder for Microsoft software and AMD processors

EXPERTISE

- **Helpdesk Support:** Responding to a broad range of hardware, software, and configuration issues
  in high-paced customer support environment.
- **Computer Repair:** Providing system- and component-level repairs for desktops, laptops,
  printers, and other computer peripherals and electronic equipment.
- **Customer Service and Sales:** Applying top-notch customer interaction skills to working with
  system users and the general public.
- **Consultation:** Advising users and customers on computing and networking components to meet
  their business and personal needs.

COMPUTER SKILLS

Platforms: Dell, Sony, HP, Toshiba, Gateway, Compaq, Acer, Emachine, Cisnet; **Processors:** AMD
XP, AMD Athlon 64/32 bit, ASUS, Chaintech; **Cases:** Lanboy; **RAM:** Crucial, Corsair Pc3200,
DDR400, Pc2700
Operating/Network Systems: Windows 9x/NT/XP/2K, Cisco routers/switches, Wireless LANs,
    modems, routers, etc.
Peripherals: Types of cameras, cell phones, PDAs, Blueray DVD, etc.
Applications: Seibel eCRM, Norton Utilities, Norton Internet Security
Development: C++, Visual Basic (academic coursework)
Office Products: Microsoft Office Suite (Word, Excel, Outlook, PowerPoint)

(continued)

(continued)

Matthew L. Chan   SSN: 000-00-0000
Announcement number: AM123219   Residence: (301) 222-3131

RELATED PROFESSIONAL EXPERIENCE

Lead Computer Technician (12/05–Present)
BEST BUY, 9031 Snowden Square Drive, Columbia, MD 21046
Full Time: 40+ hours/week
Base Salary: $27,500
Supervisor: Rachel Baker, (703) 777-4545, *may be contacted*

- Senior Computer Technician serving a high-paced metropolitan retail outlet for BEST BUY, one of nation's leading retailers of technology products and services. Lead Technical Service Group, a 9-person team providing warranty repair services for broad range of computer and personal electronics products, including desktop and laptop computer systems, digital camera equipment, cellular phones, Personal Digital Assistants (PDAs), printers, and other computer peripherals.
- Receive, log, and track help desk calls. Provide phone-based consultation and problem diagnosis for customers.
- Assign work orders to other technicians. Conduct diagnostic tests, complete on-site component repair services, and coordinate Return Material Authorizations (RMAs) with Original Equipment Manufacturer (OEM).
- Assemble customized computer systems based on customer specifications. Install, configure, and test software. Document work in progress and assist with quality-control activities by checking work of other technicians.
- Track and inventory service parts for equipment under repair. Order parts and follow company asset procedures.
- As Technical Sales Consultant, advise consumers and business customers on total solutions for their Information Technology (IT) requirements, from computing options to Ethernet and wireless LAN configurations. Manage total purchase experience, from product consultation to closing sale of equipment, peripherals, software, and maintenance services.

Key Accomplishments
- **Work Order Productivity:** Personally complete more than 100 work orders for desktop and laptop repairs each month, consistently meeting corporate productivity goals.
- **OJT:** As the senior Computer Technician, provided orientation, on-the-job training (OJT), and technical assistance to new technicians.
- **Product Certification:** Successfully completed biweekly BESTBUY product certification tests throughout the calendar year.
- **High Sales Performer of the Month:** Recognized by store management as the top sales performer three consecutive months (May–July 2006).

Desktop and Networking Administrator (6/02–8/02) *(student summer position)*
CARDEROCK DIVISION, NAVAL SURFACE WARFARE CENTER, 9500 MacArthur Blvd.,
    West Bethesda, MD 20817-5700
Full Time: 40+ hours/week
Unpaid Intern
Supervisor: Jennifer Legionnaire

- System administrator for a scientific workgroup computing environment. Participated in the planning and delivery of customer support services to the organization. Installed, upgraded, delivered, and provided troubleshooting for hardware and software components. Performed file backups and restores, system and peripherals troubleshooting, and component repair.

- 2 -

- Provided a high level of customer service for a wide variety of computer and network problems. Monitored, analyzed, and resolved end-user issues and provided informal training and assistance.
- Researched and reported on new technologies, equipment, and software with application to the Naval Surface Warfare Center.
- Completed other short-term computing projects as assigned during the summer term.

Key Accomplishments
- **LAN Configuration:** Designed and implemented a simple Ethernet-based file-sharing solution for the assigned workgroup. Previously, all desktop systems were standalone. Installed and configured a Windows 2000 server including file, print, and software update services. Configured user accounts and file shares, implemented standard Windows 2000 password and file security measures, installed and configured virus and spyware detection utilities, and trained team members on standard file-sharing tasks.
- **Macintosh Batch Code:** Completed a sample batch job using Macintosh development tools to display submarine trajectories.

Computer Technician (7/00–10/00) *(student summer position, no longer in business)*
COMP Solutions, 2900 Gateway Drive, Columbia, MD 21046
Full Time: 40+ hours/week
Base Salary: $10.00 per hour
Supervisor: Jorge Garcia

- Computer salesman and technician for a small business computer integrator providing custom desktop and laptop systems to commercial and private customers. Interviewed clients to determine system requirements, provided individual consultation and troubleshooting, sold systems and hardware/software components, and assembled and installed systems at the client home or business site.
- Provided general store administration: opened/closed the store, recorded sales transactions, maintained a computer parts inventory, and responded to both telephone inquiries and walk-in customers.

OTHER PROFESSIONAL EXPERIENCE

Retail Sales (6/02–8/02)
HECHTS, The Columbia Mall, Columbia, Maryland 21036
Full Time: 40+ hours/week *(summer employment)*
Base Salary: $8.50 per hour
Supervisor: Samantha Segal, (301) 555-1212

- Sales clerk handling cash and credit transactions in the hardware and garden departments. Assisted customers in locating merchandise, completed sales and returns, and interfaced with customers and sales associates at other Hechts stores in locating required merchandise.
- Assisted with stocking and arranging store displays.
- Followed store policies and procedures to ensure a good customer experience.

EDUCATION

BA, Information Management Systems, George Mason University, Fairfax, VA 22030, 2004
High School, Centennial High School, Ellicott City, MD 21042, 2000

Figure 14.1: Sample resume for an Information Technology Specialist.

Target Job: Senior IT Specialist (OS), GS-2210-14, from current position as Senior IT Specialist, GS-2210-13.
Resume Format: Electronic Federal Resume.
Federal career to federal career promotion.

JANET A. JOHNSON
9800 Mountain View Avenue
Falls Church, VA 22042
Residence: (703) 123-4567
Work: (703) 999-6666
jajohnson@gsa.gov
jajohnson@hotmail.com

Social Security Number: 000-00-0000
Citizenship: U.S. Citizen
Federal Civilian Status: Senior IT Specialist (GS-2210-13), Department of Education (DE),
4/2002 to Present
Veteran's Preference: 5-point preference, U.S. Navy Veteran, 1988 – 1996

OBJECTIVE: Information Technology Specialist (OS) (#PG119916DD), Department of Veterans
Affairs

CLEARANCE: Secret (2002 – Present)

CERTIFICATION: Microsoft Certified Systems Engineer (Windows 2003) 2005

PROFESSIONAL EXPERIENCE

06/2004 to Present; 40 hours per week; SENIOR IT SPECIALIST, GS-2210-13; Department of
Education; 400 Maryland Ave. FOB 6, Washington, DC 20202; $68,500; Supervisor: Barry
Gordon, (703) 444-5555, may contact

SERVE AS A TECHNICAL AUTHORITY ON THE SERVER ARCHITECTURE for the
Department of Education enterprise network. This includes Windows operating systems,
Microsoft BackOffice applications, Commercial-off-the-Shelf (COTS) applications, and
Government-off-the-Shelf (GOTS) applications.
EVALUATE, INTEGRATE, TEST, AND DEPLOY ENTERPRISE SERVER APPLICATIONS.
Serve as the lead engineer for the Microsoft System Management Server (SMS) application
suite. Maintain a laboratory test environment for Integration and Testing (I&T) of enterprise
software.
ASSIST SERVER AND CLIENT APPLICATION DEVELOPMENT throughout the Software
Development Life Cycle (SDLC) from conceptual design and development through test and
integration stages and production deployment.
PROVIDE TIER 3 TROUBLESHOOTING AND PROBLEM RESOLUTION for the production
and development environments. Interface with vendor support representatives to resolve
complex integration and operational issues.
LEAD IT PROJECT TEAMS in the planning and execution of major technology refresh
initiatives.
STAY CURRENT WITH EMERGING TECHNOLOGIES with application to the DE environment.
Research, evaluate, and develop corporate requirements and recommend hardware, software,
and LAN/WAN technologies.

KEY ACCOMPLISHMENTS
SQL CLUSTERING FOR HIGH AVAILABILITY: Led the effort to implement clustered SQL
databases to support the high availability requirements of the DE LAN (2006).
SMS UPGRADE: Led the project team tasked to upgrade from SMS 2.0 to SMS 2003 with

---

minimal interruption to the production environment. Developed and executed a detailed project plan and led a 15-person technical team through the configuration, integration, pilot, and rapid deployment stages to upgrade 80 SMS servers providing enterprise management for more than 250 servers and 5,000 client workstations (2005).
SECURITY PATCH SOLUTION: Developed, documented, and implemented a structured security patch management process in the SMS 2003 environment (2003).

04/2002 to 6/2004; 40 hours per week; SENIOR COMPUTER SPECIALIST, GS-2200/12; Department of Education; 400 Maryland Ave. FOB 6, Washington, DC 20202; $62,750; Supervisor: Kevin Muller, (703) 123-4567, may contact

PROVIDED SENIOR TECHNICAL SKILLS ON WINDOWS OPERATING PLATFORMS and enterprise server applications implemented throughout the DE enterprise network.
CONFIGURED AND TESTED ENTERPRISE-WIDE SERVER SOFTWARE SOLUTIONS and effected the rapid deployment of new applications. Procured, assembled, and configured standard system builds to support enterprise hardware/software deployments.
LED THE MONITORING AND IMPLEMENTATION TEAM, tasked with 7x24 performance and availability monitoring of DE servers and applications.
ADMINISTERED OVER 30 MICROSOFT SQL AND RELATED LAN SERVERS. Implemented system upgrades and hot fixes to ensure the optimal response, reliability, and security of DE IT resources.
PROVIDED TIER 3 TROUBLESHOOTING AND PROBLEM RESOLUTION for both the production and development environments including escalation to vendor support representatives.
DEVELOPED AND IMPLEMENTED EFFECTIVE CONTINUITY OF OPERATIONS (COOP) planning to ensure continuity of business operations.
COORDINATED AND LED TECHNICAL PROJECTS to evaluate requirements and researched and recommended technical standards and solutions.

KEY ACCOMPLISHMENTS
SQL UPGRADE: Led the upgrade from SQL 6.5 to SQL 7.0. Interfaced with organizations throughout DIT to coordinate upgrades to 15 servers and more than 100 production databases (2003).
STORAGE AREA NETWORK (SAN): Implemented SAN solutions using Dell equipment. Consolidated file systems for more than 90 servers to provide 2 TB of high-reliability data storage (2003).
SINGLE SIGN-ON: Resolved complex issues to design an Extranet Single Sign-On solution for the Department of Education (2002).

06/1996 to 04/2002; 40 hours per week; SYSTEMS ANALYST; Solution Soft, Inc.; 22100 Jefferson Ave., Newport News, VA 23602; $57,000; Supervisor: Denise Greenlea, (957) 888-9999, may contact

INSTALLED AND MAINTAINED WINDOWS-BASED OPERATING SYSTEMS over an Ethernet Local Area Network (LAN).
PERFORMED DAILY NETWORK ADMINISTRATIVE TASKS including server maintenance and backups, user account creation, group memberships and access, email administration, and security monitoring and configuration.

(continued)

KEY ACCOMPLISHMENTS
STANDARD DESKTOP CONFIGURATION: Designed, documented, and implemented a standard desktop configuration used for more than 350 desktop systems across the corporation (1998).
REMEDY PROBLEM MANAGEMENT: Researched, recommended, and installed a centralized ticket management solution using the Remedy Helpdesk application (1997).

EDUCATION

BS, Computer Science, University of Maryland, University College, College Park, MD 20742, 1998
High School, Central High School, Bridgeport, CT 06606, 1988

SELECTED PROFESSIONAL TRAINING

MS Implementing and Managing Microsoft Exchange Server 2000, 40 hours, 2002
MS Implementing and Supporting Microsoft IIS 5.0, 24 hours, 2002
MS Windows 2000, Directory Services—Implementation and Administration, IKON Office Solutions, 40 hours, 2001
Veritas Volume Manager for NT, Veritas, 24 hours, 2001
MS SQL Server 7.0, Database Administration, Learning Tree International, 40 hours, 2000
MS Windows 2000, Designing a Directory Services Infrastructure, IKON, 40 hours, 2000
MS Windows 2000, Advanced Administration, IKON, 24 hours, 2000
MS Windows 2000, Installing and Configuring File/Print/Web Servers, IKON, 40 hours, 2000

COMPUTER SKILLS

Platforms: Windows Operating Environments (Windows 9x/NT/XP/2000), SAN, Hewlett-Packard server equipment
Network: Cisco routers/switches/hubs, Ethernet, Token Ring, TCP/IP
Enterprise Applications: Microsoft BackOffice (SQL, SMS, SNA, Exchange, IIS), Active Directory, Group Policy Design, SMS, SMS Wakeup, Remedy, WebFocus, PeopleSoft, Sharepoint, Trend Micro
Office Products: Microsoft Office Suite (Word, Excel, PowerPoint, Outlook), Outlook Web Access (OWA), Lotus Notes

AWARDS/ACHIEVEMENTS

Mission Achievement Award, FBI, 2004
Special Act Award, FBI (2), 2002
Special Service Award, FBI, 2002
Special Act Award, FBI, 1999
National Defense Service Medal, Department of the Navy, 1996
Navy and Marine Corps Achievement Medal, Department of the Navy, 1995

Figure 14.2: Sample resume for a Senior IT Specialist (OS).

Summary

To review and keep it simple, study your vacancy announcement carefully for top critical skills. Make sure you are qualified for the position and present your relevant qualifications clearly. Write about your projects and accomplishments. And be sure to include customer services, problem-solving, and meeting customer needs for IT services and projects.

CHAPTER 15

Contract Specialist, Purchasing Agent, and Business Analyst Resumes

By Michael Ottensmeyer

This chapter looks at federal business specialists in the contracting series. In private industry, these business specialists are called account executives, purchasing agents and directors, contract managers and negotiators, account managers, and other business-related titles.

The contracting series, GS-1102, is part of the Business and Industry Group (GS-1100) in government for a very good reason. The occupational group includes all positions in government where the primary duties include advising on, administering, supervising, or performing work that requires knowledge of business and trade practices, products, or industrial production methods and processes. The business group involves a great deal of investigative work as well as detailed studies, collection, analysis, and dissemination of information. This group also includes the establishment and maintenance of contacts with industry and commerce. Finally, it includes advisory services, examination and appraisal of merchandise or property, and the administration of regulatory provisions and controls. For all of these reasons, the federal government needs experienced people with solid business and industry backgrounds to handle the job responsibilities of business- and industry-related jobs.

Understanding business and industrial concepts and frames of reference has been important to the United States Government since World War II, when the military came to rely heavily on industry to deliver the goods during wartime as well as subsequent peacetime, and then throughout the Cold War period from about 1948 until 1989 when the Berlin Wall fell. People who work in federal contracting (or "acquisition," as it is most often called now) must have a solid grasp of the ways of the business world outside government because they interface on a daily basis with large and small businesses. For instance, contracting and purchasing agents in government are the linchpins between their agencies and industries that supply goods and services to keep them running. Contracting professionals work with internal customers to learn about the requirements; then they work with external vendors/suppliers to buy what is needed to fulfill those requirements. Communication is a big part of the job of the federal contracting specialist because both parties (inside experts and outside companies) need to know what goods and services must be delivered at the right time (and at the right price) to meet the federal agency's mission. In short, the contract specialist/purchasing agent in the federal government must be a business-savvy negotiator who has the ability to communicate in business terms that are understood by both parties to major government contracts.

The "Government-to-Business" Imperative

Contract Specialists are in greater demand in today's federal sector than they ever have been before. This is because the newest imperative in federal contracting is to shift work functions from government to business. President Bush announced in November 2002 that up to 850,000 additional federal jobs would be contracted out. This bombshell announcement means that the ever-evolving field of government contracting has changed even more dramatically. Now, contract specialists in government must know how to buy entire government functions from the outside to take over huge chunks of what the government agencies used to do in-house. For example, outside corporations are now contracted to provide millions upon millions of dollars worth of military base maintenance functions (repairing roads and buildings, replacing electrical wiring, doing plumbing, and so on) that used to be performed exclusively by military members and full-time permanent Department of Defense career civilian employees.

As thousands upon thousands of former federal jobs have been contracted out to private industry across all government agencies, federal contracting professionals have learned to approach their jobs not only from the perspective of "how to buy goods and services," but also from the perspective of purchasing entire functions to increase their agency's economy and efficiency. In the past, an agency would look to purchase materials only to perform internal ("organic") agency functions. Today's federal agency looks for alternative methods of getting the bulk of the work done as well. Agencies are ever vigilant for the potential to "contract out" their work to get it done better, faster, and more efficiently than before. This is so important that federal executives at the highest agency levels are now evaluated in their yearly performance reviews based on their openness to contracting out inefficient functions to the private sector.

As a direct consequence of the new federal imperative to achieve real-world business results, and the continual improvement of processes for getting the work of federal agencies accomplished, Contract Specialists have been forced to go back to school and learn more about the technical aspects of the business world. Federal agencies require Contract Specialist candidates to have a four-year course of study leading to a bachelor's degree with a major in any field; **or** at least 24 semester hours in any combination of the following fields: accounting, business, finance, law, contracts, purchasing, economics, industrial management, marketing, quantitative methods, or organization and management. Some agencies, such as the Department of Defense, now require Contract Specialists to have a college degree that includes no less than 24 semester (or equivalent) hours of business coursework.

Internal promotion candidates' resumes and KSA statements for advancement to higher levels of pay and responsibility have become far more detailed and sophisticated. Candidates must be able to demonstrate their business savvy in writing. Outside job candidates for positions as Contract Specialists (GS-1102 series), Purchasing Agents (GS-1105 series), and Contracting Support employees (GS-1106 series) must show that they are true business professionals who work with and manage contracts. They need to clearly demonstrate a keen insight into the essential elements of government contract management, as grounded in essential business concepts.

Skills for Contracting Experts

What skill sets do contracting experts in federal agencies need to demonstrate? The following sections list these skills by candidate type.

Federal Employees Seeking Positions in the Contracting Series

You need to know the technical skills of contracting, as well as the transferable business management and communications skills required to negotiate and monitor large-scale service and product provision contracts. It will help if you can show that you have done investigative work as well as detailed studies, collection, analysis, and dissemination of information in your present job or in recent jobs. You also need to demonstrate that you have studied business at the associate or bachelor's degree level. Include this information in your resume and in KSA statements.

Federal Contract Specialists Seeking Advancement or New Positions in the Same Field

An important first step is to carefully examine exactly what you do in your job everyday. This sounds a bit obvious, but you'd be surprised how many contract specialists in government are so busy performing the work of their positions every day that they don't think about highlighting their acquired business skills in their promotion and advancement applications/resumes. Because most federal agencies now use some form of "self-nomination" for promotion actions, contract specialists are well advised to stop and think occasionally about what skills they can bring to the table when it comes to applying for promotion. You will be amazed to learn that it's really a lot! You are a key person when it comes to providing essential services to the American public and the internal customers you serve each day. Write your resume and KSAs with the dual focus of managing contracts and making sure that the high-quality services you bring to your agency have a positive affect on bottom-line business outcomes.

Military Members with Contracting Experience Considering Federal Jobs in Contracting

Good news! If you are about to exit the military service and have professional contracting experience, you might qualify for the GS-1102 series in the federal government based on your experience and expertise gained in the military, even if you have not completed a college degree and even if you do not have 24 semester hours in business. This is a relatively new waiver procedure based on the fact that federal agencies are hurting for qualified professionals with experience. (See figure 15.1 at the end of this chapter.)

Private-Industry Professionals Considering Federal Jobs in Contracting

It helps to understand exactly how contract specialists do their work, and to understand that, even though the title of the job is "Contract Specialist," the position involves more than contracting. In private industry, this work involves the same skills needed by business managers, operations managers, financial managers, senior accounts managers, program managers, or professional staff persons in a contracting department. If you have this kind of experience, there is a good chance that the federal government can use your skills now more than ever!

You need to write a great resume that highlights your business experience and makes you stand out as someone the federal agency of your choice wants to hire to negotiate contracts with private firms. You can do it, and you can compete successfully for these excellent career opportunities in government.

OPM's Classification Standards

To write an outstanding federal resume, it helps to study the official classification standards for the occupation itself. The official Office of Personnel Management (OPM) Occupational Standards, although not new, are written broadly enough to cover the work that is done today. Here is an abstract from the online version of the GS-1102 series classification standard, as published by OPM, describing the typical duties of the 1102 series:

The procurement process begins with the determination of requirements needed to accomplish the agency mission. The program office is responsible for the initial determination that the requirements can or cannot be fulfilled from within the government, such as from existing stock or in-house capability, for preparing preliminary specifications or work statements, for recommending delivery requirements, and for ensuring the availability of funds. The document transmitting this data to the contracting office is a procurement request. The contracting office provides assistance in developing acceptable specifications, work statements, and evaluation criteria; determines the method of procurement and contractual arrangement appropriate to the particular requirements; and conducts the contracting process.

The contracting office first screens the procurement request to ensure its completeness for contracting purposes, and then develops an overall plan designed to obtain the requirements in the most economical, timely, effective, and efficient manner.

The plan embraces the entire procurement process from the inception of a program to completion of the contract. It may be simple or complex, depending on the circumstances of the particular requirement. It includes such fundamental considerations as funding, contracting method, contract type, source competence, number of sources, source selection, delivery, government-furnished property, possible follow-on requirements, and contract administration. It should include the means to measure accomplishments, evaluate risks, and consider contingencies as a program progresses. It should also include market research and analysis and other considerations as necessary to achieve the program objective.

New Competencies Needed for Contract Specialists in Government

Two of the most important competencies for government contract specialists are computer literacy and the ability to work independently.

★ **Computer literacy:** As in any other career field in government or the private sector, contract specialists today need computer literacy. This is the biggest new requirement, in addition to the requirements addressed earlier in this chapter. Computer literacy is necessary because contracts in the federal government today are accomplished on computers. Each system for contracting is different. Some agencies use more complex computerized contract writing software than others; however, the bottom line is that contract specialists are "administratively independent" in the 21st century and do not have contract clerks to type up lengthy contracts for them, as in the old days.

★ **Ability to work independently:** Along with the new administrative independence comes more professional independence, as well as heavier workloads with fewer people in the typical contracting office. Today's specialists need to be true self-starters who are willing to learn the process extremely well and take a contracting requirement from start to finish pretty much on their own. Contract specialists who expect to take their time and learn while others carefully supervise their work are not going to be happy in government today. There is simply no need for professionals who cannot take the ball and run with it.

Other important competencies and skills include the following:

★ **Quality assurance:** Continual review of the Statement of Work against the services being provided. (This is not done by contract specialists. It's done by QA specialists, GS-1150 series, who interface with contracts folks.)

★ **Problem-solving and follow-up:** Answering questions concerning performance, expectations, timing, and cooperation with government employees. (This is not new; it has been done all along.)

★ **Customer service:** Continual communication with project managers and contract officer technical representatives (the government employees who work "hands-on" with the contractor). (This is not new; it has been done all along.)

★ **Teamwork:** Working in combination with project managers, employees, and supervisors. (This is not new; it has been done all along.)

★ **Creativity:** As daily problems occur, contract specialists resolve them with contractors and other government employees to keep projects going for the good of the project and the government's investment. (This is not new; it has been done all along.)

Examples of the Types of Contracts Negotiated and Managed

Once again quoting from the online version of the GS-1102 series standards, contracting work in the federal government includes the following specialty areas:

- **Supplies:** Commodities range from commercial off-the-shelf products, components, or spare parts, to unique items requiring fabrication to specification.

- **Services:** Services include professional or nonprofessional, such as research for a specified level of effort, field engineering work requiring specialized equipment, the delivery of a series of lectures, or provision of janitorial services to perform specific tasks in specific locations. When contracting for services, competition may be based on both price and technical considerations.

- **Construction:** This includes construction of public buildings and repair or alteration of building structures, hospitals, prisons, mints, dams, bridges, power plants, irrigation systems, highways, roads, trails, and other real property. Construction contracts have a variety of special requirements that must be followed.

- **Automatic Data Processing Equipment and Telecommunications:** ADPE acquisition with supporting software, maintenance, and services is governed by a separate statute and special regulations. Telecommunications consist of local and intercity telephone services, radio service, audio and visual service, and equipment associated with these services. In ADPE and telecommunications contracting, competition is based on both price and technical considerations.

- **Research and Development:** Research and development contractors are selected primarily for technical considerations, although a thorough evaluation and comparison of all relevant business, price, and technical factors are required for meaningful source selection. Technical evaluations are directed both to the proposal itself and to the contractor's capabilities in relation to it.

- **Major Systems:** Major systems are the combination of elements, such as hardware, automatic data-processing equipment, software, or construction that will function together to produce the capabilities required to fulfill a mission need. Major systems acquisition programs are directed at and critical to fulfilling an agency mission; entail the allocation of relatively large resources; and warrant special management attention. No two are identical and involve such differences as time, cost, technology, management, and contracting approach. Major systems are designated as such by the agency head according to a variety of criteria established by the Office of Management and Budget and by the individual agency. Examples of large procurements, some of which are designated as major systems and are subject to major systems acquisitions policies and procedures, are federal office buildings; hospitals; prisons; power generating plants; dams; energy demonstration programs; transportation systems; ship, aircraft, or missile systems; space systems; and ADP systems designated as major systems.

Sample Contracting-Series Resume

The sample contracting resume is filled with keywords for the acquisition community, including the following: manage and administer all facets of the contract process from pre-award to post-award, including acquisition strategy, acquisition planning, procurement package input and validation, solicitation, and much more. It is written in true acquisition language. Be sure to research keywords like these and use them in your resume.

Target Job: Contract Specialist, GS-1102-13, from current position as Subcontract Administrator.
Resume Format: Electronic resume.
Private industry to federal career transition.

George A. Daimlar
7555 Effington Circle
Alexandria, VA 22315
Work: (246) 555-1212
Home: (703) 555-1010
E-mail: daimlar@aol.com

Citizenship: U.S.
Federal Status: N/A
Veterans' Status: 5 points
Military Status: U.S.A.F., 1992-1996
SSN: 000-00-0000

QUALIFICATIONS SUMMARY

Senior supervisory legal assistance attorney and contract attorney with 15+ years of progressive, professional experience in private industry, government, and the U.S. military. Licensed to practice law in four states and the District of Columbia. Successful track record as advisor and legal counsel to government agencies, military organizations, and administrative boards. Direct and decisive. Skilled in all aspects of contract negotiations. Strong oral and written communications skills. Excellent organizational, analytical, and research capabilities. PC proficient. Juris Doctorate and Master of Law degrees.

CONTRACT PROCUREMENT: Currently administering more than $1 million in contracts for five U.S. military installations. Outstanding record of performance in contract administration and procurements, including four years of experience as Judge Advocate General for the U.S. Air Force, Strategic Air Command (SAC). Expert knowledge of federal contracting laws, regulations, policies, and procedures, including Government Procurement Procedures and Federal Acquisition Regulations (FARs). Demonstrated ability to manage and administer all facets of the contract process from pre-award to post-award, including acquisition strategy, acquisition planning, procurement package input and validation, solicitation, negotiation, contract award, administration, and closeout/termination. Experienced in all contracting/procurement methods and types. Strong skills in working with logistics managers, product quality managers, engineers, and other subject matter experts and stakeholders.

PROFESSIONAL EXPERIENCE

SUBCONTRACT ADMINISTRATOR
07/2005 to Present
Brown and Root Services, a division of Halliburton Company
6452 Landsdowne Centre, Alexandria, VA 22315
Salary: $60,000; 40+ hrs/wk
Supervisor: Greg Jones, (703) 555-4545, may contact

CONTRACT ADMINISTRATION: Recruited to Brown and Root, a federal government contractor, to manage and administer all facets of competitive contract process for Military District of Washington (MDW) Job Order Contracts (JOC). Provide leadership and expertise for contract administration and procurements for five U.S. military installations. Manage more than 30 multi-year contracts in excess of $1 million. Negotiate, draft, and administer contracts for diversified goods and services; repairs; construction projects; contractor services; and professional services, including architectural, engineering, and consulting.

(continued)

(continued)

Manage and administer all contractual actions from pre-award to post-award, including initial planning, contract awards, and administration. Initiate, create, manage, negotiate, and manage master agreements with subcontractors. Prepare bid proposal packages. Initiate formal change orders, contract amendments, invoicing, and certified payrolls. Analyze and research market conditions, contractors, and services to monitor changing costs and to obtain best prices for goods and services.

COST PRICE / BID ANALYSIS: Format and abstract bids. Draft bid tabulations to determine best-qualified bidder. Review proposals against previous history, actual and estimated expenditures, and established rates. Determine price reasonableness or negotiation position. Calculate pricing using "R.S. Means Facilities Construction Cost Data Book." Negotiate best value. Conduct post-proposal and pre-evaluation meetings. Initiate requests for purchases/invitations to bid. More than 85 percent of bids are competitive; remaining bids are divided between fixed bids and sole-source selection.

QUALITY CONTROL: Monitor QC performance to ensure timely closeout of delivery orders and contracts. Coordinate project specifications and requirements with QC and Delivery Order Managers. Draft Statements of Work (SOW) and Price Breakdown Sheets.

POST-AWARD ACTIONS: Execute post-award actions, including cost reimbursement and incentive arrangements. Provide business advice and contract guidance. Review and analyze settlement proposals and recommend allowable costs. Lead post-award conferences. Procurement Administration: Build and maintain a procurement system to support the real-time financial needs of the project. Analyze all procurement requests to determine requirements, contracting methods, and types.

KEY ACCOMPLISHMENTS

+ Minimized contract response time through efficient subcontract management and fast-track selection.
+ Established and administer internal Quality Control and Improvement programs.
+ Mentor and consistently utilize successful local area subcontractors.
+ Improved work performance, ensuring quality consistency by using pre-qualified, proven performers.
+ Initiated agreements with subcontractors to respond within two hours to minimize response time for corrective actions.
+ Gained thorough knowledge of Indefinite Determination/Indefinite Quantity (IDIQ), FARs, Competition in Contracting Act (CICA), Buy American Act, Balance of Payments Program, the Contract Work Hours and Safety Standards Act, and the Davis-Bacon Act.

CONTRACT ATTORNEY
09/2003 to 07/2005
LawCorps
1819 L Street, NW, Washington, DC 20036
Salary: $70,000; 50+ hrs/wk
Supervisor: Lee Fox, (202) 555-5996, may contact

LEGAL RESEARCH: Supervised 25+ attorneys and oversaw document production for government and regulatory investigations and civil discovery. Researched, analyzed, and evaluated legislation related to antitrust, acquisitions, and mergers. Prepared written and documentary responses to regulatory review of large-scale corporate transactions. Researched complex legal and factual issues. Reviewed contracts, trade secret, non-disclosure, and licensing and patent agreements for legal sufficiency.

KEY ACCOMPLISHMENTS

+ Chosen as project leader for complex acquisition case.
+ Consistently rated as "excellent" on performance evaluations.
+ Selected for Privilege Review Team for FTC/DOJ antitrust and mergers/acquisitions.
+ Based on successful track record for document review and preparation, selected as member of Quality Control review team.

ASSISTANT ATTORNEY GENERAL
09/1996 to 05/2002
New Hampshire Office of Attorney General
Consumer Protection & Antitrust/Transportation and Construction Bureaus
33 Capitol Street, Concord, NH 03301
Salary: $58,000; 50+ hrs/wk
Supervisor: Charles Plowman, (603) 555-3658, may contact

TRIAL ADVOCACY: Presented before trial and appellate courts, and administrative tribunals with quasi-judicial powers. Handled a broad range of legal and managerial assignments. Attorney for seven licensing and disciplinary agencies. Conducted legal research for cases involving consumer protection, antitrust, and construction.

SUPERVISION: Supervised 44+ administrative and support employees. Conducted training classes for volunteers and interns. Worked with Department of Transportation engineers and contractors to delineate scope of work. Reviewed construction, dredging, and demolition contracts. Official representative for the licensing state agencies at hearings.

DOCUMENT SPECIALIST: Expert for administrative subpoenas, specialized expert testimony, quality of care, professional competence, and other legal issues. Researched, developed, and presented cases involving professional misconduct or malfeasance. Drafted position papers, policy statements, and memoranda relating to current and pending legislation, decisions, and orders of government agencies. Helped ensure that pre-bid documents met specifications. Monitored post-award conferences and drafted contract amendments.

KEY ACCOMPLISHMENTS

+ Successfully handled caseload (45) for seven licensing and disciplinary agencies while increasing turnaround time efficiency.
+ Devised a reusable package of step-by-step processes in the administrative resolution of disciplinary actions, ensuring uniform and consistent procedures.
+ Established the use of legal interns, volunteers, and non-legal professionals for review of cases involving specialized issues, thereby reducing cost.
+ Successfully argued three novel issues before the N.H. Supreme Court.
+ Streamlined the investigatory and hearing phases of disciplinary hearings.
+ Appointed to the Lawline Honor Roll for providing free legal services to New Hampshire citizens.

(continued)

(continued)

JUDGE ADVOCATE GENERAL (JAG)
10/1992 to 01/1996
U.S. Air Force, Office of Judge Advocate General
Pease AFB, Newington, NH 03801
Salary: $42,000; 60 hrs/wk
Supervisor: Lt. Frank Skinner, DSN: 555-3552, may contact

MILITARY LAW: Gained extensive knowledge of Contract Disputes Act (CDA), Armed Services
Procurement Act (ASPA), Federal Property and Administrative Services Act (FPASA), and Competition
in Contracting Act (CICA). High-profile, high-visibility law position supporting top-level command
personnel regarding base policies and command objectives, including personnel, regulatory issues,
Uniform Code of Military Justice, civil law, procurement, and acquisition contracts. Government counsel,
defense counsel, and investigator for general courts-martial and administrative disciplinary hearings.

LITIGATION: Managed legal assistance program serving community of 15,000 military and dependent
personnel. Litigated cases before trial and appellate courts and administrative tribunals. Supervised staff
of seven. Reviewed procurements, contracts, and acquisitions for SAC. Provided general technical and
administrative direction of Staff Judge Advocate for protests and problems for contracts awarded or
administered within Pease complex. Managed an average of 10 contracts up to $1 million. Interpreted
FARs.

ACQUISITIONS AND PROCUREMENT: Provided legal guidance for acquisitions and procurements,
including business strategy, acquisition policy, source solicitation, contract formation, negotiation (in
accordance with TINA), preparation, and interpretation of contractual documents, modifications and
changes, and contract change notices. Reviewed contracts and purchase requests for legal sufficiency.
Advised the base contracting office as to status of pending bid protests.

LEGAL RESEARCH: Provided legal counsel for personnel and disciplinary matters and inquiries
relevant to the Freedom of Information and Privacy acts. Performed legal research in the areas of military
and veterans' law, civil rights, employment discrimination, domestic law, torts, criminal law, and
contracts.

KEY ACCOMPLISHMENTS

+ Selected as Chief Legal Advisor and Consultant within Office of the Judge Advocate General.
+ Received commendation for uncovering contractor fraud. Evaluation stated: "Provided outstanding
services as base legal advisor on contracting matters. Cited by HQ AF/JA for efforts enabling the
government to assert counterclaims of fraud without a final determination by the contracting officer."
+ Initiated program to reduce time spent reviewing legal sufficiency in pre-award by improving
coordination through the Base Contracting Office.
+ Promoted to Area Defense Counsel, serving five bases.
+ Prevailed in Unfair Labor Practice case involving a recalcitrant employee and an Armed Services Board
of Contract Appeals case involving fraudulent claims submitted by contractors.
+ Developed management controls that ensured quality performance in office operations and improved
legal services.

EDUCATION

Master of Law, Law, University of Dayton School of Law, Dayton, OH 45419, 2003
Juris Doctorate, Intellectual Property, Franklin Pierce Law Center, Concord, NH 03301, 1988

Bachelor of Arts, Political Science / International Relations, Boston University, Boston, MA 02215, 1986
Diploma, Springfield North High School, Springfield, OH 45504, 1980

PROFESSIONAL LICENSES AND CERTIFICATES

Licensed to practice in:
The State and Federal Courts of Ohio, 11/1988, and New Hampshire, 04/1997
The State Courts of Massachusetts, 02/1997; and Colorado, 05/2004
The District of Columbia, 05/2005

MILITARY SERVICE

U.S. Air Force, 10/1992 to 01/1996, Honorable Discharge
Highest Military Grade Held: Captain

AWARDS AND HONORS

Military Honors and Awards:
Air Force Commendation Medal, 1995
Air Force Achievement Medal, 1992
Top Gun Award for litigation and advocacy skills, 1992

Professional Honors and Awards:
Lawline Honor Roll, 1999 (donating time and legal services to the needy and indigent).
Speaker, Continuing Legal Education (CLE) presentation in 1997; selected by New Hampshire Bar
Association to teach Continuing Legal Education courses in Administrative Law and Procedures.
Appointed Legal Customer Service Representative for LEXIS/NEXIS, Mead Data Central, 1988 to 1989
Certificate of Appreciation, University of New Hampshire, for Presentation on Trial Advocacy and
Constitutional Rights.

TRAINING

Federal Forfeiture of Assets, 3 hours, 2003
Criminal Law and Procedure, 12 hours, 2001
How to Draft, Negotiate, and Enforce TM, Copyright, and Software, 2002
Licensing Agreements, 6.25 hours, 2002
Sexual Harassment in the Workplace, 2 hours, 1996, 12 hours, 2002
Ethics for Government Lawyers, 2 hours, 1998
Appellate Advocacy CLE, 3.5 hours, 1998
Practical Skills for Windows, 5 hours, 1998
MS Word I, 14 hours, 1997
Administrative Law, 6 classroom hours, 1997
Ethics CLE, 3.5 hours, 1997
Practical Skills for Lawyers, 6 hours, 1998

Figure 15.1: Sample Contract Specialist resume.

Summary

As you develop your business-focused resume, keep in mind that the federal government really needs your business-based perspective as agencies move into the future. Don't be afraid to stress your *corporate* knowledge and your unique understanding and insight into working with both vendors and suppliers. Emphasize your knowledge of acquisition, and use the description of your current job to show how you can lead others in achieving cost-effective results for the public sector.

CHAPTER 16

Administrative Assistant and Secretarial Resumes

By Carla Waskiewicz, CPRW

Employment opportunities for administrative, secretarial, and clerical professionals are abundant in the federal government. Why? Because these important support positions are essential to the operations of virtually every government agency. A recent search of the USAJOBS Web site for clerical positions (0303) generated nearly 722 openings in various grade levels. A search for Management Assistant generated an additional 1,000 job openings.

A resume for secretarial, clerical, and other administrative support positions should focus on your abilities to carry out the duties and responsibilities detailed in the position description. However, because many other applicants might share similar skills and qualifications, your resume should highlight the unique benefits you will bring to the position and emphasize your accomplishments.

Previewing Job Postings

As you begin your federal job search, preview some postings in the various administrative support series and compare your job experience, strengths, and qualifications to see which jobs might be the best match. Here are some series to consider:

★ Secretary/Clerical, Procurement Assistant, Administrative Assistant: GS-0303

★ Management Assistant: GS-0346

★ Office Automation Assistant: GS-0326

When you read through job announcements for these positions, you will find some similarities in the job duties and some differences. For example, a recent posting for a Management Assistant position highlighted the importance of the ability to use quantitative/qualitative analysis techniques for collecting, compiling, organizing, and interpreting data, in addition to being able to provide a wide variety of clerical, technical, administrative, and management assistance.

Now take a look at the Knowledge, Skills, and Abilities requirements for this same position:

1. Ability to communicate effectively other than in writing.

2. Knowledge of office administrative practices and procedures.

3. Knowledge of statistical methods and procedures to compile and verify quantitative information.

4. Ability to gather and compile data, including numerical data for reports.

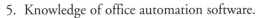

5. Knowledge of office automation software.

6. Ability to apply basic analytical methods to various aspects of assigned program or project areas.

KSAs 1, 2, and 5 are common to most administrative positions. You will see these again and again in your search for target postings. KSAs 3, 4, and 6 are more technical/analytical, so this position would be a good one for you if you have very strong analytical skills and job experience.

Other types of support positions that may require specialized experience in addition to general administrative support are EEO Assistant, HR Assistant, and Legal Assistant.

As you prepare to embark on your federal job search, make a list of all of your knowledge, skills, and abilities. This will help you to find the "best match" as you search USAJOBS for current openings. See part 4 for more information on navigating USAJOBS and interpreting job announcements.

The Importance of Soft Skills

Federal agencies seeking to hire administrative support professionals will look for a similar set of skills and experiences. They will also be looking for critical "soft skills." What are soft skills? Very simply, they are a collection of personally traits such as strong work ethic, good manners, punctuality, teamwork, friendliness, optimism, flexibility, and the ability to communicate orally and in writing in a professional, business-like manner. Your resume will make a stronger impression if you highlight some of your top soft skills as well.

Clerical/Administrative Case Studies

This chapter contains four case studies that offer excellent examples of how you, too, can make your clerical/administrative resume a real standout!

Case 1: State to Federal Career Change

Mary Stone, an Inspection Aide for the State of Connecticut, was seeking a federal position as a Secretary, GS-06 grade level, in the U.S. Attorney's office, Department of Justice. Although she had selected several potential administrative positions for which to apply, this position moved to the top of her priority list because of her extensive law-related clerical experience.

To match her resume to the position and use the right keywords, I analyzed the duties and qualifications requirements in the posting and organized them into focusing sections to be incorporated as part of her Summary of Qualifications. I used this "profile statement" to showcase her core competencies and qualifications at the start of the resume to better catch the federal hiring manager's eye. With hundreds of applications, hiring managers must quickly scan the first page of a resume to look for the most qualified candidates. I like to compare the Qualifications Summary to a billboard on the highway. You have less than 15 seconds to capture that hiring manager's attention. Why not make their job easier and improve your chances during the initial screening? Add impact to your resume by summarizing your best skills and qualifications right at the start! This summary also gives you the opportunity to develop a precise and targeted response to the "duties" section of the announcement.

Here's an excerpt from Mary's "before" resume. As you can see, her resume includes basic duties, responsibilities, and compliance information, such as salaries and starting dates, but does not effectively highlight her qualifications or accomplishments.

MARY A. STONE
PO Box 269008
West Hartford, Connecticut 06127
(860) 570-8522
e-mail: mstone@aol.com

PROFESSIONAL EXPERIENCE

STATE OF CONNECTICUT

Inspection Aide—Consumer Trades Division   (04/94–Present)
165 Capital Avenue, Room 110/Trades Division   40 hrs/week
Hartford, CT 06106   Starting Salary 28,200
Supervisor: Linda Brown (860) 712-6123   Current Salary 29,200
You may contact present employer.

Serve as the first point of contact for consumer inquiries and complaints involving work performed in the State of Connecticut by trades professionals. This includes, but is not limited to, carpenters, plumbers, electricians, painters, and other home-improvement workers, as well as ordinary everyday complaints.

Intake initial information and verify its accuracy with the complainant. Handle complaints by phone, by mail, or from walk-in citizens. Evaluate the seriousness of the complaint. Make a preliminary decision as to whether to investigate further. Forward complaints for further investigation and/or mediation. Perform all data entry so that information is entered correctly into computer database. Handle case files. Follow up through resolution of case. Assist in onsite inspections of home-improvement work. Perform Notary Public duties as required.

Court Monitor—Connecticut Superior Court   (1/00–04/01)
20 Franklin Square   40 hrs/week
New Britain, CT 06051   Starting Hourly $14.25/hr
Supervisor: Mimi Palmer (860) 515-5343   Final Hourly: $14.25
You may contact this employer.

Recorded both criminal and civil proceedings through the use of stenography machine and audio recording equipment. Utilized CD-ROM technology. Prepared certified transcripts of trials, appeals, hearings, and motions. Prepared billing and tax statements. Performed general administrative and clerical duties. Set up equipment. Maintained records. Provided auxiliary and administrative support to attorneys and court personnel.

Due to performance and to fulfill the needs of the court, asked to perform independent contractual work (described in detail later in resume). Operate this position as an adjunct to the Court Monitor Recording position (while working full 40 hours/week in Court Monitor Recording position).

Figure 16.1: Mary's "before" resume.

The "after" resume presents her key skills and abilities and the top duties requirements at a glance in bold type for greater emphasis. Her work experience follows in reverse-chronological order. The new resume format and design, with prominent qualifications summary, make her a standout candidate for the secretarial position.

Target Job: Secretary, Office Assistant, Department of Justice.
Resume Format: Paper.
State to federal transition.

MARY A. STONE
P.O. Box 269008
West Hartford, CT 06127
Home (860) 570-8522 • Work (860) 715-6887
e-mail: mstone@aol.com

Social Security No.: 000-00-0000	Citizenship: United States of America
Veterans' Preference: 10 points	Federal Status: N/A

OBJECTIVE

Secretary, Office Assistant, Justice Department, United States Attorney's Office, New York City, NY; Announcement #02-SDNY-19D, GS-0318-06.

SUMMARY OF QUALIFICATIONS

Experienced Office Administrator with 11+ years of diverse experience in government and private industry. Outstanding organizational and office administration skills, including financial management, personnel management, database expertise, and technical support capabilities. Excellent oral and written communications skills. Skilled in all aspects of office operations. Able to establish priorities and implement decisions to achieve both immediate and long-term goals.

- **Administrative Expertise:** Maintain administrative office flow. Track and maintain files; manage correspondence and information; maintain inventory. Procure office equipment and supplies.
- **Secretarial Skills:** Keyboard 69 words per minute with an error rate of 3. Experience with stenography, audio recording devices, and duplicating and facsimile machines.
- **Computer and Database Skills:** Create, establish, and maintain databases in support of operations using a LAN and desktop computers. Proficient in Word, PowerPoint, and Excel.
- **Finance and Accounting:** Experience with budget, payroll, and accounting.
- **Specialized Training:** AA degree, Liberal Arts; Certificate of Secretarial Science; Certificate of Court Reporting; Notary Public.

PROFESSIONAL EXPERIENCE

INSPECTION AIDE	April 1994 to Present
State of Connecticut, Consumer Trades Division	40 hours per week
165 Capital Avenue, Room 110, Hartford, CT 06106	Current Salary: $29,200/year
Supervisor: Linda Brown, (860) 712-6123. May be contacted.	Starting Salary: $28,200/year

Provide administrative, technical, and customer service support for all consumer inquiries and complaints for work performed by trades professionals in the State of Connecticut. First contact for all customer complaints. Coordinate all administrative functions and manage customer service complaint process to ensure smooth and efficient operation and problem resolution.

- Receive telephone calls and walk-in visitors, record intake information, and verify accuracy of information with complainants.
- Review all complaints to determine level of action. Respond to inquiries and recommend further investigation and/or refer complaints to managers for further investigation or mediation.
- Prepare and maintain all data entries and ensure accuracy of entries to computer database.

Figure 16.2: Mary's "after" resume.

Case 2: Transitioning from Private Industry to Government

Barbara Taylor was working as a Business Process Analyst for a federal contractor that provides administrative support services for special events, meetings, and conferences. She was seeking to transition to a federal position as a Management Assistant with the Department of Housing and Urban Development. Here is a summary of the target skills from the description of duties for the announcement:

Coordinates administrative matters.

Works with senior staff to consolidate administrative reports.

Initiates necessary correspondence.

Develops methods of operation or improvements in administrative practices and work routines.

Performs research and gathers background data for use by senior staff.

Researches and assembles materials for meetings, conferences, and presentations...

There were also four KSAs required for the application, including knowledge of office procedures and filing systems; knowledge of quantitative methods and research methodologies; knowledge of computer software sufficient to create tables and graphs...; and skill in oral and written communication to effectively communicate with managers, employees, and the public...."

Take a look at the first page of Barbara's "before" resume. You can see that it begins with her education and then includes short summaries of her qualifications. The summary for her current position as Business Process Analyst is brief and does not effectively showcase her many qualifications.

Barbara Taylor
2000 Quarters, Apt. E
Quantico, VA 22134
703-699-8888

EDUCATION:	Park University, B.S. Degree Candidate (Management)
	Dale Carnegie Training (12-week course)
	Situational Leadership Training (2-day course)
	Merchandise Assistant Training Program (6-week course, JCPenney)
	U.S. Navy Administrative Data School, Meridian, MS
	Event Management Training (1-week course)
	Calvert County Community College, LaPlata, MD (1994-1995) Completed Computer Courses

EXPERIENCE SUMMARY:

18 years of professional experience.

- Experience with various computer software systems from MS Office 2000, Word, Excel, MS Project, Lotus Notes, WordPerfect, Quicken, PowerPoint, Harvard Graphics, MS Publisher, Access, FoxPro, R-Base, D-Base, Flowcharting 3, TSO/ORACLE, Group Systems, Scheduling System, Internet, and e-mail.

- Developed and maintained company employee database in Access to track employee reviews, goals, and personal information.

- Several years of experience managing events from concept to completion.

- **Business Process Analyst,** 2002-Present:

  Provide required resources and expertise to support the planning and execution of events; conduct AGC events and presentations and provide facilitation and process support in diverse areas to ensure smooth and successful execution. Determine the purpose and requirements of the customer to include, but not limited to, identification of the participants, and any unique support required, appropriate technology systems; Prepare an activity security plan and prepare a plan outlining the resources and staffing required to meet customers' requirements/objectives.

Figure 16.3: Page 1 of Barbara's "before" resume.

Now, take a look at the first part of her new resume. Here are some of the improvements we made to make her qualifications really stand out:

★ Because Barbara had more than 18 years of valuable administrative experience, her new resume needed to focus on her core qualifications and career accomplishments. Her education was still important, but it needed to go at the end of the resume instead of at the beginning.

★ To better market Barbara's qualifications, we started her resume with a comprehensive Professional Profile section, a summary statement that encapsulated all of her best administrative management skills. Then, under a Core Qualifications subheading within this profile, we organized her skills and abilities in separate categories. These categories were highlighted in bold, italic type to add impact.

★ Next, within those categories, we incorporated keywords from the duties description in the job posting, as well as some of the knowledge and abilities from the KSAs, such as Communications Skills. This great focusing section now makes it easy for the selecting official to see at a glance just how qualified Barbara is for this job.

★ Finally, one of the most important additions to her resume was a list of accomplishments for each position she held. Showcasing accomplishments is the most effective way to set yourself apart from the competition and show a potential employer what you have achieved on the job. Just think about it; if you were a hiring supervisor with dozens of resumes to read, which candidate would you select for an interview: the candidate who simply lists what they do each day on the job, or the one who clearly shows quantifiable accomplishments or project successes? A resume is a marketing document. Marketing yourself as the best candidate will increase your chances of landing an interview *and* a new job!

Target Job: Management Assistant, GS-0344-07, from current position as Business Process Analyst.
Resume Format: Paper federal resume.
Private industry to federal career transition.

BARBARA N. TAYLOR

2000 Quarters, Apt. E
Quantico, VA 22134

Day: (202) 781-1000   E-mail: btaylor@yahoo.com   Evening: (703) 630-3222

Social Security No.: 000-00-0000   Citizenship: U.S.A.
Federal Status: N/A   Veterans' Preference: N/A

OBJECTIVE: Position: Management Assistant **Grade:** GS-0344-07.
Announcement No: 00-DEU-03-0002

PROFESSIONAL PROFILE: Organized, articulate Administrative Professional with 18+ years of progressively responsible experience in the strategic areas of administrative operations, information management, and events/meeting planning. Excellent organization, research, and communications capabilities. Demonstrated ability to prioritize tasks, meet time-sensitive deadlines, and work independently to achieve goals.

CORE QUALIFICATIONS

- *Administrative Expertise:* Comprehensive executive-level administrative and technical expertise. Skilled in developing, implementing, and managing office procedures and systems. Extensive experience providing informational, logistical, and technical support for meetings, conferences, and special events.

- *Computer and Database Management Skills:* Broad-based computer software knowledge and database management expertise. Proficient in MS Word, Excel, PowerPoint, Access, Goldmine, Outlook, Publisher, and Graphical User Interface (GUI) systems.

- *Report and Document Preparation:* Expertise creating Excel spreadsheets, tables, graphs, charts, correspondence, and multimedia presentations. Valued for ability to organize computer data files to improve productivity and manage information.

- *Research and Analysis:* Qualitative and quantitative analysis of information for senior management using Excel spreadsheets. Adept at researching, analyzing, extracting, and archiving data for development reports and subject-matter files.

- *Communications Skills:* Polished oral and written communications skills. Well-developed interpersonal skills. At ease interfacing with top executives, government leaders, clients, customers, and vendors.

PROFESSIONAL EXPERIENCE

BUSINESS PROCESS ANALYST
COMPUTER SCIENCE CORPORATION (CSC.COM)   **May 2002 to Present**
1201 M Street, Washington, DC 20376   40 hours per week
Supervisor: Erin Gantt, (202) 675-4993, may be contacted.   Current Salary: $47,000
(A federal contractor providing conference/special events services)

(continued)

(continued)

BARBARA N. TAYLOR, SSN 000-00-0000   Page 2 of 2

Administrative Assistant and Events Representative. Provide comprehensive administrative, clerical, and technical support for the Admiral Gooding Center, Command Events Planning Branch of the Naval Sea Systems Command (NAVSEA). Manage and coordinate administrative functions to ensure the smooth and efficient operation of conference facilities and services. Report to the Director of Events Planning.

- Organize and coordinate logistics and provide administrative and technical support for special events, meetings, conferences, and seminars at the center. Maximize use of software applications, including Excel and PowerPoint, to create project correspondence, produce support materials, and record program documentation.
- As Events Assistant, serve as key client interface and on-site technical representative from pre-event planning to post-event follow-up. Use state-of-the-art computer technology (GUI) to hyperlink client information to PowerPoint and other software to create multimedia presentations. Play integral role in planning meetings. Key contact for high-ranking military personnel.
- Assist with basic accounting/finance functions. Track bank card transactions and purchase orders. Review financial reports to ensure accuracy.
- Answer and screen telephone calls; greet and register incoming visitors; and disseminate information to customers, the public, and staff. Conduct facility tours.
- Administer workflow and establish and maintain subject-matter files. Provide secretarial/clerical support. Track and document project status using spreadsheet applications.

Key Accomplishments:
- Improved data collection, documentation, and access, and reduced errors by consolidating six spreadsheets into one. Also created pivot tables to extract requested data more efficiently.
- Utilized Word and Excel to create and implement a more efficient system for tracking and documenting conference/meeting project status and follow-up.
- Assisted with financial report review and uncovered a $30,000 calculation error. Revised and improved the report implementing Excel software.
- Consistently exceed performance standards. Valued by management and staff for increasing internal efficiencies and cutting administrative costs by creating new ways to automate office procedures and duties.

[Barbara's previous positions here]

EDUCATION AND TRAINING

     Park University, B.S. Degree Candidate (Management), Quantico, VA 22134

     Dale Carnegie Training (12-week course), June 2002

     Situational Leadership Training (2-day course), March 2002

     Merchandise Assistant Training Program (6-week course, JCPenney), May 2001

     Event Management Training (1-week course), August 1999

     U.S. Navy Administrative Data School, Meridian, MS, March 1995

     Calvert County Community College, LaPlata, MD, 56 credit hours, 1994–1995

Figure 16.4: Barbara's "after" resume.

Case 3: Moving Up from One Federal Job to Another

Experienced administrative professional Carol Deeter had worked for the U.S. Department of Agriculture for more than 10 years. Prior to working in the federal government, she had also worked for more than 20 years in private industry. Her goal was to move from a Grade 7 position to a Grade 8. When applying for previous grade changes, Carol had always submitted her government form SF-171. OPM officially eliminated this form in 1995, but many federal employees are still using it. A paper resume is a much more effective way to present a candidate's job history and skills. To apply for the new grade level, Carol wanted to convert her lengthy SF-171 to a federal resume to better showcase her experience and qualifications.

This excerpt from Carol's new federal resume (the first two pages) starts with a comprehensive Skills Summary. As detailed in the previous examples, this section incorporates many of the duties from the job posting she selected, such as market research, database analysis, and statistical analysis. Also included are important administrative/office-management skills that she will bring to the job, such as "Valued by senior executives for ability to manage offices, improve systems, meet deadlines, and develop and implement new administrative procedures."

Within the Skills Summary, we also highlighted her important "soft skills," such as "self-motivated," and her desire to expand her computer software knowledge. This helps to demonstrate that she is an experienced and competent administrative professional, and that she also has drive and initiative. She not only gets things done, but she makes things better. She achieves results and is always willing to take on new responsibilities. Those are just some of the qualities that make her stand out!

Finally, in her present job, we featured her responsibilities using a subhead format. Instead of providing a long list of job duties, this approach helps to better organize her responsibilities and makes the resume easier to read. Her accomplishments are clearly highlighted in a separate section. With the new resume format, it is easy to pinpoint her most significant accomplishments and skills.

Target Job: Secretary, GS-0318-08, from current position as Secretary, GS-0318-07.
Resume Format: Paper.
Federal to federal career promotion.

CAROL F. DEETER
3535 Signal Road
Alexandria, Virginia 22304
Home (703) 755-6555 • Work (202) 699-1111
e-mail: carol.deeter@wdc.usda.gov

Social Security No.: 000-00-0000
Citizenship: United States of America
Veterans' Status: None
Federal Status: Secretary, GS-318-07, 1997 to present

OBJECTIVE

Secretary, GS-0318-08, U.S. Department of Agriculture, Farm Service Agency, Washington, DC, Announcement #F2-FSA-042.

SKILLS SUMMARY

Secretary, Administrative Specialist, and Office Manager with more than 30 years of federal and private-industry experience. Excellent oral and written communication skills, demonstrated interpersonal skills, and proven organizational and administrative expertise. Skilled in market research, statistical analysis, and database management. Valued by senior executives for ability to manage office, improve systems, meet deadlines, and develop and implement new administrative procedures. An integral staff professional, skilled in assisting with program functions, training personnel, and communicating with and supporting program director.

- **Finance/accounting support expertise.** Experience formulating, justifying, and executing budgets. Ability to prepare budget reports, cash-flow analysis, accounts payable and receivable, and payroll.

- **Coordinate office processes and procedures.** Maintain smooth flow of paperwork. Research, analyze, process, and track files, documentation, correspondence, and information. Procure and manage equipment inventories and supplies.

- **Plan and manage workload and projects.** Ensure compliance and quality control. Effectively serve staff needs for information, scheduling, and administrative support.

- **Eager learner. Career-focused and self-motivated.** Seek to increase knowledge base and computer skills through professional development. Able to establish priorities and implement decisions to achieve both immediate and long-term goals.

- **Database expertise.** Proficient in Word, Excel, Access, and PowerPoint. Ability to establish and maintain databases in support of operations. Track record of implementing filing systems to improve internal operations.

Carol F. Deeter, SSN: 000-00-000

PROFESSIONAL EXPERIENCE

SECRETARY (GS-0318-7/10)   December 1997 to Present
U.S. Department of Agriculture   40 hours per week
Farm Service Agency, Outreach Programs Staff
1451 Rockville Pike, WOCII, Room 2009, Rockville, MD 20850
Supervisor: Cindy Harn, Director; yes, please contact at (202) 722-2222
Ending Salary: $38,954 per year; Starting Salary: $28,000 per year

- **Provide broad-based administrative support** to the supervisor and multicultural support staff. Coordinate administrative functions to ensure the smooth and efficient operation of the office and its programs. Provide the Women Outreach Coordinator with essential information and resources to promote the staff's outreach efforts to women's farm organizations.

- **Coordinate internal and external office communications and documentation:** Review and analyze incoming mail and distribute mail to director and staff. Evaluate all correspondence to ensure conformance to administrative and security requirements. Review and type all correspondence, reports, publications, and other materials from rough draft to final form, ensuring accuracy, proper formatting, and spelling and grammar. Maintain and update files supporting State Quarterly Reports and programs.

- **Supervise support staff:** Control and expedite work assignments to staff members. Prepare, maintain, and transmit time and attendance reports. Train and supervise summer intern staff.

- **Create and manage schedules and workflow:** Maintain supervisor's calendar and use own initiative to prioritize and schedule appointments.

- **Manage multiple administrative requirements:** Receive visitors, screen and field incoming telephone calls, and direct inquiries to proper departments. Monitor and maintain office-supply and operating-forms inventories. Administer travel arrangements for all staff members, including travel orders and airline, hotel, and car-rental reservations.

- **Support meetings and presentations:** Arrange and coordinate monthly meetings with National Outreach Council Members, including setup and participation in the monthly teleconference with State Executive Directors (SEDs) and Outreach Coordinators. Assist in preparation of outreach training documents.

    Accomplishments:

    ➢ Volunteered to serve as interim Women's Outreach Coordinator when position was vacant. Independently researched women's farm organizations nationwide and prepared statistics that helped establish a women's program file. When new coordinator joined staff, provided orientation and resources and developed information in support of the staff's outreach efforts.

    ➢ Assisted in the preparation of SED's Outreach Training documents in Atlanta; St. Paul; and Washington, DC.

    ➢ Created database of state directors and contact information for office distribution.

Figure 16.5: Carol's new resume.

Case 4: Transitioning from Private Industry to Federal

Debra Jones had worked in customer service support positions with a major airline for more than 15 years. She had also been very involved in the International Association of Machinists, a labor union for airline industry employees, both as a Union Steward and in administrative support roles. Although Debra had enjoyed her career, recent changes in the airline industry over the past several years had negatively impacted employee salaries and benefits and caused staff reductions. Debra was seeking to transition to federal service and contribute her many years of private-industry experience to the public sector.

Debra's diverse private-sector experience, at first glance, was not an obvious match to one specific federal job title. However, once we analyzed her private-sector experience and training, it became much more clear. Take a look at the list of core competencies we created to feature in her new federal resume:

Administrative/secretarial experience

Labor relations

Equal Employment Opportunity, personnel liaison

Confidential automated database systems/Security Screening

Travel coordination

Inventories and procurements

Document preparation and records maintenance

Customer service

Staff training experience

Her soft skills included very strong skills in meeting deadlines, working with the public, problem solving, and organization skills. Her long career in the airline industry demonstrated her dedication and flexibility to take on new positions wherever she was needed.

Based on these core qualifications and skills, we targeted the following positions with grade levels ranging from GS-4 up to GS-6: Administrative Assistant, Office Assistant, EEO Assistant, and Procurement Assistant (OA).

To ensure that her new resume included the right keywords for all these targeted positions, I excerpted the federal duties and qualifications and asked her to match them to her job history. I then incorporated the federal language into her new resume. Her qualifications summary, like the ones we featured in previous resumes, showcases all her most important knowledge, skills, and experience. Next, we added at least one accomplishment to every position. Notice the diversity of the accomplishments, as well. This helps to demonstrate clearly the value she will bring to her new federal position.

Debra began applying for federal jobs with her new electronic resume. She successfully landed her new federal position within three months and started her new career as a Procurement Assistant (OA), GS-0303-04, with the Department of Energy.

Target Job: Target Job: Procurement Support Assistant, GS-0303-04, from current position as Customer Service Representative.
Resume Format: Electronic federal resume.
Private industry to federal career transition.

DEBRA ANN JONES
1234 Center Street
Baltimore, MD 21117
Evening: 410-692-7942
Day: 410-692-7942
deb50@hotmail.com

PROFESSIONAL EXPERIENCE

SERVICE DIRECTOR
CUSTOMER SERVICE REPRESENTATIVE (CSR), 4/1995-Present
Freedom Airlines, Premier Club
BWI Airport
Salary: $40,000; Hours per week: 40
PO Box 66140, Baltimore, MD 21204
Supervisor: Harvey Stewart, 410-601-6746, may be contacted

MANAGE AND EXECUTE broad range of SPECIALIZED SERVICES for members of Freedom Airline's Premier Club, an exclusive traveler's club that provides complementary and fee-based personalized travel assistance and business support services to international and domestic travelers. Serve as Service Director or CSR depending on fluctuating schedules and personnel availability.

FIRST POINT OF CONTACT TO PASSENGERS. Manage daily operations. Research and verify credentials using automated system: Interface daily with more than 1,000 high-value customers, including VIPs, government leaders, foreign dignitaries, and business executives. Effectively manage service demands that fluctuate throughout the day depending on passenger volume, flight and airport conditions, and security priorities. Greet and screen incoming customers. Manage ticketing and seat assignments and coordinate services. I collect, verify, and document fees. Provide individualized service to special-needs passengers.

LEAD AND DIRECT UP TO 10 CUSTOMER SERVICE EMPLOYEES in fast-paced environment. Assign and prioritize work. Manage productivity. Use Timatic database system to support security screening. Examine, verify, and process credentials, passports, visas, and other legal documentation. Conduct system searches. Verify requirements relevant to country of origin. I ensure compliance with federal regulations. Coordinate supplies with contract food vendor. Track and analyze visitor statistics. Benchmark supply orders. Inventory supplies. Manage budget.

LIAISON TO SECRET SERVICE, FBI, AND GOVERNMENT AGENCY PERSONNEL. I coordinate logistics for travelers requiring high security assistance. Personally coordinate as many as 20 high-profile travelers monthly. Resolve customer complaints and problems. Seek to find a positive, acceptable resolution to every problem. Field questions on club services, fees, flight arrangements, and security.

MANAGE BUSINESS SUPPORT SERVICES AND FACILITIES. Schedule conference facilities. Maintain calendar. Review facilities and operations daily. Ensure all services and equipment are operational, clean, and orderly. Coordinate maintenance. Document and maintain accurate records on membership applications, conference room bookings, fees, facility maintenance, and food/supply inventories and orders.

(continued)

(continued)

ACCOMPLISHMENTS:

In 2000, I successfully passed a capability test required for leadership role as Service Director.

I provided accurate, error-free credential documentation for more than 11 years.

Effectively and efficiency processed and serviced an estimated 1,000 passengers per day in 2005.

Received 14 complimentary letters from passengers over two years for providing exceptional customer service.

During 2000-2001 collateral assignment as Baggage Service Director, I received Leadership Award for effectiveness and diplomatic handling of a high volume of security issues post 9/11.

REGIONAL KEY ACCOUNT REPRESENTATIVE, 4/1995-11/1998
Freedom Airlines, Cargo

MANAGED 25 MAJOR CORPORATE FREIGHT ACCOUNTS. Served as inside sales person and point of contact to customers. Priced, estimated, scheduled, and tracked international and domestic air freight shipments using the Apollo automated system. Teamed with account executive to manage corporate accounts and service accounts through sales calls. Worked closely with freight workers to expedite shipments. Recorded and tracked shipments to ensure all deadlines were met.

ACCOMPLISHMENTS:

Increased revenue by 78% with major corporate account through direct, personal contact with company president and by exceeding performance expectations in expediting shipments.

Established and fostered collaborative relationship with U.S. Mail account executive that was instrumental in retaining a high-revenue contract. Managed and flawlessly executed U.S. Mail distribution, representing $252 million in total revenue.

UNION STEWARD, 7/1999-Present
INTERNATIONAL ASSOCIATION OF MACHINISTS (IAM), District 200
531 Preston St., Ste. 103, Baltimore, MD 21201
Assistant General Chairperson: George Jensen, 301-534-7778, may be contacted

EMPLOYEE LIAISON: Concurrent with Freedom Airlines customer service duties, represent and negotiate on behalf of 900 IAM employee members in District 200. Serve as liaison to union representative, Grievance Committee Representative, Assistant General Chair of IAM, and corporate contacts for a broad range of employment issues, including Workers Compensation, EEOC, and denial of benefits.

Attend meetings and take and transcribe proceedings. Summarize all proceedings in written reports or testimony for presentation to the committee and chairperson. Defend the contract agreement to ensure it is not compromised. Continually strive to ensure that issues concerning both employees and management are fair and equitable. Liaison to Pension Benefit Guarantee Corporation (PBGC) for complex pension termination issue.

ACCOMPLISHMENTS:

Successfully represented 50 employees to reduce charges and save jobs.
Catalyst for work rule improvements, including better control of shifts and hours.

Led negotiations that reduced proposed cuts in pension benefits.

Selected to serve as media spokesperson. Appeared on national news outlets, including ABC and PBS, effectively presenting and discussing bankruptcy issues.

EMPLOYEE ASSISTANCE PROGRAM (EAP) (1/2000-8/2005)
Represented more than 900 employees of the IAM. Served as liaison between employees, Freedom Airlines, and union for a range of confidential employee problems, including domestic and child abuse, illness, and mental health issues. Worked in tandem with company representative and union steward to seek solutions to retain employee jobs during crisis situations. Helped employees find professional help.

ACCOMPLISHMENT: Instrumental in helping an employee to effectively communicate excessive time off during an illness and retain job without loss of seniority.

SPECIAL ASSIGNMENT, EXECUTIVE SECRETARY (1/2000-12/2000)
Selected to coordinate the opening of Baltimore District Office for Union President. Planned, organized, and managed all facets of the start-up. Selected vendors, reviewed bids, and ordered all supplies and office furniture to maximize use of start-up budget. Managed and prioritized incoming mail, incoming/outgoing correspondence, telephones, meetings, travel, purchasing, and billing. Liaison to Executive Board.

ACCOMPLISHMENTS:

Reduced overhead costs by more than $2,600 annually by switching to new vendors and selecting less-expensive supplies.

Organized new filing system of executive board records. Ensured all union dues were collected on time and accurately recorded.

TRAINER/FACILITATOR, 2/2000-5/2000
Freedom Airlines, Premier Club
BWI Airport
Salary: $40,000; Hours per week: 40
PO Box 66140, Baltimore, MD 21204
Supervisor: Ralph Polson, 410-773-6016, may be contacted

SPECIAL ASSIGNMENT, TRAINER/FACILITATOR (2/1990)

One of three facilitators selected by supervisor to lead Customer Satisfaction Training Program for 90 CSRs. Led videotaped scenarios demonstrating a range of challenging customer situations to help staff improve handling, response, and overall performance.

ACCOMPLISHMENT: Contributed to the development of content for a Customer Service Manual that was distributed to Premier Club agents system-wide.

(continued)

(continued)

EDUCATION

Graduate, Ferndale High School, 1968, Ferndale, MD 21405

TRAINING

University of Maryland, Women's Leadership Conference, Institute of Labor and Industrial Relations, 5/2005

Employee Assistance Program (EAP), International Association of Machinists, Las Vegas, Nevada, Training Seminar, 10/2000; Los Altos, CA, 9/2001

EAP, Joint Training Seminar with International Association of Machinists and Freedom Airlines, Pittsburgh, PA, 5/2002 and Seattle, WA, 5/2003

Conflict Resolution and Effective Management Techniques, 2001
Timatic Training Series

ADDITIONAL INFORMATION

QUALIFICATIONS SUMMARY:

CUSTOMER SERVICE / OPERATIONS SUPPORT PROFESSIONAL with more than 20 years of experience meeting and dealing with the public in a fast-paced environment. Liaison to VIPs, government officials, federal security representatives, business executives, and other dignitaries. Extensive administrative, general operations management, and labor relations experience. Areas of expertise include the following:

ADMINISTRATIVE / SECRETARIAL: Managing and scheduling conference facilities. Receiving and screening a high volume of visitors and callers. Managing business support services. Interpreting and applying rules, regulations, and procedures. Maintaining files and records. Transcribing minutes for meetings. Keyboarding speed: 40 w.p.m.

COMMUNICATIONS: Very strong oral, written, and interpersonal communications skills. Ability to clearly communicate factual and procedural information orally and in writing.

ORGANIZATIONAL: Strong skills and experience in quickly assessing current processes and recommending efficiencies. Proven track record of managing multiple tasks and meeting deadlines, often in high-pressure situations.

PROBLEM SOLVING: Action and results-oriented with the ability to solve complex problems with creativity. Keen analytical and research skills.

LABOR RELATIONS: Extensive knowledge of collective bargaining agreements, employee policies, and labor relations procedures. Point of contact for media relations.

STRONG TECHNICAL AND COMPUTER SKILLS: Expertise examining, preparing, processing, and executing electronic searches and verifying legal documents using national security and proprietary database management systems. Proficient in Word.

Figure 16.6: Debbie's new resume.

Summary

Now that you've seen some examples of how other candidates improved their federal administrative resumes, here are the most important points to remember:

1. Be sure to do a skills matching. Analyze the target posting for keywords and make a list. Many administrative positions share similar descriptions. Be sure to include those keywords in your new resume. Be sure to highlight any experience you have that matches the job posting.

2. Make a list of qualifications unique to you. Think about what sets you apart and include that information in your resume.

3. Don't forget to highlight your "soft skills."

4. Create a strong Profile statement.

5. Make sure your critical skills are on page 1 of your resume.

6. Try to list at least one accomplishment in each position.

7. Be sure to include information on your resume in the following areas:
   • Professional Memberships
   • Licenses, Certificates, and Military Service
   • Education and Training
   • Computer/Technical Expertise
   • Language Proficiencies
   • International Travel
   • Special Skills
   • Volunteer/Community Service

CHAPTER 17

Management and Program Analyst Resumes

The Management and Program Analyst position is the least well known to private-industry applicants and possibly the most prevalent management position in government. Many current federal employees strive to move into the Management Analyst occupational series so that they can be promoted to higher grade levels, work on projects that will improve and enhance government services to the American public, and have diverse and challenging work. You will see in this chapter that the Management Analyst positions are all different and you will need to read each vacancy announcement to determine whether you are qualified for a particular position. Some positions are very technical, requiring subject-matter knowledge; others are general and require basic skills in program or management analysis, writing, and oral communications skills.

According to Ligaya J. Fernandez, Senior Research Analyst for the Office of Policy and Evaluation at the U.S. Merit Systems Protection Board:

> The Management and Program Analyst positions are very important in government...yes, these positions are critical in government. The government does not provide products to the public. The government provides services. These services are based on programs that government policymakers have determined the American public needs and wants, and so they pass laws to make sure that these services are provided to the people. Once the laws are passed, the executive branch of government implements them. Management and Program Analysts are involved in the process of passing and implementing the laws...they actually do the analytical work required, from which important decisions are made.

> Decisions are based on information. Information (or data) has to be gathered, organized, and analyzed. And Management and Program Analysts do the gathering, the organizing, and the analyzing of information so that decisions can be made. Many are involved in program funding; and so many program analyst jobs require an understanding of financial management.

> Once a law is passed and implemented, the government also needs to know if the program is working the way Congress said it should work. They need to know if the program is cost-effective or if improvements are needed. Answers to these and other questions are very important to the policymakers. And the people who are assigned the task of answering questions like these are the **Management and Program Analysts.** They gather essential information, organize and study it, analyze it, and then make recommendations to government officials by way of formal reports.

> The requirements for, and responsibilities of, a Management and Program Analyst differ from job to job depending on grade, organization, location, etc. Reading the vacancy announcement very carefully is key to understanding what the job is all about. Some will require specialized subject-matter knowledge; but generally, they don't. What is required is knowledge

and skill that would enable them to perform analytical and evaluative work regarding the agency's operation or management of its programs.

The basic qualification needed for these types of jobs is the knowledge of the theories, function, and processes of management so that analysts can identify problems and recommend solutions. (And so, there really is no specific education required for these jobs, although coursework that includes math, statistics, economics, accounting, and finance is very helpful.) These types of jobs also require knowledge of the different analytical tools and evaluative techniques needed to analyze qualitative and quantitative data.

In sum…I would say the importance of this series is this: Important government program decisions are made based on what Management and Program Analysts recommend, so candidates for these jobs better be good!

Now *that* is an important position! Read Ligaya Fernandez's and other Management Analyst Reports at www.mspb.gov. Read their excellent and informative reports and newsletters to view excellent Civil Service public policy writing, qualitative and quantitative analysis, recommendations, and solutions.

The Management and Program Analyst, According to OPM

We have heard from a government expert and Senior Personnel Policy Analyst from www.mspb.gov about how important the Management and Program Analyst is in terms of keeping the "wheels of government" rolling and on track. So now let's examine the actual basic position description for this critical government employee.

> ★ **Note:** Management Analysts are also usually known as Project Managers.

The following is taken from OPM's USAJOBS Web site (www.usajobs.gov):

> Management and Program Analysis Series include positions which primarily serve as analysts and advisors to management on the evaluation of the effectiveness of government programs and operations or the productivity and efficiency of the management of federal agencies or both. Positions in this series require knowledge of: the substantive nature of agency programs and activities; agency missions, policies, and objectives; management principles and processes; and the analytical and evaluative methods and techniques for assessing program development or execution and improving organizational effectiveness and efficiency. Some positions also require an understanding of basic budgetary and financial management principles and techniques as they relate to long-range planning of programs and objectives. The work requires skill in: application of fact finding and investigative techniques; oral and written communications; and development of presentations and reports.

Some Management Analyst positions are very specific and technical to the agency mission, where the Analyst would also serve as Senior Expert, Subject Matter Expert, Advisor, and Consultant to senior executives. Other Management Analyst positions are more general in description without requiring subject-matter expertise. These positions offer opportunity for career changers who are not subject-matter experts in the mission of the organization. Here are four excerpts from Management Analyst announcements. Two are very technical and specific; three are general.

Recruiting a Subject-Matter Expert and a Management Analyst

Dept. of the Army, Field Operating Agency of Army Staff, Management Analyst, GS-13/13

Provides guidance, leads, and coordinates the work of a group of Force Integrators (materiel managers, equipment managers, force documentation analysts) with responsibility for development, implementation, and enforcement of policies and procedures applicable to a wide variety of Army manpower and equipment requirements and authorization documentation programs, systems, and projects.

Homeland Security, Transportation Security Administration, Program Analyst SV-0343-J/K Annual Salary Range (J Band) – $77,550 - $120,203 Annual Salary Range (K Band) – $92,708 - $143,703

PRINCIPAL DUTIES AND RESPONSIBILITIES: J BAND: The incumbent serves as the program analyst in Acquisition and Program Management Support Division, AA-Office of Acquisition, Transportation Security Administration, Department of Homeland Security. The incumbent serves as a program analyst and subject-matter expert regarding Project Management, Program Control, and project implementation for the Division Director. The incumbent provides consultative and advisory services to management to (1) evaluate program effectiveness and analyze gaps between actual and desired program results (2) provide solutions to eliminate or minimize the gaps between actual and desired program results, and (3) partner with the staff to ensure program guidelines and procedures are implemented and practiced.

Recruiting a General Management Analyst—Perfect for Career-Change Opportunities

Office of Postsecondary Education, U.S. Department of Education, Management and Program Analyst GS-343-9-12. MORE THAN ONE POSITION MAY BE FILLED

Conducts studies of work processes and procedures. Identifies problems, reviews production standards, and makes tentative recommendations for problem resolution. Reviews reports and studies to ensure that user requirements are met and appropriate rules and regulations are utilized. Assists in the development of directives and the design, development, documentation, and implementation of various reporting systems. Researches laws, regulations, policies, precedents and identifies best practices. Uses software to produce graphs and charts of financial, operational, or program performance.

Recruiting an Efficient Administrator and Management Analyst Who Can Improve Performance—Excellent Career Change Announcement

Department Of Health And Human Services Agency: Agency for Toxic Substances & Disease Registry, Management and Program Analyst, SERIES & GRADE: GS-0343-09/11 SALARY RANGE: 43939 - 69116 PROMOTION POTENTIAL: 11

The incumbent evaluates the efficiency and effectiveness of administrative functions. Identifies procedural problems in program operations, using quantitative or qualitative methods. The incumbent also completes data abstraction by analyzing and evaluating environmental public health documents with the purpose of ensuring the Agency's mission and performance measures are met. Completes quality assurance reviews and data verification functions on the abstracted documents to ensure the program is capturing the information efficiently and accurately. Retrieves information and pulls reports from databases and various other systems to ensure the Agency's performance measures are being met. Consolidates researched information and presents findings. The incumbent also presents findings orally and in written reports outlining findings, methods used, and makes recommendations for program improvement.

Recruiting a Management Analyst Who Can Develop New Methods for Programs—Good Career Promotion Announcement

Department: Department Of Education Agency: Office of Special Education and Rehabilitative Service Sub Agency: U.S. Department of Education, Management and Program Analyst, GS-343-12, Promotion Potential: 13

The incumbent conducts detailed analyses of complex functions and work processes of broad administrative or technical programs and makes recommendations for improvement in the effectiveness and efficiency of work operations. Develops new methods, organizational structures, and management processes. Counsels and advises program managers on methods and procedures, management surveys, management reports, and control techniques.

What Are the Critical Skills of a Management and Program Analyst?

A great way to tell whether you can qualify for a Management Analyst position is to find and read the Job-Related Questions and determine how you would assess your skill level. Also note any Essays that are required and decide whether you can write good project summaries for the essays.

The following vacancy announcement Assessment Questions for Management and Program Analyst were part of this U.S. Coast Guard announcement. These questions represent the Management Analyst series for a Generalist with these basic skills, hopefully at the highest level (or near). There are no Subject Matter Expert questions here. How would you rate on these questions? Could you cite an example of a project that demonstrated each of the critical skills?

Announcement Number: 06-0461-HQAP-D1

Vacancy Description: Management and Program Analyst GS-0343-13

Open Period: 07/05/2006 - 07/26/2006

(continued)

(continued)

Series/Grade: GS-0343-13

Salary: $77,353.00 TO $100,554.00

Promotion Potential: GS-13

Hiring Agency: United States Coast Guard

Duty Locations: 1 vacancy in Washington DC Metro Area, DC

For more information, Contact: USCG Applicant Support, 866-656-6830 Support@QuickHire.com

All Grades

1. Which of the following best describes your experience applying analytical and evaluative methods and techniques to studies concerning efficiency/effectiveness of program operations or substantive administrative support functions or organizational structures?

   1. I have not had experience, education, or training in performing this task.

   2. I have had education or training in performing this task but have not yet performed this task on the job.

   3. I have performed this task on the job with close supervision from supervisor or senior employee.

   4. I have performed this task as a regular part of the job, independently and usually without review by supervisor or senior employee.

   5. I have supervised performance of this task, and/or I have trained others in performance and/or am normally consulted as an expert for assistance in performing this task.

2. Have you demonstrated clearly superior data analysis capabilities?

   Yes   No

3. Have you collected appropriate sources of data, analyzed collected data, and reported on findings?

   Yes   No

4. Which of the following best describes your experience developing procedures for accessing and obtaining program analysis information available from various databases?

   1. I have not had experience, education, or training in performing this task.

   2. I have had education or training in performing this task but have not yet performed this task on the job.

   3. I have performed this task on the job with close supervision from supervisor or senior employee.

   4. I have performed this task as a regular part of the job, independently and usually without review by supervisor or senior employee.

   5. I have supervised performance of this task, and/or I have trained others in performance and/or am normally consulted as an expert for assistance in performing this task.

5. Which of the following best describes your experience communicating information to management for effective evaluation of program operations and milestones?

   1. I have not had experience, education, or training in performing this task.

   2. I have had education or training in performing this task but have not yet performed this task on the job.

3. I have performed this task on the job with close supervision from supervisor or senior employee.

4. I have performed this task as a regular part of the job, independently and usually without review by supervisor or senior employee.

5. I have supervised performance of this task, and/or I have trained others in performance and/or am normally consulted as an expert for assistance in performing this task.

6. Which of the following best describes your experience preparing and presenting recommendations and solutions regarding program management issues to high-level agency personnel?

1. I have not had experience, education, or training in performing this task.

2. I have had education or training in performing this task but have not yet performed this task on the job.

3. I have performed this task on the job with close supervision from supervisor or senior employee.

4. I have performed this task as a regular part of the job, independently and usually without review by supervisor or senior employee.

5. I have supervised performance of this task, and/or I have trained others in performance and/or am normally consulted as an expert for assistance in performing this task.

7. Which of the following best describes your experience effectively communicating written and oral recommendations regarding programs, personnel, budget, or facility requirements:

1. I have not had experience, education, or training in performing this task.

2. I have had education or training in performing this task but have not yet performed this task on the job.

3. I have performed this task on the job with close supervision from supervisor or senior employee.

4. I have performed this task as a regular part of the job, independently and usually without review by supervisor or senior employee.

5. I have supervised performance of this task, and/or I have trained others in performance and/or am normally consulted as an expert for assistance in performing this task.

8. Which of the following statements best describes your experience using basic and advanced evaluation tools to analyze a wide range of processes with long-term goals and results?

1. I have not had experience, education, or training in performing this task.

2. I have had education or training in performing this task but have not yet performed this task on the job.

3. I have performed this task on the job with close supervision from supervisor or senior employee.

4. I have performed this task as a regular part of the job, independently and usually without review by supervisor or senior employee.

5. I have supervised performance of this task, and/or I have trained others in performance and/or am normally consulted as an expert for assistance in performing this task.

9. Which of the following best describes your experience designing tracking and reporting systems to correlate workloads, production, and other performance indicators?

1. I have not had experience, education, or training in performing this task.

2. I have had education or training in performing this task but have not yet performed this task on the job.

3. I have performed this task on the job with close supervision from supervisor or senior employee.

(continued)

(continued)

    4. I have performed this task as a regular part of the job, independently and usually without review by supervisor or senior employee.

    5. I have supervised performance of this task, and/or I have trained others in performance and/or am normally consulted as an expert for assistance in performing this task.

10. Which of the following best describes your experience planning, developing, reviewing, and implementing program objectives and activities for national and/or regional programs in a team environment?

    1. I have not had experience, education, or training in performing this task.

    2. I have had education or training in performing this task but have not yet performed this task on the job.

    3. I have performed this task on the job with close supervision from supervisor or senior employee.

    4. I have performed this task as a regular part of the job, independently and usually without review by supervisor or senior employee.

    5. I have supervised performance of this task, and/or I have trained others in performance and/or am normally consulted as an expert for assistance in performing this task.

11. Which of the following best describes your experience analyzing, extracting, summarizing, and identifying significant trends and issues?

    1. I have not had experience, education, or training in performing this task.

    2. I have had education or training in performing this task but have not yet performed this task on the job.

    3. I have performed this task on the job with close supervision from supervisor or senior employee.

    4. I have performed this task as a regular part of the job, independently and usually without review by supervisor or senior employee.

    5. I have supervised performance of this task, and/or I have trained others in performance and/or am normally consulted as an expert for assistance in performing this task.

12. Which of the following best describes your experience using qualitative and quantitative techniques to analyze and measure the effectiveness, efficiency, and productivity of programs, as well as applying complex fact-finding analytical and problem-solving methods and techniques to identify interrelated program problems, draw conclusions, and recommend solutions?

    1. I have not had experience, education, or training in performing this task.

    2. I have had education or training in performing this task but have not yet performed this task on the job.

    3. I have performed this task on the job with close supervision from supervisor or senior employee.

    4. I have performed this task as a regular part of the job, independently and usually without review by supervisor or senior employee.

    5. I have supervised performance of this task, and/or I have trained others in performance and/or am normally consulted as an expert for assistance in performing this task.

13. Which of the following best describes your highest level of experience developing communication materials that present agency programs and policies suitable for various audiences?

    1. I have not had experience, education, or training in performing this task.

    2. I have had education or training in performing this task but have not yet performed this task on the job.

    3. I have performed this task on the job with close supervision from supervisor or senior employee.

4. I have performed this task as a regular part of the job, independently and usually without review by supervisor or senior employee.

5. I have supervised performance of this task, and/or I have trained others in performance and/or am normally consulted as an expert for assistance in performing this task.

14. Please describe your experience preparing briefings, reports, memoranda and letters:

(Essay Question)

15. Select the statement below that best describes your experience writing technical information that is logical, precise, innovative, and well organized for various audiences:

1. I have independently prepared written materials of a technical nature containing complex recommendations in a clear and concise manner for senior management or high-level officials.

2. I have prepared written materials of a technical nature containing complex recommendations in a clear and concise manner for supervisor's review.

3. I have drafted written material in a clear, concise and well-organized manner.

4. I have not had experience in performing this task.

16. Choose the statement(s) that describes the communication/briefing skills you have used as a regular part of your job:

Check all that apply

1. Developed written materials for briefings, meetings, or conferences.

2. Written clearly, logically, concisely, and persuasively for varied audiences.

3. Drafted policy and procedural materials for dissemination to field or operating-level components.

4. Drafted reports, memoranda, and correspondence for signature by higher-level officials.

5. Communicated organizational strategies, goals, objectives, or priorities on a regular basis.

6. Explained or justified decisions, conclusions, findings, or recommendations.

7. Composed complex correspondence or other written work such as manuals, books, management reports, or articles.

8. Reviewed reports for accuracy, adherence to policy, organization of material, clarity of expression, and appropriateness for intended audiences.

9. Briefed managers/executives outside of my organization.

10. Provided internal briefings on a highly controversial issue.

11. Provided external briefings on a highly controversial issue.

12. Developed comprehensive materials for briefings, meetings, or conferences for agency and departmental leaders, Congress, the media, and the general public.

13. None of the above.

17. Describe your experience using research, analysis, and writing skills to resolve complex issues:

(Essay Question)

A Significant Management Analyst Skill: Qualitative and Quantitative Analysis

Many job seekers will find this terminology in vacancy announcements. A recent workshop attendee at the Drug Enforcement Administration asked me in a course, "What does an announcement mean when they ask for experience in qualitative and quantitative methods?" This is a good question. I see this in many announcements. Think about when you measure qualitative and qualitative numbers about a program, budget, or office performance.

> 1. Knowledge of qualitative and quantitative methods for analyzing workload trends and survey data; assessing and improving complex management processes and systems, and program effectiveness.

A Management Analyst designs and conducts quantitative and qualitative analyses to evaluate and report on cost/benefit matters, financial issues, and organizational performance. The differences in qualitative and quantitative analyses are in the way data or information is collected in conducting a study. Simply stated, it is a difference between the use of numbers and words when conducting a study or evaluation. Quantitative analysis involves the utilization of questionnaires, tests, and existing databases. Qualitative analysis employs observations, interviews, and focus groups.

Collecting information using quantitative techniques is typically used to evaluate obvious behavior, and this methodology permits comparison and replication. And in most instances, it is believed that the reliability and validity of a study may be determined more objectively than when using qualitative techniques.

Utilizing qualitative methodologies to conduct an evaluation permits the consideration of concepts that were not part of the predetermined subject areas. Therefore, using qualitative techniques in conducting a study can be more exploratory in nature.

In summary, if you are applying for any kind of analyst or technician position, it would be very good to mention the type of qualitative and quantitative skills you have and the types of information you have analyzed.

Create a Project Map of Your Accomplishments and Projects That Match the Top-Level Skills

Most program and management analysts in government manage multiple projects in their jobs. The best way to write an impressive management analyst federal resume is to write about the projects you have managed. You can follow the Project Map in table 17.1 to create a project list that answers the following six critical skills for a management analyst. You could prove your competencies with examples. You can use a project list in the Duties section of your federal resume. With USAJOBS, you can include your project list in the Additional Information section.

Table 17.1: Project Map

KSA or Special Qualification	Project Examples
1. Quantitative and qualitative analysis	
2. Improving operations for more efficiency and effectiveness	
3. Recommending solutions; acting as an advisor or consultant	
4. Project management skills	
5. Writing and verbal communications	
6. Customer services/contract management	

Use Projects and Accomplishments to Prove Your Top-Level Skills

Expand your project map into narrative descriptions of your projects and analytical tasks. Define your projects and accomplishments with quantifiable numbers for excellent, impressive, on-target content for your resume. The projects or stories will be useful for interview preparation as well because most federal interviews are now behavior-based and require specific examples or stories as answers.

Here is a highly effective project outline that you can use to build your own project list:

Title of the project (or story):

Your role, name of task, project description, and date:

Budget (if this is appropriate):

Challenge/situation:

Observations, challenge, and description:

Recommendations, solutions, and actions:

Results—how did things improve?

Sample Project Description

Here is a sample of a project description for your resume, which includes the critical skills of a Management Analyst:

TITLE OF PROJECT (STORY): IMPROVED BALANCE OF WORKLOAD TO IMPROVE PATIENT SERVICES

Your role, name of task, project description, and date: Director of Customer Service for a Health Services Organization providing patient intake and care for more than 500 patients per month. Upon initial hire, I discovered the need to analyze workload balance and improve performance of 20 Patient Care Representatives. I utilized an off-the-shelf customer assessment system, Customer Service & Support Services survey tool, which includes behavioral-based questions to analyze performance. I interviewed and assessed workload on an individual basis to determine the workload imbalance that was affecting morale and efficiency of services. (2006)

(continued)

(continued)

> **Budget** (if this is appropriate): n/a
>
> **Challenge/situation:** I examined workflow and monitored staff to observe and collect information on such reported problems as unbalanced workloads (i.e., some staff assigned more tasks than others in their peer groups) and sensitive issues related to individual poor performance. In some instances, poor performance was the cause of the unbalanced workloads.
>
> **Observations, challenge, and description:** My observations and information collected indicated that some of the less productive workers were actually being given less work to do because they did not perform well, which further exacerbated the problem of workload balance and demoralized those workers who did perform well. In the final analysis, it appeared that good workers were being punished for their productivity by getting more to do, and the poor performers were being rewarded for their lack of ambition by being given less to do.
>
> **Recommendations, solutions, actions:** I confronted individual performance problems and made recommendations, reprimands, and, if necessary, terminations. In addition, I made recommendations on modifying workloads and individual assignments. Among my recommendations was the implementation of incentives for promoting productive and cooperative performance. Finally, I recommended changes in the existing processes and procedures for getting work done for such activities as telephone quotas, overflow calls, back-up ACD groups, workflows, implementations of new procedures, manual development, management and staffing assessments, training, and using interviewing tools.
>
> **Results—how did things improve?:** Within six months of the initial analysis, I directed a small team to development new processes and procedures for workflow, such as telephone quotas, overflow calls, back-up ACD groups, workflows, implementations of new procedures, manual development, management and staffing assessments, training, and using interviewing tools. The 20 employees plus 5 new hires had increased their intake by 33 percent by the end of 60 days. Workload was shared effectively and total volume of calls handled was up 25 percent. I received a $2,500 bonus for my analysis and recommendations within a short period of time.

(439 words; 2,994 characters with spaces)

Shorter Versions

Here are two shorter versions of the story for your federal resume (150 words or less):

> **Director of Customer Services—Improved Balance of Workload to Improve Patient Services.** Analyzed the performance of 20 telephone and in-person patient representatives to assess workload balance and quality of services. Utilized an off-the-shelf Customer Services & Support Services Survey tool, as well as individual interviews and workflow analysis of the staff. I created Excel spreadsheets to analyze customer services, interview times, and productivity. I discovered unbalanced workloads due to excellent and poor performance. The high-performing employees worked twice as hard as the low-performing staff. **RESULTS:** I redistributed the workload, retrained staff, fired two employees, and carefully analyzed productivity. Finally, I recommended changes in the existing processes and procedures for getting work done for such activities as telephone quotas, overflow calls, back-up ACD groups, workflows, implementations of new procedures, manual development, management and staffing assessments, training, and using interviewing tools.

(141 words)

Here's another shorter version for three-page resume builders:

> **<u>Director of Customer Services—Improved Balance of Workload to Improve Patient Services.</u>** Analyzed the performance of 20 telephone and in-person patient representatives for workload balance and customer services. Utilized an off-the-shelf Customer Services & Support Services Survey tool, individual interviews, and workflow analysis of the staff. I created Excel spreadsheets to analyze unbalanced workloads. Discovered that high-performing employees worked twice as hard as the low-performing staff. **RESULTS:** I redistributed the workload, retrained staff, and fired two employees. Recommended new procedures for telephone quotas, overflow calls, back-up ACD groups, workflows, implementations of new procedures, manual development, management and staffing assessments, training, and using interviewing tools.

(106 words)

Critical Points of this Story for Behavior-Based Interview Preparation

Memorize and practice this "story" for a behavior-based interview. This example would be perfect for a question having to do with analysis of work or employee performance, customer services, or employee communications.

> Director of Customer Services—Improved Balance of Workload to Improve Patient Services.
>
> - Analyzed the performance of 20 telephone and in-person patient representatives for workload balance and customer services.
> - Utilized an off-the-shelf Customer Services & Support Services Survey tool, individual interviews, and workflow analysis of the staff.
> - Created Excel spreadsheets to analyze unbalanced workloads.
> - Discovered that high-performing employees worked twice as hard as the low-performing staff.
> - RESULTS: I redistributed the workload, retrained staff, and fired two employees. Recommended new procedures for telephone quotas, overflow calls, back-up ACD groups, workflows, implementations of new procedures, manual development, management and staffing assessments, training, and using interviewing tools.

(106 words)

Example Behavior-Based Questions

Here are examples of the types of questions you might be asked in a behavioral interview:

★ Can you describe a time when you needed to analyze employee performance and workload in order to improve performance and productivity?

★ Can you describe a time when you had to improve productivity with available staff and needed to give recommendations to improve staff performance?

★ Can you give an example of a situation where you discovered an imbalance in workload of employees and had to resolve this problem?

Federal Employees Seeking Career Change with Career Ladder Management Analyst Positions

The Management Analyst series is an excellent choice for career development and new challenge. Because these positions vary among agencies and offices, you can write your current resume featuring your projects and skills that are similar to what is described in this chapter. Changing careers into a Management Analyst position will involve analyzing the top skills needed in the target position and highlighting those same skills in your job.

Transitioning from Specific Positions

Here are some tips for transitioning from specific positions:

★ If you are currently an **Administrative Assistant,** you would write about your special projects, database development, research, problem-solving, setting up more efficient systems, and giving recommendations to the supervisor to improve operations.

★ If you are currently a **Lead Accounting Technician,** GS-8, and hope to change series and move up a grade, you would emphasize your problem-solving, special projects, research and analysis, consulting and advising customers about more efficient methods of accounting information management, and special reports, including spreadsheets.

★ If you are currently a **Housing Management Specialist,** GS-12, and would like to move into the Management Analyst series at a GS-12 or GS-13 level, you would want to emphasize your projects, partnerships with agencies, consulting services to housing entities, problem-solving, analysis of programs, skills in spreadsheet design, and briefings written and given on housing topics. The focus of the project is on the analytical skills, not the content of housing.

Changing Levels

Changing careers at the GS-9 or GS-11 level is easier than at the higher grade levels, because usually the qualifications for the positions are more general, such as this one:

> One year of specialized experience that equipped the applicant with the particular knowledge, skills, and abilities to perform successfully the duties of the position, and that is typically in or related to the work of the position to be filled. This experience must be equivalent to the GS-9 level in the federal government. Examples of such experience may include: analyzing the effectiveness of programs; analyzing the efficiency of operations; participating in studies to increase efficiency; preparing work plans and reports based on existing procedures or observations of activities; preparing materials for workflow and operational analyses, studies of costs, or equipment utilization; reviewing operational plans and current and incoming work projects; making recommendations for improving work methods; advising on the adequacy of budgets; and determining the need for work standards and control systems.

More Hints for Writing a Management and Program Analyst Resume

Here are some more tips to keep in mind as you write your resume.

Research the Mission of the Office or Agency

Considering the mission of the office or agency will help you write more compellingly. Research the challenges of the agency or office to consider their analysis and project priorities. For instance, if you

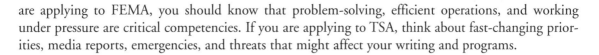

are applying to FEMA, you should know that problem-solving, efficient operations, and working under pressure are critical competencies. If you are applying to TSA, think about fast-changing priorities, media reports, emergencies, and threats that might affect your writing and programs.

Add the Numbers and Quantify Your Information

In order to write a "qualitatively correct" Management Analyst resume, you will need numbers to demonstrate that you can track information, demonstrate results, prove performance and efficiency, and present data. Because Management Analysis is all about information management, your resume should demonstrate these skills at the basic resume writing level. Which example below is better?

BEFORE: Without specific numbers or ALL CAPS HEADLINES, and the focus on projects is non-existent:

02/07/2002 to 10/31/2006; Hours Per Week: 40-52; Transition Services Supervisor; Pay Grade GS-203-11, Salary: $59,000; U.S. Army, Military Personnel Division, Fort Myer, VA 22211; Supervisor: Sam Jones, 703-696-0296; Contact: yes.

Responsible for preparing, processing, and reviewing all personnel actions related to retirements and separations. Principal reviewer of all enlisted and officer personnel action requests for reassignments, early release, and resignations. Facilitate monthly installation retirement and separation briefings, conduct exit interviews, and assist in publication of orders. Coordinate retirement processing with support stations and counsel retirees, spouses, and family members. Coordinate with Information Resources Management on any software or hardware systems needed to implement, manage, and provide reporting on Human Resources initiatives. Supervise staff of six personnel and one civilian for planning, coordinating, training, managing performance, monitoring, mentoring, and counseling subordinates.

Identify developmental training needs of subordinates. Maintain records and compile statistical reports concerning awards, transfers, and performance appraisals. Maintained full accountability for equipment and property. Directed and guided administrative and personnel requirements for opening and closing several offices. Promote sound management principles and policies to ensure compliance.

Developed and managed database required to process retirement and separation actions. Developed and published Standard Operating Procedure handbook used as guide for all Transition Personnel, which resulted in achieving 100 percent success rate for cross-training. Cross-trained office personnel on various personnel systems, increasing retirement processing.

AFTER: With impressive numbers, specifics, ALL CAPS HEADINGS for easy reading, and targeted skills:

02/07/2002 to 10/31/2006; Hours Per Week: 40-52; Transition Services Supervisor; Pay Grade GS-203-11, Salary: $59,000; U.S. Army, Military Personnel Division, Fort Myer, VA 22211; Supervisor: Sam Jones, 703-666-6666; Contact: yes.

TRANSITION SERVICES SUPERVISOR FOR FORT MYER MILITARY COMMUNITY SERVING OVER 10,000 PERSONNEL. Supervise a military personnel staff of six and one civilian for planning, coordinating, training, managing performance, monitoring, mentoring, and counseling subordinates. Prepare, process, load, and review all personnel actions

---

(continued)

(continued)

related to retirements and separations during a high level of personnel activity. Principal reviewer of all enlisted and officer personnel action requests for reassignments, early release, and resignations. Facilitate monthly installation retirement and separation briefings, conduct exit interviews, and assist in publication of orders. Coordinate retirement processing with support stations and counsel retirees, spouses, and family members. Coordinate with Information Resources Management on any software or hardware systems needed to implement, manage, and provide reporting on Human Resources initiatives.

DESIGN, DEVELOP, AND PRESENT TRAINING. Identify developmental training needs of staff to manage a high level of personnel actions. Maintain records and compile statistical reports concerning awards, transfers, and performance appraisals. Maintained full accountability for equipment and property valued at over $300,000. Directed and guided administrative and personnel requirements for opening and closing several offices. Promote sound management principles and policies to ensure compliance. RESULTS: Increased accountability of property as well as efficiency of staff with new focused training.

ACCOMPLISHMENTS: Developed and managed database required to process over 3,000 retirement and separation actions over three-year period. Developed and published Standard Operating Procedure handbook used as guide for all Transition Personnel, which resulted in achieving 100 percent success rate for cross-training. Cross-trained office personnel on various personnel systems, increasing retirement processing by 30 percent (June 2003). Developed and managed database required to process over 3,000 retirement and separation actions (November 2003).

How Does Your Private-Sector Job Involve Management Analyst Skills?

Just because your private-industry job title is not "Management Analyst," does not mean you couldn't qualify for a Management Analyst position in government. The following are the private-sector occupations that match the public-sector Management and Program Analyst job:

- ★ Advertising Director
- ★ Business Analyst
- ★ Business Process Engineer
- ★ Category Analyst
- ★ Configuration Analyst
- ★ Database Administrator
- ★ Marketing Analyst, Market Researcher
- ★ Operations Manager
- ★ Program Analyst
- ★ Program Manager
- ★ Programmer Analyst (playing down the IT part of your work)
- ★ Project Manager
- ★ Quality Systems Administrator
- ★ Research Analyst
- ★ Sales Executive (focus on marketing, analysis, and program management)
- ★ Strategic Analyst
- ★ Systems Analyst
- ★ Web Project Engineer
- ★ Writer-Editor

A Sample Management and Program Analyst Resume

Here is a full resume written for the Management and Program Analyst position.

Target Job: Management and Program Analyst, GS-0343-12, from current position as Management Analyst, GS-0343-11.
Resume Format: Electronic federal resume.
Federal to federal career promotion.

Christine Salome Dietrich
5058 Rock Glen Rd.
Arlington, VA
Home: 703-222-5656
Office: 202-555-6565
E-mail: christine_dietrich@yahoo.com

SSN: 000-00-0000

01/2006 to Present; 40 hours per week; Management Analyst; GS-0343-11; last promoted N/A; permanent employee; not on a temporary promotion; Commander Navy Installations Command, Arlington Detachment; BLDG 410; Al Reynolds, (202) 333-4545; may contact supervisor.

During the Program Manager of Commander Navy Installations Command's two-month absence, I served as Acting Program Manager, continuing to implement significant change, efficiency, service initiatives for a growing customer base (military families in transition), and quality of staff work, with a dramatically decreased budget for the Family Employment Readiness Managers located at 62 military bases worldwide.

PROGRAM MANAGEMENT: Management Analyst for the Navy Headquarters Family Readiness Programs, including Navy Family Ombudsman Program and Deployment Readiness Program.

PLAN AND DEVELOP STRATEGIC INITIATIVES that have led to improvements and delivery of Family Readiness Programs at 62 delivery sites worldwide. I continue the management of improved programs and initiatives for Family Employment Readiness Program Managers and military families worldwide. Evaluate effectiveness of programs and efficiency of management. Plan and conduct in-depth studies, analyze data, and develop policy recommendations.

CUSTOMER COMMUNICATIONS: Extensive communications, problem-solving, and program implementation with program personnel located at U.S. Navy Fleet and Family Support Centers worldwide. Prepare and present briefings and presentations on analytical findings and recommendations; represent agency at meetings and conferences.

FAMILY READINESS STAFF TRAINING: Develop, oversee, coordinate, and present numerous program initiatives that directly impact retention, readiness, and career progression. Maintain contact within DoD and professional community to utilize latest ideas, methodologies, and issues.

DATA MANAGEMENT AND ANALYSIS: Administrator of Ombudsman Registry. Serve as advisor on development of the database. Oversee database implementation, evaluation, and quality control. Conduct formal and informal surveys of field sites. Consolidate and analyze statistical data and trends utilizing data to develop reports for Navy Leadership, DoD, and Congress regarding the status of Ombudsman Program. Additional responsibilities include developing contract modifications, approving and administering user access levels, and ensuring command data is accurate.

ACCOMPLISHMENTS AND SPECIAL PROJECTS:

+ POLICY IMPROVEMENTS AND MODIFICATIONS: Navy Family Ombudsman Program and Deployment Readiness Program. Researched issues that required modifications to regulations and policy development. Analyzed issues; identified best course of action; determined potential impact on retention, readiness, and subordinate organizations; and provided recommendations for corrective actions.

(continued)

(continued)

+ OMBUDSMAN PROGRAM MANUAL. Served as Subject Matter Expert for the revision of the Ombudsman Program Manual and Instructor's Guide. Reviewed and provided recommendations and corrections to revised OPNAVINST, Ombudsman Program Manual, Ombudsman Instructor's Guide, and Ombudsman video, Second Edition.

+ SURVEY DESIGN AND DEVELOPMENT: Created three surveys to be completed by Ombudsmen, Fleet and Family Support Center Ombudsmen Coordinators, and Command Leadership. Collected and reviewed data, analyzed data, and exported into spreadsheets and PowerPoint for use at the annual Ombudsman Quality Management Board meeting for discussion on how to improve the Navy Family Ombudsman Program.

04/2002 to 01/2006; 40 hours per week; Spouse Employment Assistance Program (SEAP) Specialist; GS-0101-11; last promoted 04/2003; permanent employee; not on a temporary promotion; Commander Navy Installations Command, Arlington Detachment; BLDG 410; Al Reynolds, (202) 333-4545; may contact supervisor.

PROGRAM MANAGEMENT: Specialist (2002-2004) for Family Readiness Programs. Programs included Family Employment Readiness (formally SEAP), Volunteer, Navy Family Ombudsman Program, and Deployment Program for the Department of the Navy.

Principal program assistant to Fleet and Family Support Center (FFSC) Program Manager. Co-managed all aspects of FFSC operations, including planning, formulation, organization, program evaluation, training, consultation, publicity, and coordination of programs in the Fleet and Family Support Centers, all Navy installations, other military services, DoD, and private sector. Developed and wrote assigned portions of instructions, policy, program guidance, and materials for Family Readiness Programs.

TECHNICAL ADVISOR / SITE VISITS: Technical advisor for the program within NAVPERSCOM and on DoD working groups on Family Readiness Program issues. Assessed and evaluated Family Readiness Program services effectiveness, conducting site visits at FFSCs worldwide. Assisted in design and implementation of quality assurance and evaluation measures for Family Readiness Programs through IGs, site visits, and reports. As subject matter expert, advised field managers and counselors on Family Readiness Programs issues, to meet customer assistance goals. Reviewed and maintained resource directory on resource materials in support of programs. Subject matter expert for inquiries regarding Family Employment Readiness, Ombudsman, Volunteer, and Deployment Programs.

MANAGEMENT ANALYST / REPORTS: Tracked Navy-wide family employment efforts and consolidated and developed reports for Navy/DoD leadership and Congress. Consolidated and analyzed statistical data and trends from Fleet and Family Support Center field sites and Headquarters for Family Readiness Programs. Wrote three- to five-page documents summarizing professional career qualifications, accomplishments, knowledge, skills, and abilities. Edited, proofed, and reviewed content for consistency in grammar and style. Improved readability of documents through use of Plain Language and a focus on accomplishments. Analyzed and reviewed client position descriptions, evaluations, mission statements, and existing application packages.

TRAINING COORDINATION: Developed, oversaw, coordinated, and implemented training workshops and conferences on Family Readiness Programs to FFSC staff.

BUDGET: Impact Card Holder (2002-2004) responsible for managing monthly budget of credit card purchases. Annually, assisted in development of $1.2 million budget. Distributed field support money when available and reviewed all field staff's requests for unfunded money for appropriateness and future program effectiveness.

ACCOMPLISHMENTS:

+ Continuously partnered with Navy Personnel Research, Studies and Technologies (NPRST) group within Navy Personnel Command to develop studies and gather metrics on impact of SEAP on recruiting, retention, and readiness. Created first quarterly report for SEAP, identifying SEAP trends and documenting return on investment.

+ Selected as one of four representatives across Navy for DoD Spouse Employment Working Group to advise and consult on development and implementation of curriculum and desk guide for DoD Family Employment Readiness Program. Co-authored Federal Employment chapter of the FERP desk guide.

+ Selected as representative for Fleet and Family Support Programs to advise and consult on development and implementation of Ombudsman Resource, Instructor, and Participant Guides.

+ Hurricane Katrina relief efforts: Worked with Task Force Navy Family (TFNF), recruiting and coordinating movement of supplemental staff from other FFSCs to assist evacuees at Community Support Centers. Provided training and individual instruction on the use of case management system.

01/2000 to 04/2002; 40 hours per week; Employee Assistance Manager; GS-0101-09; last promoted Not Specified; permanent employee; not on a temporary promotion; Fleet & Family Support Center, 348 Kinkaid Road, Annapolis, MD 21402; Regina Helms, 410-222-7878; may contact supervisor.

Program Manager of military spouse and family employment program. Provided comprehensive employment assistance for Department of Defense personnel, relocating military spouses and children, and at times retirees and separatees.

COMMUNITY OUTREACH: Designed and facilitated workshops and briefings. Developed procedures to ensure quality of course content, instruction, and materials. Wrote monthly newsletter on employment, spouse appreciation, and volunteerism. Designed marketing strategies to ensure target population was aware of services. Participated in creation of community organization to effectively coordinate job readiness resources and network with peers.

CAREER COUNSELING: Interviewed and advised spouses on career, occupational, volunteer, and educational issues. Compiled work and experience profiles on clients. Used career inventories and aptitude assessments to help clients focus their interests and goals. Made referrals to civilian volunteer opportunities as needed.

STATISTICAL ANALYSIS: Compiled monthly and quarterly statistical program reports for FFSC and Navy Personnel Command as needed.

02/1996 to 07/1999; 40 hours per week; Social Services Representative; GS-0187-09; last promoted Not Specified; permanent employee; not on a temporary promotion; Fleet and Family Support Center, NAS Sigonella PSC 824 Box 2650 FPO AE 09623-2650; Jasmine Wright, 901-777-8989; may contact supervisor.

(continued)

(continued)

PROGRAM MANAGEMENT: Led mental health/social services clinician of New Parent Support Program. Provided prevention services to at-risk families with children ranging from newborn to five years of age. Prepared annual budget, procured supplies, and hired and trained staff. Prepared and implemented policy statements and operating procedures.

COMMUNITY OUTREACH / TRAINING: Developed and presented educational briefings, trainings, and workshops on child abuse prevention, parenting, pregnancy, birth control, and sexual assault. Provided information and referral services to community-based resources. Maintained networking system with community agencies and utilized media to increase awareness.

CASE MANAGEMENT: Conducted home visits to assess families and progress, teach problem-solving techniques, and provide support. Reported suspected instances of abuse or neglect. Prepared client files and tracked data for statistical reporting and analysis. Provided liaison for medical staff and community resources to identify and assess referrals and community needs.

EDUCATION

Kutztown University, Kutztown, PA 19530; Bachelor in Psychology, 1987

Archbishop Carroll High School, Radnor, PA; 1983 High School Diploma

TRAINING

08/2006: Accreditation Team Training
02/2006: Performance cash award for Task Force Navy Family
02/2006: Core Ombudsman Training Team
10/2005: Performance and cash award for successful conference coordination
04/2005: Ombudsman Basic Training
04/2003: 10 Steps to a Federal Career Certification Training
04/2002, 2003, 2004, 2005, 2006: DoD Spouse Summit Conference
04/2002, 2003, 2004, 2005, 2006: Association of Job Search Trainers Conference
10/2001: Mid-Atlantic Career Counseling Annual Conference, 24 hours
09/2000: Intermediate PowerPoint, 8 hours, Computer Wisdom
08/2000: Introduction to Excel, 8 hours, Computer Wisdom
08/2000: Introduction to Word, 8 hours, Computer Wisdom
07/2000: Myers-Briggs Type Indicator Qualifying Workshop, 40 hours, Otto Kroeger Associates.
06/2000: Spouse Career/Life Course Training, 40 hours, Department of Navy
06/2000: Introduction to PowerPoint, 8 hours, Computer Wisdom
08/1999: Navy Family Advocacy Program Biennial Conference, 36 hours, Navy Family Advocacy Program
03/1999: New Parent Support Training, 16 hours, Department of Navy
02/1999: National Conference, 24 hours, Prevent Child Abuse America/Healthy Families America

Figure 17.1: Sample Management and Program Analyst resume.

Summary

Follow the advice of the HR specialist: "Your resume should explain the nature of experience, accomplishments, education, and training opportunities that best illustrate how, to what degree, and with what impact you have applied/used each of the knowledge, skills, and abilities needed for successful performance in this position. Your description may include examples of accomplishments, problems resolved, risks/threats averted, or processes improved as a result of your efforts." Consider the supervisor who is hiring, think about their programs and challenges, and determine how you could contribute to analyzing the performance and results of the program. Write about your successes in the past, be specific, and add numbers.

CHAPTER 18

Human Resources Management Resumes

By Susan Custard

One of the most challenging and rewarding occupations in the federal government can be found in human resources management (HRM). The changes to the occupation can easily be identified in the changing work environment, and in the new competencies required to successfully perform the work. Whether you are a current practitioner or looking to enter the field, this period of change is a good time to evaluate your own career plans, assess the value you bring to the organization and the occupation, and begin to look at new opportunities in the field.

HR has been changing over the last decade, and is currently being challenged in the areas of automation, streamlining, standardization, and most critically, evolving client expectations. Management expectations are now focused on HR's changing role in being strategic, which can be defined as leading the organization in meeting business goals and objectives through effective utilization of human capital. Additionally, employees are now seen as customers of HR, changing the paradigm of "management advisory service." HR employees seeking to further their careers need to clearly articulate their value to the organization in providing service to management and employees that meets strategic goals and objectives.

Necessary Competencies and Skills

With the strategic focus now expected of HR, there are many initiatives underway throughout the federal government to support HR employees (and those seeking to enter the occupation). There has been significant direction from the Chief Human Capital Officer's (CHCO) Council regarding the new competencies required of HR staff to be effective in a field that is ambiguous at best. For example, the CHCO Council recently sponsored a competency and skills assessment for all GS-201 (Human Resources Management) positions throughout the federal government.

In order to prepare for positions within the new HR paradigm of strategically focused, customer-oriented service to managers and employees, HR employees and "wanna-bes" should be focused on developing or enhancing their competencies as described in the following list:

1. **Classification:** Knowledge of classification concepts, principles, and practices related to structuring organizations and positions and determining the appropriate pay system, occupational grouping, title, and pay level of positions.
2. **Compensation:** Knowledge of compensation concepts, principles, and practices, including pay and leave administration and compensation flexibilities.

3. **Employee Benefits:** Knowledge of HR concepts, principles, and practices related to retirement, insurance, injury compensation, and other employee benefits programs.

4. **Employee Development:** Knowledge of employee development concepts, principles, and practices related to planning, evaluating, and administering training, organizational development, and career-development initiatives.

5. **Employee Relations:** Knowledge of laws, rules, case law, regulations, principles, and practices related to employee conduct, performance, and dispute resolution.

6. **HR Information Systems:** Knowledge of HR management concepts, principles, and practices related to identifying and analyzing HR processes, translating functional requirements into technical requirements, and delivering and maintaining HR information systems.

7. **Labor Relations:** Knowledge of laws, rules, regulations, case law, principles, and practices related to negotiating and administering labor agreements.

8. **Performance Management:** Knowledge of performance management concepts, principles, and practices related to planning, monitoring, rating, and rewarding employee performance.

9. **Recruitment/Placement:** Knowledge of HR concepts, principles, and practices related to identifying, attracting, and selecting individuals and placing them into positions to address changing organizational needs.

In addition to the technical competencies in the preceding list, OPM has identified key "soft skills" that HR specialists need to be effective in the new world of HR. The new HR is focused on a less regulatory or bureaucratic approach, and is changing to a consultant, client-centric delivery model. At the full performance level (GS-12), HR staff should highlight experiences that will develop or enhance their skills in the following areas:

Attention to detail	Creative thinking
Change management	Customer service
Decision making	Flexibility
Influencing and negotiating	Integrity and honesty
Interpersonal skills	Oral communication
Planning and evaluation	Problem solving
Reasoning	Risk management
Self-management	Tolerance for stress
Teamwork	

Applying for HR Jobs

So—what does this mean to you if you are interested in an HR career?

To begin with, you need to develop a clear emphasis on developing both the technical and "soft" skills in the preceding lists in order to further your career. And, most importantly, you need to be able to articulate these skills in a well-developed application. HR people, who should be among the best at self-marketing through the application process, are generally among the poorest in the government. How can you coach and mentor applicants through the selection process, giving them feedback on improving their applications, without taking your own advice?

As you decide to apply to pursue other HR opportunities by applying to vacancies, you need to develop a marketing plan that will ensure that you address the technical expertise required, combined with clear descriptions or evidence of your possession of the required competencies. Your marketing plan needs to incorporate three aspects of the application process:

★ **Self-assessment:** Complete a self-assessment of your competencies, and determine your strengths and weaknesses. This might involve getting feedback from management, customers, peers, or others who can provide you with an honest and direct assessment of your skills.

★ **Resume and KSAs:** Develop an effective resume and KSA responses that reflect your technical competence and demonstrate your ability to effectively consult (provide options to management) and assess risk.

★ **Interviews:** Be prepared for an intensive, behaviorally based interview process for any position you apply for. The interview is where you'll have your best opportunity to show you are part of the new HR.

Resume Development: Your Personal Marketing Tool

Follow the steps in part 1 to develop your resume. Additionally, once you have a completed resume, get lots of feedback. You might have forgotten a key experience, or a peer or manager might be able to point out critical strengths to build into your resume. Finally, review your resume against each job announcement to ensure that you are addressing the specific competencies required for that position.

See the HR Management resume at the end of this chapter for a place to get started.

Putting It All Together: Writing KSAs in the CCAR Format

To write effective KSAs for the HR Specialist or Assistant job, follow the advice outlined in chapter 9. That chapter outlines the "CCAR" format, a special template OPM recommends for SES candidates who are writing their KSA statements (known as Executive Core Qualifications, or ECQs). "CCAR" stands for *Context* (what work environment were you in?), *Challenge and Action* (what was the problem you faced and what did you do to resolve it?), and *Result* (how did your actions improve the situation?). The underlying theme of the CCAR format is that specific examples or stories that illustrate problems you've resolved, cases you've handled, actions you've taken, and accomplishments you've achieved will always make you stand out above applicants who merely state that their experience has provided them with the needed KSAs.

As you work with the factor-level descriptions in the HR classification standards, write down the accomplishments that illustrate your knowledge and your ability to perform the tasks the standards call for. What guidelines do you use? If you can't apply them directly, do you interpret them? If you do, how does your interpretation affect the quality of service you deliver? Can you write a paragraph about a work assignment you've had that required you to interpret unclear guidance? With a little practice, you'll soon be giving examples of problems you've solved instead of just telling the job rater, "My job requires me to interpret a variety of guidance that is not always clear."

Eight Emerging KSAs for the HR Career Field

As more agencies transition toward the "new role" model of HR management, new KSAs will begin to be used in vacancy announcements. Although no one can predict exactly how these KSAs will be worded, the following suggested KSAs begin to capture the changes and competencies needed in the new HR. When reviewing these proposed KSAs, you should challenge yourself with developing draft responses, which may assist you in your self-assessment, and identifying those areas where you need skill development or enhancement.

★ How HR management and development contributes to the agency's ability to reach its strategic goals and objectives.

★ How HR professionals collaborate with managers to design and implement strategic approaches to overall agency objectives.

★ How HR professionals develop and recommend options best suited to particular missions, labor markets, and work technologies.

★ How HR organizations invent and adapt their processes and programs to the agency's mission.

★ How HR professionals provide advice about the latest practices and developments that might help achieve mission results and maintain a strong performance culture for the workforce.

★ How HR organizations integrate methods and options from different HR functions to streamline operations and make them more relevant to clients and customers.

★ How HR professionals work across multiple functions to tailor solutions to various HR challenges.

★ How HR information systems development is used to affect management's and employees' expectations about timely, quality service; for example, using the Internet to educate the workforce about HR programs and options.

As you develop your KSAs, be aware that in the future many HR candidates will be called on to illustrate how they have played one or more of these roles in their own HR organizations. Look for opportunities within the context of your current job to lead change, and you will automatically become a stronger candidate for the "new role" HR job of the future.

Interviewing: Practice Makes Perfect

Based on the preceding sections, you should be prepared for a competency or behavior-based interview. In a behavioral interview, the interviewer will ask you questions in which you will demonstrate your behavior in a given situation. You can't get enough practice in preparing for an interview, so choose your questions and start talking! Here are some sample questions to challenge you.

Customer Focus:

> Describe a time when you found yourself in a position where you had to "recover" with clients—how did you handle it, and were you successful?

Business Acumen:

> How do you go about developing the required knowledge of the business of your service organization(s)? How does your level of knowledge impact your ability to provide advice and service?

Working as a Member of a Team:

> What are your team-player qualities? Give examples.

Integrity and Trust:

> Have you ever been asked to violate a policy or procedure to get something for a client?

Priority Setting:

> If you have competing client priorities, what do you do?

Other:

Of the four functions that this job encompasses (classification, compensation, staffing, and recruitment), which would you rate yourself highest in and why?

If you had a chance to create a work environment in which you would be most successful, what would it be?

What is your most significant accomplishment in the world of HR?

How would you go about developing and implementing a knowledge transfer plan?

What do you know about our position classification program? Why do you want to be a part of it? What do you think will be the biggest challenge in doing the work?

What do you know about our position management program?

What do you know about our overall HR program? How do you think you can add value?

HR is undergoing significant change management. On a scale of one to ten, how would you assess your ability to manage change? Why?

Using the same scale, how would your boss assess your ability to manage change? Why?

How have you added value to your job over time?

How do you feel that you can contribute to an environment of teamwork?

What did you do to make your last job interesting and more challenging?

Tell us about a suggestion you made on the job to improve how things worked. What was the result?

Sample HR Management Resume

Following is a sample resume for an HR assistant position.

Target Job: Human Resources Assistant, GS-0203-07, from current position as Human Resources Benefits Administrator.
Resume Format: Electronic federal resume.
Private industry to federal career transition.

Becky Wallace
8990 Mountain View Ct.
Seattle, WA 98101-5150
Telephone: 206-333-1212
E-mail: beckyw@verizon.net

SSN: 000-00-0000

SKILL SUMMARY: More than 20 years of Administrative and Management experience. Human Resources Benefits Administrator and support, responsible for office management, word processing, record keeping, mail processing, computer operations, database and spreadsheet management, multi-line telephone protocol, voice and electronic mail, filing and archiving, customer service, scheduling, and accounting. Experienced in supervision and training. Proficient in operating computers, office machines, telephone systems, copiers, 10-key, typewriter, and communication console.
4 years Washington Army National Guard active guard/reserve (AG/R); Honorable Discharge.
6 years active United States Air Force; Honorable Discharge.

WORK EXPERIENCE

Feb. 2002 to Present: ABC Contracting, 210 Business Center Blvd., Seattle, WA 98101

Human Resources Benefits Administrator: Feb. 2002 to present. 40 hours/week. Salary: $29,000/yr. Supervisor: Bradley Smith, Personnel Manager, 206-444-5656. May be contacted.

Perform functional specialties of human resources; specifically, employee benefits, wage and pay administration, and staffing support. Apply knowledge of methodology and performance of work assignments involving HR activities, processes, policies, and regulations.

BENEFITS ADMINISTRATOR. Primary resource and point of contact for benefits information. Enroll eligible employees into company benefit plan(s). Serve as primary source of expertise and assist employees with health insurance claims, issuance of flexible spending accounts, and disability checks. Accountable for all COBRA notifications. Provide information for medical providers to file forms for workers' compensation. Process benefit invoices. Implement new benefit program; verify calculation of monthly premium statements for all group insurance policies and maintain statistical data relative to premiums, claims, and costs. Resolve administrative problems with carrier representatives. Research annual list of present, new, and former pension plan participants for all pertinent data. Submit data and documents to appropriate manager.

RETIREMENT BENFITS EXPERT. Enroll employees in and maintain 401(k) program. Coordinate 401(k) Pension Plan procedures. Initiate commencement of 401(k) benefits. Maintain files of 401(k) history, data, correspondence, reports, and forms. Initiate record keeping and retrieval methods in compliance with government regulations. Submit information to Human Resource Manager for actuarial valuation of 401(k) pension plan. Prepare and forward appraisal forms to supervisor for completion; record, file, and follow up on completed forms; set up new appraisal dates.

PAYROLL DEPARTMENT LIAISON. Coordinate and process new employee setups and terminations. Compute salary changes, prepare status forms, coordinate all data with Payroll Department Manager. Prepare status changes for hourly, general, and automatic increases. Ensure prompt processing of personnel claims for disability, vacation, sick time, and personal days. Review employee claims for unemployment insurance benefit to determine eligibility. Follow up on claims for unemployment to keep penalties to a minimum.

ADMINISTRATIVE OFFICER. Prepare monthly reports on hires and terminations for HR Manager and General Manager. Manage correspondence, including composing, typing, and proofreading HR correspondence such as personnel reports, performance standards, appraisals, awards, benefit providers' response, and employee response letters. Edit correspondence for style, tone, grammar, spelling, and enclosures. Compose routine letters, perform necessary research; as needed, develop document formats. Maintain records of salaried personnel attendance, vacation, sick time, and personal days. Assist in the preparation of the affirmative action plan and EEO. Under limited supervision, perform complex clerical duties following established procedures in the following areas: group life and health insurance, benefit plans, short-term/long-term disability insurance, records maintenance, and nonexempt and exempt merit reviews. Initiate medical and option forms and affidavits; monitor timeliness and completeness of these actions.

Purchasing Agent/Material Handling Specialist. Jul. 2001 to Feb. 2002. 40 hours/week. Salary: $30,000/yr. Supervisor: Melanie Poteck, Project Manager, 206-444-5656. May be contacted.

PURCHASING AGENT. Managed and coordinated purchase of goods and services. Hired, supervised, and evaluated purchasing department personnel of 15. Approved selection of major vendors. Trained buyers to assess vendor capabilities, develop sources, and evaluate vendor performance. Negotiated terms of major contracts and blanket orders. Recommended major purchases of materials on the basis of anticipated changes in prices or on unusual availability situations. Balanced cash flow considerations against possible price savings.

Ensured purchasing documents were completed properly and terms and conditions of purchase were appropriate. Supervised accurate record keeping, including price histories. Established policies and procedures, including the maintenance of low inventories, and avoidance of shortages of necessary raw materials and supplies. Responsible for payroll, A/P, A/R, invoicing, and vendor relations. Accomplishments: $1.6 million profit after completing two jobs for Intel simultaneously. Resulted in permanent placement.

MATERIAL CONTROL HANDLING/LOGISTICIAN/WAREHOUSEMAN. Extensive, long-volume traffic control; shipping; receiving; procurement; maintenance; distribution; and replacement of personnel and equipment. Managed daily operations including shipping, receiving, warehouse, and inventory control. Identified and resolved critical problem areas to ensure efficiency and timely project completion. Increased department competency through extensive training and strategic staff reengineering. Specific technical skills and knowledge include Order Fulfillment—Quickly and accurately picked numerically coded stock. Inventory updated via computer. Delivered items to the shipping section. Selected packing methods, materials, containers, and labeling best suited to ensure safe transit. Receiving/Expediting— Unpacked incoming shipments, checking that material received agreed with packing slip specifications and quantities. Rejected damaged goods and arranged for their return to vendor. Transferred incoming goods to proper storage area or department within one day of arrival to avoid backlogs. Data Entry/inventory Control—Used computer to enter incoming/outgoing material and track status of inventory and shipment.

Jan. 1999 to Jul. 2001. Office Manager/Payroll Clerk. 40-80 hours/week. Salary: $10/hr. Premier Temps (temporary service) hired for ABC Contracting.

OFFICE MANAGER/BOOKKEEPER: Responsible for A/P and A/R. Maintained journal entries. Generated checks and reconciled accounts. Verified invoices and maintained cash disbursements and cash journal receipts. Maintained general ledger and chart of accounts, and produced financial statements. Assisted in audits. Budgeted and managed assets. Maintained payroll and taxes. Supervised two people.

(continued)

(continued)

May 1999 to Jan. 2001. Owner/Operator. 20-40 hours/week. Salary: varied. Virtual Secretarial Services, Seattle, WA.

SECRETARY/OFFICE MANAGER. Monitored and managed all affairs and aspects of business operations, including hiring/firing personnel, budgeting, customer service, clerical support, and cost control. Managed time effectively by prioritizing workflow to meet deadlines. Accurately typed, transcribed, formatted, edited, and printed a variety of materials in rough draft or final form from written material or computer disks, in various office settings, and on time. Typing examples included all correspondence, legal documents, financial statements, letters, reports, memoranda, tabulated data, charts, rosters, mailing lists, form letters, inventories, vouchers, and forms. Received incoming telephone calls and directed to proper party or took messages as needed. Troubleshot as necessary. Established and maintained automated and paper filing systems to expedite tracking of documents. Increased work efficiency with computer software including AppleWorks, Calendar Create, DacEasy Accounting, Enable 4.0, FmLight, FormTools, FoxPro, Harvard Graphics, Lotus 1-2-3, Microsoft Word 95/97, Microsoft Works 98, Microsoft Money, Norton Utilities, QuickBooks Pro, Quicken 5.0, Smartware, and WordPerfect.

Jul. 1997 to Jan. 1999. Project Manager, Best Farming Systems, 143 Madison Ave., Redmond, WA 98052
Supervisors: Roland and Jen Rizzo, 206-555-4545. May be contacted.

CONSTRUCTION MANAGEMENT. Supervised all aspects of construction of $10 million feed mill designed and built by Best Farming for Washington Farms, Inc. Strong organizational skills to perform critical path schedules. Hired/fired laborers and directed subcontractors; monitored work for quality control and safety issues. Ordered construction supplies; negotiated with vendors for lower costs and delivery service; approved accounts payable. Facilitated communication among subcontractors, employees, and management. Supervised 25 people.
Accomplishments: Oversaw construction of a $10 million feed mill. First woman sent into the field by corporate office.

MILITARY EXPERIENCE:

Apr. 1995 to Jun. 1997. Hours per week: 40-60. Salary: $25,000/yr. Unit Supply Sergeant/Unit Clerk, United States Army - Washington Army National Guard, Detachment One, Supply and Transportation, 495 Support Battalion. Supervisor: Brenda Rowe, 206-222-4545. May be contacted.

Later hired full-time under the active guard/reserve program (AGR), as Unit Supply Sergeant and Unit Clerk. Supervised 76 people.
Accomplishments: 100 percent damage-free deliveries. No losses or thefts reported. The first woman full-time Unit Supply Sergeant in Washington.

Dec. 1993 to Apr. 1995. 1 weekend/month, 2 weeks/year. Material Control Handling Specialist, Washington Army National Guard Reserves.

May 1987 to Nov. 1993. Hours per week: 40. Salary: $775 bi-weekly. Command & Control Specialist/Search & Rescue Coordinator/Training Noncommissioned Officer/Maps Monitor/Operational Reports Specialist, United States Air Force, E-5, Airlift Command Center (ALCC) at McChord AFB, WA.
Accomplishments: Successfully completed 450+ missions, resulting in saving 385 lives.

EDUCATION
Unit Supply/Unit Clerk Certificates, Washington Army National Guard, Seattle, WA, 1995
Introduction to Accounting, 8 semester hours, Washington State University, Seattle, WA, 1998
Clerical Certificate, Vocational-Technical School, Olympia, WA, 1987
GED, State of Washington, 1987

AWARDS:
Good Conduct Medal, Dept. of the Army, Jun. 1993; NCO Development Ribbon, Dept. of the Army, Jun. 1992; National Defense Service Medal, Dept. of the Army, Jun. 1993; National Guard Attendance Ribbon, Dept. of the Army, Apr. 1992; Dale Carnegie Public Speaking Award, Jul. 1988; Overseas Long Tour Ribbon, Dept. of the Air Force, Nov. 1989; Good Conduct Medal, Dept. of the Air Force, Nov. 1992; Commendation Medal, AAC/RCC, Dept. of the Air Force, Aug. 1990; Longevity Service Award Ribbon, Dept. of the Air Force, Mar. 1990; Junior Noncommissioned Officer of the Year (71 It ARRS), Dept. of the Air Force, Feb. 1993; Outstanding Unit Award, Dept. of the Air Force, Sep. 1990; Senior Airman Below-the-Zone, Promoted to E-4, Dept. of the Air Force, Aug. 1989; Commendation Medal, 22nd AF, Dept. of the Air Force, May 1989; Training Ribbon, Dept. of the Air Force, Jun. 1987

OTHER INFORMATION:
Detail-oriented, efficient accounting professional with a strong background in all areas of the accounting system. Exceptional analytical and organizational skills. Self-motivated, with the ability to work independently and make thought-out decisions. Excellent verbal and written communication skills. Previously held Clearance: Top Secret - USAF and Secret - US Army

Figure 18.1: Sample Human Resources Assistant resume.

Summary

The HR occupation and work environment are constantly changing. In order to continue to advance your HR career, you should focus on developing the critical technical and "soft skills" required, with a special emphasis on understanding how the broad use of all HR functions together can contribute to your organization's success. With these skills in hand and an effective marketing campaign, your success in finding new and challenging positions in the HR field will be assured.

Special Federal Job Seeker Strategies: SES, Military, and Wage-Grade Transitions

CHAPTER 19

Senior Executive Service, Executive Core Qualifications

In an effort to develop a corps of executive managers with the talent, foresight, and flexibility required to lead a soon-to-be-reformed federal service through a new era, Congress, through enactment of the 1978 Civil Service Reform Act, created the Senior Executive Service (SES). Congress envisioned the SES as a cadre of exceptional leaders recruited from the top levels of government and private industry, who would move among agencies and share their broad background and experience to create new efficiencies and innovations government-wide.

Managerial experience gained solely in the federal government would no longer be the most important criterion for gaining a senior position in an agency, nor would the Best Qualified new leader necessarily be the career civil servant who spent his entire career in one agency. The reality is that the majority of SES positions continue to be filled by career civil servants. Nonetheless, it is remarkable that unlike virtually all other governments around the world, high-level professional positions within the United States government still remain open to those who have gained their experience outside the federal civil service.

A Profile of the SES

The SES has changed in many ways during the past 20-plus years, but it is still the leadership cadre of the federal service. Of the 6,800 members of the SES, 88 percent are career civil servants. The remainder are noncareer appointments (usually political) or appointments for a limited term. Almost half of SES positions are based in the Washington, D.C., metropolitan area. The composition of the SES reflects various federal agencies' functional requirements. Forty-five percent are in administrative or management fields. Another 12 percent provide legal services. Engineering, science/math, and other fields each account for 12 to 14 percent. Twenty-six percent of the SES are women, and nearly 14 percent are minorities.

The first word of "Senior Executive Service" is appropriate: It *is* a senior service, with 30 percent of its membership eligible for retirement between now and 2008. Retirement remains the primary method of attrition in the SES.

Ten years ago, the National Performance Review formally recommended that the SES develop a "corporate perspective" that supports government-wide cultural change. This recommendation might have been a veiled acknowledgment that Congress' vision of the SES as a mobile corps of flexible executives had yet to be implemented in practice. Several years later, the Office of Personnel Management revised the Executive Core Qualifications (known as ECQs, listed later in this chapter), which are the five main rating factors used to evaluate an SES candidate's "corporate perspective." OPM has recently updated the "leadership competencies" that define the ECQs; this minor change is the only change seen in the ECQs since their inception.

The ECQs are defined in tables 19.1 and 19.2. Each ECQ definition has been modified to provide a clear explanation of the ECQ's requirements. The most significant changes in the ECQs are the addition of the "fundamental competencies," which are considered as an inherent part of the skills of each ECQ. Additionally, the competencies for several ECQs have changed. Leading People has changed, with the addition of "Developing Others" as a competency; many of the other ECQ competencies have been moved into the "fundamental competencies," including Interpersonal Skills (Building Coalitions and Communication), Written Communication (Building Coalitions and Communication), Continual Learning (Leading Change), as well as the addition of "Public Service Motivation."

Table 19.1: Executive Core Qualifications

Leading Change	Leading People	Results Driven	Business Acumen	Building Coalitions/ Communication
Definitions				
This core qualification involves the ability to bring about strategic change, both within and outside the organization, to meet organizational goals. Inherent to this ECQ is the ability to establish an organizational vision and to implement it in a continuously changing environment.	This core qualification involves the ability to lead people toward meeting the organization's vision, mission, and goals. Inherent to this ECQ is the ability to provide an inclusive workplace that fosters the development of others, facilitates cooperation and teamwork, and supports constructive resolution of conflicts.	This core qualification involves the ability to meet organizational goals and customer expectations. Inherent to this ECQ is the ability to make decisions that produce high-quality results by applying technical knowledge, analyzing problems, and calculating risks.	This core qualification involves the ability to manage human, financial, and information resources strategically.	This core qualification involves the ability to build coalitions internally and with federal agencies, state and local governments, nonprofit and private-sector organizations, foreign governments, or international organizations to achieve common goals.
Competencies				
Creativity and Innovation	Conflict Management	Accountability	Financial Management	Partnering
External Awareness	Leveraging Diversity	Customer Service	Human Capital Management	Political Savvy
Flexibility	Developing Others	Decisiveness	Technology Management	Influencing/Negotiating
Resilience	Team Building	Entrepreneurship		
Strategic Thinking		Problem Solving		
Vision		Technical Credibility		

Fundamental Competencies: These competencies are the foundation for success in each of the Executive Core Qualifications: Interpersonal Skills, Oral Communication, Continual Learning, Written Communication, Integrity/Honesty, Public Service Motivation

Table 19.2: Executive Core Qualifications and Competency Definitions

ECQ 1: *Leading Change*

Definition: This core qualification involves the ability to bring about strategic change, both within and outside the organization, to meet organizational goals. Inherent to this ECQ is the ability to establish an organizational vision and to implement it in a continuously changing environment.

Competencies

Creativity and Innovation	Develops new insights into situations; questions conventional approaches; encourages new ideas and innovations; designs and implements new or cutting-edge programs/processes.
External Awareness	Understands and keeps up-to-date on local, national, and international policies and trends that affect the organization and shape stakeholders' views; is aware of the organization's impact on the external environment.
Flexibility	Is open to change and new information; rapidly adapts to new information, changing conditions, or unexpected obstacles.
Resilience	Deals effectively with pressure; remains optimistic and persistent, even under adversity. Recovers quickly from setbacks.
Strategic Thinking	Formulates objectives and priorities, and implements plans consistent with the long-term interests of the organization in a global environment. Capitalizes on opportunities and manages risks.
Vision	Takes a long-term view and builds a shared vision with others; acts as a catalyst for organizational change. Influences others to translate vision into action.

ECQ 2: *Leading People*

Definition: This core qualification involves the ability to lead people toward meeting the organization's vision, mission, and goals. Inherent to this ECQ is the ability to provide an inclusive workplace that fosters the development of others, facilitates cooperation and teamwork, and supports constructive resolution of conflicts.

Competencies

Conflict Management	Encourages creative tension and differences of opinions. Anticipates and takes steps to prevent counterproductive confrontations. Manages and resolves conflicts and disagreements in a constructive manner.

Competencies

Leveraging Diversity	Fosters an inclusive workplace where diversity and individual differences are valued and leveraged to achieve the vision and mission of the organization.
Developing Others	Develops the ability of others to perform and contribute to the organization by providing ongoing feedback and by providing opportunities to learn through formal and informal methods.
Team Building	Inspires and fosters team commitment, spirit, pride, and trust. Facilitates cooperation and motivates team members to accomplish group goals.

ECQ 3: Results Driven

Definition: This core qualification involves the ability to meet organizational goals and customer expectations. Inherent to this ECQ is the ability to make decisions that produce high-quality results by applying technical knowledge, analyzing problems, and calculating risks.

Competencies

Accountability	Holds self and others accountable for measurable, high-quality, timely, and cost-effective results. Determines objectives, sets priorities, and delegates work. Accepts responsibility for mistakes. Complies with established control systems and rules.
Customer Service	Anticipates and meets the needs of both internal and external customers. Delivers high-quality products and services; is committed to continuous improvement.
Decisiveness	Makes well-informed, effective, and timely decisions, even when data are limited or solutions produce unpleasant consequences; perceives the impact and implications of decisions.
Entrepreneurship	Positions the organization for future success by identifying new opportunities; builds the organization by developing or improving products or services. Takes calculated risks to accomplish organizational objectives.
Problem Solving	Identifies and analyzes problems; weighs relevance and accuracy of information; generates and evaluates alternative solutions; makes recommendations.
Technical Credibility	Understands and appropriately applies principles, procedures, requirements, regulations, and policies related to specialized expertise.

(continued)

(continued)

ECQ 4: Business Acumen

Definition: This core qualification involves the ability to manage human, financial, and information resources strategically.

Competencies

Financial Management	Understands the organization's financial processes. Prepares, justifies, and administers the program budget. Oversees procurement and contracting to achieve desired results. Monitors expenditures and uses cost-benefit thinking to set priorities.
Human Capital Management	Builds and manages workforce based on organizational goals, budget considerations, and staffing needs. Ensures that employees are appropriately recruited, selected, appraised, and rewarded; takes action to address performance problems. Manages a multi-sector workforce and a variety of work situations.
Technology Management	Keeps up-to-date on technological developments. Makes effective use of technology to achieve results. Ensures access to and security of technology systems.

ECQ 5: Building Coalitions/Communication

Definition: This core qualification involves the ability to build coalitions internally and with other federal agencies, state and local governments, nonprofit and private-sector organizations, foreign governments, or international organizations to achieve common goals.

Competencies

Partnering	Develops networks and builds alliances; collaborates across boundaries to build strategic relationships and achieve common goals.
Political Savvy	Identifies the internal and external politics that impact the work of the organization. Perceives organizational and political reality and acts accordingly.
Influencing/Negotiating	Persuades others; builds consensus through give and take; gains cooperation from others to obtain information and accomplish goals.

Fundamental Competencies

Definition: These competencies are the foundation for success in each of the Executive Core Qualifications.

Competencies

Interpersonal Skills	Treats others with courtesy, sensitivity, and respect. Considers and responds appropriately to the needs and feelings of different people in different situations.
Oral Communication	Makes clear and convincing oral presentations. Listens effectively; clarifies information as needed.
Integrity/Honesty	Behaves in an honest, fair, and ethical manner. Shows consistency in words and actions. Models high standards of ethics.
Written Communication	Writes in a clear, concise, organized, and convincing manner for the intended audience.
Continual Learning	Assesses and recognizes own strengths and weaknesses; pursues self-development.
Public Service Motivation	Shows a commitment to serve the public. Ensures that actions meet public needs; aligns organizational objectives and practices with public interests.

The Changing Competition for SES Positions

Competition for SES positions will become more intense in the next 10 years. It is not unusual for HR professionals to report receiving 55 to 60 applications for each SES announcement. Not only are numerous baby boomers seeking the promotions that will cap careers that began in the late 1960s, but agencies reduced the number of SES positions during the mid-to-late 1990s as a result of the National Partnership for Reinventing Government—the successor to the National Performance Review.

Most SES reductions were achieved by cuts in the Department of Defense (closures of major installations resulted in many workforce cuts) or by eliminating positions that were on the books but had not been filled. In other instances, agencies eliminated one position only to create another—redesigning jobs to align with "reinvention" initiatives. Such restructuring, however, tended to be at the margins of the SES. Most executive positions lead core agency programs that would require statutory changes to modify or eliminate. In an era of divided government, such changes are difficult to effect.

Who Should Apply?

In most cases, new SES members rise through career-development ladders within single agencies or departments. They might serve within different agency components during their careers, but the federal service generally still adheres to the principle of advancement within a profession. A new SES manager in the Environmental Protection Agency's water program, for example, is more likely to come from within that program than from any other program in the EPA. Although most agencies have SES attorneys, an immigration law attorney is unlikely to transfer into an SES position in the antitrust division at the Department of Justice. Demonstrating relevant skills is the surest route to entering the SES, and that is usually done most credibly at the agency where the position will be filled.

There is no substitute for substantial experience. Entrants who rise through career ranks to the SES frequently have 15, 20, or even 30 years of experience, most of which was gained within their own agencies. They typically have at least a college education, and frequently possess graduate degrees and other forms of professional development training. Many will be identified and nurtured—or mentored—through their agency's SES candidate-development programs or through other well-recognized channels, such as the Federal Executive Institute. Their experiences will include broadening through a number of detail assignments at other agencies. Nearly all successful SES applicants will have a succession of outstanding performance evaluations and demonstrate a record of developing other people to ensure that their organizations continue to work well in their successors' hands. In addition to this sustained superior performance, it usually helps to have pulled one or two major projects out of the fire under emergency or adverse circumstances.

An important dimension of an SES application, as with most federal positions, responds to the question, "What have you done lately?" Federal human capital officers and selecting officials are looking for progressively responsible performance at or near the level for which one is applying. Typically, the SES applicant will be able to describe five to seven years of experience at the GS- or GM-15 level.

Successful SES applicants must demonstrate an ability to think at least two bureaucratic levels above the advertised position. An SES appointment usually requires the approval of an agency head and the Office of Personnel Management, so a Senior Executive applicant must be able to speak that executive's language.

An SES opening in any agency signals some organizational change—maybe an experienced executive is retiring or agency leaders are creating a new position to address a perceived problem. Knowing the agency and its needs is critically important. You can strengthen your SES application if you know what the agency leadership believes its problems to be and can demonstrate that you have the experience to tackle those issues. You need not be an insider to gain familiarity with an agency's mission and requirements; however, you bear the burden of demonstrating that experience and knowledge you gained elsewhere provides enough background for you to perform effectively.

Finally, senior executives at or above the SES job level being filled usually rate SES applicants. You will be a stronger candidate if these executives already know you and are familiar with your significant accomplishments, and if you effectively represent these accomplishments in your ECQ statements.

If the preceding description fits you, consider applying for the SES. Vacancies for SES positions are listed on the www.USAJOBS.gov Web site. The vacancy list is updated regularly. Many individual agencies also advertise SES positions on their Web sites.

Requirements for Successful Applicants: Remember the Basics

As you begin to develop your SES package, keep in mind that regardless of the federal agency to which you apply, staffing an executive position is much more complex than staffing other types of federal jobs. Because of the high visibility and broad impact to the agency, nearly all SES selections require agency-level approval. Before you can even hope to get an interview, your application must survive the initial and secondary screening phases it will pass through in the agency's HR office.

One seasoned HR professional who has staffed many SES jobs and has reviewed hundreds of applications offers the following advice to those applying from both within and outside the government.

Read and Follow the Instructions

Follow the application instructions. As obvious as this might seem, an appalling number of applicants are eliminated at the initial screening phase because they simply fail to submit the required documents.

"We received 55 applications for our agency's SES General Counsel position last year," our HR professional reports. "Of those 55, over half were eliminated because they did not submit proof that they were licensed to practice before a state bar—even though the announcement stated clearly that applicants who did not submit such documentation would receive no further consideration."

If you're an attorney applicant with many years of service, you might think such a requirement is unnecessary, or perhaps even nitpicky: After all, you've worked as a civil-service attorney for 30 years. Surely the personnel office "knows" you're licensed to practice before a state bar. Or, at worst, if they don't have record of this, surely the personnel office will call you or your agency's personnel office and ask for it. Remember this: Forty to sixty candidates are applying for only one job. It is an enormous task for the HR specialist to review these applications and whittle them down to a manageable number of candidates for senior managers to interview. If you fail to include the information required in the vacancy notice, it is an easy way for them to disqualify you from further consideration. Don't let this be you. Follow the application instructions to the letter.

Make the Length "Just Right"

Think Goldilocks. Or maybe Procrustes (the mythological host who adjusted his guests to the size of the bed). Make sure the length and substance of each document in the package is neither too long nor too short. "Internal applicants tend to submit way too much information," our HR advisor says. "They've been with the government a long time and think they have to include everything they've done since they were a GS-5." On the contrary, statements should describe experience that is directly relevant and closely focused to the job requirements. "On the other hand," our advisor continues, "external candidates tend to submit only one-page resumes, often with no cover letter, and seem to feel we are lucky to get even that."

The SES selection process, a very daunting one even for internal candidates who are familiar with lengthy staffing procedures, is often incomprehensible to external candidates. "The government loses a lot of good talent because of the process," our advisor notes, "they simply get frustrated and go away. OPM is working on streamlining the process, so we hope it will get better." In the meantime, external candidates must take the time to describe their experiences in-depth and explain how it relates to the vacant position. Otherwise, HR professionals simply will not have enough information to determine that an external candidate is highly qualified for the job.

Balance the Strengths and Weaknesses of Your Background

Both internal and external candidates need to balance the inherent strengths and weaknesses of coming from either a federal or private-sector background. To be effective as a senior leader, SES positions require a mix of both worlds: Candidates must know the internal workings of government systems— how the bureaucracy works—but they also must have the ability to bring new ideas and approaches to the agency.

What Does the SES Announcement Require?

The normal SES package contains a cover letter, a strong federal resume (study parts 1 and 2), special statements addressing as many as three sets of technical and managerial factors listed in the vacancy notice, and most importantly, statements showing that the candidate possesses the five Executive Core Qualifications (ECQs) established by OPM—the managerial skills that are the prerequisites for entry into the SES. Unless the resume and the statements demonstrate that you possess the Executive Core Qualifications, even exceptional technical qualifications will not be enough to develop a successful SES application.

As a reminder, from table 19.1, the five Executive Core Qualifications (ECQs) are as follows:

★ Leading Change

★ Leading People

★ Results Driven

★ Business Acumen

★ Building Coalitions/Communication

In addition to the five ECQs, each agency can define both mandatory and desirable technical qualifications for any SES position advertised. These qualifications vary according to the position. For example, an applicant for Assistant Administrator of the Federal Aviation Administration for airway facilities must be able to demonstrate professional knowledge of the design and engineering of radio navigational systems. Firsthand flying experience using this system might strengthen those qualifications, but that would be a desirable, rather than a mandatory, technical requirement.

Nearly one-third of SES applications are rejected for not describing the advertised qualifications for the position. Of the remaining two-thirds, the quality of the ECQ statements determines who will be grouped among the Well Qualified, and ultimately, who will gain interviews for the position. It is not unusual for agencies to report a final list of only 3 to 12 Well Qualified candidates from a pool of 60 applicants. With competition this intense, your core qualifications statements must stand above the crowd.

Are All ECQs Created Equal?

A frequently asked question we receive from SES candidates is, are some ECQs more important than others? In a recent government-wide survey, OPM asked career senior executives how the ECQs ranked in order of importance to their current federal jobs. The majority responded as follows:

1. Leading People
2. Building Coalitions/Communication
3. Results Driven
4. Leading Change
5. Technical Competence (based on your Mandatory Technical Qualifications Narratives)
6. Business Acumen

These results confirm that communications and "people skills" continue to be the most important characteristics required of senior leaders in the federal service. The survey went on to conclude that Business Acumen was also emerging as a more desirable characteristic of future government leaders.

The core qualifications demand more than managerial experience. A candidate must demonstrate keen business acumen, the ability to foresee and overcome challenges to successfully lead change, and the ability to gain others' support and cooperation to reach results. It is not enough to discuss the duties of positions you have held or to make conclusive statements that you have managed large staffs or held jobs that gave you these abilities. You must provide concrete examples of the problems you faced, how you solved them, and how your effort improved the organization. As one personnel officer responsible for SES positions commented, "I want to know not merely what the applicant claims to have done; I need to know when and where it was done to make the case credible." In short, to be a successful SES applicant, you must master the art of writing powerful ECQs. Let's get started!

Writing Executive Core Qualifications

Writing Executive Core Qualification statements is like writing KSAs for other types of federal jobs. Unlike the KSA statements, however, the ECQs are exactly the same government-wide. Consequently, the statements will be applicable to virtually any SES position for which you apply. Although writing and polishing the statements requires significant time and effort, your initial investment will pay off, particularly if you apply for more than one vacancy.

Writing ECQs is no different from any other writing challenge: Well-written material that keeps the reader's interest gets more attention than sleeper prose. Still, the challenge of consolidating 20 years of accomplishments into five pages is significant—especially if you have had too many successes to fit into the allotted space.

Basic Principles

Here are some basic principles that will help you write successful ECQ statements:

1. **The basics of effective writing still apply.** Use the active voice. Your responses must convey what you did and what difference it made. Avoid passive constructions and bureaucratic phrasing: Say "I decided and directed" instead of "I was given responsibility for."

2. **Demonstrate the application of your knowledge.** Whereas KSAs require you to state what you know (knowledge) and what you have done or can do (skills and abilities), Executive Core Qualifications require you to demonstrate effective *application* of what you know. Effective statements require more than an explanation of your personal growth. In each ECQ, describe the effects you and your work have had on other people, other organizations, and agency policies. If you have held a job requiring interagency coordination, bring it to the evaluators' attention.

3. **Demonstrate executive performance.** This is not the place to write about how you gained your skills. Many of the KSA statements written for lower-level positions are effective because they show "progressive responsibility"—that is, they describe how increasingly complex work assignments prepared them for the next job up the ladder. The SES needs people who can demonstrate through what they have already done that they are in a position to take charge *now*. Well-qualified applicants must be able to describe how they used or obtained available resources to bring about significant changes or accomplishments while heading agency programs. In addition, OPM suggests explaining how recent education or training enhanced your skills in particular factors. If you mention education or training courses, detail work assignments, or other skills-enhancement efforts, make the link specific and stress the recentness of the information or experience gained.

4. **What have you done for me lately?** The SES needs people who are ready to lead in today's environment. Use recent examples as much as possible. Examples within the past three years are fine, but if you have to go back more than five years, the achievement must be spectacular. If your responses to Executive Core Qualifications dwell on accomplishments at the GM-13 level, they will be less favorably received than comparable GM-15 accomplishments.

Helpful Hints for Developing ECQs

Executive Core Qualifications are most effective if they are consistent continuations of the resume and any other documents in the application package. They should summarize—concisely—a record that demonstrates that you are ready for SES responsibilities. Effective statements of the Executive Core Qualifications combine breadth of accomplishments, a record of supervising other people in the successful completion of substantial tasks, and a record of applying current skills and training to challenging circumstances.

In describing your achievements, try to give different examples for each of the ECQs. A candidate with a true likelihood of success will have numerous achievements in each category. As you sift through your experience, ask yourself, "Will this example be a better illustration of Leading People, Results Driven, or Building Coalitions/Communications?" Review the core qualifications as a group, sort through your resume and supporting notes, and make the hard choices about where your achievements best fit into the factors.

The samples in this chapter include the words "Context, Challenge, Action, and Results." You can include these words in the text of your narratives if you choose. This storytelling outline approach can help the Quality Review Board members read your text more easily. Several SES Recruiters have recommended that including the CCAR terms helps with readability if the flow is not interrupted.

Remember that most SES applications are reviewed by agency Executive Resources Boards, whose members are familiar with your accomplishments and the conditions facing the agency at the time. Your responses need to remind people of these achievements in a credible, consistent way.

---

5. **Be concise.** OPM seeks one to one-and-a-half pages for each qualifications statement. You are writing executive summaries, not autobiographies. If you need more than one page, make certain that every word is important to convey your full leadership abilities. As much as possible, avoid repetition and use different achievements for each of the ECQ statements.

6. **Be specific.** Use precise numbers to describe budget, personnel, dates (time frame), and other factors. Avoid the "various," "numerous," and "several" quantifiers that make people guess about how much. You need to show that you are familiar with the results and how they were achieved so that your reader can understand the environment you were working in and the significance of the accomplishment.

7. **Keep the resume builders in mind.** Some SES applications are copied and pasted into the USAJOBS builder now. You should read the character limits and instructions for submitting the USAJOBS federal resume, ECQs, and technical factors online.

Here's an example of a keyword Profile statement from a federal resume, which could be placed in the Additional Information field (see chapter 5):

PROFILE:

Senior program manager with 20-year background creating and managing innovative, cost-effective, large-scale, and long-term programs. Extensive governmental reengineering and streamlining experience. Strong strategic sense with the ability to balance short-term priorities against long-term organizational mission and goals. Excellent communication, leadership, and negotiation skills. National network of professional contacts in and out of government.

Use OPM's Recommended Format

OPM recommends that SES applicants use a structured format to address each Executive Core Qualification factor. Using this format helps candidates focus the relevancy and impact of their own experiences on the five ECQs all agencies expect their senior leaders to bring to the table. The format is known by the acronym *CCAR,* which stands for

★ Challenge

★ Context

★ Actions

★ Result

Let's analyze the components of this format to learn the best way to write your ECQs.

Challenge

What was the specific problem you faced that needed to be resolved?

★ The problem should have existed at a large organizational level, with agency-wide, government-wide, or national effects.

★ Resolution of the problem should have required more than one individual's actions. Leadership means, at minimum, that you have the ability to get other people to follow when you set direction.

Context

Define the other factors or limitations (people, institutions, procedures) that made the challenge of executive caliber.

★ The problem should require redefinition of goals, changes in conditions, or the need to persuade other people/organizations to comply with your changed direction.

★ Be specific about factors that made the challenge substantial: resources, people, laws, regulations, deadlines, and complexity.

Actions

What did you do that made a difference?

★ Express your achievement in a team environment, but focus on your leadership role with the team.

Result

What difference did it make?

★ Performance and accountability are the key factors. Your participation must be seen as the critical factor in realizing some goal or action that someone else wanted and/or needed done.

As we take an in-depth look at the five ECQs, keep the CCAR format in mind. The format will prompt you to write about specific results instead of citing general information about job responsibilities.

The Anatomy of an ECQ

Now that you're familiar with the fundamentals of writing the ECQs, let's take an in-depth look at the five ECQs and the specific types of information you should include in the statements.

ECQ 1: Leading Change

Definition: This core qualification involves the ability to bring about strategic change, both within and outside the organization, to meet organizational goals. Inherent to this ECQ is the ability to establish an organizational vision and to implement it in a continuously changing environment.

Your *Leading Change* statement needs to articulate an understanding of the mission and vision of the organization that you have led. Think up the organizational ladder. Describe your achievements in terms of how the head of the agency would have seen the challenge and why it should have been considered important.

If you have participated in a major transformation of an organization—for example, taking a nuclear weapons program from a production focus to an environmental clean-up mission—this is the time to highlight your account of how you achieved the change.

Emphasize the continuity factor here. It is important to realize that sometimes missions change even when authorizing laws and regulations stay the same. Convey the scope of the challenge and describe your role in transforming the organization.

Sub-factors of the *Leading Change* ECQ are the following:

★ **Creativity/Innovation:** Have you implemented a new way to solve an old problem?

★ **External Awareness:** What is or was happening outside your agency that affected your programs, or how did your agency's programs affect others and what did you do to improve the situation?

★ **Flexibility:** Did you identify and work different options to reach a desired result? Was it possible to use one authority versus another to get around a longstanding problem?

★ **Resilience:** Did you overcome obstacle after obstacle to change an agency policy, program, or operating procedure?

★ **Strategic Thinking:** Did you develop and execute a long-range plan to improve the agency?

★ **Vision:** Did you predict a cause-and-effect situation and then act to take advantage of changing circumstances? Or, did you propose and then implement a change?

The questions attached to each of these sub-factors are not the only way to address the ECQs; they are just examples to get you thinking about how you can describe what you've done to lead a substantive change in your agency.

ECQ 2: Leading People

Definition: This core qualification involves the ability to lead people toward meeting the organization's vision, mission, and goals. Inherent to this ECQ is the ability to provide an inclusive workplace that fosters the development of others, facilitates cooperation and teamwork, and supports constructive resolution of conflicts.

Leading people includes supervisory responsibilities—but you should express these in terms of coaching, mentoring, and motivating for success. Stress good communication skills, the ability to convey instructions, the ability to delegate responsibilities, and your success in planning for the professional career development of your subordinates.

Working across organizations is vital. Your ability to reach out, gain the support of other organizations, integrate the working of other managers, and represent your organization is critical. Your description of this ECQ should signal the reader to expect a strong statement about coalition building in the fifth ECQ factor.

Workforce diversity is part of the *Leading People* factor. Government requires an ability to work with all races, creeds, sexes, colors, religions, and nationalities. This factor should affirm a solid commitment to the professional development of women and minorities, describe affirmative employment achievements, and discuss overcoming challenges in this arena. Recruiting and retaining highly qualified people is one dimension of the presentation. Demonstrating your ability to train other team members who are highly regarded in the organization is also a big help.

Diversity also should highlight the need to integrate a complex range of professional skills. Scientific, human resources, legal, public affairs, and other talents need to be melded to achieve complex missions. If you are a mathematician, how did you get your public affairs office to understand the importance of what you accomplished? If your skill is legal, how did you develop a mastery of the technology that your agency uses?

Sub-factors of the *Leading People* ECQ are the following:

★ **Conflict Management:** Have you effectively resolved conflicts between working groups, either within or outside your organization? What happened to cause the conflict, and how did you resolve it?

★ **Leveraging Diversity:** Have you used the diverse makeup of your staff to understand the perspective and needs of both your incumbent work force and the customer base the agency is designed to serve?

★ **New Leadership Characteristic—Developing Others:** Describe the steps or programs that you have managed in order to ensure that employees have the right skills at the right time, and in the right place.

★ **Team Building:** Have you been able to foster trust and support among staff members to achieve a better program?

ECQ 3: Results Driven

Definition: This core qualification involves the ability to meet organizational goals and customer expectations. Inherent to this ECQ is the ability to make decisions that produce high-quality results by applying technical knowledge, analyzing problems, and calculating risks.

This factor relies on presenting strong numerical achievements. When possible, cite before-and-after data. In defining challenges, use performance indicators that were considered unsatisfactory (that is, things you had to change). When describing results, compare the differences and describe the resources that you brought to bear to make a difference.

You don't need to base changes solely on program results; they also can be brought about in terms of context. If your actions built alliances, strengthened relationships, or overcame resistance, that too is a result.

Mention successes during organizational changes—for example, sustaining productivity despite reduced resources. Mention policies and procedures you developed to incorporate new assignments while sustaining the organization's current productivity.

Describe methods you developed to define nonessential factors and reduce or eliminate bureaucracy while sustaining results. For example, if OSHA currently measures an agency's performance by how well it complies with rules, and you are successful in changing that approach to now measuring agencies in terms of reductions in accident rates or reductions in time lost due to illness and injury, you should highlight this change in focus here.

What changes or processes did you institute—for example, monitoring mechanisms—to identify future opportunities for improvement and to provide incentives to sustain improved performance? What measures did you take to correct performance problems that preceded your leadership?

Sub-factors of the *Results Driven* ECQ are the following:

★ **Accountability:** What did you do to ensure that performance or outcomes could be measured or quantified? What happened?

★ **Customer Service:** How did you improve it?

★ **Decisiveness:** Were you forced to make a difficult decision? How did you decide which option was best? What happened as a result of taking that approach versus another?

★ **Entrepreneurship:** How have you shown your ability to make smart business decisions?

★ **Problem Solving:** What was the problem and how did you resolve it? If various solutions were possible, don't forget to discuss why you used the approach you selected and why the outcome using this particular approach was superior.

★ **Technical Credibility:** Why did this particular result work better than other alternatives? Did the solution help give customers confidence in your program or agency?

ECQ 4: Business Acumen

Definition: This core qualification involves the ability to manage human, financial, and information resources strategically. Highlight budget data, numbers of people, size of the constituency served, and methods of reducing costs/increasing efficiency here. You should also discuss your familiarity with procedures for establishing and justifying budgets, securing resources, and managing finances.

Demonstrate the effective use of information technology for your activities. The critical factors here are not the abilities to use word processors and spreadsheets, but to define System Development Life Cycle strategies and other factors associated with the acquisition and management of technology resources. The Executive Review Board must be able to see that you know how to apply information technology to the design and management of the organization that you will supervise.

If you have corrected major administrative weaknesses—financial management and accounting procedures, security deficiencies, or potential vulnerabilities of organizations—this is the place to discuss those achievements.

Sub-factors of the *Business Acumen* ECQ are the following:

★ **Financial Management:** Have you managed large program budgets to reach agency goals?

★ **Human Resources:** Have you reorganized or restructured your human resources to better the organization and the services it provides to customers?

★ **Technology Management:** How have you applied information technology to the design and management of your organization?

ECQ 5: Building Coalitions/Communication

Definition: This core qualification involves the ability to build coalitions internally and with other federal agencies, state and local governments, nonprofit and private-sector organizations, foreign governments, or international organizations to achieve common goals.

Just as the *Leading People* factor addresses your ability to communicate down the organizational chart, this one emphasizes your ability to reach out to other organizations. This factor should highlight your ability to work with nongovernmental organizations, the media, professional associations, and at least other substantial organizations within your agency.

Written and oral communications are both required here. The question should not focus on your ability to write, but on your ability to set direction for others who will draft the correspondence, memoranda, speeches, and other material.

Working on interagency committees and coordinating multi-agency policy development and reporting groups are examples of achievements that you should describe in this factor. Effecting change might require bringing other agencies' perspectives back to your organization and winning support for something that serves the public interest, even if it generates resistance within the agency.

This factor asks you to convey that you are in charge of an organization and that you can convince others that your agency's positions on critical issues are well based. If you have testified before Congress or other legislatures, have spoken to state and local governments, or have represented the U.S. on international working groups, these are the experiences to include here. Again, the focus needs to be on the results that were realized from your efforts.

Sub-factors for the *Building Coalitions/Communications* ECQ are the following:

★ **Influencing/Negotiating:** How were you able to bring together two or more factions to reach a mutually acceptable resolution to a problem?

★ **Partnering:** Have you been able to establish solid working relationships with groups that might have been at odds with your organization or agency?

★ **Political Savvy:** Were you able to broker a desired outcome or make your organization look good in the face of a potentially nasty outcome?

Sample ECQ Statements

The following pages contain samples of core qualifications statements developed for various jobs. Some are actual statements taken verbatim from SES applicants. Others are composites of various statements. Study these samples to get an idea of how to compose your ECQs.

Two Examples in the CCAR Format

You will notice in the first two examples that the statements are broken out into the CCAR format. The later examples, however, drop the specific "challenge-context-result-action" labels. They flow as one narrative describing the challenge the candidate faced within a limiting context and the action(s) the candidate took to reach the desired results.

As you are first learning to write the ECQ statements, it will help you to organize and label the information under each of these specific CCAR headings. After you work and rework the material into polished narratives, however, the format will come to mind automatically and you will no longer need the CCAR "training wheels." The final product should resemble the last two examples at the end of this chapter. Quality Review Board and Agency SES Panel Members appreciate seeing the CCAR headings. They can improve readability of full-page narrative statements.

ECQ 1: Leading Change
or
ECQ 3: Results Driven

This is an example of an accomplishment that could be categorized under either the *Leading Change* or the *Results Driven* ECQ. Which category do you think it fits best? The answer might depend on the resume, the technical qualifications statements, or other types of accomplishments the candidate plans to use in the application package. The answer might also depend on the problems or perceived problems the senior leaders in this specific agency will expect the selectee to address: Does this program already operate behind the power curve and need leadership to bring it up to speed, or have agency plans been in place for several years and now agency leaders need to see results? This is where knowing the agency and its needs is critical.

> *[BRIEF INTRO]:* I led major organizational changes to improve the agency's performance in meeting its EEO and Civil Rights goals.
>
> *[CONTEXT]:* As Branch Chief for Equal Opportunity and Civil Rights, National Institutes of Health,
>
> *[CHALLENGE]:* I discovered that the agency needed to establish the parameters for, design, and implement a comprehensive study of the agency-wide affirmative-action program.
>
> *[RESULT]:* Within six months, I was able to develop a multiyear employment plan for the central (headquarters) EEO Office.

[ACTION 1]: I directed a staff of six specialists to elicit and analyze information from 22 component organizations that comprised the National Institutes of Health. The information was consolidated into a comprehensive document, which outlined a long-range plan for increasing minority representation by 10% within a five-year period. I presented this plan to key agency officials, who approved the plan and submitted it without changes to the Public Health Service for implementation.

[ACTION 2]: In carrying out this project, I established strong and compatible working relationships with agency managers and staff in the 22 components (Personnel, EEO, and Executive Officers in each component). *(Provide specific examples of what you did to establish these relationships.)*

[ACTION 3]: I also led a similar effort for the preeminent Biomedical Research Institution, garnering the respect of key management officials in the agency, the Public Health Service, and the Department of Health and Human Services.

[RESULT]: As a result, the agency established a series of employment objectives for a five-year period between xxxx and xxxx. During the first two years of the plan, employment of women and minorities rose 6% agency-wide.

[RESULT]: As senior agency leadership continued to emphasize the importance of affirmative action and hold the 22 components accountable through interim assessments and annual evaluations, the NIH was lauded by OPM for its successes and has since served as a model for the rest of the department.

[RECOGNITION]: As a result of my efforts, I received the Public Health Service's EEO Special Achievement Award.

ECQ 2: Leading People

This candidate used specific percentages to support her results statements. Anytime you can quantify the outcome of your efforts, it will strengthen your credibility with the reader and make you stand out over other applicants who claim their actions resulted in nonspecific "overall improvements."

[INTRO]: Throughout my career, I have recognized the value of motivating and rewarding employees. For the past 15 years, I have developed performance plans, training plans, professional development plans, and counseling; taken disciplinary actions; worked with unions; and hired and promoted employees.

[CONTEXT]: As the Director of the Office of Affirmative Action and Human Resources Special Programs, Library of Congress, my initial assignment was to

[CHALLENGE]: completely restructure and refocus the entire organization. I was advised that the organization was not productive, lacked skills, and had low morale.

[ACTION]: I developed a plan to identify the organization's resources and needs, analyze the work flow, increase productivity, improve service, enhance communication, and improve morale. My challenge was to get the staff to buy into the study and contribute to its development.

I worked hard to get the staff involved. Using positive feedback and active listening techniques, I was able to establish good rapport with all staff members and get them to buy into the process fully. Together we identified specific staff responsibilities. I worked with staff to increase their understanding of the tangible benefits of an organizational assessment. For example, I was able to persuade each staff member that assessing individual

(continued)

(continued)

and overall program responsibilities and resources would provide critical information for future budget requests.

[RESULTS]: I was able to complete the study and achieve major organizational changes within three months. The major changes were (1) I established an automated work-flow analysis and tracking system to manage, measure, and monitor responses to requests; (2) strengthened internal communications by establishing regular staff meetings; (3) strengthened external communications by providing monthly briefings on programs and activities to clients and agency leadership; (4) developed an interactive, dynamic Web site to further communicate goals and advertise accomplishments; (5) promoted team-building activities to strengthen group cohesiveness and maximize organizational resources; (6) trained staff in their new responsibilities and arranged for cross-training to enhance flexibility and mobility; and (7) established production standards and submitted staffing proposals to supplement existing resources.

[RESULTS]: Over a two-year period, and based on documented surveys and feedback I received, I measured a 65% improvement in service to clients. My staff exceeded the established production standards by 25% in all critical functional areas. As a result, morale went up, customer service improved, and I was able to regain our organization's credibility with our agency's senior managers.

The Author's Own Leading Change ECQ

Coming from private industry and wondering how to compete with federal applicants on the ECQs? The author provides an example of the "Leading Change" ECQ from her own experience. Imagine that the author is applying for an SES position with the Office of Personnel Management or Department of Homeland Security, where they need innovative HR professionals to improve recruitment systems.

LEADING CHANGE

Introduction: My track record as a leader of change and an innovator in support of federal employment recruitment and career advancement programs is characterized by several significant accomplishments. During my more than two decades as a successful change agent and consultant to federal human resources and training organizations, I have accepted training and educational challenges—working with employees in large federal organizations. **Context:** As a small-business owner specializing in federal careers with an emphasis on consulting on writing the long, verbose, cumbersome, and unflattering SF-171s, I was prepared to take on the challenge of making the federal application process better. **Challenge:** In 1995, Vice President Gore and his reinvention of government organization, National Performance Review (NPR), enacted an important piece of federal personnel legislation. One of the by-products of this legislation was that resumes would be accepted in government, and the badly outdated Standard Form 171 (SF-171) would be eliminated. In light of this critical legislative step forward, I took the following **actions:**

- I spoke with personnel expert Betty Waters at the United States Department of Agriculture (USDA), who was on the panel that determined that resumes would be accepted. She told me that the panel had authorized the development of a small brochure with printed guidelines for the new resume, the Optional Form 510, or OF-510. Although this brochure would affect almost 2 million federal employees and their careers, it would NOT contain a sample format for the new resume.

- I met with Dick Whitford, Director of Employment Information Services at the Office of Personnel Management (OPM), to discuss the format of the new "federal resume." He had no specific ideas as to how the resume should be formatted and presented. I then waited for OPM to create a style guide, or manual, for employees to follow. Nothing was forthcoming.

- As an expert in the former SF-171 federal application process, I decided to take matters into my own hands and design a "user-friendly" model of the federal resume that would meet the required OF-510 guidelines referred to above. I wasted no time in setting up interviews with federal human resources experts concerning their preferences for the new federal resume. I compared the SF-171 and the instructions in the Optional Form 612 (OF-612) with the conventions of a standard private-sector resume and designed the new resume for the federal government. This new federal resume would be different from the private-industry resume in that it would be longer, include more details, and have a consistent, conservative chronological format. This consistent style would please federal human resources professionals, who were accustomed to systematic forms that contained a great deal of "regulatory compliance" information.

- After I developed the first federal resume format, I proceeded to write a book to support my theories about the new federal resume, along with its features and benefits. The book included 10 hard-copy samples as well as a cutting-edge PC disk, with Word samples/templates. I mortgaged my house for $50,000 to finance publication of the first 5,000 copies of my 250-page book in July 1995. The copies sold in two years (despite severe federal cutbacks and two separate government furloughs during the same time period). I subsequently negotiated a publishing agreement with JIST Publishing of Indianapolis, a successful career book publisher. The book, entitled *The Federal Resume Guidebook,* is now utilized in human resources offices, libraries, and career centers throughout the U.S. to help job seekers apply for federal jobs. I will publish the fourth edition in 2007.

As a direct **RESULT** of my initiative, I brought about a major change in a critical federal process that federal insiders were essentially unable to achieve. Specifically, the large and cumbersome federal human resources bureaucracy saw the need for major change in hiring practices when the Clinton/Gore administration announced the National Performance Review. But, despite their awareness of the need for rapid systemic change, they were unable to act quickly from "within" the system. In contrast, my entrepreneurship and desire to help federal employees write their first federal resumes enabled me to develop a successful training and education curriculum given in more than 100 federal agencies since 1995.

I am now recognized as the pioneer designer of the federal resume throughout government, including the Office of Personnel Management, federal human resources offices, career centers, and training offices. I am introduced in a variety of forums as the "federal resume guru," and am regularly hired as a "sole-source trainer" in more than 100 government agencies. Since 1995, I have written seven books on the subject and have been published or quoted in more than 150 national newspapers, Web sites, and columns.

Summary: Thousands of federal employees and first-time applicants have now gained the confidence as well as the tools to write consistent federal-style resumes to apply for jobs as a result of my books, training, and media presence. In recognition of the outstanding results of

(continued)

(continued)

> my innovative approach, countless federal human resources experts now see me as an unofficial government spokesperson for recruitment and federal jobs. I am an advocate on behalf of working for the federal government and continue to support recruitment while advocating for the applicant, making the hiring process easier through a streamlined, systematic, and flattering resume format and career-motivation printed materials.
>
> Finally, in recognition of the long-term and significant impact of my writings on the federal hiring process, Mr. Paul Light, Vice President and Director of Government Studies, *The Brookings Institution,* recently wrote the following about my latest publication, *Ten Steps to a Federal Job:*
>
> "Despite all the efforts to the contrary, finding a federal job is still a tough climb. *Ten Steps to a Federal Job* is the best guide you can find for the challenge."

Summary

As you develop your specific application package for each SES job, review and study this chapter on writing the ECQs. Developing these statements is a challenging process, but it is supported by a formula that you can learn. Because mastering the ECQ statements is critical to qualifying for an SES job and being selected for an interview, the time you spend learning how to structure your statements is an investment that has the potential to pay huge dividends.

CHAPTER 20

Military to Federal Resume Conversions

By Diane Burns, CCMC, CPRW

Military members need to prepare federal resumes to look and speak the same as those of their civilian counterparts. However, after being in the military for many years, they often speak "military," using plenty of military acronyms and jargon that needs to be translated to meet corporate or civil-sector requirements.

> ⭐ **Note:** For more samples and information for writing military federal resumes, refer to *Military to Federal Career Guide* by Kathryn Troutman.

Translating Your Resume to Civilian Speak

Service members have the added challenge of looking for civilian keywords that help their resumes qualify in the federal system, but they also need to spend extra time learning what their military terms, acronyms, and jargon translates to in the corporate world. Service members should translate military rank, career history, job titles, military occupational specialties and career fields, and training courses; and use their award, training, and performance rating justifications to glean accomplishments.

Translating Military Terms

The following are a few sample translations for rank, responsibilities, and acronyms. Sometimes service members tell me that they don't know what an acronym means because they never spelled it out. If you don't know what it means, ask someone or look it up. Federal resumes need to have all acronyms spelled out at least once in the first reference. Each branch of service has its own set of acronyms for individual systems. Some acronyms might be the same, but the meaning is very different.

Military Speak	Civilian Speak
Rank	
Senior Officer (Naval Commander, Army or Air Force Major)	Chief Executive, Administrator, Chief of Staff, Senior Executive/Vice President, Chief Administrator, CEO, COO, CFO
Senior Enlisted (E-7 to E-9) or Junior Officer	Program/Project/Plant Director, Manager, or Coordinator
Enlisted (E-5 to E-6)	Team Leader, Training Manager, Instructor
Responsibilities	
Commanded	Directed, supervised, or guided
Provisioning Chief	Logistics management
Briefings	Presentations, seminars, or public speaking (communications)
Acronyms and Terms	
Battalion	250 personnel
ANOC	Advanced Noncommissioned Officers Course (Leadership and Administration Course)
COMSEC	Communications security
AcofS	Assistant Chief of Staff
OCONUS	Outside continental United States
PCS	Permanent Change of Station (a move or transfer)
PAC	Personnel Actions Center
AORS	Areas of Responsibility
ATRRS	Army Training Requirements and Resources System
Pathfinder	Army Intelligence Database System
SGT	Sergeant
CPT	Captain (very senior officer in the Navy; junior officer in the Army)

Keywords

Service members are proud of their duties, titles, training, leadership roles, and awards. However, military members need to further translate accomplishments into qualitative and quantitative sentences that are chock-full of keywords. A quality, translated sentence can be very successful in describing years of leadership and management credentials.

Here's a sample translation for operations management (extracted from a resume written by a military member):

Before:

> Support the 76th aircraft wing providing services to 12 carrier air wing squadrons and 32 reserve squadrons, supported commands, and a special project unit. Manage inventory and a budget.

After:

> Supervise a staff of 35 shop personnel providing maintenance services to 12 major customers and 32 tenant units encompassing 87 worldwide sites. Orchestrate logistical support and inventory requirements controlling a bench stock of 2,400 items. Execute a $60 million operational budget.

The first sentence includes only three keywords (inventory, budget, and manage), and it is confusing to the reader. A civilian without any knowledge of aircraft wing, reserve squadrons, or supported commands will not fully comprehend the credentials behind the candidate. The sentence will be vague and complicated to a civilian recruiter. With some strong questioning and a thorough review of "what you actually do on the job," you can write a strong qualitative or quantitative sentence that shows the employer what you managed and what value you have to offer the organization.

The second sentence includes at least 11 keywords: supervise, staff, shop, personnel, maintenance, services, customers, logistical, inventory, bench stock, and budget. Moreover, it describes for the reader how vast the needs are to coordinate logistical requirements for the 76th aircraft wing. Additionally, the second sentence captures the reader's attention with specific accomplishments and numbers. This translation is strong and factual.

Uncovering and Quantifying Accomplishments

The second sentence was derived from a line of questioning using the information provided in sentence one:

What is the 76th aircraft wing?

> 12 major customers and 32 smaller customers in 87 sites around the world.

Do you have a team to accomplish this support?

> Yes, I supervise 35 personnel.

Tell me about the inventory you control.

> Well, it is pretty big; I coordinate logistical support for the 87 sites with a bench stock of 2,400 items.

Tell me about your budget. Is it significant?

> Yes, $60 million, which includes pricey aircraft maintenance parts.

This line of questioning helps unfold skills, accomplishments, and credentials that are otherwise lost in military speak.

Also, remember that if you convert your paper copy (formatted resume) to an electronic Resumix version, the Resumix system will not understand the military terms in the first sentence. Furthermore, the second sentence quantifies the military terms and adds keywords that are critical for a candidate seeking employment in logistics or supply discipline management.

Remember, this is only one sentence in a three- to five-page electronic resume. Each sentence needs to carry its weight in order to match the skills required for a specific federal series. Military members should research private-industry job announcements as well as federal job announcements to learn how to properly translate military terms.

When a military sentence (full of military acronyms and military terms) is properly converted to a civilian sentence, there is almost no recognition that the applicant is from the military—and private-industry officials will be able to understand and appreciate your qualifications.

Service members who prepare early to exit or retire from military service can learn to write a successful civilian-language, skill-based federal resume, maneuver the federal application process, and land a second career with the federal government.

Focusing Your Resume

Often, military clients tell me that they can do anything: they are leaders and they have managed personnel, human resources, logistics, computer repairs and LANS, accounting and budgets, supply systems, commissary operations, aircraft maintenance, security requirements, instructors, health care—and the list goes on. Interestingly, they might perform many of these duties under the job title of Ammunition Specialist, Administrative Specialist, or Field Artillery Surveyor. Very often, the work completed on the job and the skills and training acquired are very different from the job title or occupational field.

Unfortunately, the federal resume system does not favor "jack-of-all-trades" resumes. In order for a candidate to be deemed "Best Qualified," his or her federal resume must meet requirements for a position within a federal series. So, for example, one client told me he was an accountant and was seeking accounting positions based on his work with budgets in the military. However, he began to apply for different positions such as Force Protection Manager and Security Operations Manager. This client was not qualifying for any positions in the security series because his resume was focused toward accounting and auditing. We rewrote his federal resume to incorporate both accounting and security operations, focusing on his military background and highlighting specific accomplishments in both accounting and security. As a result, he began to qualify for jobs in the security series.

In order to focus your federal resume and target critical skills required in the federal vacancy announcements, you need to review the duties and qualifications in the vacancy announcements and highlight keywords, in the same manner that you develop keywords from your military language. Train yourself to highlight keywords in vacancy announcements and use the same words when you translate your background. For example, here is a sample section of a federal vacancy announcement for an Intelligence Specialist. The keywords are marked in bold.

> **Instructor** experienced in one or more of the following **Counterintelligence (CI)** and **Human Intelligence (HUMINT)** disciplines: Department of Defense (DoD) **surveillance tactics, CI and/or HUMINT operations, tradecraft,** DoD CI **Counterespionage (CE) investigations,** and the employment of special investigative techniques. The selected applicant will **develop, update, and present classes** on the aforementioned subjects at various skill levels. He/She will also participate in **role-playing** practical exercises, and serve as an **operational mentor.**

Then be certain to use the keywords in your federal Resumix, while translating your military language and focusing on your key accomplishments. As you develop the federal Resumix, use small paragraphs and lots of nouns, and outline the format using all caps to lead off on sentences start new paragraphs. Be sure to personalize the resume by using "I" in your accomplishments occasionally.

Sample Resumes

Following are two sample resumes for military-to-federal transitions.

Sample Federal Resume 1: Counterintelligence Specialist Seeking Federal Employment

Most candidates need one resume that targets one to three similar federal series codes. For example, the following resume highlights an Army Counterintelligence Specialist seeking federal employment in intelligence operations (0132) or security management or operations (0080). Her military training and on-the-job experience includes Motor-Pool Manager, Instructor, Analyst, Supply Manager with Line Items, and Personnel Actions Clerk. This candidate also told me that she has a background in retail management and that she could easily see herself as an HR Manager.

Realistically, she will qualify and rate the highest in the intelligence and security series with agencies that post for such types of positions. She applied for jobs with the CIA, FBI, Department of State, Department of Transportation, Homeland Security, and others. She submitted both an electronic Resumix for appropriate agencies and a formatted resume for the agencies that do not yet accept the Resumix.

> **Note:** Each agency has different application and resume requirements; consequently, military candidates need to read the application procedures carefully for each agency to which they want to submit an application. Also, application procedures may change at a moment's notice, so re-read application procedures at the time of submission and nomination.

Introductory Material

Jane's resume begins with the required federal elements. Note that she used both her home and work phone numbers and her e-mail address to ensure that she can be easily reached. Because she is leaving the military, her employer knows she is pursuing other employment and she does not have to worry about confidentiality.

Jane needs to include her military dates of employment and veterans' preference because some military personnel receive special preference in the hiring process based on service dates, service during wartime, campaign or expeditionary medals, or disabilities.

Professional Profile

Next, Jane's resume includes a profile section that provides an overview of her qualifications in intelligence and security. Note that in the profile section and throughout the resume, Jane spelled out a number of acronyms familiar to counterintelligence. She referred to commanders and generals as high-level decision makers. She ensured that the resume included references to the required KSAs on the application (in other words, analysis and presentation skills, coordinating activities with other law enforcement agencies, analyzing and evaluating intelligence programs, policies, and knowledge of software applications). We included a final profile bullet about her interpersonal skills with descriptors, leading off with "I."

Security Clearance

A qualifying factor for this critical position is the ability to obtain and retain a TOP SECRET (TS) security clearance with SCI (Secret Compartmented Information) access, having completed a SSBI (Single Scope Background Investigation). Consequently, we included this very important factor at the beginning of her work experience section. We listed her entire current access because the position is dependent on this access level. We also added her last periodic reinvestigation (PR) date so that federal employers know that she is very current and will not need another periodic investigation for several more years.

Professional Experience

In the Professional Experience section, Jane included the federal requirements for each job in reverse-chronological order. Because she is a service member, we included her rank (E-6) and full dates (MM/DD/YYYY). We were sure to include, "yes, you may contact my current employer." Because there is no threat of a confidentiality breech, Jane gladly listed her current supervisor's name and phone. Each description entry is broken down into two parts: Scope of Operations and Accomplishments. The Scope of Operations helps the reader see the special or collateral duties the military member might perform, as well as offers insight to daily responsibilities. The Accomplishments section offers specific accomplishments and highlights special activities or projects.

Once again, acronyms are spelled out, except for well-known acronyms, such as CIA and FBI.

Professional Development

Jane's military training and professional development is very applicable to the security field positions she is seeking. We listed her training in reverse-chronological order and included course length and graduation dates.

Awards

Finally, we listed some of Jane's awards. The titles of the awards are not as significant as the accomplishments pulled from the award justifications that are incorporated into the resume text. The awards indicate her drive to excel and attain recognition. She can describe the nature of the awards in an interview.

Target Job: Intelligence Operations Specialist, Transportation Security Agency.
Resume Format: Paper.
Military to federal career transition.

JANE MYERS

1280 Patriot Lane
Columbia, MD 21451

410-555-1256 (h) / 410-555-4312 (w)
E-mail: janem@hotmail.com

Social Security Number: 000-00-0000
U.S. Citizen: Yes
Veterans' Preference: 5 points; U.S. Army (E-6); Military Service: 05/1997 to Present
Federal Employment Status: N/A

OBJECTIVE: Announcement Number: TSA-02-112
                Intelligence Operations Specialist, SV-0132-00/00

PROFESSIONAL PROFILE

- Five years of direct experience as a Counterintelligence (CI) Special Agent for the Department of the Army, conducting critical counterintelligence, counterterrorism (CT), counterespionage (CE), and security investigations and operations to protect national security. Engaged in intelligence collection and analysis to develop reports and threat assessments. Initiated and coordinated investigative operations. Conducted interviews and interrogations.

- Specific knowledge of Technical Surveillance Countermeasures, National Security, Foreign CI Investigations & Operations, Human Sources (HUMINT) Operations, Personnel Security Investigations (PSIs), Communications Security (COMSEC), Computer Espionage & Security, Technology Protection, and Force Protection.

- Member of the worldwide foreign surveillance team conducting sensitive investigations and surveillance operations resulting in arrests of suspected terrorists.

- Skilled computer operator. Maintain databases, prepare PowerPoint presentations, write Standard Operating Procedures (SOPs) for data entry, and train users. Proficient with MS Office (Word, Excel, Access), Outlook, Exchange 5.5, and Windows 98/ME/2000/NT.

- Superior oral and written communications. Compose reports, investigative and operational plans, summaries, updates, incident accounts, memos, and briefings. Deliver briefings before high-level delegations, conduct platform instruction and training sessions, and present security awareness seminars.

- I possess excellent interpersonal skills. I am energetic, easily adaptable to changing conditions; able to determine new and innovative methods to interact positively in difficult situations; relate well with various people and individuals of diverse backgrounds; and apply direct, action-oriented approaches to solving problems.

CLEARANCE

TS/SCI/SSBI (current/active) PR updated 05/2006

Page 1 of 4

(continued)

(continued)

JANE MYERS　　　　　　　　　　　　　　　　　　410-555-1256 (h)
Announcement: TSA-02-112　　　　　　　　　　　　　SSN: 000-00-0000

PROFESSIONAL EXPERIENCE

Surveillance Case Officer (E-6)　　　　　　　　　02/12/2000 to Present
Foreign Counterintelligence Office　　　　　　　　　Hours per week: 50+
U.S. Army, Detachment 26　　　　　　　　　　　　Salary: $2,500 per mo.
Fort Belvoir, VA 22340　　　　　　　　　　　　　　Supervise: 25
Supervisor: Matt Eve; Phone: 410-555-5555
Yes, you may contact my current employer.

- Plan and conduct worldwide physical surveillance operations against Foreign Intelligence Services (FIS) in support of national-level Human Intelligence (HUMINT) requirements and counterintelligence operations and investigations to identify suspects involved in compromising national security.
- Review surveillance processes, requirements, and cases. Approve or disapprove surveillance measures.
- Employ state-of-the-art surveillance equipment to train subordinates. Lead and control ground operations for specific missions, supervising 25 team members.
- Conduct regular liaison with representatives from various counterintelligence and law-enforcement agencies including the FBI, CIA, DoA, and other national agencies.
- Compose and review reports and other written documents.
- Conduct briefings and debriefings. Prepare PowerPoint presentations for briefings and class instruction.
- Serve as Communications Security (COMSEC) Custodian.
- Plan and lead training scenarios. Advise, evaluate, and counsel students at CI training school.
- Collateral Assignment, Assistant Supply Manager: Manage and account for $1.4M worth of equipment, purchasing requirements, and logistical support for the surveillance team.

Specific Accomplishments:
- Since 9/11, the surveillance team has worked overtime on additional counterterrorism operations and investigations. Also, I work closely with local law enforcement to handle multiple arrests.
- Develop Surveillance Detection Routes (SDR) in support of Offensive CI Operations.
- Engaged in a number of surveillance activities: foot, mobile, public transportation, map reading, tradecraft and operation activity recognition, note taking and report writing, aerial surveillance, night surveillance, stakeouts, and boxing.

Special Agent/Security Specialist (E-5)　　　　　02/12/1998 to 02/12/2000
U.S. Army　　　　　　　　　　　　　　　　　　　Hours per week: 40+
Detachment 7　　　　　　　　　　　　　　　　　Salary: $2,500 per mo.
Fort Meade, MD 21067　　　　　　　　　　　　　Supervised: 8
Supervisor: Joe Brown; Phone: 410-555-5555

Operations Officer/Training and Operations (S3)
- Managed and coordinated all CI taskings from subordinate organizations and input all data into database, including Polygraphs, Technical Support Countermeasures, Information Warfare Branch, and counterintelligence activities in support of the Department of the Army (DoA) and DoD military units and civilian contractors. Enforced Department of Army Intelligence and Security Command procedures and policies.
- Supervised mission database and daily operations stats, and provided operational input/reports to headquarters. Managed in-house database software.

Page 2 of 4

- Managed and controlled physical security of sensitive areas and proper operation of access devices. Assisted in local adjudication and granting of access to sensitive compartmented information and assisted in processing of periodic reinvestigations for DoA personnel.
- Provided security and computer forensics to computer investigations and collection efforts.
- Trained personnel in completion of Electronic Personnel Security Questionnaire and led security training for more than 250 personnel.
- Maintained excellent liaison with program managers, operations officers, and other unit representatives regarding issues of multi-disciplined CI technical assets.
- Prepared weekly and special PowerPoint slides for meetings.
- Constructed and wrote weekly operations reports, monthly unit status reports, and quarterly civilian law-enforcement operations reports.
- Supervised, mentored, and counseled eight subordinates. Fostered cohesive working team. Assisted personnel with travel orders and requirements.

Specific Accomplishments:
- ➢ Selected to supervise a team (normally assigned to a more senior agent) to support the Presidential mandated DoD War Crimes Disclosure Act declassification project. The project digitized over one million counterintelligence investigative and operational files and then declassified and released more than 15,000 of the files to the National Records Administration. Managed all Quality Control reviews for declassification of files.
- ➢ Developed a Fire and Safety Program and prepared for and passed Safety/Fire Inspection. Conducted security inspections ensuring compliance with DoD and Army security policies, procedures, and regulations.
- ➢ Located and removed more than 300 corrupted computer files within one week of hire.
- ➢ Created a Standard Operating Procedure (SOP) for data entry.
- ➢ Devised and implemented a cross-training plan for the section, which ensured assignment completion (devised training for agents in Personnel Security Investigations and Subversion and Espionage Directed Against the Army (SAEDA) briefings.
- ➢ Maintained and accounted for $600,000 worth of equipment.

Special Agent (E-4)   02/12/1997 to 02/12/1998
U.S. Army   Hours per week: 40+
A. Co. 518th MI BN Korea   Salary: $ 2,300 per mo.
Supervisor: MAJ Donna Merson   Supervised: 6

- Provided covering agent support and security assistance to all staff sections and elements within U.S. Forces Korea and headquarters. Supported two exercises. Conducted security briefings and answered questions related to suspicious activity to more than 20,000 individuals stationed in Korea.
- Assisted with cyber-counterintelligence investigations to detect, prevent, and neutralize threats to national security.
- Conducted liaison with federal, state, and local law-enforcement agencies.
- Organized and maintained counterintelligence files and databases.
- Debriefed or interviewed witnesses and sources to extract pertinent information concerning investigations. Coordinated, implemented, and maintained debriefing programs with federal agencies. Debriefed DoA personnel for information of intelligence value.
- Wrote investigative plans, reports, summaries, updates, and closure reports. Produced intelligence reports to answer national-level intelligence requirements.
- Managed barracks requirements: Created a detail roster, enforced standards, and coordinated building work orders.

(continued)

(continued)

JANE MYERS   410-555-1256 (h)
Announcement: TSA-02-112   SSN: 000-00-0000

Specific Accomplishments:

➤ Served as Investigations Team Leader/Personnel Security Investigations (PSIs) Case Control Manager and directed investigative actions of six agents completing more than 2,000 leads and closing 486 cases.

➤ Personally closed 120 PSIs and conducted 300 leads, accounting for 40% of total PSI production.

➤ Acted as Lead Investigator on six espionage investigations and supported one other by completing two Intelligence Memorandums for Record (IMRs).

➤ Selected among a pool of 37 peers to participate in two counterintelligence surveillance exercises.

➤ Selected as Soldier of the Quarter (Battalion level).

EDUCATION

Pursuing Master of Science of Strategic Intelligence, Joint Military Intelligence College, Washington, DC; Enrolled Fall 2006

Bachelor of Science, Health Administration, University of Maryland, MD, 1996 (GPA: 3.8); Dean's List; Women's Business Honor Society

Diploma, Canyon Area High School, Columbia, MD, 1992

PROFESSIONAL DEVELOPMENT

Basic Non-commissioned Officer Course (BNOC), 8 weeks, 2001 (Distinguished Graduate)

Basic Surveillance Course, Joint Training Academy, 200 hours, 2001

Driver Enhancement Training, Police and Correctional Training Commissions, 1 week, 2000

Basic Tactical Pistol Class, 40 hours, 2000

Counterintelligence Training Center Surveillance Course, 2 weeks, 2000

CI/HUMINT Automated Tool Sets (CHATS), 1 week, 1998

Korea Surveillance Training Course, 2 weeks, 1997

Primary Leadership Development Course, Noncommissioned Officer Academy, 4 weeks, 1997

U.S. Army Counterintelligence School, Counterintelligence Agent, 17 weeks, 1996

AWARDS

Received special letters of commendation from senior members of the FBI and national-level intelligence agencies for supporting a successful and highly sensitive operation, 2002

Army Commendation Medal, 2002

Army Achievement Medal, 2001, 2000

Certificate of Achievement, 1998 (for skillful investigative techniques)

Figure 20.1: Sample Intelligence Operations Specialist resume.

Sample Federal Resume 2: Logistics, Operations, and Supply Management Candidate

The next resume is for a retiring Army Lieutenant Colonel who was deployed to Iraq during Operation Iraqi Freedom II and to New Orleans after hurricanes Katrina and Rita. After his senior-level work in operations and supply management in combat areas, he is pursuing positions in logistics and homeland security.

Introductory Material

Bob's resume begins with the standard required information: name, address, phone number, and e-mail address. Bob's Resumix is formatted for Army CPOL with 12,000 characters for the employment section. Although the CPOL Resumix does not allow for a separate opening summary or profile, you can include it with the experience section, just before the job descriptions. Bob will also be able to use this resume for QuickHire applications.

Employment Experience

The CPOL Resumix allows for 12,000 characters, including spaces, for the Employment section. Once you are in the builder, you can simply copy and paste the entire Employment section into the employment block. Be sure to include the required elements: full dates, job title, salary, supervisor's name and phone number, and employers' addresses.

In the Professional Experience section, Bob included the federal requirements for each job in reverse-chronological order. Again, because he is a service member, Bob's rank (Lieutenant Colonel) and proper dates (MM/DD/YYYY) are included. Because Bob's retirement is no secret, he is giving permission to contact his supervisor.

Note that Bob lists the full dates of his military employment first, then divides the experience by appointment with the date and location. Under each, he lists the duties of the jobs, followed by his special assignments and accomplishments. This allows the rater to see not only what his assigned responsibilities were, but also what he accomplished personally while he held the job. Additionally, he's included a quote from a supervisor from a recent performance appraisal. Because of Bob's long military history, it's important to focus on the recent and relevant experience and stay within the character limits. To do this, he summarized and combined some of his earliest assignments.

Education

Following Experience is Education, which allows 2,000 characters. Bob states his formal education, including high school and both colleges he attended. For his bachelor's degree, he also included courses that might be relevant to jobs for which he is applying.

"Other"

The next block in the CPOL builder is for "Other." "Other" might include specialized training, clearances, licenses/certifications, a profile, awards, memberships, languages, volunteer jobs, community service, presentations, and any other information relevant to the announcements, including KSA factors or screen-out factors. The CPOL builder does not allow for attachments or provide spaces for essay questions, so all KSAs noted in a CPOL vacancy announcement should be incorporated into the Experience and/or Other section. The character limit for this section is 6,000, including spaces.

For the "Other" section, Bob will include his most recent and relevant training, awards, and computer proficiencies.

Target Job: Supervisory Logistics Management Specialist, U.S. Army.
Resume Format: Electronic.
Military to federal career transition.

Bob J. Becker
345 Rock Glen Rd.
Nolanville, TX 76559
Residence: 254-333-0303
E-mail: bobjbecker@comcast.net

SSN: 000-00-0000
Citizenship: U.S.
VEOA / VRA Eligible
Security Clearance: Top Secret, held since 1990, recertified 2005

PROFILE: Logistics and operations professional with more than 20 years of expertise in all aspects of personnel and supply movement. Currently manage supply logistics program for active-duty and reserve troops in 3rd U.S. Corps. Excellent strategist and administrator, able to lead staff to achieve challenging short- and long-term goals. Superb communications skills, able to establish trust with internal staff and external customers, including other military branches, federal agencies, and state and local authorities; Joint Service Officer since 2001. Demonstrated crisis management skills, able to critically assess situation, options, and outcomes and make sound decisions. Skilled in developing and implementing policies and procedures and managing projects and programs.

PROFESSIONAL EXPERIENCE

U.S. Army
07/1983 to present; 40 hrs/wk

06/2001-present
Lieutenant Colonel
HQ, 13th Corps Support Command
Ft. Hood, TX 76544
Salary: $100,500
Supervisor: Colonel Mark Kimmel, 254-222-2020. May be contacted.

Deputy Support Operations Officer

LOGISTICS MANAGEMENT OPERATIONS: Directly support Global War on Terrorism, preparing, planning, and managing logistical operations for 200,000 active-duty and reserve troops assigned to Ft. Hood and geographically separate 3rd Corps units. Evaluate and implement all aspects of logistics assistance mission activities. Integrate logistics including financial, transportation, road network planning, supply chain support, and material life cycle management. Develop logistics operations to support task force operations, equipment, and personnel. Ensure supplies and equipment are in place with troops and arrange for re-supply as needed. Coordinate with other military organizations and government agencies to secure goods.

DIRECT AND SUPERVISE logistics and administrative personnel, with 14 managers directly reporting. Train employees on technical regulations, policies, and procedures. Set priorities and assign tasks. Guide employees to resolve difficult technical issues and problems. Mentor and coach employees to ensure best performance and career satisfaction. Monitor and evaluate performance; implement / recommend corrective actions. Recognize staff performance in multitasking, deadline management, problem-solving, and teamwork.

PROGRAM MANAGEMENT: Develop reports and provide status information for U.S. Army leadership use in operations planning and decision making. Expedite requests, cancellations, shipment changes, and general logistics information to Command group and subordinates. Identify and evaluate current and potential logistics problems, determining cause and developing corrective or preventive action plans. Research and assess readiness posture data; plan detailed assessments of situations adversely affecting readiness, including retail / wholesale logistics systems, and management of equipment / weapons systems. Evaluate policies, procedures, operations, and systems; develop and implement improved concepts and systems. Measure / evaluate program effectiveness and productivity.

01/2000-06/2001
Division Support Command Operations Officer, 1st Cavalry Division

SPECIAL ASSIGNMENTS

Hurricanes Katrina, Rita, 09-10/05
Deployed for Joint Task Force Katrina to provide mission support to relief efforts. Sent in 4 days after Hurricane Katrina to establish warehousing and distribution operations center for active-duty military. Grew assignment to support city of New Orleans to receive and distribute FEMA aid to local emergency workers and residents. Analyzed situation and developed action plan. Assumed distribution management: Established priorities and coordinated and moved supplies to distribution points. Worked directly with local officials to support recovery operations. Established system for logistical support--received water, life support, vehicles, etc., for 18,000 firefighters; federal, state, and local employees; and Army National Guard. Controlled supplies and synchronized distribution. Devised and implemented forward planning for short- and long-term recovery and most efficient use of funds and resources. After system was in place, turned over management to city officials and continued in advisory role. Throughout assignment, led staff of 15, logistically supporting 25,000 active-duty Army service members. Upon arrival of Rita, deployed to Lake Charles and Cameron Parish. At end of duty assignment, ensured situation had transitioned from crisis management to recovery planning and operations.

Iraq, 01/04-12/04
Supervisor: Colonel Leslie Smythe, 254-333-4040.

Deputy Commander, Corps Distribution Command (promoted from Director of Logistics). Served in Iraqi combat zone, supporting Operation Iraqi Freedom II. Managed logistics support for 7 subordinate peace and wartime battalions of 1,600 troops.

Operations Logistics Management: Provided daily leadership for Corps Distribution Center, logistically supporting all U.S. branches and Multi-National Command forces in Iraq, approximately 318,000 personnel, comprised of U.S. forces, Iraqi security forces, and U.S. and foreign contractors. Implemented standard automated Army Supply system in combat environment. Developed, implemented, and synchronized logistics operations, achieving total logistics distribution visibility. Designed and oversaw construction of COSCOM Distribution Command Center, state-of-the-art mission control center in the Iraqi theater logistic hub providing total logistics asset visibility / force tracking, linking material commodities with convoy movements. Orchestrated movement from crisis supply system to sustained system, establishing routines and standard logistical practices, distribution, transportation and supply management procedures. Enforced standard ordering practices and ensured time and mission-critical stocking were fulfilled. Built confidence of other military branches to rely on Army supply system.

Originally, supply system was not set up, as a short operation was anticipated. When apparent the operation would be longer, a coordinated supply management needed to be instituted. Additionally, situation changed in April, escalating from "dangerous" environment to mid-intensity conflict.

(continued)

(continued)

Reconfigured strategies to reduce troop and supply exposure: Reorganized convoy structures, armored vehicles, and changed and increased delivery routes to reduce predictability.

As principal operations officer, developed daily orders for staff of 300 (with 30 reporting directly), moving all classes of supply. Executed mission analysis, order production, and current operations through agile logistics applications. Resynchronized communications and operational procedures and ensured support battalions with different missions communicated effectively. Developed staff, maintained morale, and resolved problems. Prepared reports and presented briefings to command staff; kept subordinates abreast of changes and critical issues. Assumed Brigade Commander duties as required.

MOBILIZATION / DEMOBILIZATION: Crafted deployment order and plans to move 13th COSCOM operation to Iraqi theater from 45 separate locations. Executed logistical support plan for 600 troops. At completion of tour, handed over operations to new unit, coordinated return logistics, and reestablished operations in Ft. Hood. Spearheaded reintegration of Brigade forward and rear elements and jump-started homestation training plans. Managed enrollment of unit equipment into reset or reconstitution programs to get them ready for future missions.

Saudi Arabia, 07/02-07/03
Supervisor: Colonel Theodore Steedman, 703-333-2020.

Assistant Chief of Staff, Operations (originally assigned to Logistics). Initially in place to coordinate logistical support for U.S. and Saudi Arabia National Guard air defense systems. After terrorist attack on contractors, mission escalated to combat level. Commanded and controlled Patriot missile operations in Saudi Arabia, Kuwait, Bahrain, and Qatar, leading the multi-functional hybrid Air Defense Artillery Brigade. Executed force protection, training, and combat operations in support of Operation Iraqi Freedom and Desert Spring. Directed reception, staging, and onward movement of all Air defense and combatant elements in sector. Developed, planned, rehearsed, and executed situational training exercises. Synchronized operational activities with higher and subordinate commands and managed multiple installation and tactical combat missions.

RECENT SUPERVISOR COMMENTS: "He is a tremendous officer, leader, coach, and mentor to all who know him...[his] performance was exemplary. As the Corps Distribution Brigade's Deputy Commander, he took the Brigade and its staff to the highest level, managing complex, tough logistics support missions while superbly providing support to seven subordinate battalions during OIF II." (Colonel Leslie Smythe)

11/1996-12/1999
Scott AFB, IL 62225
Salary: $72,500
Supervisor: LTG Calvin Kipley (retired), 618-444-4040.

Joint Transportation Staff Officer

Senior Duty Officer, Mobility Control Center. Planned, coordinated, controlled, and monitored global strategic transportation operations DOD-wide. Responsible for near-term planning and analysis for emerging contingencies, operations, and exercises. Coordinated multi-modal air, land, and sea transportation for supported CINCs and for Joint Staff directed operations and contingencies. Action officer for Crisis Action Team; developed contingency operation plans in support of the Joint Staff and National Command Authority. Controlled $3.5M of CJCS Exercise Commercial Ticket Program funds directly supporting worldwide movements. Managed 14 exercises, including Contingency Readiness

Exercises and Joint Chiefs of Staff-directed events. Provided liaison and developed rapport with foreign nations to support mutually beneficial policies and sustain international DOD operations.

07/1990-08/1996
Germany

Held several logistics and transportation positions during assignments in central Germany.

27th Transportation Battalion Movement Control Executive Officer. Executed deployment, redeployment, and sustainment missions for U.S. and allied forces throughout central region. Controlled CIA's collection and shipment of former Warsaw Pact equipment from East Berlin to the U.S.

37th TRANSCOM Highway Operations Officer and S4 Logistics Officer. Directly managed dispatch, use, and readiness of Army's largest truck command. Managed fleet of 850 tractors and 2,900 trailers with ancillary engineer and maintenance equipment.

Joint Transportation Company Commander, Central Army Group. Directed staff to plan and manage operation of transportation systems supporting all NATO activities in Germany, Benelux, and Denmark. Commanded multinational / functional transportation company with 200 soldiers and civilians, controlling central region temporary duty travel and wartime / exercise tactical transportation. Managed $7.5M budget for commercial highway, rail, barge, and containers, U.S. and NATO exercises and unit deployments.

SPECIAL ASSIGNMENTS

Joint Task Force Provide Hope, Rwanda. Executed USEUCOM humanitarian aid mission to Rwanda. Controlled Arrival Departure Airfield Control Group (A/DACG) at Rhein Main, GE. Planned loads; staged and dispatched aid / forces.

Bosnia, 12/95-07/96
Brigade Operations Officer. Deployed to sustain U.N. mission to establish local police force in support of Daytona Peace Accords. In hostile fire zone, controlled sole logistical supply route for Task Force Eagle. Executed reception staging and onward movement. Planned and executed force protection, collective training programs, unit readiness, intelligence operations, and physical security. Directed logistics sustainment for 23,000 soldiers.

Early assignments:

Company Commander, 1987-1990, Ft. Bragg, NC
403rd Transportation Terminal Transfer Company. Provided surface lift, tactical airfield seizure control groups, and material handling equipment. Managed A/DACG at Pope AFB and CRP warehouse.

Battalion Platoon Leader / Staff Officer, 1983-1987, Germany

EDUCATION

BA, Business, Texas Technical University, Lubbock, TX 1983, 83 credits; GPA: 2.51
Relevant Coursework: Managerial Communication (3 credits); Organization and Management (3 credits); Advanced Organization and Management (3 credits); Business Law (3 credits); Behavioral Science in Business and Industry (3 credits); Principles of Marketing (3 credits); International Politics (3 credits);

(continued)

(continued)

Business Statistics (4 credits); Personnel Administration (3 credits); Advanced Personnel Administration (3 credits); Organizational Behavior (3 credits); Labor Relations (3 credits); National Income Analysis (3 credits); Management and the Business Environment (3 credits); Job Evaluation and Wage Administration (3 credits); Corporation Finance (3 credits); Production / Operations Management (3 credits); Administrative Policy (3 credits)

AA, Business, Grayson County College, Denison, TX 1980, 67 credits; GPA: 3.12

Diploma, Sherman High School, Sherman, TX 1978

TRAINING

Individual Terrorism Awareness, 1 week, 07/2002
Middle East Orientation, 1 week, 04/2002
3L Skill Identifier, Joint Service Officer, 2001
Air Mobility Course, 2 weeks, 1999
Joint Operations Planning and Execution System (JOPES) Course, 1 week, 1998
Joint and Combined Staff Officers Course, 12 weeks, 1997
Command and General Staff Officers Course, 40 weeks, 1993
Combined Armed Services School, 8 weeks, 1990
Transportation Officers Advanced Course, 23 weeks, 1987
Junior Maintenance Officers Course, 6 weeks, 1987
Transportation Officers Basic Course, 20 weeks, 1983

AWARDS / RECOGNITION

Bronze Star Medal (2), 2004, 2003
Campaign Medal, Iraq, 2004
Meritorious Service Medal (4), 2003, 2002, 1997, 1995
Army Achievement Medal (3), 2003, 1988, 1986
Armed Forces Expeditionary Medal (2), 2002, 1996
Global War on Terrorism Expeditionary Medal, 2002
Global War on Terrorism Service Medal, 2002
Army Commendation Medal (4), 2002, 1990, 1986, 1985
Defense Meritorious Service Medal (2), 1999, 1993
Joint Service Achievement Medal (3), 1999, 1991, 1988
Joint Meritorious Unit Citation, 1999
NATO Medal, 1996
Superior Army Unit Citation, 1996

COMPUTER PROFICIENCIES

Word, Excel, PowerPoint, Outlook; Military Specific

Figure 20.2: Sample Supervisory Logistics Management Specialist resume.

Summary

The foregoing examples illustrate some of the ways you can convert military experience into a federal resume. Remember to frame your experience in terms that are familiar to the federal human resources rater and the qualifications standards. Follow this simple rule and you will be well on your way to developing a winning military federal resume.

CHAPTER 21

Wage-Grade to General Schedule (GS) Transitions

When writing "keyword and skill" electronic resumes, job seekers are concerned that they will not be able to write a career-change resume. Because the electronic resume system is read by a computer initially, rather than a human resources professional, the words in the resume must be clear. There will be little chance to influence a reader with an entire package presentation.

Can a Supervisory Submarine Hatch Mechanic get unstuck from his current series? The answer is *yes*. In this chapter, you'll find out how. The example of the Hatch Mechanic's ability to select skills, nouns, and verbs that are transferable from the specialized field of submarine hatch work to general maintenance, supervision, and team leadership in a production shop environment is interesting and can help you learn how to target new jobs with selected relevant skills.

Case Study: Ship Fitters at Pearl Harbor

Ten ship fitters attended one of my Resumix resume-writing workshops at Pearl Harbor Naval Base. They were positive they were stuck for the rest of their careers as hatch mechanics. And they were determined not to use "flamboyant language" that was meaningless in their resumes to change jobs. But could it even be done?

Jeff was the Pearl Harbor Naval Shipyard's expert on submarine hatches. He had 16 years of repairing, installing, troubleshooting, upgrading, scheduling, training, quality assurance, purchasing parts, and endless communication to schedule the on-board ship repairs. But he wanted to do something new. He really wanted to move out of the specific submarine-hatch area. How could he refocus his skills away from the submarine-hatch world and into a different mechanical world where he could use his transferable skills? What job would that be? And what were his transferable skills? He would consider an inspector or quality-assurance job, or a production controller job in a Navy shipyard. He had many transferable skills in addition to the specialized ones in the area of submarine hatches.

But the second challenge was the Resumix system. How could Jeff "fool" the Resumix system into thinking he could do something besides work on sub hatches? Did he have to fool the system? Would the human resources recruiters and managers find him if he tried to present himself as someone other than a submarine-hatch mechanic? He didn't want to be lost forever in the database. Could he come up with a good set of skills that would be truthful for his new career-change objectives?

Together in the workshop we analyzed the transferable skills that a supervisory hatch mechanic uses every day to see whether the skills would fit in another career—without being flamboyant or untruthful. Then we made a list of keywords and skills.

I asked the 10 ship fitters "What percentage of time do you spend fixing stuff versus talking to people?" They said 70 percent talking and 30 percent fixing. "Wow," I said, "70 percent?" (This demonstrates extensive use of communications skills.)

Then I had to know more. "Who are you talking to?" I asked. One said, "It takes about two hours to do a 30-minute job because I have to talk to the ship captain, engine mechanics, and plant operators to schedule the on-site repair with security, parts, and other trade cooperation." (This demonstrates customer service, liaison, scheduling, coordination, and planning skills.)

"All right," I said, "this is communications skills, teamwork, interpersonal skills, customer service, job planning, and scheduling. These are some of the keywords you can add to your resumes. And they are all transferable skills that you could use in any mechanic or mechanic supervisor position."

We were getting somewhere. So we kept making this list. Here's what we created. These keywords and skills should be integrated into a career-change Resumix resume, along with some of the technical descriptions.

Teamwork–Team Leader (40%)

- ★ Leadership
- ★ Project coordination and planning
- ★ Planning and scheduling
- ★ Contractor liaison and oversight
- ★ Training

Customer Service (30%)

- ★ Problem-solving, negotiating solutions
- ★ Systems and problem analysis; devising solutions

Quality Control (30%)

- ★ Quality assurance
- ★ Research (parts, warranties, new equipment)
- ★ Purchasing/ordering
- ★ Inventory and equipment control
- ★ Security systems implementation

After you have your list of keywords, you should create an outline with three to five major work areas. Then describe your duties in each area. This is the best way to create a great skills list that will be transferable to your next field. You can also add percentages to each of your major skill areas so that the human resources staff can see how you spend your time at work.

The submarine-hatch mechanic now felt like it was possible for him get away from being the "hatchman." As long as he analyzes the duties of his target position and adds those skills to the list, he should qualify for a new position.

> **Note:** In today's facilities services operations departments, many employees are competing to keep their jobs and offices. If you believe that your organization will become privatized or downsized, you should begin to write your resume and plan for your next career now. Research the jobs that are not being privatized or downsized and target these positions so that your job will be safer.

Strategies for Writing a Winning Wage-Grade Resume to Compete to Keep Your Job

With the advent of computer technology and the reduction of personnel office staff, applying for federal jobs as a first-time applicant or for promotion/career change for current federal employees has changed drastically over the past five years. Application forms that ask specific questions and are completed with pen and ink are practically obsolete. The federal sector now utilizes software called Resumix, USAJOBS, and other online applications. What each has in common is the requirement for the individual to be proactive in seeking employment or in managing his or her career by submitting an online resume.

The software applications make qualification determinations. If the applicant does not use the correct language on the resume, he or she might miss the opportunity for employment or promotion. Federal Wage System (FWS) employees are sometimes at a disadvantage in using these systems because they often do not have access to computer terminals at work and do not have the time to do research to properly prepare a resume.

Also, many tradesmen/women are not writers. They work with their hands, building, fixing, and maintaining things. They are not writers, editors, or job analysts. So, online resumes, transference of skills, and job analysis of new positions are difficult, to say the least. But it is a *must* for anyone who wants to survive in government after privatization activities or to be promoted.

It is vitally important that the resumes of current federal employees in the FWS classification, seeking promotion or a change in career field, reflect the correct language tailored to the applicable software. Another stumbling block is that one size does not fit all. Your resume must be targeted toward the position for which you are applying; therefore, you might need to rewrite it depending on the type of position that is vacant.

Journeyman wage-grade employees, due to their extensive shop-floor experience, are often sought as prime candidates for some GS positions, such as Equipment Specialists and Production Controllers. However, they must stress in their resumes the correct knowledge, skills, and abilities they possess if they are to be considered for these career changes. FWS employees are an extremely valuable asset. They often have the capabilities to progress into production-chief positions and high-grade general-schedule positions; but in today's environment, that might be more difficult if the employee doesn't take a proactive approach.

The Most Desired Jobs for Former WG, WS, WL, WD, and WN Employees

In many cases, foremen, work leaders and planners, and estimators are usually WS, WL, WD, or WN grades, which are blue-collar positions. Some activities have converted these schedules to GS grades. Here are some GS jobs that blue-collar workers can move into most effectively by transferring their existing skills:

★ Administrative Clerk

★ Data-entry positions

★ Production Controller

★ Material Specialist

★ Buyer

★ Planner/Estimator

★ Work Leader/Supervisor

★ Quality Assurance Specialist

★ Surveillance Specialist

★ Occupational Safety and Health

If a WG worker goes into a GS job, they can expect to be in an office environment, even if they are in the shop, because they will be sitting at a desk working on a computer. That means for a WG to be successful as a GS, he or she will need some sort of computer and keyboarding skills.

Researching Your Transferable Skills and Keywords

Look for position descriptions and vacancy announcements, and the skills they list. A great source for position descriptions or a classification standard is the Army's Fully Automated System for Classification (FASCLASS), which you can find online at http://cpsfc.belvoir.army.mil/fasclass/inbox/.

Another excellent source are the Classification Standards from the Office of Personnel Management at www.opm.gov.

After you create your list of skills, make sure that the statements and skills are true. For example, there is a statement in the introduction for Heavy Mobile Equipment Mechanic that might or might not be true of an employee's job: "...assist heavy mobile equipment mechanics in the complete overhaul and repair of major systems, such as engines, transmissions, drive lines, and hydraulic utility systems." If you did not assist mechanics, or if there are some systems listed that you did not work on, you should delete these. Also, do you ensure proper "calibration"? We included this word in the keyword list, but it does not appear anywhere in the materials. Is another word more accurate?

Here is a list of keywords from three WG-10 announcements that we will try to integrate into the resume:

Pre-shop analysis

Major systems and components

Disassembly

Diagnosing malfunctions

Placing in operable condition for pre-inspection

Utilizes gauges and instruments

Performs rebuild, repair, assembly, adjustment, troubleshooting, applicable functional test of major mechanical systems and components for...

Defective units

Repairs/replaces

Assembles

Performs limited functional test

Hand tools

Measuring instruments

Micrometers

Dial indicators

Torque wrenches

Blueprints/schematics

Technical publication

CMWR

Checkout

Adjustment

Tune-up

Examines vehicles; starts, performs operations checks

Detects malfunctions

Here's a list of keywords and skills from the KSAs in the announcements:

Mechanical makeup operating and working relationship of heavy mobile vehicles

Troubleshooting

Analysis

Vehicle systems

Assemblies

Parts

Diesel

Gasoline

Transmissions

Hydraulic systems

Technical manuals

Diagrams

Schematics

DMWRs

Work orders

Micrometers

Dial indicators

Dial bore gauges

Ignition timers

Fuel pump testers

Here are the keywords from a second announcement that are different from what we've already listed:

[Listing of types of heavy equipment]

Traces and locates defects, causes of mechanical problems

Determines type and extent of repairs

Selects repair specs and procedures

Routine welding

Transitioning from a WG Career to a GS Career

What does it take to change career paths from a WG career to a GS career? It might take going backward in grade so that you can begin a new career track. It might take some education and specialized training (read the announcements and occupational series to find out what is required). It will take specialized experience in your selected area. You must make a concerted effort to develop the skills and gain the experience needed while you're in your current job. Ask for and take on additional projects in order to gain specialized skills.

You might have to perform two jobs while you are transitioning from one career to another—the one you are paid for and special projects in your new career area. Analyze skills, training opportunities, and project opportunities; network with people who are in the new area; and build your resume to support the job change.

Checklist for Writing a Wage-Grade Resume

The following checklist was created by Mark Reichenbacher, who specializes in writing WG civilian resumes for the Resumix system. He is highly analytical in developing keyword lists and skills from classification standards and announcements. He selects the keywords that will best fill the "skills bucket" for the target grade and announcement. He then carefully crafts a three- to five-page resume with good descriptions of job functions, specifics of jobs, accomplishments, awards, and recognitions.

You can use this checklist to write a wage-grade resume for a lateral position, as well as one geared toward a promotion. The analysis and keywords can also be developed so that you can target a GS position. The GS positions require less "hands-on" technical skills and more planning, estimating, project-coordination, communications, and problem-solving skills. Write your resume to include the skills that will be required in your *future* position.

1. Assess Your Skills and Research Relevant Positions That Fit These Skills

A WG employee (or any other employee) should make an assessment of his or her skills and then look for relevant positions that fit those skills. You can make a list of your skills based on your position description and the services you provide to your customers.

2. Review Your Work Experience for Relevance

Look at each position in your work experience. Are they relevant to the target positions? Should they be combined? Should the resume be arranged in reverse-chronological order for the most relevant presentation of the jobs? Should any positions be left out? How many jobs have you had over the last 20 years?

3. Analyze Your Work Experience for Jobs, Grades, and Special Assignments

Target the resume to qualify for two grade levels if that is appropriate. You can capture extra job skills in "special assignment" sections that can help you qualify for a higher grade level. Add hours per week to the special assignments.

4. Analyze Work Experience for Numbers

How many employees, square feet, numbers of items, numbers of helicopters, numbers of job tickets, dollars, budgets, percentages, money saved, hours billed? These numbers help describe the work in context and are also important in describing accomplishments and special projects in specific terms.

5. Write Accomplishments and Special Assignments

Write about specific projects that resulted in performance awards or customer-service letters. Have you improved the efficiency of your shop operations? Write about new projects and complex situations. Did you work on special projects? Were you a member of a team to redesign a work process? Were you involved with new construction, capital improvements, or tenant build-outs? If so, describe them in the corresponding work experience block, using the CCAR formula, which is explained in chapter 9, "New Essay Writing: The KSA Way."

6. List Education

Add your college course hours and list your college or professional training programs in the Education section. You might have to consider returning to college in order to change careers. If you have a college degree, even if it is an associate's degree from a community college, you will have a big advantage over other WG employees with no college.

7. Include Job-Related Training

Computer and keyboard training will be helpful in any desk or trades job. You might need to give a quote, pull up an order, create a receipt or bill of sale, or research an online manual for repair. New training can help you change occupational series.

8. List Certifications

Under the Certifications heading, list training courses that resulted in professional licenses or certifications, and include the month and year when the certification was achieved. List first those that are current and essential to your current work.

9. Cite Awards

When listing awards, list them by importance. Check to see whether the order of importance is accurate. For instance, it's difficult to tell how an "Official Commendation" is regarded in terms of importance unless you state the reason for receiving the commendation. Also, a Letter of Appreciation is received for a reason. If you have room in the Awards section, write a sentence about why you received the award.

10. Remove Redundancies in Work Descriptions, Awards, and Training Courses

Because the Army resume format is only three pages, you will have to be concise when writing your duties, skills, and accomplishments. Maximize your three pages by avoiding redundant information.

11. Include Other Experience and Summary of Important Experience

In a Summary statement, you can summarize your experience, knowledge, skills, and abilities (one for each sentence). This is a good place to pick up anything that might not be covered elsewhere. Also, you can include the strongest statements from your appraisal. Put them in some logical sequence. You can add volunteer, non-profit, association, and community activities in this section.

12. Core Competencies

Don't forget any core competencies that can be added to this section; for example, flexibility, resourcefulness, proficiency in oral and written communications, or being a valuable team member. Refer to chapter 8 to determine your competencies that would be impressive to the selecting official.

13. Talk to Your Human Resources Office

Ask about other occupational series that will be available (not privatized) for people with skills that match your experience. Take your list of skills and new resume with you and discuss those with the HR staff. Ask about positions that can lead to a promotion.

14. Get Help from Professionals

If writing is not one of your best skills, get professional help with writing, editing, and determining your skills and accomplishments. Your resume is your future and career. It's worth your time and investment.

Sample Resumix Resume for a Wage-Grade Transition

This Electrician, WG-10, is seeking a new position in Planning, Inspection, and Supervision where he can utilize his technical skills as well as his teamwork, planning, inspection, and supervisory experience.

*Target Job: Vocational Instructor (HVAC), GS-1712-09/11, from current position as Air
  Conditioning/Refrigeration Mechanic, WG-5603-10.*
Resume Format: Electronic federal resume.
Federal WG Career as HVAC Mechanic to Federal GS Career promotion as HVAC Instructor.

WAYNE C. HART, JR.
3719 Three Mile Road
Annapolis, MD 21403
Contact Phone: (000) 000-0000
Work Phone: (000) 000-0000
E-mail: wchart@aol.com

EXPERIENCE

08/1998 to Present; 40 hours/week; AIR CONDITIONING / REFRIGERATION MECHANIC; WG-5603-10; U.S. Naval Academy, Public Works Department, 121 Blake Rd., Annapolis, MD 21402; Jeffrey Bloom, (000) 000-0000; may contact supervisor.

As ACTING FOREMAN for the A/C Shop, I SUPERVISE and LEAD a MULTI-TRADE TEAM in the installation, repair, maintenance, testing, and adjustment of air-conditioning, refrigeration, and HVAC equipment. I SUPERVISE PREVENTATIVE MAINTENANCE TEAMS. Serve as Acting Foreman approximately 45 days per year.

INSTRUCTOR FOR HVAC AND TRADES HELPERS. Developed on-the-job training program for new hires, as well as specific training for development of skills within the trades. Recognized by the Foreman for ability to instruct, give direction, and ensure safety on the job. Lead monthly classes on diagnosing problems, equipment utilization and care, inventory and parts ordering, estimating, cooperating with trades, warranty research and communication with manufacturers, quality assurance, and project management efficiency. I also instructed workers in customer services and problem solving with employees and office managers. Since 1998, I have been the sole instructor for an ongoing crew of 10 HVAC Mechanics; plus an average of two to three new hires per year; plus contractors working on major projects.

I use knowledge of and instruct HVAC workers in PRINCIPLES AND THEORIES related to refrigeration cycles, equipment functions, testing, repair, and maintenance procedures for a variety of equipment and systems that achieve regulated climatic conditions, including compressors, motors, condensing units, electric controls (contractors, relays), heat pumps, cooling towers and refrigeration liquid (gycol / water), and wall converters.

Perform quality CUSTOMER SERVICE AND NEW PROJECT INSTALLATION, REPAIRING AND MAINTAINING domestic and industrial air-conditioning and refrigeration equipment at multiple facilities. I TRAIN new hires and HVAC staff in customer services techniques supporting a variety of customers, including staff and managers from main campus, critical buildings, single and multi-unit residences, research labs, dining halls, stores, and ice rink.

QUALITY EXPERIENCE DIAGNOSING AND TROUBLESHOOTING equipment malfunctions. I PLAN and SUPERVISE and DELEGATE TASKS to HVAC team for the installation, repair, and maintenance of HVAC equipment, such as chillers; large A/C package units; rooftop commercial A/C units; rooftop split systems; heat pumps; central A/C systems; window A/C units; air dryer systems; computer room A/C systems; dehumidifiers; ice machines; electronic air cleaners; refrigeration and freezer systems; commercial walk-in boxes; drinking water fountains; medical centrifugals; and electrical, pneumatic, and pressure controls. Replace compressors, coils, water-cooled and air-cooled condensers, and system and equipment controls.

(continued)

(continued)

I COMPLETED and SCHEDULED preventative maintenance on 255 central A/C units 40 percent ahead of schedule (9 days vs. 15) and LED A TEAM of riggers, electricians, and helpers to replace a vital commercial 50-ton compressor unit within 36 hours.

I ORDERED, INVENTORIED, and ORGANIZED all parts and materials for newly opened A/C parts shop. I kept records for EPA regarding refrigerant types and amounts and locations where used.

05/1994 to 07/1998; 40 hours/week; AIR CONDITIONING/REFRIGERATION MECHANIC; $10 per hour; Thomas R. Owens A/C and Heating Contractor, Mitchellville, MD 20710; Thomas Owens, (000) 000-0000; may contact supervisor.

INSTALLED AND REPAIRED air conditioners, heat pumps, oil burners, and refrigeration units. Installed sheet metal and flex ductwork. I used manifold gauges, multi-meter testing equipment, tube cutters, hand tools, electric saws, drills, and sheet-metal cutters. I used EXPERT KNOWLEDGE of all repair skills including brazing, soldering, plumbing, wiring, etc.

EDUCATION
Southern High School, Harwood, MD; 1992 High School Diploma
Anne Arundel Community College, Arnold, MD; Business Management, 2003; 3.32 GPA; 18 credits
RETS Electronic School, Baltimore, MD; 2-year Certificate in HVAC, 1995; 3.0 GPA; 56 credits

PROFESSIONAL TRAINING
Manitowoc 2000 Training; 40 hours; 2005
Liebert Small Systems / Monitoring Course; 40 hours; 2004
A/C Refrigeration Units; 40 hours; 2003
Carrier Electronics for Technicians; 24 hours; 2003
Carrier Commercial Rooftop Split & Package Systems; 40 hours; 2003
Liebert Environmental Training Class; 40 hours; 2001
Carrier Reciprocating Liquid Chiller Course; 40 hours; 1998
EPA Refrigeration Certificate Training; 8 hours; 1997

PROFESSIONAL LICENSES / CERTIFICATES
Certificate, EPA Refrigeration; 1997
License, Refrigerant Handling & Recovery, Universal; 1997
Certificate, Refrigeration, Climate Control, and Clean Air; 1996

PROFESSIONAL RATINGS, AWARDS, AND RECOGNITIONS
Outstanding rating; 02/2006
Performance Awards; 2002, 2003, 2005, 2006
Special Act Award, 10/2004; led team to exemplary performance and gave extra hours during emergency outage

OTHER INFORMATION

PROFILE: HVAC/R Expert, with more than 10 years of experience. Expert at every phase of heating and air conditioning, chillers, and boilers: design, installation, and troubleshooting. Skilled in control systems design and installation, analog, and DDC. Proficient A/C systems programmer; expert in Manitowoc, Liebert, and Carrier systems. Skilled in verbal and written communications, training, and supervision.

Figure 20.1: A sample Vocational Instructor resume.

Summary

Resume writing can be challenging for trades professionals. They are highly skilled in a variety of hands-on tasks, but writing, marketing, editing, and salesmanship are usually not part of their daily activities. But without a good resume, promotions might not occur, jobs might disappear, and job offers might not happen. It's worth the time and effort to create lists of skills, accomplishments, training, and customer comments when a promotion or job change is near.

Federal Career Management Strategies

CHAPTER 22

Strategies for Moving Up

The timing for your federal career advancement couldn't be better. Despite private-sector layoffs and reorganizations over the past decade, job opportunities within the federal government are on the rise. Why? Three main reasons:

- ★ The federal workforce has aged and significant numbers of federal employees are retiring now or will be eligible soon.

- ★ Staffing reductions and technology advances have combined to cause agencies to require new skills mixes as they restructure their programs and different work methods to operate in a leaner environment.

- ★ Nearly every agency must now address new demands for technological, information management, and other skills to meet changed or changing workplace requirements.

First, the retirement dilemma. The statistics are mind-boggling. The *Wall Street Journal* reported that roughly half of all government workers are eligible to retire by 2006 according to recent demographics by the Office of Personnel Management, and about one-fifth of those eligible are expected to do so. More federal workers today are in their 60s than are in their 20s! Agencies that play key roles in the war on terrorism are among those facing large retirement hits: 30 percent of workers in the Federal Bureau of Investigation and 36 percent of those in the Federal Emergency Management Agency could retire by the end of 2006. Such turnover will cause a growing number of vacancies.

What about earlier government reduction efforts? Doesn't this mean that fewer positions are now available? Ironically, the reduction of nearly 17 percent of government positions during the 1990s created an unexpected shortage in many critical program areas. To reach mandated reduction quotas by the deadlines imposed by Congress, some agencies accomplished their reductions without a lot of thought. In these agencies, disproportionate numbers of employees with important corporate knowledge or valuable expertise left the federal workforce. These agencies often later discovered that their indiscriminate means of reducing staff had created mismatches between remaining staff and the work that had to be done. Even agencies that planned their reductions well were forced to restructure to cope with fewer resources to accomplish their missions. Many agencies are still struggling to recruit and/or train employees who can do the work now needed to carry out their missions. Although there might be fewer actual numbers of positions in the federal workforce, there are now many opportunities for candidates with the competencies—or knowledge, skills, and abilities—to perform today's more complex work.

Along with the problems caused by government downsizing, the war on terrorism has created an increased government-wide demand for special skills. Federal agencies are now seeking candidates for jobs in the growth fields of law enforcement, intelligence, physical security, cybersecurity, computer technology, and foreign languages. Studies show that the federal government will need about 16,000 more technology professionals over the next decade and hundreds of experts in Asian, Middle Eastern, and other languages. These skills will be needed in agencies that handle commerce, transportation, military operations, diplomacy, law enforcement, intelligence, and counterterrorism.

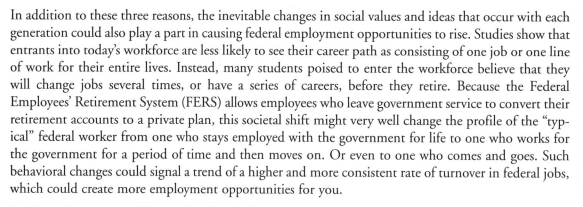

In addition to these three reasons, the inevitable changes in social values and ideas that occur with each generation could also play a part in causing federal employment opportunities to rise. Studies show that entrants into today's workforce are less likely to see their career path as consisting of one job or one line of work for their entire lives. Instead, many students poised to enter the workforce believe that they will change jobs several times, or have a series of careers, before they retire. Because the Federal Employees' Retirement System (FERS) allows employees who leave government service to convert their retirement accounts to a private plan, this societal shift might very well change the profile of the "typical" federal worker from one who stays employed with the government for life to one who works for the government for a period of time and then moves on. Or even to one who comes and goes. Such behavioral changes could signal a trend of a higher and more consistent rate of turnover in federal jobs, which could create more employment opportunities for you.

In short, the stars are aligning for those who want to move up in the federal government. To take advantage of this situation, you need a plan! The rest of this chapter shows you how to formulate one.

Setting Goals Makes the Difference

If you want to position yourself to move into a new job or gain a promotion, you need to do something that makes the difference between staying where you are and moving up. What makes the difference? You must set goals, develop and follow a plan, believe in yourself, and recognize that no one is going to come along and just promote you or hire you away into your dream job.

Your career development strategy needs to be about you: your dreams, your talents, your goals, your needs, and your skills. You must know what you want. If you don't know what you want, who else does? Make a commitment to invest an hour each week in long-term planning and goal-setting for your career development. You could spend the time in self-assessment, rewriting your resume, researching vacancies, or pursuing self-development activities. Whatever you do, the investment in yourself will be like money in the bank, especially if you do land a new job or a promotion. Here are some ideas about how to develop a career strategy.

Step 1: Know Thyself

What are your personal limits? Are you willing to relocate? If you are not willing or able to move to another geographic locale to pursue your federal career, you will be limited to the federal job market in your area. There is nothing wrong with staying in your current area; you just need to be realistic about what types and grades of jobs you can expect to land, and develop your strategy accordingly.

What about changing agencies? Some individuals are deeply loyal to their current agency and wouldn't dream of going to another to advance their careers. Again, this is fine; just know that you must factor in the turnover rate in your organization and the number of people who might compete with you for vacant jobs. For instance, suppose you are not mobile and don't want to switch agencies. You are in your mid-40s and aspire to an SES job, but the supervisors and managers at the top agency levels above you are also in their mid-40s and also aspire to an SES job. Your career strategy will have to be much different than that of the candidate who is willing to relocate and switch agencies.

Step 2: Start with a Statement of Your Dream Job

Don't worry that you probably aren't qualified for your "dream job" right now—that's why you're developing a plan. Don't make your job description too specific. Think about the characteristics of your dream job rather than a specific job title. Do you want a job that uses your communication skills? Provides overseas travel? Helps other people? Doesn't require computer savvy? Try describing what your perfect day on this job consists of—not in terms of the duties, but more in terms of the work situation. Are you working alone or with others? Are you supervising other people? Do you have flex time and/or flexi-place? Approaching what your dream job looks like from this point of view rather than from a job title will help you see other job possibilities besides ones you already know about.

Step 3: Expand Your Picture

What kinds of jobs would have some, if not all, of the characteristics you like? If you can't get from where you are to your dream job in one leap, what interim jobs or situations would move you in that direction? The best way up is not always straight up—sometimes you have to move sideways first. Factor that into your plan.

Step 4: Consider the Obstacles

What stands in your way? Are you missing certain credentials? Does your experience not fit your goals? Don't be in too big of a hurry to conclude that you need an extra degree. What you might actually need is different skills.

Step 5: Make a Plan for Overcoming Each Obstacle

You must recognize and face the obstacles in your way before you can overcome them. If you don't have the right degree or it's not from the right school, how can you get or demonstrate that you have the right skills and competencies? If you had a bad experience in a previous job, how can you overcome it, learn from it, put it behind you, or turn it into an asset? If you don't know the right people, how can you meet them?

Step 6: Develop a Timeline

After you identify your goals, the obstacles to those goals, and how you can overcome each obstacle, don't stop there. You need to make a timeline for achieving those goals and visualize yourself at the goal line on the due date. How do you do this?

Go back to step 5, where you described how you will overcome the obstacles to your goal. Break down your plan into phases or steps. For instance, do you need additional education or training? How much time will it take? What is the one thing you can do during your hour of career-strategy planning this week to move yourself toward this goal? Do you need to enroll in a class? If so, what steps do you need to take to line up the enrollment? Do you need to find a source for the training or education? Choose a source? Contact the source? Ask yourself, "What do I need to do first," and then, "What do I need to do before *that*?" Keep going until there is nothing to place in front of the very first task. Then, assign a date and time to each task, and complete the task by the assigned date. Before you know it, you'll have stepped over the obstacle and will be on your way to the next task.

One hour a week doesn't seem like a lot of time, and it isn't. But that's all you need to focus on at this point. In one hour, you could write a draft of the six steps discussed in the preceding sections. In one hour, you could read a couple of chapters in a good career-development book. In one hour, you could meet with a career transition center counselor. In one hour, you could attend an evening lecture by a notable person in your field. In one hour, you could gather all the material you need for your resume. In one hour, you could search the Web for government job announcements. In one hour, you could read your agency's Web site to review new programs and mission statements. In one hour, you could work on a draft of your federal resume.

Of course, you could put in more than one hour a week, but you don't have to. The advantage of spending one hour a week is that it keeps you from feeling overwhelmed by a long-term project. You will be amazed at how much progress you've made after just a few sessions. Setting up and going through this process gives you a feeling of immense control and personal security. If there's a setback in your agency, you don't have to panic: You're already on your way to something better. If you don't like a particular offer or work situation, you don't have to let desperation drive your decision. You can continue to develop yourself. Invest the time in yourself. It *will* make the difference.

Some Tips on Networking: It *Is* Who You Know!

Zig Ziglar, in his book *Top Performance,* tells this story: A little boy tried in vain to move a heavy log to clear a path to his favorite hideout. His dad finally asked him why he wasn't using all his strength. The boy explained he was straining as hard as he could. But the father disagreed. "Son, if you were using all your strength, you'd have asked me for help."

We tend to overlook the many sources of help, forgetting that even the legendary "self-made" people seldom made it on their own. We need others' help to reach our goals. And most people really like to be asked for their help. Besides, most important jobs require teamwork, so now is the time to get started cultivating this skill.

Where to Look for Help

Who can help? Besides the obvious supervisors, mentors, and coworkers, survey your friends and acquaintances. Don't overlook the people you meet at training seminars or those in your social circle outside work. Talk to others about your dreams and goals and ask them what they might be able to contribute. You'll be surprised at the range of contacts and advice you'll get. Here are some more ideas of ways to network and meet people who might be able to help:

★ **Attend courses, workshops, and seminars.** Ask your supervisor or manager to authorize agency payment for training to develop skills that will make you more valuable in the future to your agency. This will make you more upwardly mobile. Ask your supervisor about an agency-sponsored career-development program that could make you more competitive in advancing in government. Take a few minutes to introduce yourself to the leaders or speakers. They always like to hear positive things about their presentation, and many are willing to share additional advice and tips with a participant who is willing to listen.

★ **Get involved in professional associations and meetings where people in your desired field or industry hang out.** Introduce yourself. Most people are happy to share; everyone likes a receptive audience. Use the "information interviewing" techniques developed by Richard Bolles in his seminal book *What Color Is Your Parachute?,* which is updated annually.

★ **Write letters to people who have achieved what you want to achieve.** Some may reply with helpful guidance.

★ **Read government news Web sites** (such as www.govexec.com, www.federaltimes.com, and www.fendonline.com) and pay attention to articles, people, job titles, agencies, missions, and e-mails. If you read an article about new hiring in your career field, write to the author of the article about how you can get more information on these jobs or this executive. People (even executives) can be very helpful if you e-mail them and tell them you are looking for a promotion or first-time position in government.

Networking Do's and Don'ts: Project the Right Image

As you expand your social circle and range of contacts during your job search, keep the following tips in mind to ensure that your encounters with others are successful:

★ Remember that you are "on" at all times. Be aware that the way you dress, how well you groom yourself, your speech, and your behavior all contribute to the impression you make on others. Always be courteous. You never know who is watching.

★ Follow up with the people you meet and let them know that you appreciate their help. Written thank-you notes have all but gone the way of the dinosaur. If you want to really stand out, write them.

★ Keep plenty of business cards and a one-page marketing resume on hand (see "The One-Page Resume: A Networking and Self-Marketing Tool," later in this chapter). Make sure these items are professional looking, on good paper stock, and are in good condition. They should never be bent, soiled, or have notes written all over them. The information should be current. If your business address or phone number has changed, have the cards and resume reprinted. If you have to cross out information to update these items, it might make the recipient wonder whether you keep up-to-date on your other business matters as well.

★ As you go about looking for your next job or career-broadening opportunity, never badmouth your current or former employers or coworkers. Even if your current supervisor is Simon Legree and your coworkers have horns, complaining about their shortcomings will only make you look like a whiner and a gossiper. Take the high road. Say that you appreciate the opportunities and experience your current job provides, but that it is time to broaden your skills and meet important career goals.

As you put together your personal long-range career plan, remember that networking is probably the single most important component of that plan, no matter what your goals are. The more people you know, the more likely it is that you will hear about a vacant job through someone else. Use all your strength: Ask for help.

Know Your Agencies

As you go through the exercise of describing your dream job, the characteristics of that job should help you identify specific agencies that have those types of jobs. For example, if you are interested in the environment, the Environmental Protection Agency and Department of Interior both have missions requiring substantial involvement in environmental protection issues. If you do not know which agencies might have the types of jobs you're interested in, you could spend the first few sessions of your weekly career-strategy planning hour browsing the Office of Personnel Management's (OPM) job posting site, www.usajobs.gov. You can find links to most of the agency Web sites at www.firstgov.gov.

Learning about various government agencies and what they do will help you meet new people, pinpoint various agencies' issues, and ask intelligent questions during job interviews. Reading the daily newspaper, the *Wall Street Journal,* and the *Federal Times* will also help keep you up-to-date on current events and might help you spot employment trends. Read the Federal Diary article in the *Washington Post* or at www.washingtonpost.com daily for up-to-date news on agencies, people, and change in government.

As you click through OPM's USAJOBS Web site, you will notice a category called Top Job Searches (www.usajobs.gov/infocenter/topjobsearches.asp). This page features the hot jobs for federal hiring on one particular day.

Being Proactive: Eliminating the "Wait-and-See" Mentality

By now, you've figured out that you are in a very unique era in the history of federal career opportunities, and this is the ideal time to plan how to take advantage of it. What else can you do to move things along in your favor?

While you are planning your next career move, remember the following strategies as you look for your chance to make the transition:

★ **Do a good job where you are.** If you aren't giving your current job 110 percent, prospective employers will assume that you won't give their job your full effort, either.

★ **Be willing to do everything.** Supervisors cite an employee's attitude as "90 percent of the reason" they select or promote them.

★ **Volunteer for details.** They not only broaden your experience, but brand you as a "can-do" team player that managers can count on. With work methods and technology changing rapidly in virtually all agencies, your value to the organization goes up exponentially when you show flexibility in accepting new and different work assignments.

★ **Emphasize your additional strengths.** When applying for other jobs, figure out what need the agency would fulfill by hiring you. Then present your talents in a manner that shows why hiring you would help meet the agency's need.

★ **Network with everyone.** Establish relationships with program managers and human resources professionals, not just with colleagues in your own office. A strategic network of people will keep you in mind for vacancies and will inform you when they hear about one.

★ **Try to make an impact on the bottom line.** Let's say you are a budget analyst seeking promotion in another agency, and one of that agency's strategic goals is "improved integration of budget and program performance indicators." Showing in your application or KSA essays how you have achieved or contributed to this in your current job will put you high on the list of eligible promotion applicants. Work hard to make a difference, and then be sure to show what you have done when it comes time to compete for advancement. And don't forget that making your supervisor look good, in addition to doing a good technical job, is a time-honored way to move ahead quickly.

★ **Don't dally.** If you need to gain experience on an interim job to get to your ultimate goal job, don't get complacent by staying in the interim job too long. Use it to gain valuable experience to build your resume and develop needed relationships. Then continue to carry out your plan to reach your goal.

★ **Assess your personality.** Search out computerized personality tests or arrange to take one of the more well-known self-assessment indicators such as the Myers-Briggs test to identify your strengths and weaknesses. These tests touch on personal behaviors, attitudes, values, and skills and will help you determine where to concentrate your self-development efforts. Do you need to be more flexible or learn to communicate better? Knowing your strong and not-so-strong suits will help you develop career goals in alignment with your natural talents.

★ **What have you done for yourself lately?** Your own personal development, continuing education, and technical training are some of the most important career strategy factors over which you have direct control. You cannot afford to sit back and wait for your agency to provide official training opportunities for you. Get busy and take the initiative! Don't have much money to spare? Go to OPM's Web site and find the Gov Online Learning Center. This government-wide resource is dedicated to developing the federal workforce. It provides high-quality e-training products and services—free! Everyone can find a way to develop their knowledge and skills, even if money is an object.

The One-Page Resume: A Networking and Self-Marketing Tool

An important component of your career planning strategy is to design a one-page "calling card" resume that you can use while networking. Informing others of your background, interests, and special talents is a smart way to pre-market yourself for task forces, teams, details, and other career opportunities. The one-page resume is not intended to take the place of a job application or another more serious marketing package, but it does help others remember you when they hear about opportunities that might interest you. The one-page resume can also be used as a short biography or to provide information others might use to introduce you for speeches or award presentations.

The following sections give tips on writing the various parts of a one-page marketing resume.

Profile

This is where you have the chance to make a good "first impression" by summarizing your experience and strengths. Give the reader a picture of you in as few sentences as possible—ideally, four to five at most. This is not the place to talk about your interest in a career change or advise that you are "willing to learn new skills." You are using this resume to inform others of your background and strengths, not to apply for a job. Besides, telling others that you are willing to learn new skills is best done orally. Stating this in writing gives the impression that you do not have anything definite in mind. A good summary profile statement might include something like this:

> Professional with 10 years of experience analyzing employees' training needs and recommending to managers optimal ways to meet those needs. Collaborated with high-level managers and contractors to coordinate formal training courses, select and present material, and provide guidance concerning the best candidates to attend the training. Recognized as a highly effective program coordinator with excellent oral and written presentation skills.

You can tweak this statement to incorporate other skills you might want to emphasize, such as budget management, but try to keep the profile statement to no more than five or six lines in length.

Professional Experience

A simple outline will do here. Include current and past job titles, employers, and dates worked on each job. If you have more than 10 years of experience, combine everything over 10 years old into one statement and summarize it. An exception to this rule would be if you accomplished something so spectacular on an old job that you received special recognition for your initiative.

Education and Training

List all college and graduate degrees. Do not list individual training courses unless they provided you with a unique skill or credential. Keep your professional training up-to-date. Add current training in computer systems, teamwork, customer services, or other relevant courses.

Publications or Written Works

This section highlights written communications skills. List all published works regardless of how long ago they were published.

Professional Presentations

Oral communication skills are important in every job. If giving presentations was an extensive part of your work, summarize and list the most impressive presentations.

Honors and Awards

List special recognition for unusual accomplishments and give a brief statement describing what you did to earn the award. Combine serial performance awards, such as "Seventeen sustained superior performance awards, 1995–2006." Also, list any private-sector honors and awards if they reflect an individual talent and are relevant to a federal job, such as winning a Toastmasters contest.

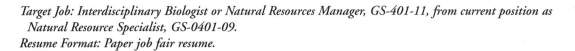

Target Job: Interdisciplinary Biologist or Natural Resources Manager, GS-401-11, from current position as Natural Resource Specialist, GS-0401-09.
Resume Format: Paper job fair resume.

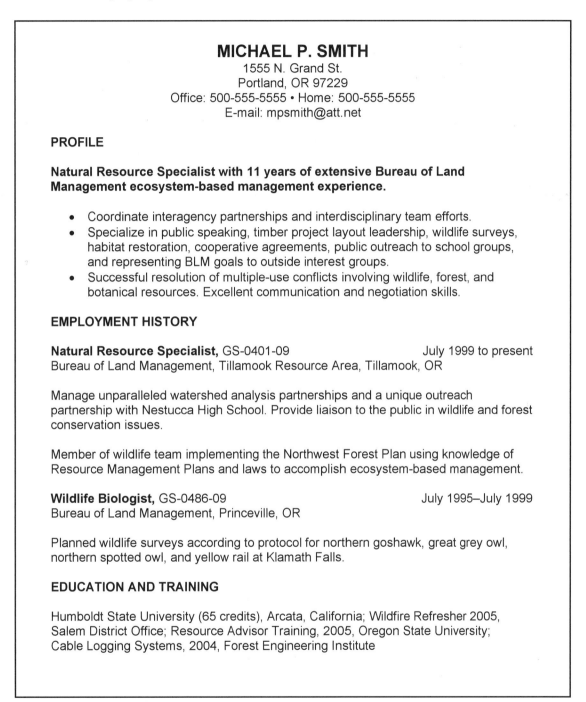

MICHAEL P. SMITH

1555 N. Grand St.
Portland, OR 97229
Office: 500-555-5555 • Home: 500-555-5555
E-mail: mpsmith@att.net

PROFILE

Natural Resource Specialist with 11 years of extensive Bureau of Land Management ecosystem-based management experience.

- Coordinate interagency partnerships and interdisciplinary team efforts.
- Specialize in public speaking, timber project layout leadership, wildlife surveys, habitat restoration, cooperative agreements, public outreach to school groups, and representing BLM goals to outside interest groups.
- Successful resolution of multiple-use conflicts involving wildlife, forest, and botanical resources. Excellent communication and negotiation skills.

EMPLOYMENT HISTORY

Natural Resource Specialist, GS-0401-09   July 1999 to present
Bureau of Land Management, Tillamook Resource Area, Tillamook, OR

Manage unparalleled watershed analysis partnerships and a unique outreach partnership with Nestucca High School. Provide liaison to the public in wildlife and forest conservation issues.

Member of wildlife team implementing the Northwest Forest Plan using knowledge of Resource Management Plans and laws to accomplish ecosystem-based management.

Wildlife Biologist, GS-0486-09   July 1995–July 1999
Bureau of Land Management, Princeville, OR

Planned wildlife surveys according to protocol for northern goshawk, great grey owl, northern spotted owl, and yellow rail at Klamath Falls.

EDUCATION AND TRAINING

Humboldt State University (65 credits), Arcata, California; Wildfire Refresher 2005, Salem District Office; Resource Advisor Training, 2005, Oregon State University; Cable Logging Systems, 2004, Forest Engineering Institute

Figure 22.1: A sample one-page marketing resume.

Summary

Strategies for moving up should be an everyday plan of action. Each time you volunteer for a detail, impress a supervisor, or help a customer, you are creating a good platform for a promotion or new position. You can really boost your strategies for moving up in government if you have a great resume and learn to interview well. The next chapter gives strategies for preparing for the interview.

CHAPTER 23

Preparing for a Behavior-Based Interview

Congratulations—you have been selected for an interview! To increase your chances of success, you'll first need to do some preparation, including understanding different interviewing styles and typical questions you might encounter. In this chapter, we focus on the most common type of interview—and the one that requires the most preparation—the behavior-based interview. We also touch on key things to know about other interviewing methods, as well as provide a checklist for how best to prepare and practice.

Managers and human resource professionals have many different interviewing techniques and processes at their disposal. Although you can't always be certain which type of interviewing method you'll be facing—although it doesn't hurt to ask in advance—you can be prepared by understanding what's at the root of all interviewing approaches. All interviewers want to develop an understanding of you as a candidate to determine whether you are the best "fit" for the position. They want to know whether you have the skills, desire, and personal qualities to do the job effectively and to work well with others in the organization.

The format they choose to gain that understanding depends on the nature of the position, the interviewer's own style and preferences, and whether the organization mandates a particular interview format and set of questions, or lets interviewers design their own format and write their own questions.

Federal Job Interview Styles

Interviews may be conducted in person, over the phone, or both. Interviews in person may include an interview panel (more than one interviewer) in addition to one-on-one interviews. Interview methods may fall into one of several categories or may combine elements of various categories. The most common interviewing methods include

- ★ Behavioral interviewing
- ★ Technical interviewing
- ★ Competency interviewing
- ★ Combination interviewing
- ★ General interviewing

All of these interview methods call for some preparation on your part, with behavioral- and competency-based interviews requiring the most preparation because they require that you provide examples of your performance. Examples aren't always easy to think of on the spot, so it's best not to go in cold and try to "wing it"! When you are contacted for the interview, it is appropriate for you to request information regarding the type and method of interviewing that will be conducted. If you're not able to find out which method will be used, it's best to get familiar with all the methods but focus most of your efforts on preparing behavioral examples.

Let's look at brief definitions of each interviewing method in the list. Then, later in the chapter, we'll explore behavioral and competency interviewing in more depth.

Behavioral Interviews

A behavioral interview involves questions that are situational in nature; in other words, questions that attempt to determine how applicants will react to certain situations, or how they have done so in the past. Behavioral interviews are designed to forecast your future behavior on the job, based on your past behaviors.

Technical Interviews

Technical interviews focus on examining the applicant's technical or functional skills and knowledge. Technical interviews enable interviewers to verify the claims made on a resume.

Competency Interviews

Some organizations define the competencies, or behaviors, necessary for success in a position and then build interview questions and discussions that will explore applicants' strengths and weaknesses in the defined areas. These competency-based interviews may have the look and feel of a behavioral interview because they often involve asking for actual examples of how you have demonstrated various competencies.

Combination Interviews

The combination interview may involve any of the three interview techniques described so far, as well as general interview questions. Combination interviews require that applicants be alert to the types of questions being asked so that they provide the right style of answer and that they be agile enough to "go with the flow" of an interview that changes course from time to time.

General Interviews

A general interview is based on a range of questions asked of the applicant, and may cover a variety of topics related to skills, competencies, experience, and credentials. Questions in general interviews are often heavily resume-based, prompting you to talk more about certain work experiences or other items on your resume. A general interview may also be informal, such as meeting for coffee or having a networking meeting for information that turns into an interview for employment.

General interviews may also include many questions that could easily be answered with a "yes" or "no." Resist that temptation! If asked a seemingly "yes/no" question such as, "Are you proficient in PowerPoint?" follow your "yes" reply with examples of how you've used that tool or how you've added value to prior work settings because of your level of proficiency.

Here are some examples of general questions you may be asked:

★ Why did you leave or are you leaving your last position?

★ What do you know about our organization?

★ What are your goals? Where do you see yourself in five years?

★ What are your strengths and weaknesses?

★ Why would you like to work for this company?

★ What is your most significant achievement?

★ How would your last boss and colleagues describe you?

★ Why should we hire you?

★ What are your salary expectations?

Open-Ended and Behavioral Questions

From the Merit Systems Protection Board Report

This report was written by MSPB, which is a small federal agency that writes reports about Civil Service and the Merit Hiring System. You can read many reports about federal hiring, assessment processes, and the Outstanding Scholar program at www.mspb.gov.

FOR THE SUPERVISORS: Ask effective questions. As we've indicated, effective interview questions are based on job analysis to ensure that they are job-related. Effective interview questions are also usually **open-ended and behavioral,** so that they will elicit useful responses.

APPLICANT INSIGHT: Open-ended questions are questions that require the candidate to provide details, and cannot be answered in one word (such as "yes" or "excellent"). Such questions are much more effective than closed-ended questions at developing insight into a candidate's experience and abilities.

For example, the closed-ended question, "Can you write effectively?" can be answered with an uninformative "Yes"—a response that sheds little light on the candidate's level of performance in this area.

An open-ended question such as, "Describe the types of documents you have written, reviewed, or edited," requires the candidate to provide specifics, and provides much more insight into the candidate's writing accomplishments.

There is a place for the closed-ended question. For example, to learn whether a candidate is willing to travel frequently or can start work on a given date, it is perfectly appropriate to ask a closed-ended question.

Behavioral questions are just that: questions that ask the candidate to describe behaviors—responses, actions, and accomplishments in actual situations. The case for the behavioral question is more subtle than the case for open-ended questions. Although research indicates that both behavioral questions ("What did you do?") and hypothetical questions ("What would you do?") can be effective, many researchers and practitioners generally recommend the behavioral question for two reasons. First, behavioral questions can provide greater insight into how the candidate will perform on the job, because the best predictor of future behavior is past behavior. Second, behavioral questions may be more reliable than hypothetical questions. Because the response can be verified through reference checks or other means, it is more difficult to fabricate an inaccurate or untruthful answer to a behavioral question than to a hypothetical one.

Read the entire report here: www.mspb.gov/studies/interview.htm

---

Practice Your Best Success Stories for the Behavior-Based Interview

Behavior-based, or behavioral, interviewing is the structured, practical interviewing approach that many federal agencies have formally adopted as a best practice. In a behavior-based interview, you will be asked to describe past experiences that demonstrate your competencies as related to the available position(s).

How Should You Prepare for a Behavior-Based Interview?

Take some time to think of examples from your past experiences that demonstrate skills needed for the job you are seeking.

For example, you might be asked for a past work situation in which you demonstrated such competencies as attention to detail, teamwork, effective communication skills, or problem solving. Making the logical link from demonstrated past competences to skills needed on the new job is what behavior-based interviewing is all about.

Pull your examples primarily from paid work experience relevant to the positions you'll be interviewing for, but don't hesitate to look for examples from other areas of your background, such as education or volunteer experiences, as long as they demonstrate relevant competencies.

DLA's Formula for Behavior-Based Questions

The Defense Logistics Agency (DLA) uses this formula for the behavior-based interview questions:

J Job Related

O Open Ended

B Behavioral Based

S Skill and Competency Based

DLA also provides a list of competency examples that can be prepared before an interview. These are general behavior-based competency questions. Most of the DLA questions are actually technical in nature and support the position under consideration.

Sample Competency-Based Interview Questions

Let's look at typical competencies employers seek and some questions they might ask to explore those competencies. As you review these, think about your own experience and start compiling examples you have to demonstrate these skill sets.

★ **Attention to Detail:** Describe a project you have worked on that required a high level of attention to detail.

★ **Communication:** Tell me about a time when you had to communicate with others, such as co-workers or customers, under difficult circumstances.

★ **Conflict Management:** Describe a situation in which you found yourself working with someone who didn't like you. How did you handle it?

★ **Continuous Learning:** Tell me about a time you recognized a problem or weakness as an opportunity.

★ **Customer Service:** Discuss a situation in which you demonstrated highly effective customer service.

★ **Decisiveness:** Tell me about a time when you had to stand up for a decision you made even though it made you unpopular.

★ **Leadership:** Describe a time when you exhibited participatory management (participatory management at DLA is when managers share information, gain consensus, and work toward participation and established performance goals).

★ **Planning, Organizing, Goal Setting:** Describe a time when you had to complete multiple tasks. How did you prioritize and manage your time?

★ **Presentation:** Tell me about a time when you developed a lesson, training, or briefing and presented it to a group.

★ **Problem Solving:** Describe a time when you analyzed data to determine multiple solutions to a problem. What steps did you take?

★ **Resource Management:** Describe a situation in which you capitalized on an employee's skills.

★ **Teamwork:** Tell me about a time when you had to deal with a team member who was not pulling his or her own weight.

More Examples of Behavior-Based Questions

- Can you describe a time when you led a change in your organization?
- Can you tell me how you work as a member or leader of a team?
- When have you had to be adaptable in your job and how did you do it?
- Can you describe a customer service situation that was challenging?
- Was there a time when you were under pressure to be more productive, and if so, how did you change your work methods?

A Step-by-Step Approach to Preparing for a Behavior-Based Interview

Now that you have an idea of how a behavioral interview sounds, you're ready to start preparing for your own. Generally, your preparation will involve reviewing the announcement, preparing to answer typical questions, and practice, practice, practice.

Specifically, there are six steps to follow to prepare for your interview. These steps, as outlined here, are based on a curriculum taught at federal agencies throughout the U.S. to prepare employees for better interview performance. This formula is also used by the author in coaching individuals for interviews, and applicants frequently report that they were well prepared, confident, and felt like they "knew the job" as a result of following these steps.

Step 1: Find and Analyze the Target Announcement, Line by Line

Locate the announcement of the position for which you'll be interviewing, or any other job description you've been provided with, and analyze each sentence in the duties and specialized skills section (see chapter 11 for more on finding and analyzing vacancy announcements). Be sure to save any announcement for which you apply! Note the underlined text in the announcement sample that follows. This is an example of key language to pay special attention to. Start thinking about how your experience and skills relate to these job criteria, and jot down examples from your background to provide evidence of these credentials.

Position: Supply Systems Analyst, GS-2003-7/9/11 to 12 or 12
Salary: $35,452.00 - $81,747.00 Per Annum

Organization/Location:
DLA, Defense Energy Support Center, Facility & Distribution Commodity Business Unit, Optimization Division, (DESC-FL)/FORT BELVOIR, VA

Major Duties: Continually performs <u>analysis of existing fuel storage and distribution</u> systems throughout the <u>world,</u> from original acquisition to final shipment to customers, to determine the total cost of the system as well as strengths and weaknesses.

Knowledge of and experience in working with various <u>DoD fuel-supply systems</u> (product refineries, fuel storage terminal, fuel distribution systems and procedures, and military customer locations and product requirements.

Performs detailed <u>economic and cost/benefits analyses</u> in order to conduct studies of DoD fuel logistics operations and programs.

<u>Factors analyzed</u> include, but are not limited to, transportation cost, customer consumption quantities, economic order quantities, inventory-level requirements, facilities costs (both recurring and those requiring amortization), and risk of system failure.

<u>Evaluates potential alternatives</u> to current fuel storage and distribution systems to determine if they justify detailed analysis.

Alternatives may be provided by the senior supply systems analyst, but may also be developed by the incumbent.

Step 2: Be Prepared; Write and Give Examples of Skills and Competencies

Your behavior-based "stories" are essentially the same as your KSAs. If you have written KSAs for the position, you will be nicely prepared for a behavior-based interview. You can use the same KSAs and examples in the interview. Talk about them with animation and enthusiasm, and they will demonstrate your past performance in a positive way. (See chapter 9 for more on writing KSAs.)

Make sure that you have written at least five stories to prepare for your interview, using examples that are related to the criteria you have analyzed in the position announcement. Then, turn each of your KSAs or interview stories into seven or eight talking points that make it easier to practice and memorize your stories. It is important to practice speaking your interview stories, so that you will be fluent in and easily remember your best examples.

The following exercise helps you develop interview answers for behavior-based questions that could be asked during an interview.

Be sure to give your story a name to make it easier to remember. Story names should be interesting and descriptive, such as these:

Saved USACE $20 million…

Discovered Missing Funds…

Designed New Database, Saving Time…

Led Team Under Tight Deadline…

Supervised During a Time of Huge Transition

Title of Your Example/Story: _____

What competencies are represented by this example?

Review chapter 8 to find two to three competencies that are demonstrated by this example.

Your Interview Story:

_____

_____

_____

_____

Context:

_____

_____

_____

_____

Challenge:

_____

_____

_____

_____

Action:

_____

_____

_____

_____

Results:

_____

_____

_____

_____

Step 3: Study the Structured Interview Scoring System Used by Interviewers

This interview scoring plan is an example of what an interviewer will follow in order to grade your answers to interview questions. As you can see here, you will get a top score of five points if your example of Interpersonal Skills demonstrates that you can communicate controversial findings in a challenging situation.

Competency: Interpersonal Skills

Definition: Shows understanding, courtesy, tact, empathy, concern; develops and maintains relationships; may deal with people who are difficult, hostile, distressed; relates well to people from varied backgrounds and situations; is sensitive to individual differences.

Lead Question:

Describe a situation in which you had to deal with people who were upset about a problem.

Probes:

- What events led up to this situation?
- Who was involved?
- What specific actions did you take?
- What was the outcome or result?

Benchmark Level	Level Definition	Level Examples
5	Establishes and maintains ongoing working relationships with management, other employees, internal or external stakeholders, or customers. Remains courteous when discussing information or eliciting highly sensitive or controversial information from people who are reluctant to give it. Effectively handles situations involving a high degree of tension or discomfort involving people who are demonstrating a high degree of hostility or distress.	Presents controversial findings tactfully to irate organization senior management officials regarding shortcomings of a newly installed computer system, software programs, and associated equipment.
4		Mediates disputes concerning system design/architecture, the nature and capacity of data management systems, system resources allocations, or other equally controversial/sensitive matters.

Benchmark Level	Level Definition	Level Examples
3	Cooperates and works well with management, other employees, or customers, on short-term assignments. Remains courteous when discussing information or eliciting moderately sensitive or controversial information from people who are hesitant to give it. Effectively handles situations involving a moderate degree of tension or discomfort involving people who are demonstrating a moderate degree of hostility or distress.	Courteously and tactfully delivers effective instruction to frustrated customers. Provides technical advice to customers and the public on various types of IT such as communication or security systems, data management procedures or analysis, software engineering, or web development.
2		Familiarizes new employees with administrative procedures and office systems.
1	Cooperates and works well with management, other employees, or customers during brief interactions. Remains courteous when discussing information or eliciting non-sensitive or non-controversial information from people who are willing to give it. Effectively handles situations involving little or no tension, discomfort, hostility, or distress.	Responds courteously to customers' general inquiries. Greets and assists visitors attending a meeting within own organization.

Source: United States Office of Personnel Management

Step 4: Research the Agency and Office to Learn the Latest News and Challenges

Research the agency and office carefully. Print pages from their Web site. Find and memorize their mission. Find out who their customers are. Try to find out any new challenges or changes occurring in the office or agency.

Step 5: Plan and Practice

★ Don't cut corners! Take the time to prepare properly.

★ Practice with a tape recorder or video camera if you can. Listen to your voice. Watch your body language. If recording is not an option, consider practicing in front of a mirror or with a friend who can give constructive feedback.

★ Check out the Web site of the agency you're interviewing with and conduct research on their size, services, products, key leadership, and more.

★ Prepare a one-minute response to the "tell me about yourself" question.

★ Try to find out which kind of interview to expect—behavioral, technical, and so on—by asking when you schedule the interview.

★ Write at least five success stories to answer behavioral interview questions.

★ Prepare answers to the most common interview questions that present your skills, talents, and accomplishments.

★ Remember that nothing will make you look worse than not knowing what you put on your own resume. Study your resume carefully and be able to speak about it knowledgably.

★ Have ten questions prepared for you to ask the interviewer, but ask only ones that are not addressed during your discussion.

★ Prepare a list of references that might consist of former managers, professors, friends of your family who know you well (but not family members), or people who know you through community service. Contact each person to get their permission for inclusion on the list. You also want them to be aware of the types of positions you're seeking and provide them with a copy of your resume so that they'll be prepared to praise you in a way that's relevant to the employer.

Step 6: Be Confident

Here are steps to consider before the interview:

★ As you prepare to leave for the interview, make sure to take a printed copy of your reference list, paper and pen for note-taking, and directions to the interview site.

★ Arrive 10 to 15 minutes early for your interview.

★ Stand and greet your interviewer with a firm handshake.

★ During the interview, be conscious of your body language and eye contact. Crossed arms appear to be defensive, fidgeting may be construed as nervousness, and lack of eye contact may be interpreted as being untrustworthy. Instead, nod while listening to show you are attentive and alert. And most importantly, do not slouch.

★ Think before you answer and have a clear understanding of the question…if you don't, ask for clarification.

★ Express yourself clearly and convey confidence but not conceit. Keep your answers two to three minutes long.

★ Show a sincere interest in the organization and position.

★ Focus on what you can contribute to the organization rather than what the employer can do for you. Don't ask about salary or benefits until the employer brings up the topic.

★ Do not place blame on or be negative about past employers.

★ End the interview on a confident note, indicating that you feel you are a good fit for the position at hand and can make a contribution. Ask about next steps, as most offers are not extended on the spot.

★ Thank the interviewer and ask for a business card so that you'll have the necessary contact information for follow-up.

After all interviews, promptly and carefully write gracious letters to thank the interviewers for their time and to remind them of the valuable qualifications you bring to the job. If you've been told that a decision is going to be made within a day or so, e-mail your note right away rather than mailing. On the other hand, if you know that the interviewing and decision-making processes are likely to take a while, or if you know that the organization you have interviewed with prides itself on personalized service, then you may want to mail a handwritten message on a nice card or word-processed letter on quality paper. Either way, don't miss this last chance to market yourself!

Summary

Congratulations! You are much closer to achieving your next career position with the federal government. If you have prepared for the interview by analyzing the job, mission, and agency carefully, and by practicing your interview stories and answers, you just might find yourself receiving a job offer!

Epilogue

This book is a compilation of all the most recent federal job search knowledge, strategies, and lessons I've learned during my years of training federal employees in getting promoted and advising federal job seekers on their searches. If you have success with your search and land a federal position, please write to me at kathryn@resume-place.com to share your success!

—Kathryn K. Troutman, Author

More Sample Federal Resumes

Target Job: Accounting Technician, GS-0525-07, from current position as Accounting Technician, GS-0525-05.
Resume Format: Electronic DFAS and USAJOBS Resume.
Federal to federal career promotion.

CAROLINE MARTIN
5512 Dolphin Avenue, Sarasota, FL 34230
Daytime phone (200) 555-6405
carolinemartin@sfl.com

Social Security Number: 000-00-0000
Veterans' Status: N/A
Citizenship: United States

OBJECTIVE: Accounting Technician, Defense Finance & Accounting Service
GS-0525-05/07, Job Announcement number: D00107

EMPLOYMENT HISTORY:

JOB 1
ACCOUNTING TECHNICIAN, May 2004–Present, DFAS Accounting, GS–525–05, 40 hours/week. 4411
Summerville Road, Sarasota, FL 34230. Salary: $31,250/year. Supervisor: Johanna Gary (200) 555-6414; may
contact current supervisor.

COORDINATE COLLECTION EFFORTS AND ENSURE THAT ACCOUNTS RECEIVABLE are recorded, aged,
collected, transferred, written off, or closed out as required. Handle all correspondence to maintain due diligence
for each receivable. Perform follow-up and analysis on payments posted and on outstanding receivables.

RECEIVE, CLASSIFY, AND RECORD MORE THAN $25 MILLION OF INCOMING AND OUTGOING
TRANSACTIONS for Defense Department appropriations, obligations, expenditures, and reimbursements with
99.8% accuracy on a daily basis. Utilize the Intra-Governmental Payment and Collection (IPAC) System to
accurately collect and disburse funds to and from other DFAS field organizations and federal agencies quicker
and in greater detail, with 100% accuracy. Complete routine and complex claims in order to process, pay,
record, and report transactions, in accordance with the Prompt Pay Act of 1982 with 99.9% accuracy.

RESEARCH AND ANALYZE HISTORICAL FINANCIAL DATA to identify disparities and incompatible
information in existing data and conduct remediation as appropriate. Coordinate with internal and external
departments to resolve out-of-balance situations. Summarize transactions, determine the appropriate accounts
and methodology for processing, and prepare control documents or other posting documents reflecting the
entries to be made.

VALIDATE, MONITOR, CONTROL, AND MAINTAIN ACCOUNTING TRANSACTIONS and accounting
records/ledgers to ensure audit trails and accuracy in procedures. Monitor fund balances. Balance and maintain
the subsidiary and general ledger accounts. Prepare and post journal vouchers. Reconcile subsidiary ledgers to
control/summary accounts. Reconcile data from suspense by submission of correction cards once accurate data
has been verified. Evaluate source documents and supporting files for sufficiency, veracity, acceptability, and
completeness of information. This includes verifying mathematical precision, expenditure limitation, valid
authorization, and accuracy of accounting data. Make appropriate accounting adjustments to finalize and
validate these lines of accounting into the U.S. Government Standard Finance accounting system (STANFINS).
Monitor and input accounting accrual adjustments as needed to comply with standard accounting procedures.

REVIEW AND ANALYZE OPERATING PROGRAMS, PRACTICES, AND PROCEDURES related to receiving,
controlling, validating, recording, and reporting accounting transactions affecting the asset, liability, revenue,
expense, and budgetary accounts of supported organizations to ensure compliance with generally accepted
accounting policies, new operating procedures, and revised regulations. Review, analyze, and act upon initial
output concerning daily block balancing and editing in the form of the Daily Preliminary Balance Listing. The
Daily Preliminary Balance Listing validates all Financial Accounting Office (FAO) input data after source
documents have been processed and keypunched. Propose new procedures and methods or modify existing
procedures and methods to resolve current problems and enhance the validity, accuracy, and integrity of
accounting processes. Advise lead technician/supervisor of recurring, extraordinary, or unusual
situations/problems and assist in the resolution of these situations. Assist in the implementation of new
procedures or policies to ensure compliance with established financial accounting requirements.

Caroline Martin, SSN 000-00-0000, Candidate Annct.: D00107

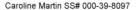

Caroline Martin SS# 000-39-8097   Page 2

ACCOMPLISHMENTS:
+ Developed innovative approach to the accounting of receivables, in accordance with the Statement of Federal Finance Accounting Standards (SFFAS) and the Department of Defense Financial Management Regulation (DODFRM). This allows for more control, more timely resolution, and reduced errors.
+ Cleared $500,000 of incorrect transactions in a timely manner, and maintain incoming transactions on a daily basis.
+ Resolved over $300,000 of erroneous or incorrect records using thorough research of all available systems in less than three months and with 99.8% accuracy.

JOB 2
ACCOUNTING TECHNICIAN, March 1998–May 2004, DFAS Travel, GS–525–05. 40 hours/week, 318 Marlin Drive, Sarasota, FL 34230. Salary: $30,000/year. Supervisor: Frank Johnson (200) 555-6698, Permission to contact.

PRIORITIZED AND PROCESSED TRAVEL VOUCHERS submitted on DoD Forms 1351-2 and SF-1164. Utilized knowledge of accounting procedures related to appropriation funding, allotments, obligations, and disbursements to process travel claims. Computed, with 99% accuracy, disbursement of travel entitlements for transportation, meals, lodging, and other reimbursement for international and U.S. travel. Was assigned the most complex travel claims due to high level of accuracy and understanding of federal regulations.

ACCURATELY CLASSIFIED, ANALYZED, EDITED, AND SUMMARIZED documentation to compute accurate and timely payments. Ensured correct personal information on travel card and conducted comparisons of travel entitlements and payment documents. Reconciled disparities, corrected errors, and initiated corrective actions for travel vouchers. Balanced and reconciled detail and summary accounts. Maintained strict compliance with the Prompt Payment Act (PPA) and Performance Measurement Indicators (PMIs). Knowledge of DFAS' automated accounting computer systems, such as the Defense Joint Military Pay System (DJMS). Using automated disbursing systems, Standard Finance System Redesign Subsystem 1 (SRD1) and Operational Data Store (ODS), performed quality-control reviews. Office leader in training and mentoring. Provided technical expertise to customers, including high-level officials. Conducted four training sessions, covering 150+ attendees, on travel entitlement, claims processing, and voucher and order preparation. Audited transactions computed by other technicians to ensure accuracy of computations and adherence to regulations before payments were uploaded for disbursement.

VALIDATED ACCOUNTING DATA to determine the general ledger accounts, journals, and subsidiary accounts affected. Responsible for single-source entry of the accounting line for all travel entitlements. Used Windows Integrated Automated Travel System (Win IATS) to validate allowances and reimbursable expenses, adhering to Department of Defense and Joint Federal Travel regulations. Corrected accounting data and expenditure limitations. Researched and analyzed historical financial data to identify disparities in existing data. Maintained, reconciled, and validated accounting records and ledgers.

PERFORMED IN-DEPTH REVIEW AND RESEARCH of previously paid or disapproved travel vouchers. Prepared checks and electronic transfer payments.

ACCOMPLISHMENTS:
+ Expedited and simplified computation of travel vouchers by creating an Excel spreadsheet for official travel distances, which is still currently in use.
+ Reported to Ft. Stewart, GA to coordinate the completeness, accuracy, validity, and appropriate accounting classifications of over 5,500 hurricane evacuation travel claims with budget and finance officers.
+ Developed training guidelines for logging and computation of vouchers and conducted training of new personnel.

(continued)

(continued)

JOB 3
ADMINISTRATIVE ASSISTANT, October 1997–March 1998, Orion Bus II. 40 hours/week. 2098 MacLaren Road, Tampa, FL 33601. Salary: $24,000/year. Supervisor: Robin Parrow, (200) 555-7828, Permission to contact.

Temporary position performing clerical and secretarial duties for management and supervisors. Composed and drafted reports, performed typing and transcription duties, and compiled data for programs and procedures. Software utilized included Visibility; MS Word, Excel, PowerPoint, and Access.

JOB 4
TRAVEL CONSULTANT, October 1995–October 1997, B. Charles Company. 40 hours/week. 44 14th Street, Rome, NY, 13440. Salary: $22,000/year. Supervisor: Brandon Eliot, (212) 555-4400, Permission to contact.

Assessed clients' needs, built sales rapport, and made recommendations on travel destinations and best values. Employed SABRE database, published sources, and computer resources to research and stay abreast of weather, current offerings, and travel document requirements. Was on call for corporate travel emergencies and performed clerical duties as needed.

EDUCATION:

BACHELOR OF ARTS, French, August 1994. SUNY Cortland, Cortland, NY. Minors in Psychology and Math.

30 SEMESTER HOURS IN UNDERGRADUATE STUDIES, Business and Accounting, 1998–2002. SUNY Utica, Utica NY. Accounting GPA: 3.85. Relevant Coursework includes
--Fundamentals of Income Tax, BU216, 2002
--Introduction to Macroeconomics, SS185, 2002
--Managerial Accounting Problems, ACC305, 2000
--Cost Accounting, ACC370, 1999
--Business Law II, LA1b, 1998

PROFESSIONAL TRAINING:

Collections: Federal Law, March 2005
Anti-Terrorism Level 1 Awareness Training, January 2005
Accounting for Stockholders' Equity, October 2004
Business Accounting: Accounting for Liabilities, September 2004
Standard Finance System (STANFINS), June 2004
Introduction to Accounting, May 2004
Managing and Motivating Your Staff, September 2003
Introduction to Macroeconomics, December 2002
Business Accounting: Accounting for Assets, January 2002
Cost Accounting, December 1999
Windows NT 4.0, November 1999
Accounting, Intermediate II, May 1999
Accounting, Intermediate, December 1998
EEO/POSH/Ethics Training, December 1998

Caroline Martin SS# 000-39-8097

Page 4

HONORS, AWARDS, AND SPECIAL ACCOMPLISHMENTS:

Highly Successful Performance Rating, 2005
Exceptional Performance Rating 1999 through 2004
Certificate of Appreciation, August 2005
On the Spot Cash Award, 1999 and 2004
Three External Customer Letters of Appreciation, 2003
Peer Award, 2003
Certificate of Appreciation, HHC 5th Special Forces Group (ABN), April 2000

ADDITIONAL INFORMATION:

EFFECTIVELY ORGANIZE WORK AND SET PRIORITIES. Schedule performance to efficiently use available resources and punctually meet job demands. Successfully complete assignments under the pressure of changing conditions and short deadlines.

ALERT TO INCONSISTENCIES, errors, omissions, and duplications in accounting tasks and projects.

COOPERATIVE TEAM MEMBER AND SELF-MOTIVATED INDEPENDENT WORKER. Work effectively with little supervision and handle multiple tasks in a high-pressure environment.

CLEAR KNOWLEDGE OF OFFICE ADMINISTRATION AND CLERICAL PROCEDURE. Adept at establishing and maintaining filing systems and records for rapid access and retrieval.

SKILLFULLY PRACTICED AT USING AUTOMATED PROCESSING EQUIPMENT and computer software (including electronic spreadsheets) to compile reports. Software skills include Microsoft Office Professional, Windows, Internet Explorer, and Netscape.

FULLY FAMILIAR WITH APPLICATION OF COMPUTER SECURITY PROCEDURES and computer fraud prevention.

PRACTICE AND PROMOTE CONTINUAL LEARNING AND DEVELOPMENT. Train and assist other accounting technicians with techniques to correct errors. Respond to complex questions from customers and lower-graded technicians, and assist higher-graded technicians in maintaining more complex accounts.

FULL KNOWLEDGE AND EXPERIENCE WITH ELECTRONIC FUND TRANSFERS AND CHECK PREPARATION for the disbursement of funds.

COMMUNICATE EFFECTIVELY ORALLY AND IN WRITING. Competently prepare correspondence for inquiries. Handle calls professionally and efficiently.

PROFESSIONAL ATTRIBUTES include ethical conduct, creativity, manual dexterity, diligence, and time management.

Target Job: TSA Lead Screener, SV-1802-F/F, $31,100–$46,700 per year; U.S. Federal Air Marshal from current position as Screener, TSA; seeking position to use top skills in administration, security, and instruction.
Resume Format: Paper (with bold type) or USAJOBS.
Federal to federal career change.

MARK ETHERIDGE
1010 Massachusetts Avenue
Cambridge, MA 02045
Residence: 781-999-9999
Cell: 904-444-4444
Email: marketh2@yahoo.com

PROFILE: Over 20 years of experience in administration, security, and instruction. Demonstrated experience in operations and project and program management, including tracking and evaluating progress and effectiveness, developing new processes, and improving performance. Proven skills in solving problems, leading teams, and managing staff. Strong administrative skills; able to manage office workload, prepare correspondence, maintain records, and coordinate events. Excellent interpersonal and verbal communication skills; able to lead change and build trust. Held Active Secret Clearance 1991–2001.

PROFESSIONAL EXPERIENCE

TRANSPORTATION SECURITY OFFICER, SV-1802-D
Transportation Security Administration
Boston, MA
01/2006–present
40 hours/week
Supervisor: Mark James, 774-444-4445. May be contacted.

Maintain knowledge of TSA Screening Standard Operating Procedures, TSA Aviation Operation Directives, and Airport Bulletins.

VOLUNTEER AS LEAD SCREENER: Oversee screening checkpoint on daily or as-needed basis, including equipment and personnel. Calibrate equipment and perform shift maintenance. Identify, distribute, and balance workload among 5 employees, making adjustments for workflow and skill level. Schedule employee breaks, ensuring adequate coverage to efficiently and effectively screen travelers. Rotate employees to ensure attentiveness and equal workload, accomplishing goals and meeting established priorities. Monitor flow of passengers through screening checkpoint to facilitate orderly and efficient processing.

SCREENER: Screen passengers and carry-on baggage. Technically proficient operating Walk Through Metal Detector, X-ray Machine, Explosive Threat Detection, Explosive Detection System, hand-held metal detector, and other screening equipment. Ensure safe air transport of passengers and baggage. Discover, prevent, and deal with threats to aviation security through complete screening of passengers and baggage, supporting TSA mission of protecting the traveling public. Implement security-screening procedures central to TSA objectives, identifying any deadly or dangerous objects and preventing them from being transported onto an aircraft. Perform wanding and pat-down searches and screen and review ticket information. Maintain focus in stressful environment, staying alert to potentially lethal devices and threats. Make effective decisions in crisis and routine situations.

Mark Etheridge, SSN 000-00-0000, Candidate Annct: 40404   1

COMMUNICATIONS/CUSTOMER SERVICE: Build customer rapport and trust through professional and courteous communications. Answer questions and resolve simple, informal complaints of employees and traveling public; refer others to supervisor or appropriate official. Participate in information briefings on security-sensitive or classified information, and relay information to coworkers as needed. Assist management with inquiries for information or investigations. Maintain communication with supervisors regarding issues that might reveal weaknesses or vulnerability of security screening discovered during screening duties. Represent team in communications with supervisor or manager to obtain resources and supplies (e.g. computer hardware and software, etc.) or equipment repairs. Maintain logs and time sheets, including records of confiscated contraband and lost-and-found items.

KEY ACCOMPLISHMENTS/SPECIAL PROJECTS:
+ Selected to conduct off-site screening of Maryland and Duke Women's basketball teams for the Final Four Championship in April. Set up portable screening station at teams' hotel and screened players, coaches, and other staff before they were escorted by state troopers to a chartered plane. Ensured all communications were professional and exceeded customer service expectations.
+ Rotate assignment to collect, sort, mark, and store prohibited and lost-and-found items for entire airport. Complete records, both paper and electronic, for tracking purposes, and prepare prohibited items for disposal.

REAL ESTATE AGENT
09/2002–12/2005
First Coast Realty
Jacksonville, FL
Salary: Commission
40 hours/week
Supervisor: Milton Crow, 904-888-8888. May be contacted.

Complete knowledge of the real estate process, buyers and sellers. Consistent multimillion-dollar producer.

CUSTOMER SERVICE: Maintained full knowledge of real estate process from buying and selling perspectives. Interviewed clients to determine needs, objectives, and financial resources; researched property listings and recommended appropriate options. Scheduled and coordinated appointments to show homes. Provided 24/7, on-call service to clients, being available and flexible to show properties and answer questions to meet their needs. Kept current with market to determine competitive prices.

COMMUNICATIONS: Worked with buyers and sellers and their representatives, negotiating sales and conditions. Coordinated closings, overseeing document signing and disbursement of funds. Interacted with lenders, inspectors, and others to ensure purchase agreement terms were completed by deadlines. Also, served as instructor for North East Florida Association of Realtors. Taught Ethics, Fair Housing, Antitrust, and Personal Security seminars for 60–90 people. Developed curricula and prepared materials, including tests and handouts. Cohost for weekly radio show, "The Real Estate Hour." Planned topics and coordinated guest appearances; interacted with guests and callers in live radio setting.

CONTRACT REVIEW/RECORDKEEPING: Prepared and reviewed complex legal documents for clients, including representation contracts, purchase agreements, closing statements, deeds, and leases. Ensured data accuracy and completeness. Maintained confidential client records and safeguarded sensitive information.

Mark Etheridge, SSN 000-00-0000, Candidate Annct: 40404   2

(continued)

(continued)

KEY ACCOMPLISHMENTS:

+ Initiated new training programs for North East Florida Association of Realtors; also, implemented innovative concept of soliciting support from brokerage and mortgage companies for seminars, reducing cost to association and enabling firms to establish contacts with new Realtors.
+ Top seller for 04/2003 and 02/2004.

MASTER SERGEANT
07/1998–10/2001
U.S. Marine Corps
Salary: E-8
40 hours/week
Supervisor: Warren Wood, 910-333-3333.

Held series of progressive leadership positions in diverse areas, including administration, training and development, strategic planning, operations management, and personnel management.

SENIOR INSTRUCTOR/OPERATIONS CHIEF
Aberdeen Proving Ground, MD, 07/1998–10/2001

ADMINISTRATION: Coordinated, directed, and completed full range of clerical and administrative duties in support of training and instruction programs. Managed personnel functions, including time and attendance recordkeeping, leave approval, and maintaining personnel files. As key member of management staff, served as point of contact for executive officers and subordinate staff. Responded to inquiries and provided staff guidance on policies and procedures. Developed and implemented policies and process changes to increase efficiency and program efficacy. Updated and maintained paper and electronic files.

OPERATIONS CHIEF: Developed and implemented new accountability system to maintain inventory and track weapons and ammunition, ensuring chain-of-custody records. Oversaw programs: Substance Abuse, Driver Improvement, Weight Control, and Military Appearance, tracking performance to ensure staff met goals.

SENIOR MARINE INSTRUCTOR: Served as lead strategist for training support for 2 military occupational specialty schools, managing staff of 21 instructors with 87 students. Ensured department adhered to Marine Corps and Army regulations and standards. Developed and presented training programs and classes, ensuring materials and lectures were audience appropriate and that courses met training objectives in adult learning environment. Evaluated and counseled instructors and students on performance and proficiency, preparing formal graduations, disciplinary actions, and discharges.

OPERATIONS MANAGER
Quantico, VA, 08/1995–07/1998

INSTRUCTOR/ARMORER: Piloted logistics, operations, administration, and security for 13 individual armories with million-dollar inventories. Reviewed operations and implemented new policies and procedures to ensure tracking of weapons. Ensured new policies were understood and followed, including procedures for physical security, personnel access, and possession monitoring. Troubleshot problems and applied innovative solutions. Provided training and operations support to FBI and DEA. Led public relations and community outreach programs.

Mark Etheridge, SSN 000-00-0000, Candidate Annct: 40404   3

KEY ACCOMPLISHMENTS:

+ Brought on as Senior Military Instructor/Operations Chief at Aberdeen Proving Ground, after department failed Inspector General inspection due to poor recordkeeping, resulting in termination of predecessor. Revamped training program, armory recordkeeping policies and procedures, and drug testing program data collection. Passed subsequent inspections.

+ Revised Electro-Optical course, assessing presentation, materials, tests, course objectives, and student learning. Condensed class, eliminating extraneous information and streamlining teaching agenda and presentation. Received Meritorious Service Award, 07/2001.

+ Provided support to Coalition and Special Warfare Division in predeployment of Riverine Training Team (RTT)/Operation Rompadour to Republic of Colombia, in fighting the war on drugs. Instrumental in efficient and smooth transfer of weapons. Received Letter of Appreciation, 05/1996.

EARLY MARINE CORPS EXPERIENCE

STATE DEPARTMENT INSTRUCTOR/TRAINER
Saudi Arabia, 04/1994–06/1995

Selected to lead Small Arms Repair Course and train the trainer for this esteemed assignment. Revised, planned, coordinated, and supervised course instruction. Coordinated resources to build Saudi Royal Marines readiness, providing guidance to develop and implement training course. Formulated innovative periods of instruction and resolved numerous maintenance issues to maximize training opportunities and ensure mission success. Introduced new, cutting-edge equipment. Held additional duty of maintaining armory. Promoted strengthened relationships with allies.

INSTRUCTOR/INSPECTOR
Dallas, TX, 05/1991–04/1994

Held operations and security authority for 23 locations, personnel, inventories and budgets. Grew reserve armory section into effective, cohesive, and independent group. Team leader and liaison in multiple community programs, including Drug Free campaign and Toys for Tots drive. Communications manager with secret clearance.

GROUND ORDNANCE CHIEF
El Toro, CA, 05/1989–05/1991

Led resource allocation and operations management for 19 armory locations, inventories, and budgets in support of Desert Storm. Developed and implemented Wing Armed Awareness Safety Program (which became Third Marine Air Wing policy) and Standard Operating Procedures. Fully accountable for personnel and ordnance materials valued at more than $9 million. Streamlined arrival/departure processes of 200 aircraft and interactions among several units.

Mark Etheridge, SSN 000-00-0000, Candidate Annct: 40404   4

(continued)

(continued)

KEY ACCOMPLISHMENTS:
+ Overcame language and culture barriers to train 6 Saudi nationals as small-arms repair and weapons maintenance. Awarded Navy and Marine Corps Achievement Medal, 04/1996.
+ Successfully spearheaded design of new armory, including supervision of construction. Researched and designed weapons issue ports, resulting in improved efficiency and armory flow. Received Navy Achievement Award, 05/1994.
+ Volunteered for additional assignment during Desert Storm, staying on as 3rd MAW Embarkation Chief. Coordinated and assisted loading of 200+ aircraft; led team of 15 embarkation specialists and provided critical logistical coordination between 3d MAW units, the arrival/departure control group, and Logistics Movement Control Center. Awarded Navy Commendation Medal, 06/1991.

EDUCATION

Undergraduate Coursework, Computer Science, Park College, Parkville, MO, 1997, GPA: 3.5; 51 credits
Diploma, Westbury Senior High, Houston, TX, 1977

TRAINING

TSA Screener, 40 hours of classroom training plus 60 hours of on-the-job training, 01/2006
Substance Abuse Counseling 09/1999–10/2001
Small Arms Weapons Instructor Class, 01/1993–10/201
Advanced Course, 5 weeks, 09/1996

Advanced training in Leadership, Communications, Public Speaking, Administration, Operations, Technical Issues, Applied Management, Physical Education, and Military Science.

AWARDS

Meritorious Service Medal, 07/2001
Navy Commendation Medal, 06/1991
Navy and Marine Corps Achievement Medal with one star, 04/1996 and 05/1994
National Defense Service Medal, 02/1991
Marine Corps Good Conduct Medal with five stars, 1977–2001
Kuwait Liberation Medal, 02/1992
Armed Forces Expeditionary medal, 12/1995
Navy and Marine Corps Overseas Service Ribbon with two stars, 07/1995
Southwest Asia Service Medal with three stars, 10/1991–09/1992
Sea Service Deployment with one star, 01/1991
Joint Meritorious Unit Award, 06/1994
Navy Unit Commendation, 01/1992

COMPUTER PROFICIENCIES

MS Office: Word, Excel, Outlook, PowerPoint, Access

Mark Etheridge, SSN 000-00-0000, Candidate Annct: 40404   5

Target Job: General Attorney, GS-0905-11/12, from current position in Education; seeking position utilizing top skills as attorney, writer, analyst, and instructor.
Resume Format: Paper.
Private industry to federal transition.

STEPHANIE HAINES GLASGOW
333 East 10th Street, #34 • New York, NY 10024
Residence: 212-555-5555 • Cellular: 917-444-4444
E-mail: Stephanieglas@yahoo.com

Social Security Number: 000-00-0000	Federal Employment Status: N/A
Citizenship: United States	Veterans' Status: N/A

OBJECTIVE: General Attorney, GS-0905-11/12; Announcement: CS/05-117

PROFILE: Possess dual experience in law and education, with over 10 years of combined experience. Strong skills in research and analysis of law; particular legal background includes special education, education, employment discrimination, domestic violence, child support, and juvenile delinquency. Excellent writing and verbal communication skills, demonstrated in law and teaching experience. Reputation for thoroughness and organization in case management and hearings, as well as ability to isolate uniqueness of cases. Superb defense of cases and negotiation of settlement agreements.

EDUCATION

J.D., American University, Washington College of Law, Washington, DC 20016; May 2000

> *Relevant Courses:* Women and the Law Clinic, Criminal Trial Practice, Environmental Litigation, Constitutional Law, Employment Discrimination (including Age Discrimination Law), Special Education, Juvenile Law, Criminal Trial Practice
> *Awards and Honors:* Fellowship, Equal Justice Foundation
> *Activities:* President and Founder, Racers Running Club; Member, Equal Justice Foundation; Volunteer, Volunteer Income Tax Assistance; Volunteer, DC Bar Pro Se Divorce Clinic; Member, National Association for Public Interest Law; Troupe Member, Law Revue (Theatrical Group); Co-Chair, Health Center Insurance Ad Hoc Committee.

Ed.M., Boston University, Teaching English to Speakers of Other Languages (TESOL), Boston, MA 02215; 1994. Cumulative GPA: 3.57

> *Awards and Honors:* Certificate of Appreciation, Boston University Hillel House
> *Activities:* Volunteer, Boston University Hillel House; Teacher and Curriculum Writer of Adult Education, Immigrant Learning Center; Counselor, American Trails West teen tour

B.A., Brandeis University, English & American Literature and Sociology (double major) and Education Program (minor), Waltham, MA 02454; May 1992. Graduated *cum laude;* Dean's List: Fall 1992, Spring 1990, and Fall 1989.

> *Awards and Honors:* Letter of Appreciation, Brandeis Hillel Services
> *Activities:* President and Founding Mother, Lambda Phi Sorority chapter; Member, Improvisational Comedy Troupe, "False Advertising"; Clerk, Public Defender of Rochester, NY; Graduate, Hurricane Island Outward Bound School, Rockland, ME.

Diploma, Brighton High School, Rochester, NY; 1988

Stephanie Glasgow, SSN 000-00-0000, Candidate Annct.: CS/05-117

(continued)

(continued)

LEGAL EXPERIENCE

Interim Attorney   09/2000–12/2002
New York City Department of Education (NYCDOE)
52 Chambers Street $48,000/year
New York, NY 10007   40 hours/week
Supervisor: John Withers, 212-555-5555. Permission to contact.

Represented NYCDOE at impartial hearings arguing tuition reimbursement and special-education issues.

- Case Preparation/Management: Processed complaints and compliance reviews; performed full scope of responsibilities for each case, including witness preparation, school visits, case investigation and research, and negotiations. Drafted memoranda of law, motions, and settlement agreements. Prepared discovery and hearings. Made recommendations on jurisdictional questions, investigative plans and reports, letters of findings, and negotiation strategies. Oversaw corrective actions/implementation of decision and maintained reimbursement decision database. Monitored impartial hearing officer decisions for appropriate issues for appeals to State Review Officer and the courts.
- Legal Research: Conducted legal research/analysis of local, state, and federal statutes, regulations, and guidelines, including but not limited to Section 504 and the ADA. Engaged in research to resolve legal and policy issues when there were no clear precedents or when there were conflicting state and federal requirements.
- Legal Representation: Provided effective representation at impartial hearings and in negotiations with public and private educational institutions, local agencies, plaintiffs, and their legal representatives. Negotiated and drafted stipulations of settlement. Wrote briefs and executed oral arguments. Represented the agency to external and internal parties and served as liaison to the Corporation Counsel of New York City and to one district superintendent.
- Technical/Legal Expertise: Provided technical and legal assistance to the Committee on Special Education and the Committee on Preschool Special Education. Provided legal advice to administrators regarding issues of special education and disability laws, NYCDOE practice, and policy. Advised supervisors and colleagues on significant changes in law or procedures, as well as interpretation and application of laws and regulations.

Key Accomplishments:
- Achieved unprecedented success rate at hearings. Through detailed research and arguments, saved NYCDOE nearly $200,000 in impartial hearings alone.
- Assisted with identification of important issues for purposes of providing staff development for Committee on Special Education administrators and clinicians, and continued development and implementation of staff development program.

Student Attorney   08/1999–12/1999
Washington College of Law, Women and the Law Clinic
4801 Massachusetts Avenue, NW   Salary: N/A
Washington, DC 20016   20 hours/week
Supervisor: Anne Thomas, 202-222-4440.

Represented indigent clients in domestic violence and child-support cases. Registered and participated in the Legal Assistance by Law Students Program, DC Court of Appeals. Successfully addressed clients' concerns. Counseled clients on various issues, including real property.

2

Law Clerk 06/1999–08/1999
Public Defender Service for the District of Columbia, Trial Division
633 Indiana Avenue, NW Salary: N/A
Washington, DC 20004 40 hours/week
Supervisor: Winston Goldberg, 202-628-1111.

Supported representation of indigent defendants. Researched criminal law issues related to juvenile delinquency. Conducted investigations, served subpoenas, filed court documents, attended training seminars, and toured correctional facilities.

Legal Intern 01/1999–05/1999
National Wildlife Federation, Office of Federal and International Affairs
1400 16th Street, NW Salary: N/A
Washington, DC 20036 16 hours/week
Supervisor: Olive Thompson, 703-444-4444.

Compiled and analyzed sea-level-rise data for lobbyist. Researched and compared relevant state laws and programs, and their effect on coastal zone management and wetland protection.

Legal Intern 01/1999–05/1999
United States Consumer Product Safety Commission
Litigation Division, Office of Compliance
4330 East-West Highway Salary: N/A
Bethesda, MD 20814 10 hours/week

Researched product liability issues and tort law, drafted interrogatories, prepared information for deposition, and attended preliminary determination meetings.

Legal Intern 06/1998–08/1998
United States Department of Health and Human Services
Office of the General Counsel, Business and Administrative Law Division, Litigation Branch
330 Independence Avenue, SW Salary: N/A
Washington, DC 20201 40 hours/week

Provided full-time support to attorneys in all areas of practice. Performed legal research on a variety of issues. Observed litigation proceedings. Assisted with research pertaining to many aspects of litigation. Researched and prepared issues for briefs. Prepared interrogatories and agency information requests.

Key Accomplishment:
- Received Certificate of Appreciation, Litigation Branch of the Business and Administrative Law Division of the Office of the General Counsel of the United States Department of Health and Human Services.

3

(continued)

(continued)

EDUCATION CONSULTANT EXPERIENCE

Math Consultant   08/2003–Present
LL Teach, Inc.
P.O. Box 6256, 674 Route 202/206N, Building 4, Suite 5 $63,960/year
Bridgewater, NJ 08807   40 hours/week
Supervisor: Jim Boyers, 908-222-2222. Please do not contact at this time.

Facilitate implementation of the Jersey City Mathematics Initiative. Service a cadre of teachers within six elementary schools. Act as liaison and contact person for 30 grade-level teachers among building administrators, LL Teach personnel, and facilitators. Create demonstration and coaching sessions with teachers. Visit schools, administrators, and teachers to troubleshoot problems. Conduct four 90-minute demonstration lessons and four coaching sessions per teacher per year. Make a difference in students' self-worth, understanding of mathematics, and achievement in mathematics. Utilize presentation skills, compassion for children, passion for teaching, extraordinary patience, extreme flexibility, and tact.

CAPA Team Mathematics Specialist   02/2005
New Jersey Department of Education
Office of Program Planning and Design   Salary: N/A
P.O. Box 500   50 hours/week
Trenton, NJ 08625
Supervisor: Edward Kramer, 973-655-5558.

Served as mathematics specialist on an external evaluation team entitled Collaborative Assessment and Planning for Achievement (CAPA), assigned to one of 42 New Jersey elementary schools identified as an Abbott low-performing school. CAPA, assembled and trained by NJDOE, satisfies the standards for corrective action under the No Child Left Behind (NCLB) act. As team member, worked in concert with school districts, using thoughtful, systematic, evidence-based process to reach agreement about changes needed to make a positive difference in teaching and learning. Participated in collaborative process, demonstrating commitment to shared responsibility for student learning among state and local educators, and a commitment to continuous school improvement.

Appointed Teacher   01/2003–08/2003
New York City Department of Education
515 West 182nd Street $52,000/year
New York, NY 10033   40 hours/week
Supervisor: Phyllis Matthews, 212-927-7739.

Instructed health and hygiene to special education population and physical education to general education population at intermediate school level. Developed curriculum; prepared and presented a variety of lessons at various levels. Participated as staff member of a student running club.

PROFESSIONAL MEMBERSHIPS

American Bar Association of the City of New York, New York State Bar Association, Judges and Lawyers Breast Cancer Alert, Aerobics and Fitness Association of America

4

LICENSES/CERTIFICATIONS

Legal:
Member, Bars of New York, New Jersey, and U.S. District Court of New Jersey

Education:
Tenured Teacher: Howard County Public School System
Teaching Certifications: NYSED English 7–12 Provisional, NYSED ESOL Provisional, NYCDOE English Junior High Conditional, NYCDOE ESL Secondary Conditional, and NYCDOE ESL Elementary Conditional

TRAINING

Mediator: American University Office of Judicial Affairs & Mediation Services, Office of Student Services, 20-Hour Training in Basic Mediation, 1999

CONFERENCES

Legal Tech, New York, NY, 2004
School Law Institute: Special Education, Practicing Law Institute (PLI), New York, NY, 2002, 2001
Animal Rights Law, Washington College of Law, American University, Washington, DC, 2004

SEMINARS ATTENDED

Learning Disabilities and Second Language Learning, American University, Washington, DC, 1996
Sports Management of the Olympics, George Washington University, Washington, DC, 1996

INTERNATIONAL TRAVEL

Ontario and British Columbia, Canada; Europe (including England, France, Italy, Sweden, Switzerland, and Spain); Russia; Israel

LANGUAGES

Moderate: French, Hebrew
Beginning: Spanish, Yiddish

COMMUNITY/VOLUNTEER ACTIVITIES

Volunteer: National Down Syndrome Society, Multiple Sclerosis Society, G-d's Love We Deliver, United Jewish Appeal, Leukemia Society, NYC 2012 Olympic Bid Committee, Everybody Wins (Power Lunch) reading partnership program for children (2002)

Fundraising for Susan G. Komen Foundation, Multiple Sclerosis Society, Leukemia Society

COMPUTER PROFICIENCIES

Windows 95; MS Office: Word, Excel, Outlook, PowerPoint; Internet

PERSONAL ACCOMPLISHMENTS

Marathons—Boston: '00; Chicago: '99; San Francisco: '96; NYC: '04, '00, '97, '98, '95, '94
Triathlons—Ironman: '05, '03, '02; Olympic: '00, '99; Sprint: '00, '98, '99

5

Target Job: Economist, ZP-0110-02/02, $44,000–$64,000 from current position in Economic Development; returned Peace Corps Volunteer. Seeking position to use top skills in industry analysis, estimated methodologies, and research into source data.
Resume Format: USAJOBS.
Private industry to federal career.

JEANNA SIMPSON
655 West Lake Road
Harper's Ferry, WV 25425
Day Phone: 907-333-3333
Email: jeanna002@aol.com

Country of citizenship: United States of America
Veterans' Preference: No
Contact Current Employer: Yes

WORK EXPERIENCE COMMUNITY ECONOMIC DEVELOPMENT ASSOCIATION
Tempe, Arizona US

1/2006 - Present
Salary: 42,000 USD Per Year

Hours per week: 40

BUSINESS DEVELOPMENT CONSULTANT
STRATEGIC BUSINESS PLANNING AND CONSULTING: Evaluate internal operations and pursue business-development opportunities including strategic partnerships and grant funding. Interpret and evaluate economic information. Identify new data sources and methodologies. Collect, analyze, and document data; utilize estimation techniques. Perform tax and budget projects and prepare business investment plans.

PROJECT MANAGEMENT. Completed the following projects with economic research, planning, assembling information, performing analysis, and evaluation: (1) an analysis of the housing assistance industry; (2) clarification of CEDA's purpose, mission, and vision; (3) design and implementation of a website to reflect CEDA's new direction. Prepared reports of conclusions and outcomes for all projects.

BUSINESS ANALYSIS PROJECTS: The following deliverables are expected in 2007: (1) a strategic plan that identifies opportunity areas; (2) a work plan that outlines proposed partnerships and alliances; (3) identification of grant funds for the next fiscal year; and (4) hiring of a full-time replacement to continue projects that I launch.

ACCOMPLISHMENTS:
Successfully added new clients and projects to agency's portfolio based on expertise and business relationship management. Developed 4 new clients within the first 6 months. (Contact Supervisor: Yes, Supervisor's Name: Samantha Rogers, Supervisor's Phone: (506) 777-7777)

PEACE CORPS CAMEROON
Babadjou, Cameroon

6/2003 - 8/2005
Salary: 29,000 USD Per Year
Hours per week: 55

SMALL BUSINESS DEVELOPER
SMALL ENTERPRISE DEVELOPMENT PROJECT:

Assigned to Cameroon's Small Enterprise Development (SED) Project to analyze and develop the informal sector and influence the government and general population to ameliorate business and banking processes with the following strategies: (1) improved banking practices within host microfinance institutions (MFIs), (2) transferred business knowledge to MFI entrepreneurs, and (3) fostered development and business linkages among entrepreneurs within promising industries. The SED Project emphasizes service to women, youth, and other underserved groups whenever possible.

KEY PROJECTS/ACCOMPLISHMENTS:

1. PETIT À PETIT YOUTH SAVINGS PROGRAM: Developed Petit à Petit in the MC² microfinance network. This financial literacy project sponsored educational seminars on financial topics for neighborhood youth and allowed them to open personal savings accounts for less than a dollar.

Solicited and managed funds for program's pilot implementation; developed and executed a feasibility study that led to funding from Appropriate Development for Africa Foundation (ADAF); designed marketing materials in French (included skits, brochures, handouts, and an educational comic book); trained and directed a team of youth advocates to host seminars on financial literacy; developed step-by-step implementation plan to address accounting and management issues unique to maintaining youth accounts.

2. BAMENDA HANDICRAFT COOPERATIVE (BHC). Provided consulting direction in product development, business management, and international marketing. Expanded product line to include goods from all of Cameroon's ten provinces. Aided BHC in adding three international clients to its portfolio. Organized photo shoot of products for web marketing.

3. TREADLE PUMP. Networked with local farmers, community leaders, government officials, and NGOs to advocate for the introduction of treadle pump technology (labor-enhancing device used to create inexpensive irrigation systems) in Cameroon. Assisted in securing 1.5 million dollars to train locals in using and manufacturing the treadle pump.

4. MC² Babadjou. Assisted bank employees in learning and perfecting efficient business and banking practices. Designed and carried out computer training courses that lead to a proficiency certificate for employees who completed the program.
• Designed and implemented computerized banking practices (using spreadsheets and word processing) to integrate with manual systems. Leveraged time-saving advantages of computerization while retaining the ability to employ manual processes when necessary due to the unreliability of electricity and other factors making complete computerization imprudent. (Contact Supervisor: Yes, Supervisor's Name: John Smith, Supervisor's Phone: (202) 444-4444)

EDUCATION

Monterey Institute of International Studies (MIIS)
Monterey, California US
Master's Degree - 12/2005
Major: MBA, International Management

Relevant Coursework, Licensures and Certifications:
Peace Corps Masters International Program (PCMI): Completed joint program with the US Peace Corps emphasizing small enterprise development, language proficiency, and cultural adaptability. To fulfill program requirements, served two years in Africa with the Peace Corps before completing final semester at MIIS under a half-tuition scholarship.

International Curriculum: Graduate coursework focused on international business management. Worked with an intercultural team on a Business Plan capstone project for a domestic company wishing to extend its services abroad; worked intimately with colleagues from other cultures and gained exposure to global market challenges.

Arizona State University
Tempe, AZ US
Bachelor's Degree - 5/2005
Major: Economics
GPA: 3.7 out of 4.0
Relevant Coursework, Licensures and Certifications:
Barrett Honors College Graduate: Magna Cum Laude: 3.7 GPA.
Completed (1) 15 hours of lower-division honors credit, (2) 15 hours of upper-division honors credit, and (3) an HONORS THESIS that discussed the costs and benefits of using low labor standards to achieve ECONOMIC DEVELOPMENT goals.

International Business Certificate: Completed 30-hour international business certificate (beyond baccalaureate) focusing on three areas of competency: (1) international business, (2) cultural sophistication, and (3) language proficiency. Possess understanding of input/output accounts and the Gross Domestic Product.

(continued)

(continued)

LANGUAGES

French
Spoken: Advanced
Written: Intermediate
Read: Intermediate

ADDITIONAL INFORMATION

DISTINCTIONS

Monterey Institute of International Studies: 3.8 GPA; Half-tuition academic scholarship 2002-2003; Masters International Scholarship 2005; Net Impact 2005, affiliate. Arizona State University: 3.7 GPA, Magna Cum Laude, ASU President's Scholar 1996-1999; ASU Dean's List, every semester; National Dean's List, 1998-2000; Student Economics Association, President Fall 2000, Vice President 1999-2000; Beta Gamma Sigma National Honor Society, inducted 1998.
Peace Corps: Small Enterprise Development (SED) Steering Committee, selected member 2004; Peace Corps Trainer 2004, 2005.

PROFICIENCIES

Languages: English (native), French (written, proficient; spoken, fluent).
Computer: Extensive use of MS Word, Excel, Outlook, Publisher, and PowerPoint; past extensive use of scheduling and billing systems; high proficiency in Internet research; general knowledge of statistical analysis software.

FREELANCE EDITORIAL WORK
Editorial/Research Assistant
06/01–08/01; 08/05–present
Counseling & Consultation/Testing Support Services, Arizona State University, Tempe, AZ
Provide editorial and research support to authors writing career testing and career development curricula.

EARLY WORK EXPERIENCE

GRADUATE ASSISTANT
09/02–05/03
International Commercial Diplomacy Project, Monterey Institute of International Studies, Monterey, CA
Compiled, researched, and summarized international economics, trade, and commercial diplomacy Internet links now used as a resource for trade officials, negotiators, and students in the field; designed trade negotiation simulations that allow students and practitioners to participate in mock trade negotiation and dispute resolution exercises.

ADMINISTRATIVE ASSISTANT
08/97–07/98; 06/99–05/00; 06/01–08/02
Counseling & Consultation/Testing Support Services, Arizona State University, Tempe, AZ
Provided front-office and customer-service support for the counseling and testing center; performed data management using both Access and Excel; organized a data collection project and created outcome report for the director; created marketing materials on MS Publisher; managed intern application process under the general direction of the Training Director; and assisted on special projects.

BUSINESS INTERN
01/01–05/01
L'ESSEC, Paris, France
Assisted in the preparation of corporate training programs in France's leading business school; served as an expert on English grammar, business jargon, and American culture.

Index

Index

J

K

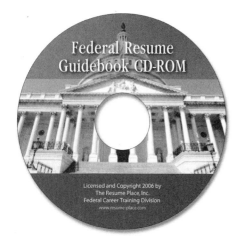
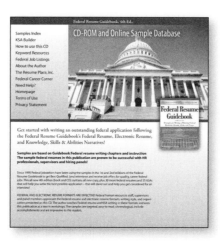